FOR KING AND COUNTRY

Alberta in the Second World War

This book belongs to

Received at
PGI - GOLF FOR LITERACY '95
The Learning Centre
Calgary, Alberta
September 29, 1995

DONATED BY
Reidmore Books Inc.

Canadian Cataloguing in Publication Data

Main entry under title:

For King and Country

Co-published by the Provincial Museum of Alberta
ISBN 1-895073-81-2

1. World War 1939-1945—Alberta. 2. Alberta—History—1905-1945. I. Tingley, Kenneth W. (Kenneth Wayne), 1947- II. Provincial Museum of Alberta.
FC3674.F67 1995   971.23'02   C95-910179-9
F1078.F67 1995

printed and bound in Canada

The Provincial
Museum of Alberta
12845-102 Avenue,
Edmonton, Alberta
T5N OM6

T · H · E
PROVINCIAL
MUSEUM
OF ALBERTA

COMMUNITY DEVELOPMENT

Reidmore Books Inc.
1200 Energy Square
10109-106 Street,
Edmonton, Alberta
T5J 3L7

Front cover: *For King and Country,* acrylic on board by Ronald Volstad, based on Charles Comfort's design for the Canadian Volunteer Service Medal, Provincial Museum of Alberta Government History Collection.

Back cover: *If the Cap Fits Wear it!* Anonymous, Second World War lithographed poster, Allan Kerr Collection.

Foreword

W. Bruce McGillivray

We Albertans know so little of our history that it both delights and frustrates to have a piece of it revealed so richly as in this book. There is delight in the response of Albertans throughout the war to the needs of King and Country. The unparalleled mobilization of human and financial resources to meet the challenges of the war reinforces our pride in western resourcefulness, and confirms even today our ability to overcome great obstacles. There is delight in the willingness of the authors to present a diversity of views on the impact of the Second World War on Alberta. Certainly, there is delight for the curatorial staff of the Provincial Museum of Alberta, that this book will be available to students in our schools who will get a glimpse into the events that shaped the lives of their parents and grandparents.

The touch of frustration comes when I wonder why we waited 50 years to bring these stories and events to a popular audience. Before we can resolve the problems facing Albertan and Canadian society, we need to understand their origin. Many current issues such as the rights and responsibilities of aboriginal Canadians, the relative precedence of treaties over federal law, the rights of women, the rights of ethnic minorities, and even gun control were raised as problems during the war. Perhaps if we were more aware of our own history we would not be facing all of these issues today.

In Canada, it is easy to lose sight of our unique history when it is overwhelmed by the American and British stories revealed in film and on television. Even within Canada, western perspectives on national events are often lost. These essays commemorate the successes and failures of Albertans, and their impact on the world as witnessed and judged by Albertans. Remarkably, they reveal 50-year old social, political and cultural attitudes that are as current as today's newspaper.

The war was a highly emotional time for Albertans. Even in retrospect, emotions make it a complex and controversial subject to describe. It is important for readers to judge the actions and attitudes presented here not by modern standards but by those of the time.

The Provincial Museum of Alberta is pleased to be a partner in this publication and to offer a visual record of the war in Alberta through our travelling exhibit "For King and Country". Both Maurice Doll, Curator of the exhibition, and Ken Tingley, editor of this book, deserve high praise for making the issues and people of the war years accessible to a new generation of Albertans.

Preface

Maurice F.V. Doll

Nineteen ninety-five marks the 50th anniversary of the end of the Second World War. Looking back over the past five decades we can trace important aspects of political geography, modern economics and popular culture to this cataclysmic event. It is in the life experience of our most recently retired generation, however, that the memory and influence of that global conflict is most vivid. Almost without exception the war provided the context and was a touchstone for all which followed in their lives.

The cover of this book is illustrated with a special painting by renowned military artist and Albertan, Ronald Volstad. It depicts Canadian men and women in Second World War uniform serving in land, sea and air forces, and as nursing sisters. The painting is based on Charles Comfort's design for the Canadian Volunteer Service Medal and is an image quite familiar to all Canadian veterans who volunteered for Second World War service. However, this image may not be as familiar to new Canadians, or to the two generations of Albertans born after the war who now make up 80 per cent of the province's population.

The painting introduces the Provincial Museum of Alberta's travelling commemorative exhibit *For King and Country: Alberta in the Second World War* and reinforces the theme of volunteer service. The scope of this exhibit goes beyond that of other commemorative projects in Canada and presents a particularly Albertan perspective. The exhibit and this complementary publication are an attempt to focus equally upon overseas service and that on the home front. They examine the experiences of thousands of men and women in the Army, Navy and Air Forces, and of the thousands of civilians who backed them up at home.

Though the war was global in nature, our response to it was typically Canadian and in certain instances, uniquely Albertan. The book explores Canadian active service overseas, and contributions made by Albertans in the Battle of the Atlantic, in the air war and in the campaigns in Italy and northwestern Europe. This is balanced by home-front activities centring on the British Commonwealth Air Training Plan, the role of Alberta women in the war and the strong American presence in Alberta with the building of the Alaska Highway, the Northwest Staging Route and the Canol Pipeline. In addition, alternative views of the war are presented in terms of the experience of Japanese-Canadian internees, German POWs and those of a uniquely Albertan war-time organization, the Veterans Volunteer Reserve.

This publication from the outset was designed to complement the exhibit. While it mirrors the exhibit, it expands beyond and introduces several more themes which could not be satisfactorily dealt with in an exhibition format.

Ken Tingley, our editor, must be congratulated for his diligent work in pulling together in only six short months, a publication which met all the demands made of him. It is a work of which we are proud and which, I am sure, will have a useful life well beyond the four years scheduled for the travelling exhibition.

This publication lets us hear the voices of the participants, be they Second World War veterans recounting their personal experiences or more contemporary historians presenting a more detached account. Ideally, we would prefer to have added more voices to the chorus, both in the exhibit and in this publication. We were naturally limited to the artifacts at hand and, in the case of this publication, to the availability of authors kind enough to volunteer articles upon extremely short notice.

Veterans are already aware of the influence the war had on their lives, but it is hoped that for the rest of us born later, the impact of the war will not be forgotten.

Acknowledgments

Many individuals and groups assisted in bringing this project to completion. Provision of funds, donation of time and materials, support from archives and museums, generous gifts of time and talent in preparing articles, and outstanding service from people within the Provincial Museum of Alberta have all played a significant role in the development of the exhibit *For King and Country: Alberta in the Second World War* and the accompanying publication of the same name.

Gene Bince and Terry Collins of the Department of Veterans Affairs supported this endeavour by allowing Maurice Doll to address a joint meeting of the presidents of the Edmonton and area branches of the Royal Canadian Legion. The Royal Canadian Legion, Kingsway Branch 175 and Norwood (Alberta) Branch 178 donated funds to start the publication project for "King and Country." The Ladies' Auxiliary to the Royal Canadian Legion, Montgomery Branch 24 and the Edmonton and District Historical Society also supported the project financially. Individuals made generous contributions as well: thanks to James A. Bell, Mr. and Mrs. Jack Campbell, Coral A. Davids-Fry, Murray Kelcher, and Mr. and Mrs. Ted Turton. K.J. Clark Photography and Lab Services also offered financial support.

Many individuals made special contributions of time and effort. Contributors to the publication worked diligently under time constraints to produce quality articles. Mr. Ron Volstad, an enthusiastic supporter of the project, donated his original painting for use on the cover of the book and in headlining the exhibit. Mr. Allan Kerr of Milarm Ltd. provided artifacts and lent two dozen original Second World War posters for the exhibit, one of which appears on the back cover of this book.

Excellent graphic materials enhance the exhibit and the publication. A number of individuals writing articles contributed original photographs, and these are noted in the text of the book. Several institutions and individuals were very cooperative in this respect too. Thanks to: Bill Kent of the Canadian War Museum (CMW); Dr. Dave Leonard, Brock Silversides, Marlena Wyman and Dennis Hyduk of the Provincial Archives of Alberta (PAA); Pat Molesky of the Glenbow Archives (GA); Bruce Ibsen of the City of Edmonton Archives (EA); Alf Bogusky, Edmonton Art Gallery (EAG); Lorraine Mychajlunow of the Alberta Association of Registered Nurses Archives (AARNA); Alexander Makar of the Ukrainian Canadian Archives and Museum of Alberta (UCAMA); The Red Deer City Archives (RDMA); The University of Alberta Archives (UA); The Imperial War Museum (IWM); National Archives of Canada (NAC); Sir Alexander Galt Museum and Archives, Lethbridge (SAGMA).

Material for the book came to the Museum on a variety of word processing programs. We thank Sheila Tingley for her work in translating these to a standard format during the editing of the articles.

A strong creative team at the Provincial Museum of Alberta worked to produce the publication. Numerous individuals made contributions critical to the success of both components of *For King and Country: Alberta In The Second World War*. Dr. Bruce McGillivray, Assistant Director [Curatorial] was an energetic supporter from the beginning, and also worked to secure funding for and to promote the project. Dr. Philip H.R. Stepney, Director of the Provincial Museum of Alberta, provided leadership and support. Carolyn Lilgert was dedicated in preparing the design for the cover of the book. Her work enhances the outstanding painting provided by Ron Volstad for the book's cover illustration. Special thanks to Dr. James Burns for his meticulous copy editing and to Dr. Bruce McGillivray and Maurice Doll who also acted as copy editors. Mark Steinhilber, responsible for the book layout, has worked tirelessly and made many excellent suggestions. Computer scanning by Steve Fisher and cartography by Wendy Johnson have added significantly to the final product. Typists Colleen Steinhilber and Laura Pretula provided support and superior service throughout the production of the book.

Finally, we would like to thank the many contributors to the publication *For King and Country: Alberta In The Second World War*. They generously donated their time and effort under the tight time constraints imposed by the project. It was their articles which finally made the book possible.

Contents

Introduction

Ken Tingley

Nineteen ninety-five marks the fiftieth anniversary of the end of the Second World War. Victory in Europe Day [VE Day] marked the formal end of the European conflict on 8 May 1945. On 15 August 1945 Victory over Japan Day [VJ Day] was celebrated throughout most Allied countries on the day following the Japanese acceptance of the terms of surrender. During that spring and summer the growing realization that the world had been fundamentally changed swept through the global community. Shock at the atomic bomb attacks on Hiroshima and Nagasaki, revelations of the genocidal inhumanity perpetrated in the death camps of Eastern Europe, the horrendous casualty lists, and the massive dispersal of populations, all symbolized the brutal nature of the war. At the same time, a sense of euphoria and optimism found expression among the returning veterans as they turned their energy toward postwar reconstruction and civil re-establishment. One thing was obvious to all, and that was that the world had changed. Certainly Canada had been changed by its wartime experience, and so had Alberta.

The Provincial Museum of Alberta is marking the end of the Second World War through a travelling exhibit which opened in Edmonton on 4 February 1995, and which will be seen in many Alberta communities. *For King and Country: Alberta in the Second World War* examines the many ways in which the war affected the people of Alberta, and shaped the society in which they lived. This book was published to complement the exhibit, and to allow several of those who served in uniform to communicate directly to the reader the nature of their experience. Every effort has been made to allow these men and women to speak in their own voice as they describe their experiences, with as little editorial interference as possible. Other articles were written to provide a context for such memoirs, and to define the wider historical circumstances within which the individual was swept up. The experiences of Albertans, both overseas and on the home front, are examined, as are the experiences of those men, women and children who became involved on the Alberta home front as prisoners of war or evacuees.

Alberta's contribution to the war was significant. The facts presented in the exhibit speak eloquently of that contribution. Albertans served in every theatre of war, in such distinguished units as the Loyal Edmonton Regiment, Calgary Highlanders, King's Own Calgary Regiment, South Alberta Regiment and Lord Strathcona's Horse (Royal Canadians). Of the 50,844 Albertans who served in the Canadian Army, many paid the supreme sacrifice or were wounded during the war. A surprising 22 per cent of the Royal Canadian Navy was recruited from the prairie provinces during the war. Alberta's two naval divisions accounted for a significant number of these: HMCS Nonsuch in Edmonton recruited 3588 sailors, while HMCS Tecumseh in Calgary recruited 3899. Many others enlisted in the Merchant Marine or in the Royal Navy. Alberta also contributed 19,499 men and women to the Royal Canadian Air Force, while the Royal Canadian Air Force (Women's Division) recruited additional provincial women into its ranks.

On the home front, the most immediately visible effects of the war came with the British Commonwealth Air Training Plan [BCATP] facilities built rapidly across Alberta to provide the highly trained technicians and aircrews needed for the modern Allied air forces. Flying Instructors' Schools were located in Vulcan and Pearce; Flying Training Schools in Calgary, Fort Macleod, Claresholm, Vulcan, Medicine Hat and Penhold; Bombing and Gunnery Schools in Lethbridge; Air Observer Schools in Edmonton and Pearce; and Elementary Flying Training Schools in Lethbridge, High River, Edmonton, De Winton, Bowden and Pearce.

In addition to the BCATP, the "friendly invasion" of American construction and service personnel following the Japanese attack on Pearl Harbor on 7 December 1941 was responsible for a massive impact on many areas of the province. This was especially true of Edmonton, which became the supply, communications and transportation centre for the three most significant projects designed to ensure northwestern continental defence. The Alaska Highway, Northwest Staging Route, and Canol Pipeline Project all emanated from Edmonton, which truly lived up to its sobriquet "Gateway to the North" as the armies of engineers, technicians and construction workers were funnelled through on their way to Alaska. During peak activity over 33,000 Americans could be found in Alberta, northeastern British Columbia, and the Yukon Territory.

Edmonton was the major staging area for construction and supply of the Alaska Highway, Northwest Staging Route and Canol Pipeline. These projects had a significant impact on Northern Alberta as well.

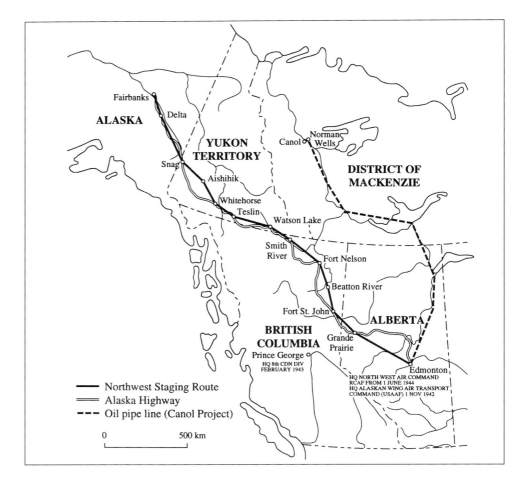

When Maurice Doll, Curator of Government History at the Provincial Museum of Alberta, approached me to edit a book which would contain articles reflecting aspects of the Alberta wartime experience, I had some concern that it might prove difficult to find enough material to cover this fairly broad subject. Articles which already had been completed, or almost completed, were required to accommodate the looming deadline. However, we were pleasantly surprised to find a number of veterans who were prepared to write accounts of their experiences, as well as many historians and researchers who already were involved in research, or completing projects dealing with a wartime theme. This was particularly true of several aspects of social history associated with the Alberta home front. Finally, the book presents an overview of Alberta during the Second World War, as seen from various perspectives, and reflects the numerous and sometimes divergent ways in which this complex series of events was experienced.

Albertans who served their country overseas are represented by several writers. Harris Field recounts his experiences with the Edmonton Regiment in Italy, and takes the reader on a night patrol. Dr. David Lewis brings an immediacy to his account of the infamous Dieppe Raid, in which most of the 2nd Canadian Division was killed, wounded or captured in August 1942. Miss Jessie Morrison gives a moving account of her time with the No. 10 Canadian General Hospital near Bayeux, France following the D-Day landing of 6 June 1944. Rodney Pike takes the reader on dangerous and vital convoy duty along the North Atlantic shipping lanes. Stan Reynolds describes his education as an RCAF pilot, while Phyllis Patterson evokes the feelings of a young prairie woman who enlists in the RCAF(WD).

The military accomplishments of the Calgary Highlanders at the Walcheren Causeway, during the Battle of the Scheldt Estuary in The Netherlands, is meticulously detailed by Dr. David Bercuson, who recently published *Battalion of Heroes: The Calgary Highlanders in World War II*. Donna Zwicker describes recruitment among Alberta women for the Canadian Women's Army Corps, RCAF(WD) and "Wrens." James Dempsey, Director of the School of Native Studies at the University of Alberta, assesses the effect upon the province's native community of their recruitment into the armed forces, and their experiences in uniform. Carrielynn Lamouche also provides an appreciation of the Métis men who served Canada in uniform.

Although Alberta was far from the major theatres of war, it nevertheless played a significant role in the global air war and continental defence. Dr. Carl Christie, Senior Researcher for National Defence Headquarters Directorate of History, places the Northwest Staging Route within its continental context, and indicates its importance to the Allied cause through Lend-Lease flights to the USSR, as well as its immediate impact on Alberta, and its more lasting influence upon international aviation. Mark Hopkins, Curator at the Alberta Aviation Museum, describes in more detail the overwhelming impact of the war upon the Edmonton Municipal Airport. Patricia Myers indicates the pervasive influence of the British Commonwealth Air Training Plan upon the urban centres, large and small, throughout Alberta. Frank Chiovelli also reveals a little-known aspect of the war, the Japanese balloon bomb offensive against North America during 1944 and 1945. Over two dozen balloon bombs were recovered in Alberta, while others drifted inland to central Canada during this campaign.

Most Alberta women found that their lives during wartime were changed in many ways. Some of these were immediate and obvious, and others more difficult to assess. Catherine Cooper Cole provides an account of women struggling to cope on the home front while many of the men were serving in the armed forces. Donna Zwicker, in addition to her article on Alberta women in uniform, acknowledges the pervasive role women filled in volunteer war work at home. In many ways the women of Alberta "kept the home fires burning" during the six war years.

The social and economic impact of the war on Alberta communities was quite striking. Dr. David Leonard, Provincial Archivist of Alberta, describes the way popular culture changed in Edmonton between 1939 and 1945, and how these changes were accelerated during the "American occupation" of 1942-1945. Jeff Keshen, an SSHRC Postdoctoral Fellow at the University of Alberta who is studying the impact of the war on the "morals and morale" of the Canadian home front, provides an absorbing account of wartime concerns in Alberta. Steven Boddington and Sean Moir give a valuable overview of the "friendly invasion" of Edmonton by Americans during major construction projects such as the Alaska Highway, Canol Pipeline Project and Northwest Staging Route. Bob Oliphant, a commercial artist who worked in Edmonton at this time for Bechtel, Price Callahan and Kansas City Bridge Company, gives a personal flavour to his memories of those days. Michael Dawe, Archivist for the Red Deer and District Museum and Archives, describes how the war came to Red Deer and changed it virtually overnight. Bruce Ibsen, City Archivist for the City of Edmonton Archives, writes an amusing account of wartime bureaucracy and injured civic pride, in which he answers the question, "Why was there no HMCS Edmonton?"

While most Albertans were drawn together by the war effort as they struggled toward a common goal, several groups and individuals experienced the war in ways which isolated them from their fellow Canadians. David Goa, Curator of Folklife at the Provincial Museum of Alberta, questions how the Japanese-Canadian community of southern Alberta could adapt to wartime and postwar conditions with so little animosity. He suggests that those who experienced the war as evacuees sent to work in the sugar beet fields near Lethbridge, Taber and Picture Butte, used Buddhist and Neo-Confucian beliefs to adapt in ways which allowed them to continue with their lives. John J. Kelly describes the Prisoner of War Camps in southern Alberta where German POWs were interned, while Dan Duda provides an account of the executions of August Plaszek and Karl Lehmann by the Gestapo group which dominated the internal operations of the Medicine Hat camp. Peter Melnycky writes a moving account of the Ukrainian-Canadian contribution to the war. My article indicates how the Veterans Volunteer Reserve perpetuated nativist sentiments formed among most of its members during the First World War, and how these were implemented in the "enemy alien" settlement blocs of Alberta. Finally, Dr. Reginald Roy, prominent Canadian military historian, provides an overview of Western Canada during the Second World War.

During the Second World War, Canada had a population of just over eleven million. Yet over a million Canadian men and women served in uniform between 1939 and 1945. Countless others served on the home front in farm fields, munitions factories and volunteer war services. By the end of the war the RCAF was one of the largest air forces in the world, with personnel numbering over a quarter million; this was sufficient to operate an entire bomber group, No. 6 Group. The Royal Canadian Navy became the fourth largest in the world as it provided the corvettes and frigates for convoy duty in the Battle of the Atlantic. The Canadian Army distinguished itself from Dieppe to Normandy, from the Battle of the Scheldt Estuary to Italy. The British Commonwealth Air Training Plan has been judged by many historians to be the single greatest Canadian contribution to the Allied victory. Albertans participated in all these campaigns with distinction, and their contributions were an important part of the war.

Many of us born after the Second World War experienced the events of that great violent upheaval through the lives of our close relatives, as I did through my father, Francis D. Tingley [RCAF 1940-1945] and father-in-law, Robert E. Whitson [RCAF 1941-1945]. Sometimes they told us about their experiences; more often they did not. Sometimes distorted views of wartime events came to us through the movies. We remembered on Remembrance Day. But as years passed, and the wartime veterans became grandfathers or great-grandfathers, the memories of the young grew more vague, and Remembrance Day memories less clear. This may be reason enough to recall the events of fifty years ago. By shaping our society, they still affect us all.

Albertans Overseas

The Calgary Highlanders at the Walcheren Causeway: October, 1944

David J. Bercuson

As the Battle of the Scheldt Estuary neared its climax in late October, 1944 the 5th Canadian Infantry Brigade of the 2nd Canadian Infantry Division drove westward across the length of Zuid Beveland. This peninsula, connected to the mainland of Holland by a narrow isthmus, formed much of the north bank of the Scheldt Estuary, the waterway from the North Sea to the all-important port of Antwerp. The British Army had liberated Antwerp and its important docks early in September, 1944, but had allowed the Germans to fortify both banks of the Scheldt, bring up reinforcements, and mine the waterway. Until the shores of the Scheldt were cleared of the enemy, the mines could not be swept. Until the mines were swept, the waterway and the port of Antwerp could not be used by the Allies. Since the Allied armies were still trucking supplies hundreds of kilometres from the beaches of Normandy to the fighting fronts, an acute supply crisis had arisen. There were shortages of everything from food to gasoline. Antwerp was the key to resolving that crisis and the Scheldt was the key to Antwerp.[1]

British Field Marshal Sir Bernard Law Montgomery, in command of 21st Army Group, had given the job of securing the Scheldt Estuary to the 1st Canadian Army. Now that battle was about to climax with a three-pronged assault to capture the island of Walcheren, just to the west of Zuid Beveland, where the last German bastion remained by the end of October. One of the infantry battalions of the 5th Brigade was the Calgary Highlanders, a militia regiment that had been mobilized in September, 1939 and that was largely made up of men and boys from southern Alberta and western Canada (the other two battalions were from Montreal — the Black Watch and the Régiment de Maisonneuve).

On the south bank of the Scheldt Estuary the port of Breskens had been liberated 21 October as troops of the 3rd Canadian Infantry Division pushed the German garrison there westward towards Zeebrugge. The final shots on the south bank would not be fired until 2 November when the German guns at Cadzand were put out of action, but possession of Breskens meant that the last phase of the operation — the assault on Walcheren — could proceed once all of Zuid Beveland was secure.

To help the 2nd Canadian Infantry Division complete the occupation of Zuid Beveland, the British 52nd (Lowland) Division had started to cross over to Zuid Beveland from the south bank of the Estuary on the evening of 23 October. They then advanced towards the western tip of the peninsula where they would meet the Canadians. On the Canadian front, the 4th Brigade had cleared the final German positions to the immediate east of the narrow causeway connecting Walcheren to Zuid Beveland in the early hours of 31 October.[2] The next phase of the attack plan originally drawn up by Canadian Lt. -Gen. G. G. "Guy" Simonds, temporarily in command of lst Canadian Army, called for seaborne assaults on 1 November at Westkapelle by the British 4th Special Service Brigade and at Flushing by the British No. 4 Commando and the 155th Infantry Brigade of the 52nd (Lowland) Division. At the same time, there would be an attack over the Walcheren causeway.

The causeway attack was to be essentially diversionary in nature. It was timed to coincide with the British commando landings and maintain pressure on the Germans so that they would not reinforce their positions at Flushing and Westkapelle. There is some indication that Lt.-Gen.Charles Foulkes (the acting commander of the 2nd Canadian Corps, of which 2nd Canadian Infantry Division was a part) did not decide until the last moment whether the causeway attack was to be done by the 2nd Canadian Infantry Division — which had been in constant action since the third week of September — or the 52nd (Lowland) Division, which had not yet seen combat.[3]

In late 1944 the Walcheren causeway was about one kilometre long, 40 metres wide, and 20 metres from its base to its top. It connected the eastern tip of Walcheren to Zuid Beveland over marshy salt flats of deep mud, long grasses, and runnels of water. Sometimes the flats were covered with sea water to a depth of up to five metres, but not at the end of October 1944. Atop the causeway was a rail line, a two lane blacktop road, and two bicycle paths that had once been lined with trees. There was also a set of railway tracks on the north side of the causeway. The trackbed was about 1.5 metres higher than the road and bicycle paths. The two sides of the causeway were lined with boulders secured in place by wooden stakes, designed to withstand the tides.

Map courtesy
Department of
National Defence.

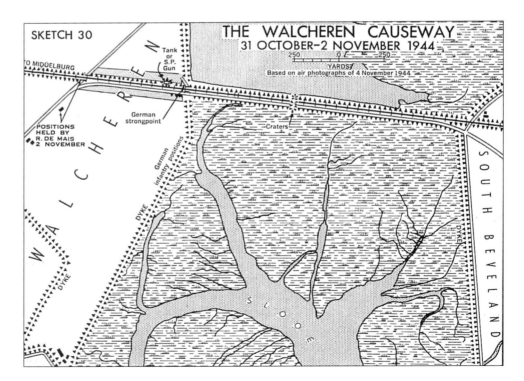

On 31 October, 1944 the causeway had been much changed by war. The trees had been almost totally shattered by shellfire. The Germans had built concrete bunkers at both ends of the causeway and in the sides of the Walcheren dykes that ran to the north and south of it. Atop those dykes they had dug firing trenches. On the causeway itself, they had prepared brick-lined slit trenches and on both slopes of the causeway, about 300 metres from the Walcheren end, they had poured concrete slabs in which they had embedded perpendicular lengths of rail cut at sharp angles and enmeshed in barbed wire. A large crater had been blown in the causeway about 300 metres from the Zuid Beveland end. Some of the Highlanders would later recall the crater as having virtually cut the causeway in two.[4] One report radioed to 5th Brigade HQ by engineers in the midst of the causeway battle on 1 November estimated that it would take five uninterrupted hours of work with earthmovers to fill it.[5] In addition, the Germans had built a large roadblock from bits of torn-up rail at the Walcheren end of the causeway, and had sited one 88mm anti-tank gun to fire down its length. They had also positioned at least two other 88s, as well as heavy mortars and machine guns, northwest and southwest of the western end of the causeway. Some members of the Highlander intelligence section were certain that one of the 88s was actually embedded in the dyke itself.[6] German artillery for miles around was also sighted in on it. The defences were manned by troops of the 70th Infantry Division, a "stomach" unit made of men with ulcers and other stomach disorders, and the tough veterans of the 64th Infantry Division who had had battle experience on the Russian front.[7] It is no exaggeration to say that the causeway was a killing ground.

In his excellent account of the battle to clear the Scheldt Estuary, J.L. Moulton claims that Brigadier H. Keefler, the acting 2nd Canadian Infantry Division GOC [General Officer Commanding], "told the 4th and 5th Brigades that whichever first reached the eastern end of the causeway ... would stop there, leaving to the other the uninviting task of crossing."[8] There is no evidence cited to support this extraordinary statement, probably because none exists. Given that the order in which brigades move anywhere is invariably determined by division's own staff, Keefler would have been 'loading the dice' had he made such a condition. It is, however, entirely possible that Keefler approached the 4th Brigade CO [Commanding Officer], Brigadier Frederick Cabeldu, with the proposition that his troops attempt the attack and that Cabeldu demurred because his men had spearheaded the division in the past two days whereas 5th Brigade had followed in reserve.[9] In later years the CO of the 5th Brigade, Brigadier W.J. Megill, would only say that he had been given an assignment, and that was that: "Foulkes wanted the end of Walcheren cleared and sealed and turned over to the Brits. That is what we tried to do."[10] In fact, the 5th Brigade war diary makes plain that Megill and his staff were not pleased that their men had been picked for the job. When the Brigade staff first heard this news on 30 October, the war diarist recorded: "This comes as an unpleasant order as we were definitely infm [informed] that we were to go no further than the WEST end of ZUID BEVELAND and in fact had been promised a weeks rest once we had done this job."[11]

The last shots in the fight to clear the eastern end of the causeway had barely died away when Highlander CO Major Ross Ellis and the other 5th Brigade COs were called to a brigade 0 [orders] Group at 1000 on the morning of 31 October and told what was in store for them.[12] Megill wanted the Black Watch to send "a fighting patrol" across the causeway as a "quick operation" because "no artillery support" was yet available; if the Black Watch could "bump a bridgehead," the way would be prepared for "a more ambitious operation."[13] That operation was to be an amphibious attack by the Calgary Highlanders. Once a bridgehead had been secured on Walcheren by the Highlanders, the Maisonneuve were to follow and drive westward on the north side of the tracks while the Highlanders advanced on the town of Arnemuiden, about two kilometres west of the causeway, on the south side of the tracks.

The Black Watch CO disregarded Megill's instructions and, instead of trying to get a patrol across the causeway, mounted a full three company assault which began at about 1040. As soon as the Black Watch approached the causeway, German mortar and shell fire began to fall on it. One group of men managed to reach within some 25 metres of the far end but the rest were pinned down and eventually ordered to withdraw after last light. Most were able to do so but those at the farthest end, including a few casualties, had to take refuge in the German-built slit trenches until evacuated by the Highlanders in the early morning hours of 1 November.[14]

As the Black Watch men on the causeway underwent their trial by fire, the Highlanders prepared for their over-water assault. They had presumably been picked for this operation due to assault training they had received months before in England, but most of the officers and men who had undergone that training were now gone. Captain Frank "Nobby" Clarke, who would command B Company during the causeway attack, was put in charge of the training, which consisted of teaching men how to get into, and out of, outlines of boats drawn in the dirt. He ridiculed the idea of a water assault on Walcheren and did not hesitate to let Ellis know,[15] but Ellis had his orders, whatever misgivings he may have had. In the end Megill decided that there was not enough water in the tidal flats to float assault boats and too much mud for wheeled or tracked vehicles. At 1830, he informed Ellis that the Highlanders would have to go over the causeway itself.

The assault plan was straightforward; after a heavy bombardment of the far end by the divisional artillery of the 52nd (Lowland) Division, the Canadian 5th Field Artillery, the heavy mortars of the Toronto Scottish, and the mortars of the Highlander mortar platoon, B Company would move onto the causeway and establish a semi-circular bridgehead about 200 metres in depth at the far end. Then D and A Companies would move through, the former pushing towards the southwest, the latter to the northwest. Ellis may not have known that the "polder," or the dyked and reclaimed marshland to the immediate southwest of the Walcheren end of the causeway, was partially flooded and that D Company would have to move atop the dyke or along it. Once all that had been accomplished, the Highlanders were to expand the bridgehead in the direction of Arnemuiden in preparation for the Maisonneuve who were to pass through them. The area would then be turned over to the 52nd (Lowland) Division which would drive deeper into Walcheren. To oversee the battle, Ellis moved his tactical headquarters to a sunken brick road running south from the causeway approach road, on the east side of a dyke. From atop the dyke he would be able to see what was happening along the causeway and on the Walcheren dyke about a kilometre away over the salt marsh. It was an exposed position, but this was the first major battle for Ellis as battalion CO and he obviously intended to show his men that he was right up with them.

The night was exceptionally clear. Clarke and his men waited at the eastern end of the causeway, anxious to start across. Signaller Frank Holm carried the Mark 18 radio set. As they waited he remarked to one of the other men: "Tonight is Halloween. I wonder if there are going to be any fireworks?"[16] Within minutes he had his answer; at 2340, the guns opened up on the far end of the causeway and the line of dykes to the north and south of it. According to Megill the 52nd (Lowland) artillery had the task of blasting the Germans from their fire trenches atop the dykes but failed to hit their targets.[17] Almost as soon as the Canadian and British artillery opened up, German artillery began to fire at the causeway. At 2400 B Company moved out, inching forward along the south side of the railbed and trying to use it as partial cover from the machine guns firing at them from the north dyke.[18]

The B Company advance was led by 12 Platoon, commanded by Lt. Walter Lefroy. John Morrison was with them, and later recalled: "We headed out and everybody was with us and out in the middle of the causeway was this enormous big crater.... When we got to the crater they put in a big barrage of mortar fire. Everybody hit the deck....When it eased up somebody said 'lets go' and away we went .... We got down on the south side and crept along there. Most of the fire was going over the top, but there was lots of it .... Eventually we got up to a big tank trap .... There were pieces of railroad track that had been cut off at a sharp angle placed in this concrete .... Before that this French fellow behind me had been killed by a rifle grenade. I actually saw it out of the corner of my eye. We went on and we could hear the Germans on the other side of the tank trap. We thought 'well, we can't take them on'. I had been hit with some schrapnel, [Corporal D.H.] Richardson had been shot through the arm, and then Lefroy got it through the chest."[19] Chewed up, 12 Platoon could go no farther.

Back on the causeway, Clarke and Holm took refuge in the crater. The shellfire was intense. Holm later remembered: "The heavy shells were the worst. The explosion would send a shock through you that would reach the very depths of your nervous system and put in doubt your ability to take it .... I swore that if I ever got out of this hellish place alive I wouldn't mind eating dirt for the rest of my life."[20] John Martin was in a somewhat more exposed position: "This shell or something came and I could just see stars, all colours of the rainbow. And some guy yelled 'I'm hit'. I said 'where are you hit?' He says 'I think in the back.' You could tell that he wasn't real bad. I was at the stage where I thought I would give anything to get out of there. I said 'you lucky son of a bitch.'"[21] The Germans also fired the 88mm at the end of the causeway, skipping shells down the roadway. The sound terrified the advancing infantrymen. The position of B Company was untenable. Clarke reported that he was unable to make progress and requested permission to withdraw. Ellis obtained Megill's sanction[22] and as B Company pulled back, they took the remaining men from the Black Watch with them. They were off the causeway by 0300.[23] It was clear the Highlanders would have to try something else and Clarke and Ellis went back to Brigade HQ to confer with Megill on what that might be.

The answer the three commanders came up with was yet another assault, but with a different fire plan. This time two field artillery regiments would concentrate their fire on a frontage of some 750 metres with a creeping barrage that would lift 50 or so metres every two minutes. Advancing behind this barrage, Major Bruce McKenzie's D Company started back at 0605 on the morning of 1 November. German shelling was still heavy but the German machine gun fire had slackened off, probably because of the creeping barrage. However, there appeared to be no let up in small arms and sniper fire as D Company crept around the crater towards the end of the causeway. At 0710 they radioed that they were nearing the German roadblock; at 0715, they were past it. Then, at 0717, they called for more artillery on their front.[24] Dawn was now breaking as the company's leading troops inched their way forward; it was broad daylight at 0950 when they radioed that they had reached the end and were beginning to fan out onto the eastern end of Walcheren Island, one platoon moving north, the other south. The first of some 43 prisoners were sent back as McKenzie radioed for the following companies to come forward.[25]

Clarke's B Company and Major Wynn Lasher's A Company were waiting on the causeway for word to move up. As D Company began to secure the bridgehead, they advanced. A Company crawled forward on the right side of the causeway [facing the Germans] and was supposed to move north once off the causeway. It made good progress at first, but then came under heavy sniper fire and was forced to hold up. B Company, on the left side of the causeway, made it across despite the bad footing and began to advance south along the front of the dyke, toward a cluster of farm buildings about 600 metres south of the D Company positions. Moving single file, they got close enough to assault the buildings, but Clarke needed covering fire to get his men over the dike and his radio was not working; he had no contact with battalion headquarters. He could literally see Ellis's position across the salt marsh but he had no way of communicating with him. Clarke would later remember his "despair and exasperation at our position because we could actually see battalion across the flood plain on the far dyke. We hoped that they would appreciate our position and act. This of course was a ridiculous and foolish hope."[26] He sent two runners to call for mortar or artillery cover, but they never reached battalion HQ.

Back at battalion HQ Ellis thought things were falling into place; at 1210 the Maisonneuve received the warning order to be ready to move across the causeway at 1305 to reinforce the Highlanders. But in fact the three forward Highlander companies were taking heavy casualties and A Company was making no progress at all. Lt. Howard 0. Schoening accompanied Lasher who went forward to get his company moving: "I had just come up beside a slit trench and was talking to Wynn Lasher and two other people. I got up ... and got hit in the right arm .... The force of the bullet swung me around and I landed beside the slit trench again. I rolled over and went into the trench .... Lasher was hit by the same burst, he was hit in the back.... Eventually I got up and so did Lasher. The firing had stopped. We started back towards where the regimental aid post was and eventually got back."[27] With Lasher and Schoening gone, A Company had no commissioned officers left on the causeway. At roughly 1545, Typhoon fighter bombers appeared over the causeway and dove on the German gun positions firing rockets and cannon.[28] Then two squadrons of Spitfires flew over to continue the air assault but the German guns were well dug in and the defenders tenacious; Highlanders continued to fall. Clarke was down to less than 25 men.

At 1545 Ellis, Captain Gordon Sellar and Brigade Major George Hees (from 5th Brigade HQ) went onto the causeway to see what was happening. Ellis looked neat and calm as he moved from position to position, talking to his men and encouraging them. Sellar would later recall: "We started up the causeway ... and with the first of these shells that came over, I dived into this hole with the two riflemen that were in there and when I looked up [Major] Ellis was standing up top talking to us. I felt rather silly and got out and stood beside him. We did this all the way up the causeway, stopped at every slit trench and talked to everybody and paid no attention to the shelling."[29] Ellis, Hees and Sellar discovered that A Company was without commissioned officers; once back at battalion HQ Hees, a staff officer with no experience in the field, volunteered to lead them. Ellis received Megill's permission and Sellar outfitted him with a helmet and a Sten gun. Then Ellis led him and the artillery observation officer, Captain Newman, who had also volunteered, out to the A Company positions.[30] Hees was shot in the arm shortly after, but led the company for the remainder of its time on the causeway. Ellis later said of Hees: "It took a lot of guts for a guy who had never been in action to go into a hell-hole like that one."[31]

Ellis returned from his second trip on the causeway at about 1730 and went to Megill's tactical HQ to discuss the situation. The problems with A and B Companies had postponed the Maisonneuve advance; now Megill told Ellis to hold "until Div[ision] decided what to do."[32] At just about that time, however, the Germans at the western end of the causeway launched a counter-attack aimed at the southern end of the D Company perimeter. Armed with flamethrowers, they threatened to cut Clarke's men completely off; he ordered a withdrawal. Across the salt marsh battalion HQ could see the Germans advancing, and called down tank and artillery fire to help, but they still had no radio contact with B Company. As B Company withdrew, D Company pulled back as well.[33]

Sergeant Emile Jean Laloge was with 18 Platoon of D Company when the counter-attack began. As German grenades sailed toward his men, he picked them up and threw them back at the Germans. When one of his Bren gunners was killed and the gun damaged, Laloge repaired the gun and opened fire at the advancing Germans. When Laloge yelled for PIAT [projector, infantry, anti-tank] fire and found out that the PIAT man was wounded, he fired that too at the enemy. His bravery and leadership earned him the Distinguished Conduct Medal.[34] Another man decorated for his role in defending against the counter-attack was L/Cpl. Richard G. Wolfe. In charge of a 2" mortar, Wolfe stayed behind to give covering fire to B Company as it pulled back. Time after time his well placed mortar bombs held up the German advance until he was captured. A day or two later the Germans sent Wolfe back to the Canadian lines with a request that their hospital not be shelled.[35] Lt. John Moffat, Clarke's second in command on the causeway, tried to move his men to better firing positions as they withdrew, but he was shot dead.[36] B and D Companies first pulled back about 300 metres from the Walcheren end of the causeway, then were withdrawn completely by Ellis. A Company and C Company remained on the causeway in the vicinity of the crater. By the time they pulled out, B and D companies were down to about 22 men each.

The Calgary Highlanders had made it across the causeway but had not been able to hold. In the end, it did not matter to the overall outcome of the battle because the fate of the German garrison on Walcheren was sealed anyway. The British landing at Flushing was a complete success and although the assault on Westkapelle was a near disaster, German resistance soon began to crumble; as the British troops drove south and east along the rim of the flooded island, the German troops between them and the causeway were held in an ever tightening grip.

Despite the success of the landings, Foulkes insisted that Keefler and Megill continue their effort to get across the causeway and as night fell, Megill laid plans for one more attack, this time by the Maisonneuve. At first Megill envisioned a full scale assault supported by a massive artillery and mortar barrage. Then, at the behest of Divisional HQ, plans were changed again. The Maisonneuve would send only two companies forward and attack for about one hour and would then be relieved by the 157th Brigade of the 52nd (Lowland) Division.[37] At 0400 the barrage and the assault began. The last Highlanders pulled back, taking their casualties with them, as the Maisonneuve advanced. One Maisonneuve company made it as far as 200 metres from the Walcheren end of the causeway before it was stopped. It would not finally leave that killing ground until early afternoon when it was relieved by the Scottish troops.

The story of the causeway does not end there. Ordered by Foulkes to make yet another assault, Maj.-Gen. Hakewell-Smith, the GOC of the 52nd (Lowland) Division, refused and sought permission to find another way. Eventually he did when his scouts discovered a place where his troops could walk across the salt marsh at night. They outflanked the Germans at the end of the causeway in the early morning hours of 3 November and quickly bypassed them, securing the western end of the causeway. Then they advanced westward. The Germans were trapped. The last shots on Walcheren Island were fired towards the evening of 8 November and the Battle for the Scheldt ended. By then the Highlanders and the rest of the 2nd Canadian Infantry Division had been pulled out of the battle and were headed for Nijmegen, Holland where they would spend most of the winter.

In the Battle of the Scheldt Estuary the Calgary Highlanders lost 107 men killed and another 327 wounded; nineteen of the dead and 45 of the wounded fell at the Walcheren causeway. The last word on this epic battle in regimental history should be reserved for the man who commanded the Highlanders there, Ross Ellis: "The actual battle itself in which the Calgary Highlanders took part didn't develop a great deal. The main accomplishment we got out of there was that we got as many as we could out alive."[38]

Notes

This paper is published by permission of the Calgary Highlanders Regimental Funds Foundation. It is excerpted from David J. Bercuson, *Battalion of Heroes: The Calgary Highlanders in World War II* [Calgary: The Calgary Highlanders Regimental Funds Foundation, 1994].

[1]The best secondary source on the battle of the Scheldt Estuary is W. D. Whitaker and Shelagh Whitaker, *Tug of War: The Canadian Victory that Opened Antwerp* [Toronto, 1984].

[2]National Archives of Canada [NAC], War Diary of the 2nd Canadian Infantry Division, 31/10/44.

[3]NAC, War Diary of the 5th Canadian Infantry Brigade (WD, 5 CIB), 30/10/44. The diary states "news suddenly arrived that the show was off and we would NOT do the op - 52 Br Div are to clear WALCHEREN IS."

[4]William J. Wright, "Adventures of a Canadian Soldier Through a Europe at War with the Calgary Highlanders" [Privately produced, 1992]. In the possession of the author.

[5]WD, 5 CIB, Message Log 1/11/44.

[6]Ed Ford to Bercuson 27 November, 1993 quoting a letter from Vosko to Mannix, 7 May, 1993, in the possession of the author.

[7]George Blake, *Mountain and Flood* [Glasgow, 1950], p. 91.

[8]J.L. Moulton, *Battle for Antwerp* [New York, 1978] p. 137.

[9]Terry Copp, *The Brigade* [Stoney Creek, Ontario, 1992], p. 156.

[10]D. Bercuson interview with W. Megill in possession of the author.

[11]WD, 5 CIB, 30/10/44.

[12]Except where otherwise cited, the story of the causeway battle is taken from WD, Calgary Highlanders (CH), 31/10/44-2/11/44.

[13]NAC, RG 24, Records of the Department of National Defence (henceforth DND Records), Vol. 10985, File 265.011, "The capture of Zuid Beveland and operations to secure a bridgehead on Walcheren Island ... " draft version. There are two versions of this document in this file, a draft version and a shorter final version.

[14]WD, Black Watch, 31/10/44; 1/11/44.

[15]Bert Reed interview with Frank "Nobby" Clarke, in the possession of the author.

[16]Frank P. Holm, *A Backward Glance* [Sault Ste. Marie, 1989] p. 33.

[17]DND Records, Vol. 10985, File 265.011, "The capture of Zuid Beveland and operations to secure a bridgehead on Walcheren Island ... "

[18]Ibid. The railbed, being 1.5 metres or so higher than the road, afforded some cover against fire from the north, but not the south.

[19]Reed interview with John Morrison, in the possession of the author.

[20]Holm, pp. 36-37.

[21]Reed interview with John Martin, in the possession of the author.

[22]The war diary is confirmed on this by Clarke to Tennant, 7 April, 1954, in the possession of the Calgary Highlanders Regimental Funds Foundation collection, Museum of the Regiments, Calgary.

[23]WD, Black Watch, 1/11/44.

[24]5 CIB message logs, 1/11/44.

[25]Ibid., WD, CH, 1/11/44.

[26]Frank "Nobby" Clarke to Jeffery Williams, 26 July, 1987, courtesy of Jeffery Williams. The letter is in the possession of the Calgary Highlanders Regimental Funds Foundation collection, Museum of the Regiments, Calgary.

[27]Reed interview with Howard Schoening, in the possession of the author.

[28]5 CIB Message logs, 1/11/44.

[29]Reed interview with G. Sellar, in the possession of the author.

[30]W.D. Whitaker interview with Ross Ellis, 21 August, 1982, courtesy of W.D. Whitaker; Williams to Bercuson, 30 March, 1992. Both documents are in the possession of the author.

[31]Ford to Bercuson, 27 November, 1993.

[32]WD, CH, 1/11/44.

[33]DND Records, Vol . 10985, File 265.11 , "The capture of Zuid Beveland and operations to secure a bridgehead on Walcheren Island ...."

[34]Glenbow Archives, Calgary Highlanders Collection, Box 4, File 41, medal citation for E.J. Laloge.

[35]Ibid., medal citation for R.G. Wolfe.

[36]Ibid., medal citation for J.D. Moffat.

[37]DND Records, Vol. 10985, File 265.011, "The capture of Zuid Beveland and operations to secure a bridgehead on Walcheren Island ... "

[38]W.D. Whitaker interview with Ross Ellis, 21 August, 1982, courtesy of W.D. Whitaker, in the possession of the author.

With the Loyal Edmonton Regiment in Italy

Harris G. Field

Included among the units in the Canadian forces in Italy during the Second World War was the Loyal Edmonton Regiment, founded at Edmonton in January 1915, under the leadership of William A. "Billy" Griesback. The Regiment as I shall call it, had distinguished service in the First World War, and survived as a Militia Unit based in Edmonton between 1918 and 1939.

When the Germans invaded Poland on 1 September 1939, the Canadian Army was in a state which might kindly be described as inadequate, although harsher critics have described it as virtually non-existent. When the Regiment was being mobilized in Edmonton that September and October, there were lots of sturdy volunteers, but experienced military personnel were limited, and there was no decent equipment or weapons.

In spite of these difficulties, the Regiment was selected as one of the nine infantry battalions forming the First Canadian Infantry Division. It also was fortunate to be brigaded with two other fine units, the Seaforth Highlanders of Canada [based in Vancouver], and the only permanent prewar infantry force in Western Canada, Princess Patricia's Canadian Light Infantry.

The first Canadian Infantry Division was sent to Britain late in 1939; with the exception of an expedition by a detachment of the Regiment to Spitsbergen in the summer of 1941, which did not meet any enemy resistance, the Canadians sat. They went on exercises, they went on schemes, they went on leave, but they went nowhere for three and a half years.

On 13 May 1943 the War in Africa ended, and questions started flying — where would the Allies' next attack be, and who would launch it? At the end of June 1943 the Division's questions were answered when it set sail for the Mediterranean.

On 10 July 1943 the Allies, including First Canadian Division Forces which were now part of Field Marshal Bernard Montgomery's Eighth Army, landed in Sicily. The long slow bitter struggle which would rage over the whole Italian peninsula now began in earnest. It is my recollection that we were told that this Division of Canadian Forces, numbering about 15,000 to 16,000 well trained and well equiped troops, were committed to the Italian campaign because in mid-1943 a strike against Italy was judged by the strategy planners to be critical. This was for several very good reasons: it could quickly knock Italy out of the war; it would open a new European front, thus relieving some pressure on the Russians, and Churchill, who distrusted the Russians, could see that a strike into Austria from Italy would keep Russian forces out of Western Europe.

As it turned out, US strategy, to the Allies' lasting regret, did not perceive this danger from the Russians, and by 1944, Allied military strength and strategic emphasis was shifted to France and North-Western Europe at the expense of the Italian Campaign.

Italy from May through September has bright hot weather which can stretch for six weeks or more with no rain. In the winter months of November through into March, it is cold, very grey, very wet, and there may be no sunshine for weeks on end.

The Italian peninsula is a very long chain of rugged mountains running parallel to both coasts from the Po Valley to the toe of the peninsula. Cutting across the mountain chains are many deep valleys with quite steep slopes which may be dry or have modest rivers in summer, but which can be torrential in winter. This landscape lends itself well to military defence, because every few miles there will be another deep gully with its water course cutting across the line of advance from the south. There is a major exception in the plain near Rome, which probably explains why the Germans made no attempt to defend it. Elsewhere, however, the defenders had plenty of ideal defensive sites. The Eighth Army was on the east side of the peninsula [the Adriatic side], with American forces on the west side. Canadian forces landed on the west side of the toe of Italy, but after the initial advances they were committed along the Adriatic coast, except for "the Hitler line" battle above Monte Cassino.

The Loyal Edmonton Regiment, Italy, on Hill 736. By war artist Will Ogilvie.

Artwork courtesy Canadian War Museum [13457].

The Italian people had little sympathy for Mussolini's commitment of the nation to a devastating war with Italy's traditional ally, Britain. At the first opportunity, in September 1943, Mussolini's government was overturned and Italy was out of the war. The German reaction was to strengthen its forces in Italy on the basis that it was essential to defend Germany's southern flank, and Italian terrain was ideal for that defence.

We Canadians were of the opinion, whether justifiably so or not, that the German forces in Italy in 1943 and 1944 were roughly equal in strength to the Allied forces. The advantage the Germans had was that they had over-land supply routes from Germany and Austria, while the Allies had to ship everything in by sea. The reason the Allies were successful in forcing the Germans back was the total domination of the air and ocean by Allied forces. These could move in daylight, while theirs could not. Consequently, concentration for a strike at any particular sector was possible for the Allies, but very difficult for the Germans.

The campaign by the Allied forces consisted of a series of diversionary tactics, trying to keep the enemy guessing as to which particular sector would be attacked in force. The Allies would regroup behind the lines for a major assault at a particular point on the front. When that assault was launched it would at first be successful, but within a few days enemy reserves would be assembled in the threatened area and the attack would grind to a halt. The whole procedure would then start over again.

Night Patrolling North of Ortona

After the battle of Ortona ended on 28 December 1943, the main thrust of the Allied attack shifted to "the road to Rome," with attacks up the Rapido River toward Monte Cassino and the American attack at the beach-head of Anzio. The Canadians were left on the Adriatic coast to hold that sector, and to do what they could to keep the Germans committed there so as to prevent those forces moving as reinforcements to other sectors. A vigorous patrol policy was initiated. Those patrols varied in strength from two- or three-man reconnaissance ["recce"] patrols, to fighting patrols consisting of up to thirty or forty men, depending on whether the patrol's objective was to gain information or to try a sneak attack on an enemy position.

The purposes varied, but patrols were intended to achieve one or more objectives: to attempt to locate exactly where the enemy defensive positions were, and what areas were covered by their "fixed lines of fire" by machine guns; to attempt to locate holes in the defensive positions; to find out which specific units or formations were holding the sector — for example, German paratroopers were formidable, and were always to be found where the German high command expected trouble; to deceive the enemy into thinking your side of "no man's land" is more strongly held than it really is; to take prisoners or inflict casualties in a surprise attack on an outpost; or to dominate "no man's land," so that if you

Canadian armour
passing through
Ortona. By war artist
Charles Comfort.

*Artwork courtesy
Canadian War Museum
[12245].*

must later traverse it in a major attack, you would find few surprises such as land
mines or wire entanglements.

Let me describe a patrol. A deep gully with the Arielli River at the bottom
separated the forces. Each night patrols would go out into the gully. As a Platoon
Commander I was expected to lead every patrol in which any of my platoon were
involved. A platoon, if up to strength, was at that time about 35 men.

On this particular mid-afternoon I was ordered to report to the Intelligence
Officer at Battalion headquarters. This was probably a mile on foot through the
mud from where my platoon was positioned in defensive locations, in trenches or
stone buildings just behind the top of the near slope of the hill overlooking Arielli
gully. The IO gave me all known data on the enemy positions in the area I was to
enter. He also stated the objective of the patrol — in this case to determine if
certain groups of buildings on the top of the far bank were occupied by enemy
troops, and if so in what strength. He stated I was to take a strong patrol in hopes
that we might isolate an enemy outpost and kill the occupants, or take them
prisoner. He also stated that if we were discovered before we could hope to
succeed in a snatch, we were to be discreet and not engage in a fire fight.
Together we went over stereo aerial photos, so that I would know the contours
and features in detail in the dark, and we also agreed on the patrol's route out and
back. I then returned to my platoon and relayed all these instructions to the ten
men which I had designated to accompany me. "Never come back the same way

you go out — you may be ambushed — be certain you come back the route agreed upon because the troops in forward positions in that area will be expecting you." It also was essential that each member of the patrol had all of the information, for who knew how many would get back safely. At night, forward troops were watching constantly for enemy patrol attack, and anyone approaching them in the dark from the enemy side might be shot if the approach was unexpected.

It was usually overcast with a light drizzle, and when night fell it was very dark. The point was again made to all members of the patrol that absolute quiet, particularly on the outward-bound leg, was essential if we were to accomplish anything. Everyone took off anything that might glitter and betray us, such as a watch.

At the appointed hour we set off through and beyond the forward positions of our defences. Half way down the exposed slope there was a sudden burst of machine gun fire right behind me. My new and somewhat nervous sergeant, who had very much wanted to come on the patrol, had inadvertently squeezed the trigger on his Tommy gun!

So much for the element of surprise! After waiting to be sure we had not attracted the attention of any enemy patrol in the area, we moved on to the bottom of the gully. The patrol was spread out — five or more feet apart in single file, with instructions passed back to each in turn in low whispers. I was constantly trying to check our position from the recollection of the stereo photos. Ahead and above us, near the hilltop, loomed a group of white buildings. We broke into two groups — one to approach straight up the gully slopes, the other to approach at a right angle to the gully slope. In this way, if the enemy detected and shot at one group, the other group could offer protection by returning the fire without risk of hitting our own people. Since the purpose of the patrol was not to engage in a protracted fire fight, once we were discovered, if we could not immediately isolate one or two people, we were to withdraw. Before we split up we agreed on the precise location where we were to reunite. On this occasion one of our men stumbled a little, and the enemy sent up flares in an attempt to see us. The flares lasted ten to fifteen seconds, and were very bright, although objects on the ground remained in deep shadow. If you were down on your knees or stomach, and you stayed absolutely still until the flare faded out, even if you were in the open you were unlikely to be detected. The enemy began firing their automatic weapons, set on fixed lines to cover the obvious approaches. We studied where that fire was going, to be certain that we could avoid it, and to report back as to where it was located. We did nothing, the individual Germans were too far away for us to effectively shoot at them, and firing at a shadowy figure in the distance would only disclose our position. The two groups then quietly withdrew to the rendezvous point. The enemy knew there was a patrol out, so we had to be very careful to avoid easy and obvious routes home, and the areas where machine gun fire had been pre-aimed.

When we were nearly back to our re-entry point on our designated route, I rather noisily hailed our forward defence so as to be challenged and respond with the password for that day. Safely back, I still had to return to the IO and fully report on all that we learned.

Our forces were often involved in counter attacks as well. In describing this type of engagement, it must be remembered that "counter attack" in military terms is an attack by one side shortly after an attack by the other side has gained some objectives. The purpose of the counter attack is simply to drive the other side from its recent gains before the gains can be consolidated.

One of the major counter attacks faced by the Regiment occurred at the Naviglio Canal in December 1944. The plains of the Po Valley inland from the Adriatic are low and flat. In the winter they resemble Sea Island at Vancouver in January — soggy! Across this plain, over many years, the Italians had built drainage canals, and at this time these had high earthen dykes on each side. In winter, with all bridges blown, the larger of these dyked canals posed formidable obstacles, and were impossible for armoured vehicles to cross, unless a military bridge could be put in place.

The Loyal Edmonton Regiment returns to Edmonton, 6 October 1945. Some arrive bearing mementoes of the Italian Campaign.

Photo courtesy Provincial Archives of Alberta [PAA Bl.987/4].

In early December 1944, the First Canadian Division had attacked such a dyke system, the Naviglio Canal, and after heavy fighting it had gained a rather tenuous hold on the far bank. The Regiment was ordered to reinforce the bridgehead, where an engineering bridge had been hastily built to get armoured vehicles across at a single crossing. On 13 December, late in the day, the forward companies crossed the canal and looked over the sector from the Hastings and Prince Edward Regiment, which had secured the foothold on the far bank. During the night, the forward companies of the Regiment passed through the Hastings and Prince Edward Regiment, and were positioned in very close proximity to the enemy positions. This proximity was revealed in the order I received during the night from the Commanding Officer. At that time I was in command of the machine gun platoon, and its water-cooled Vickers were too heavy to be moved far on foot. When ammunition supply also was involved, the weapons had to be transported by carrier to be effective. These were open-topped, armour-plated tracked vehicles. The CO explained to me precisely where the most forward company headquarters of our Regiment was located. He wanted a section of the machine guns to go to that company immediately, to be deployed by daylight for defence against counter attack. He showed me on his map where the bridge over the canal had been built, and then following the road parallel with the canal on the far side with his finger, he said "D Company headquarters is in the third house on your left." He then observed that "the fourth house, 60 or 70 feet farther, is held by the Germans." So off I went in the darkness, leading my carrier with its crew, and counting those houses very, very carefully.

By next morning we were set up with a tank in support in the company area. I had a good siting for one of the guns in an upstairs room of the typical rural Italian stone house which we were occupying. The other gun was sited on the ground floor, and protected another approach to the house. A platoon of D Company infantry was deployed in defensive positions around the outside of the house.

At noon we were advised that an attack would be launched on the enemy, who were a very short distance down the road. A bombardment was to begin at a prescribed time, and since there was a target very close to us and the infantry near the house, the gunners were afraid "a short" [a slightly defective round of artillery that lands short of its target] might join the machine gunners in the upper storey of the building, so we were all ordered to withdraw downstairs to avoid the risk.

The bombardment started on schedule, but before it started there seemed to be a lot of shell fire coming from the enemy side. Before our attack was actually launched we discovered that a major enemy counter attack was starting, and instead of attacking we were being attacked. The platoon scrambled back to their defensive positions, and my men to their guns.

By pure coincidence our preliminary bombardment caught the attackers just as they were forming up for their assault on our cluster of buildings. The casualties and confusion caused by the shelling seriously disrupted their attack.

At the time when the German infantry attack was timed to begin, a very heavily armoured German "Tiger" tank lumbered around the bend of the road about 75 yards from us, appearing from behind a building held by the Germans. The only tank support we had was the one tank stationed at the corner of the building we were in, which was guarding the approach along the road. As soon as the "Tiger" appeared, our gallant tank crew fired at it with its 6-pounder. As I watched this episode from the upstairs hole in the wall where once there had been a window, I was horrified to see the armour-piercing, 6-pounder shell bounce off the armour plate of the tank. However, the Tiger's crew were so startled by the impact that they bailed out, and of course once out they couldn't get back in because they were under direct fire from machine guns only 75 yards away. A brick wall, which was all there was between my gunners and that Tiger tank, would have provided about as much protection from the tank's armour-piercing shells as would tissue paper against a rifle bullet.

The German attack came in, but without armoured support, and having been badly beaten up by the artillery barrage, it quickly fizzled out. The platoon defending "our" building had been well deployed, and although enemy troops got within about 25 feet of the building, they got no farther.

Since our guns were blazing away from within the building, our gunners would have been sitting ducks if the enemy had made it over that last 25 feet. The following day we were able to resume the offensive and the bridgehead was firmly established.

An Alberta Nurse at Normandy

Jessie Morrison

Jessie Morrison joined the Royal Canadian Army Medical Corps in May 1941, and was posted to Nova Scotia almost immediately. Soon after this she was posted to the No. 10 Canadian General Hospital Unit and sent to England. In July 1944 she was sent to Normandy, shortly after the intense fighting of the D-Day invasion. After serving in Normandy for several months, she was returned to Canada due to RCAMC restrictions regarding length of service and age. However, she continued nursing in Canadian Military Hospitals until her discharge on 30 December 1945. During the postwar years she worked at the Colonel Mewburn and Colonel Wells Pavilions, caring for ex-servicemen there and at the Colonel Belcher Hospital in Calgary. Miss Morrison also served as Assistant to the Director at the Montreal School of Nursing Aides in 1948, and after her return to Alberta the following year, as Matron at Government House, for the Department of Veterans Affairs. She continued to work as a caregiver until her retirement in 1967. This account of her experiences in Normandy is an edited version of a transcript of a talk presented in 1979, as well as biographical material taken from an article in the Archives of Alberta Registered Nurses Newsletter *[Vol.50, No. 4, April 1994].*

Jessie Morrison, portrait taken in Providence, Rhode Island, March 1945.

In the early spring of 1944, it was evident the effort to invade Europe would take place that summer, so it was no surprise when we were ordered to leave our hospital at Watford. It was taken over by a hospital unit just arrived from Canada. We were to go to a spot in Yorkshire for field training in preparation for the real battleground, which soon would prove to be Normandy. Here we left our blue uniforms behind and went into khaki. This consisted of slacks, shirt, battle dress tunic — oh yes, we were issued a skirt too — and heavy brown boots. We spent hours on the drill square getting "toughened up," on long route marches, learning how to pitch tents, dig a slit trench, dig for a latrine, and read maps. We were in a beautiful area of Yorkshire, between the towns of Richmond and Darlington.

D-Day started as most other days. Our unit, No. 10 Canadian General Hospital, in company with No. 7, No. 8, and No. 16 CGHs, all were undergoing extensive field training, preparing us to move quickly when the order came. Even though 6 June started as other days, there was a subtle difference in the air. We had been receiving news and rumours indicating that it was only the vicious storms pounding the Normandy coast that delayed the impending invasion. The official confirmation that the invasion was under way reached us in midmorning. On hearing the dispatch, it seemed to me that a quiet solemnity replaced the usual sounds associated with our daily living. The thoughts that came to me were, "This is it. The reason for my being here. It has finally all come together."

When news of the invasion came through that memorable day, we were all caught up with the emotion of the event. Strangely, the first thought for all of us was that "we want to meet together in prayer." Within a very short time the call came to meet in the mess hall for a drumhead service. There were no denominational differences that day — we all knelt in prayer, asking that the conflict be over quickly, that pain and suffering be lessened, that we be given the grace to bear whatever might be ahead. It was a sobering moment, for we knew we would soon be doing what we had come to do — follow our troops into the battle area to give them the care and support they would need. This I do know, the faces of the boys who had been patients over the years flashed before me — army, navy and air force — so young, so vulnerable.

A few weeks later we were sent to a staging camp near Southampton, to await transportation across the Channel. We were there a couple of days. The buzz bombs were coming over with great regularity, and several fell in the camp, causing damage and casualties; several were killed but not any in our unit. Finally we were told that transportation was set, so we were off to Southampton and the Liberty Ship that would take us to Normandy. By this time we were really tough, hardened by the drill and exercise in Yorkshire. To see us in full marching order we couldn't be distinguished from the troops, except that we didn't carry guns. We wore our tin hats, carried a large pack on our backs which contained all our personal effects — most of us sneaked in a few cosmetics — our trench coat was rolled and placed on top of the pack and a ground sheet on the bottom, secured by web straps. Our gas masks were slung over the right shoulder. Mess tins, a mug and the water bottle hung from the web belt that encircled our waist. We were ready for anything.

The passage across the channel was smooth and it was a clear day. There were many different craft making the crossing — mine sweepers, sloops, and various types of landing craft. Subs were about and every now and then a depth charge would be put off that shook the ship from stem to stern. Later that day, 23 July 1944, we were ordered on deck to disembark as the ship dropped anchor some distance from the beach at Arromanche. We left the ship by climbing over the side down a scramble net. Strange looking craft called "ducks" waited to receive us; they could float as a boat where the water was sufficiently deep and then put down wheels — I think they were more like tracks — and clamber on shore. These ducks had been specially designed for the channel beaches. We had arrived at the beach head of Arromanche where our Canadian troops had gone in on "D-Day." Later the famous Mulberry floating dock was brought over from England in sections and set up here, but it wasn't there the day we arrived.

Two Canadian hospital units, No. 7 and No. 8, preceded us by a couple of weeks and were already set up and in operation, so we were taken to one or the other that first day in Normandy. Unfortunately our hospital tent and equipment had been lost a few days before we landed. It was still on a ship that had been torpedoed. When replacement came after a few days, we weren't long in setting up — the tents were put up, we organized our supplies and were soon ready to receive casualties. Our hospital tents were called "E" blocks because of their design, and could accommodate sixty or more patients each. We had over 800 beds available. It was a complete tent hospital.

When we arrived near Bayeux, it was nicknamed Harley Street because of the large number of British and Canadian military hospitals clustered in this area some seven miles behind the front lines.

The author at Bayeux, France.

Photo courtesy Archives of Alberta Registered Nurses [AARN 92.10].

At that time the Americans occupied the area to the northwest of us in the Cherbourg peninsula, the British were to the northeast, and we were in between in a very confined area. The heavy fighting at that time was around Caen, a lovely old city about six or eight miles from where we were situated. We were so close to the front that it was only a matter of a few hours, from the time that a soldier was wounded until he was cleared through the regimental aid post, field station and then sent to us to be operated on or cared for as necessary. This was one reason the casualties were not as heavy as in previous wars.

At night the sky was a blaze of light from shellfire, flares and the flash of the great guns. We were always within the sound of the guns, which continued their barrage by day and night.

The convoys of wounded came to us usually after dark and streamed in all night. Medical officers examined the patients as they arrived and assigned them to whatever service was necessary. If they needed immediate surgery they were sent to an "E" block adjacent to the Operating Room.

Others who had less urgent needs were sent elsewhere. Those in shock and poor condition were sent to the Resuscitation tent, and there received blood transfusions, plasma or whatever else was required. Everyone worked through the night and day until every patient was cared for, and hundreds passed through our hands in a single night. In the Operation Room, the surgeons, anaesthetists, nurses and orderlies worked in teams. The patients' medical records were pinned to their uniforms, and notes made by anyone who had seen the man or given him any treatment were recorded on his medical sheet.

Two days later all who could be evacuated, and this was nearly everyone, were sent to England to our hospitals there. Some were transferred by air but most went by ship. After evacuation, we would work like beavers to clean, prepare supplies and be ready for the next convoy. We worked in rotation with the other two Canadian hospitals. As they filled up, the patients came to us. So it worked in a cycle — admit all one night, usually several hundreds though not always, then operate all that night and as far into the next day as required, allow the patients to "rest" two days, then evacuate to England and be ready for another convoy that night or next day. It was a marvelously smooth organization that worked well, largely because of the spirit of the people involved. Everyone gave of their best for the good of the troops.

Our food consisted of field rations; each individual carried emergency rations in their kit, but these were not to be used except in an actual emergency. Rations were prepackaged food; "M & V" [meat and vegetables] was a staple, and was a dehydrated stew with lots of cheese. Hard tack tasted really good with cheese, when dunked in tea. We drank quarts of tea. It was unsafe to drink the water that came to us in tanks. If one did so it was at the risk of acquiring what was called the "Normandy Glide." There were worn paths in the grass around our hospital, which was located in a farmer's pasture, from the tents to the central location of our latrine. This was a canvas structure, and I think it was a ten-holer — with no roof. The air force unit stationed behind us used to fly low over our facility as they were taking off on their bombing raids and we would wave to them.

Sometimes there would be an air raid warning. We then would hasten to relieve the tension on our tents. Shrapnel that fell didn't do as much damage if it fell on slack canvas — it was very sharp.

For the most part we didn't have any baths, although the bath trucks would come around occasionally and some of the girls took showers in the truck. But we were usually too busy and the boys needed them more than we did. We were on a rationed amount of treated water which we used for washing our hands and faces; the basin was our tin helmet. After the sponge bath, panties and socks, and other items were dunked in the same water, then hung on the tent ropes to dry. Water used to clean our teeth was also treated but more heavily. This was kept in our water bottle — we drew a daily ration. Hair? Well, some of us walked to a farmer's pump a half a mile or so down the road. A few girls tried the hair-dressing parlour in Bayeaux, but that wasn't too successful because they had water problems too.

Two of our big problems were wasps and moles. The wasps were always with us. One couldn't put a bite of food in one's mouth without moving the wasps away with the other hand. Some of the boys were badly bitten in the mouth through inadvertently swallowing a wasp. And the moles! They never ceased their labours. We were two nursing sisters to a tent, old bell tents that had seen service in the Boer War. As a consequence, there was just a small area around the centre-pole where one could stand to dress. This was where the moles chose to make their excavations every night. The earth would tremble and heave, and you knew a mole was at work.

One day sometime near the end of August, we suddenly became aware that we no longer heard the guns. The battle had pushed on very rapidly. The Americans had made their big push and circled the Cherbourg peninsula. The Canadians had, after a terrific battle, closed the Falaise Gap, and the British had squeezed from the north in a pincer's movement — battle language. The enemy had beaten a hasty retreat toward and past Rouen and kept moving. In his haste he left behind all manner of vehicles and armour. Shortly after, I happened to be in Deauville, a fashionable watering place in peacetime, with many beautiful villas owned by wealthy people. It had been occupied by the Germans for several years. At the breakthrough following the Cherbourg sweep, the German troops who were in Deauville left so hastily there were remains of food on plates in these villas. They must have left at breakfast time because there were partially eaten slices of toast, part of a fried egg, and so on — it was an amazing sight.

We had many prisoners of war as patients. They were appreciative of the care they received. A German field hospital had been captured soon after we arrived in France and we received the patients. Their doctor accompanied them, and I remember how amazed he was to learn of the discovery of penicillin and to see it in use. Two young lads — and they were so young — we called Hans and Fritz were among the prisoners. They became very useful. They adored the nursing sister in charge of the prisoners of war, and called her "Schwester" Ray.

When the rains came water streamed through our tents, and we dug ditches to carry it away. We wore rubber boots to crawl through the mud — mud was everywhere. Somehow we coped. Carrying stretchers with patients in the dark though the mud was an ordeal for the stretcher bearers. Their work was made more hazardous because of the slit trenches that had been dug around each "E" block for shelter in the event of an air raid. Fortunately we never had to use them. Fortunate too that poison gas wasn't used by either side in this war. There were a few false alarms but they were just that.

By October 1944 it was getting pretty chilly in the tents. By this time we were no longer busy, since the battle had passed too far from us to receive fresh casualties. Our hospital was ordered to proceed to a place in Belgium called Turnhout. There we remained until after V-E Day. Meantime, many of the original members of the unit, of all ranks and with long service, had been sent home. This included me, and while it was great to get home we all were sad to leave before the war had finished, though it was in its last throes when we left.

It had been a marvelous experience but pray God that none of you will ever be called upon to give similar service. We were very conscious of the privilege that had been ours. We were conscious too — and appreciative — of the women who had gone before, who had built the admirable structure of the nursing service from the ground up through great effort and sacrifice.

Military hospital in Windsor, Nova Scotia, August 1945. Assistant Matron Jessie Morrison, at left, with Lt/NS Ross at right.

Photo courtesy Archives of Alberta Registered Nurses [AARN 92.10].

The Face of Service: Alberta Métis in the Second World War

Carrielynn Lamouche

Métis veterans volunteered for the same reasons other Canadians enlisted, because their friends or relatives did, to follow the patriotic impulse, for the chance of adventure, or simply to earn a secure income. "Our true destiny is not bound by the success or failure attendant upon Métis deliberation," observed James Brady. "It is bound up with continued existence as Canadians who fight [for] those liberties to which we are all devoted and the preservation of which is dependent upon our victory."[1]

The exact number of Métis participants from Alberta is not known because the nominal rolls of the Canadian Active Service Force did not make provision for ethnic origin. However, aboriginal veterans' groups estimate that approximately 1500 served in the Second World War.[2] Julia Harrison, a Métis historian, notes that you see many Métis names such as Riel, Lepine, Nolin and Trottier on Canada's Military Roll of Honour.[3] Métis soldiers were renowned in both world wars as outstanding stalkers, scouts, message senders and riflemen. The following men represent a larger group of unnamed Métis soldiers, who placed a greater cause before their own lives. Their portraits show us the face of service, and are a reminder of their patriotism and contribution to Alberta's war effort.

Métis men served in the First World War, and established a tradition of service for which they can be proud. One of the most famous Canadian snipers in the Great War was a Métis marksman who was known as Henry Louis Norwest. Norwest was born in Fort Saskatchewan, Alberta, and was of French-Cree ancestry. In his nearly three years of service with the 50th Battalion, Canadian Expeditionary Force, this Lance-Corporal also merited the Military Medal and bar, making him one of roughly 830 members of the CEF who were awarded this double honour. Sniping was a hazardous infantry role. Most snipers worked in pairs, with one partner shooting and the other observing — scanning the surroundings and reporting enemy movements. It is said that Norwest possessed all the skills required of a sniper: excellent marksmanship, an ability to keep perfectly still for long periods and superb camouflage techniques. Much of his time was spent in "No Man's Land," the dreaded area between opposing forces. As well, Norwest and his observer often slipped behind enemy lines. On 18 August 1918, only three months before the war ended, he was hit by an enemy sniper's bullet, which killed him instantly. For the members of his battalion, a genuine hero had been lost.[4]

Edward McLeod, Regimental number M29109, Killed in Action.

Photo courtesy Charles McLeod.

Fred Belcourt
*Photo courtesy
Carrielynn Lamouche.*

Joseph Collins
*Photo courtesy
Carrielynn Lamouche.*

Two decades later the country once again called upon its sons to rally to the flag, and take up arms in the cause of Canada. Fred Myles Belcourt is an example of the selfless response of Métis Canadians to the chaos spreading throughout Europe during those troubled years. Born in Heart River, Alberta, he was one of six children. Belcourt's father died when he was fifteen and, as the eldest son, Fred went to work to help support his family. It was while he was away working in the Northwest Territories that the war broke out in Europe, and Belcourt came down to Peace River to enlist. "A lot of my friends had already gone over and I didn't want to be left behind," he later recalled. He first served with the 2nd Canadian Army Service Corps and often was responsible for drilling platoons. Belcourt then went on to serve as a Lance-Corporal with the 5th Canadian Army Service Corps. In 1943, aboard a ship headed for Italy, his convoy, which included 35 other vessels, was attacked. "It was right at dusk. I looked up and saw that we were completely surrounded by enemy aircraft. I was one of 36 gunners and we positioned all the guns at a 45-degree angle and commenced firing. The enemy started dropping torpedoes, we could see them coming through the water at us." They were able to save all the vessels with the exception of a hospital ship that was hit, making it necessary for the passengers to abandon that ship. All but one nurse were rescued. The convoy scattered in all directions to evade further attacks and Belcourt went on to Italy where, with six men under his command, he braved it through heavy artillery to get amunition and supplies to the troops.[5]

Joseph Collins enlisted in Calgary on 11 August 1943. After basic training in North Bay, Ontario, he took advanced training at Camp Shilo, Manitoba. Joseph Collins served with the Winnipeg Rifles on D-Day, and in Holland during the winter of 1944-1945. He was wounded on 21 February 1945 in the Hochwald Forest, just before the Rhine River Crossing. After three months in hospital in England, he was invalided home on a hospital ship, and was discharged on 17 November 1945. After leaving hospital in Edmonton during May 1945, he returned home to Elk Point, and moved to the Elizabeth Settlement in June 1947. He married Agnes Desjarlais, and they had thirteen children, twelve of whom are still living on or near the settlement.

Neil Frederick Anderson was born at Myrtle Creek, Alberta in 1917, and worked on the family grain farm near Brièreville until he enlisted in the Army at Edmonton on 2 November 1941. He served in England, Sicily, France, Germany, Holland and Italy as a Lance-Corporal. He received a leg wound, spent time at a Rehabilitation Centre in England, and returned to Edmonton in 1946.

Charles Tomkins, born in Grouard, Alberta, was one of eighteen children, six of whom served in the armed forces. He recounts that the voyage across the Atlantic to Scotland was almost intolerable for him. With more that 8000 servicemen crowded into the ship and no sanitary facilities, they lived on a diet of salt herring for eleven days. When they landed in Scotland on Christmas Eve 1942, Tomkins was assigned to the 2nd Armoured Brigade, which was stationed in England. Later he reported to Canadian Military Headquarters in London, where he was asked to translate a message into Cree. Tomkins and his brother Peter, along with six other Cree-speaking servicemen, were then assigned to the American 8th Air Force and 9th Bomber Command as message senders.[6]

Neil Frederick Anderson

The Tomkins Brothers. From left to right: John Smith [step brother], Henry Tomkins, Peter Tomkins, Charles Tomkins, Frank Tomkins.

Photo courtesy Frank Tomkins.

At the age of fifteen Sam Sinclair, who told the recruiting officer that he was eighteen, enlisted in Edmonton. However, in a few days his mother sent a letter through the Roman Catholic Church informing the military that he was underage. "I was in trouble right off the bat. [The] only thing that saved me was that my birth certificate and my name weren't quite the same." Sinclair was allowed to stay in the army and was officially sworn in on 13 January 1943. At the age of seventeen, still underage, he was shipped overseas to England, and then on to Northwestern Europe in 1945, where he served as an infantryman with the Calgary Highlanders. When the war ended Sinclair was assigned to the occupying forces and became involved in sports. He and nine comrades won the championship in track and field, and then he went on to win the Canadian Army Middleweight title for boxing in July 1945. Once home, Sinclair began a political career that lasted for 25 years. He sat on the committee for the World's Council of Indigenous People and was elected President of the National Aboriginal Veterans Society in 1992. In recognition for his outstanding contribution of more than 25 years as a coach, trainer and manager in amateur boxing, Sinclair was inducted into the Boxing Hall of Fame in 1994.[7]

Shortly after his eighteenth birthday, Robert Berard and his sixteen-year-old brother enlisted in Edmonton. "I lied and made myself two years older so that he could say he was eighteen. He had a letter from my mother saying I was old enough to join and that's all we needed." The Berard brothers were shipped overseas as reinforcements in 1942. They were separated, with Robert assigned to the Regina Rifles and his younger brother joining the Royal Canadian Engineers. After additional training Berard was transferred to the First Corps, 13th Field Engineers and was reunited with his brother in Italy. For the next 24 months they were involved in the dangerous and painstaking job of disarming enemy mines. They also constructed the rapidly assembled Bailey bridges, upon

Group of Métis veterans. Left to Right: Jesse Norris, Robert Berard, Robert Drennen, Stan Shanks, Herb Bell.

Photo courtesy Frank Tomkins.

which the Allied armies came to rely for quick river crossings, as well as laying Canadian mines. Promoted to corporal and placed in charge of a platoon of sixteen men, Berard saw a lot of front-line action. One especially intense conflict occured at Cassino. "We took over from the Americans; they had been there for six months and hadn't moved. We had a major battle there. We had over 2700 guns firing all day and night. The next day we went in, the bombers came and bombed Cassino for two or three hours, then the fighter planes came in. It was quite a sight!" Although Berard came home and was fortunate to get a good job for the Alberta government, tragically his younger brother, having suffered the traumatic effects of shell shock, was hospitalized upon his return and died a few years later.[8]

Richard Poitras

Richard Joseph Poitras was born in St. Paul, Alberta and left his farm in 1942 to enlist in Camrose, Alberta. After taking basic training, he was shipped overseas aboard an old converted freighter, and after an attack by enemy aircraft was landed in Sicily. Poitras would spend the next few years with the 5th Medium Battery Royal Canadian Artillery as a gunner, often on the front lines breaking through enemy strongholds. Upon his return to Canada he took a one-month "Disembarkment Leave," and returned as a Lance-Corporal with the Garrison Police to serve for another nine months.[9] In 1952 Poitras began his political activities at the Paddle Prairie Métis Settlement. During the next ten years he was involved with the establishment of

Isabelle Clark Glennie married Charles Dagneault in Scotland on 13 March 1942. Charlie returned to his home town of St. Paul in October 1945, after being wounded in Belgium in May while serving with the Calgary Highlanders. He enlisted in Edmonton in December 1939, and served for the duration.

Photo courtesy Charlie and Isabelle Dagneault.

Métis Branch Housing, and was elected Vice-President of the Métis Association of Alberta, as well as being appointed to its Board of Directors. Between 1973 and 1975 he founded the Alberta Federation of Métis Settlements Associations [AFMSA], which amalgamated Alberta's eight Métis Settlements. He became the first president of the Alberta Federation of Métis Settlements Associations. Alternating the presidency for the next few years, Poitras continued his political involvement in the Métis Settlements until his retirement in the Fall of 1994.[10]

In Cree we say *"Kahgee pohn noten took"* on Remembrance Day. It means, "The fighting has ended."[11]

NOTES

The photographs used in this article were collected during research for depositions before the Senate Aboriginal Peoples Committee. We would like to thank all veterans and family members who kindly donated the photographs for use in the book. Copies of these photographs are now housed in the Provincial Archives of Alberta and with the Government History Programme of the Provincial Museum of Alberta.

[1] James Brady, quoted in Julia Harrison, *Métis "People Between Two Walls"*, p. 115.

[2] Sam Sinclair, President of the National Aboriginal Veterans Society, telephone conversation with author, October 1994.

[3] Cited by Senator Len Marchand, Address to Senate of Canada, 29 January 1994.

[4] Janice Summerby, Native Soldiers Foreign Battlefields, pp. 11-13.

[5] Fred Belcourt, conversation with author, October 1994.

[6] Charles Tomkins, telephone conversation with author, October 1994.

[7] Sam Sinclair, interview with George Pambrun, President of Aboriginal Veterans Society of Alberta; subsequent telephone conversation with author, October 1994.

[8] Robert Berard, interview with George Pambrun, President of Aboriginal Veterans Society of Alberta; subsequent telephone conversation with author, October 1994.

[9] Richard Poitras, telephone conversation with author, October 1994.

[10] Métis General Council Biography.

[11] Irene Plante [veteran's widow]; Janice Summerby, op. cit., p. 41.

Alberta's Indians and the Second World War

James Dempsey

When Canada declared war on the Axis countries in September 1939, the response from the native population proved to be as enthusiastic as that shown by most other Canadians who feared the Fascist menace. Over the next five years, Alberta's natives supported the war effort by enlisting for active service in the armed forces and contributing significantly to the home front effort. The latter was achieved by finding employment in the war factories, supplying finances for war funds, and working to increase agricultural production on the reserves.

Natives' sense of loyalty to the King of England was a strong inducement to participate in the war effort, as it had been in the First World War. But unlike the previous war, Indians ultimately became eligible for conscription, in spite of treaty stipulations to the contrary. These treaties, made between the Indians and the Crown in the 19th century, promised that Indians would not be required to participate in any of Canada's foreign wars, but they were overruled when conscription was introduced in 1944. The controversy over the conscription issue and other government policies will be examined with native Albertans' contributions during the Second World War.

Indian participation in active service betwen 1939 and 1945 was remarkable. They were represented in every rank from Private to Brigadier, and fought in every theatre of the war. Their total recorded number of enlistments reached 3090, of which 213 died in service and 93 were wounded.[1]

Indians saw action in theatres as diverse as Hong Kong, where seven men saw action against the Japanese, and the famous raids on Norway and Dieppe. At Dieppe two natives died and three were captured.[2]

Natives served in all three services, though their presence was mainly felt in the Army. Only nine Indians served in the Royal Canadian Navy, 82 enlisted in the Veterans Guard of Canada, and 29 were members of the Royal Canadian Air Force.[3] Educational requirements for the RCAF barred many Indian enlistees, which was a blow to the many who tried to join.[4] Their rejection from the Air Force, because their education was not on a par with that of non-Indians, showed that improvements were needed in the native education system if it was to provide an education equal to that of non-Indians. Undaunted, 46 Canadian Indians crossed the border and joined the United States Air Force.[5]

Indian women also joined the three armed services, with a total of 72 enlisting.[6] Some were involved in overseas duties, while civilian women worked on the home front, organizing campaign committees and clubs to aid in the war effort.[7]

Raymond Many Chiefs.

Photo courtesy Glenbow Archives, Calgary [NB-3-11].

Ontario, with the largest population among the provinces, provided the largest enlistment of natives with 1324 men and women joining up. Saskatchewan was second with 443 men, and Alberta contributed 144 enlistees.[8] The percentage of Indian participation across Canada was considered to be equal to the 35 per cent rate for eligible males which had been attained in the First World War. This fact was commented upon by the Hon. John Diefenbaker during debate preceding the conscription plebiscite, when he stated that "by percentage Canada's Indians had the highest enlistment rate of any race and if others were like them there would be no need for a plebiscite."[9] An important point to be remembered when referring to native enlistment figures for both world wars is the fact that they do not include many Indians from the far north who enlisted, enfranchised natives, nor those who missed the national registration. Bearing this in mind, estimates for Second World War enlistment could have reached the 4000 level attained during the First World War.

The Indians of Canada were in a unique situation as wards of the Federal government in that they did not have the rights or responsibilities of citizenship.[10] This exemption can be traced back to the signing of the treaties in western Canada during the 1870s. The Hon. Alexander Morris, who negotiated some of the treaties for the Crown, was specifically asked by the Indians during Treaty Three in 1873 about possible Indian involvement in wars outside Canada. "They then asked," wrote Morris, "that they should not be sent to war and I told them the Queen was not in the habit of employing the Indians in warfare."[11] One of the chiefs commented: "If you should get into trouble with the nations, I do not wish to walk out and expose my young men to aid you in any of your wars."[12] To this Morris replied: "The English never call the Indians out of their country to fight their battles."[13] Therefore, in the First World War they had not been expected to take up arms. When conscription was introduced in 1917, natives were included at first, but once the negotiations during Treaty Three were brought to the attention of the government, all Indian conscripts were discharged. Near the end of the Second World War, Canada again introduced conscription but this time Indians were not to be exempt.

In the House of Commons debates of 23 July 1943, the Hon. Mr. Nicholson asked the government what its position was regarding the treaties which were considered by the Indians as sacred and binding.[14] The Hon. Thomas A. Crerar, Minister for the Indian Affairs Branch of the Department of Mines and Resources, replied that "the Department of Justice has given a decision to the effect that as the Indians are British subjects they are liable to military service. That decision was sustained in a recent court action in the province of Quebec."[15]

The federal government, by using the War Measures Act with its far-reaching powers, and with the stamp of approval from the Department of Justice, had overruled the seventy-year-old treaties. Similarly, a year earlier, the Hon. M.J. Coldwell, MP for Rosetown-Biggar, and national Leader of the CCF party, questioned on what authority the government had acted to supersede a treaty concerning a land deal. Crerar responded by stating that "[the] Department of Justice expressed the opinion that the government had the right to acquire property under the War Measures Act."[16] These actions clearly indicated that while the Indians of Canada had the responsibilities of Canadian citizens, they were not yet recognized as having the rights of citizenship.

Why would Canada's Indians be interested in fighting a war that was on a different continent and against an enemy they never really knew? Memories of the First World War, their fathers' war, probably were still present, and there remained the strong attraction of martial glory which had been a major element in the cultures of most of Canada's native tribes. In addition many western Canadian Indians felt a unique relationship existed between themselves and the British Crown. This is illustrated by Private Dreaver from the Mistawasis Reserve at Carlton, Saskatchewan, who told an English newsman that he had three brothers in the Great War, and one had died at Vimy Ridge. He explained that his great-grandfather, Chief Mistawasis, had signed a peace treaty which Queen Victoria had also signed, and therefore he had a commitment to the Crown.[17] However, some Indians had a broader picture of the war and their responsibilities. One anonymous Indian wrote a letter to the Indian Missionary Record saying that the Indians had to

> *stand up and fight for what we believe is a righteous and a just cause. We therefore take it upon ourselves to share the burdens of our white brothers, even though it means war, and to do our utmost to overcome what may threaten to take away all that is dear to us.... We are prepared to make any sacrifice knowing that however hard and bitter it may seem, our efforts shall not be in vain.[18]*

This feeling was also expressed by a non-Indian, who stated in a newspaper article:

> *Indian participation is probably because they feel that this is their country; they are a part of the Canadian nation. And*

probably also because they have learned something of the villainies of the enemy against whom we are fighting. Those Indians who do so nobly give back some of their small treaty payment, must have a good idea why they are doing it.[19]

In the first war, recruiting was done unofficially. In the second war, however, recruiting parties officially campaigned on reserves to attract native recruits. One such Second World War recruiting party visited the Assiniboine reserve at Sintaluta, Saskatchewan, and four men enlisted in category A, forming the first group of volunteers in Canada's first platoon of Indians.[20] Sometimes recruiting also was carried out by the Indian Agent on the reserve.[21]

Canadian Indians participated in the war and were as much a part of the action as any other group. They engaged the enemy and won recognition for their exploits, receiving commendations and medals for their involvement. Such a man was Sergeant George A. Campion from Alberta who fought with the Loyal Edmonton Regiment and was awarded the Military Medal.[22]

The arrival of the Canadian forces in England drew general comments from the English press, but the Indian members of the force were singled out for particular attention. At Aldershot a British newsman stated that "a group of eagle nosed Red Indians padded down the gangway in moccasins and were known to be admirable snipers."[23] This was a reference to six Micmacs, who actually were in service boots like other members of the force, and did not really look any different from the other soldiers. The *Glasgow Evening News* called them "Maginot Mohicans," while a British naval officer present commented that "there is unmistakable red Indian characteristics in many of those individuals, don't you think?"[24]

The press also made comparisons to the current war and previous wars in which Canada's Indians had been involved. "Canada's Indians fought against the British in former years but now they fight with them, using motorcycles and uniforms instead of ponies and plume feathers, and Bren and Lewis guns over bows and arrows."[25]

Opinions and comments from non-Indians who saw action with Canada's natives were varied, though usually favourable. An officer with the Battleford Light Infantry [16th/22nd Saskatchewan Horse], who had 400 Indians under his command, stated that "they made excellent scouts and runners and knew their way around rough country."[26] Lieutenant-Colonel A.W. Embury said, "They are fine men to have with you in a tight spot," while Sgt. Norman Watson commented, "I like them. They have a sense of humour and don't frighten easily." Major Gordon Brown stated, "You couldn't ask for better men in action, especially on night patrols. They move soundlessly. They are natural hunters. Some regiments used them exclusively as scouts and snipers."[27] One consideration, however was that military confusion sometimes resulted from native names; an Indian calling himself "Teepee" Star refused to write or pronounce his name, but instead used hand gestures or drew a picture. Johnny No Name also ran into obvious problems when officers refused to believe that No Name was his real name.[28]

Neither the Indian volunteers in Canada's army in England, nor the Canadian treatment of Indians back home, escaped the notice of the German propagandists. "Lord Haw Haw," the infamous German propaganda broadcaster, mentioned the natives' arrival in England, and stated on his radio propgram, "England says her only task is to defend European culture. She has even enlisted red Indians in this defense. It is well known that London is not very discerning when choosing cannon fodder."[29] The newspaper *Vöelkischer Beobachter* in Berlin attacked the Indian Affairs Department in Canada by charging atrocities in that department.[30]

Canada's Indians were notably diligent in their support of the war effort on the home front, and their contribution to the war funds was a prime example of Indian dedication. Although they were the poorest of any ethnic group in Canada, a total of $23,596.71 was donated, with the Red Cross being the favourite fund, accounting for $13,797.50. Others were the War Effort funds, $2822.51; the Wings for Britain Fund, $2427.61 and the Canadian War Service Fund, $1787.45.[31]

The Hobbema reserves donated $2080 for ambulances from their band funds,[32] while the Blackfoot Indians donated $3050 to the Red Cross.[33] The money for such donations was raised in a variety of ways. Many bands converted large sums of band-fund interest money into war savings certificates, or turned in part of their $5.00 per year treaty money. Some donations were given directly to the interested party, while some donations were in the form of material objects such as furs. The Moose Lake Indians of Manitoba donated skins and moccasins as well as $40.00. The value of the furs brought their donation up to $3000 by December 1940.[34]

Other donations were made in the form of repaired garments and knitted socks, mufflers, and comforts bound for the soldiers overseas. Included with these items were treats and cigarettes for Indian servicemen, sent from reserves like File Hills in Saskatchewan.[35] Most of these articles were sent through one of the ten war service clubs or Homemakers' Clubs run by Indian women.[36] The federal government accepted most donations, but if the band funds were too low the offer was rejected.

The "Greater Production Campaign" that had been initiated during the First World War was reinstated during the Second World War, in cooperation with the Indian Affairs Branch of the Department of Mines and Resources. When the land controlled by Indians was examined, it was found that of the 2,159,652 acres cleared, only 210,921 acres were being cultivated. From these statistics it was thought the Indians as a group had never been self-supporting from a production standpoint, and therefore special measures would have to be taken.[37]

This attitude resurrected the old idea that the best way to use land was through farming, and since most of the Indians on farmable land had been hunters, they did not naturally take to farming. Their land had to be actively used, according to

Increases in grain
production on Indian
Reserves in western
Canada, 1943-1945.

		Wheat		Oats	
		Acres	Bushels	Acres	Bushels
Saskatchewan	1943	9,015	165,106	13,515	294,845
	1944	11,038	221,944	12,536	314,622
	1945	12,674	160,835	14,647	304,744
Alberta	1943	8,793	85,531	9,978	259,651
	1944	12,741	128,277	10,264	321,209
	1945	13,827	199,262	10,177	183,490
British Columbia	1943	3,100	61,175	3,047	72,240
	1944	3,049	46,697	3,157	70,425
	1945	3,420	76,179	3,882	97,357
Canada	1943	24,530	387,939	43,258	877,575
	1944	31,808	501,681	40,082	1,064,579
	1945	33,516	502,934	41,324	846,261[39]

*Data from Department of
Mines and Resources,
Annual Report, 1946.*

the predominant Canadian perception, or else be taken over by non-Indians as had happened during the Great War. However, efforts were made to avoid the forced sale of land that had occurred during the First World War, and the few sales which did occur were for military bases rather than farming.

Efforts taken by the government to raise production on Indian land came in the form of programmes emphasizing subsistence on gardens, use of instructional charts for farming and supplying seed, nets, cattle, bulbs, goats, poultry, and fruit trees. At the same time fishing was extended in the lake areas.

The "Greater Production Campaign" saw notable increases in British Columbia agriculture and stock-raising, but in Alberta the crops were only fair each year because the weather had stunted their growth.[38] Statistics from the government's annual reports showed a steady though gradual increase of grain production on Indian reserves during the war years.

On a smaller scale, individual families were encouraged to plant "Victory gardens." Mr. Christianson, the Superintendent General of Indian Affairs in Saskatchewan, stated in 1943 that Indians under his jurisdiction were ahead of all others in planting Victory gardens. A year later, though the gardens were increasing, actual interest had declined. Mr. Christianson attributed this to the fact that vegetables were not the Indian's natural food, and that spring planting was also the time for visiting relatives. This "wanderlust" occupied all the Agents' time as they tried to keep their wards at home with their gardens.[40] Victory gardens were also planted in Alberta, and Mrs. Lucy Swite, a former Alberta Indian, remembers the problems there as being very similar.[41] These gardens were an attempt by the government to lighten their own responsibilities to the Indians by making them more "subsistent" on their own grown food, which in turn would enable the government to cut down on its assistance to them.

In the early 1940s, as Canadian industry began to change to a wartime footing, jobs became plentiful and Indians who had suffered chronic unemployment were able to profit by the situation. The railways, packing plants, lumber mills and factories employed Alberta natives, while many also found summer jobs working on local farms.[42]

Indians were also included in the government's Selective Service Plans and relocated in other parts of the country. Two hundred men from the West who were rejected from active service were moved to Ontario forests, where they cut and peeled pulpwood.[43] Another ten were sent to munitions factories in the East, and some worked in kitchens or did domestic work because these jobs had been practically drained of labour.[44] Such abnormal movements within the native population had some detrimental effects, including the introduction of epidemics of influenza, typhoid, diphtheria, whooping cough and measles to the northern Indians of the Yukon and Mackenzie River basin.[45]

However, the war generally brought better times for Indians. R.A. Hoey, Acting Director of Indian Affairs, stated near the end of the war, that construction in the north and northwest had employed many Indians, who also had benefitted from a 35 per cent increase in the price of furs.[46]

Indian contributions to Canada's war effort were officially acknowledged by government officials and in ceremonies during the war. In November 1941 when Prime Minister W.L. Mackenzie King visited Regina, he met with Indian leaders and commented on their attitude towards Canada's war effort. King stated that "he was proud to see the real natives of Canada lining up in the war effort, and that they were accomplishing what was most desired: the complete unity in the Dominion's war effort."[47] On the King's Birthday list of 2 June 1943, a number of natives were cited for showing excellent leadership and loyalty to the British Crown, and for serving as fine examples to Indians throughout Canada.[48]

Government policies and measures taken during the course of the war at times overrode not only their exemption from conscription but other rights Indians had acquired from the treaties. On 1 May 1942, Ottawa announced that Indians would be subject to the provisions of the national war services regulations, including compulsory military training.[49] A year later, in July 1943, during a Commons Debate, T.A. Crerar defined his government's position on taxation of natives. He stated that "the Indians are not subject to income tax upon income they derive from the reserve, but if an Indian, for instance, a medical doctor who practices

Ernest William
Omeasoo.

Photo courtesy Glenbow
Museum Archives
[NA-3591-5].

his profession outside the reserve, he is liable to income tax."[50] These conditions exist even to this day.

Indian reaction came in the form of a protest march to Parliament Hill on 23 October 1943. The protesters left a petition with J.W. Pickersgill, Prime Minister Mackenzie King's private secretary. It stated that Indians were exempted from paying income tax by Proclamation of King George I, and that Queen Victoria also had signed a treaty granting Indians military exemptions. Their petition further noted that Canada's natives already supported the war effort by donations and by voluntarily joining the services.[51]

Other accusations were made by opposition Members of Parliament concerning government policies towards Indians. The Hon. John G. Diefenbaker outlined one such problem for Indians in Canada.

> *I want to speak of the situation concerning the Indians in this country. They have not been mentioned during this debate; they very seldom receive any mention; but if all the people of this country had enlisted as generally as have the Indians, there would have been no need for a plebiscite or of discussion along the lines on which I am speaking.... [The] reserves have been depleted of almost all the physically fit men. The Indians in service ask, "Why are we discriminated against? Why are the ordinary rights to go to refreshment places and so on which are allowed to other members of the army denied to us? Why is it that dependent's allowances for wives of other soldiers is $35.00 while the wife of an Indian receives $10.00 and $15.00 a month.[52]*

Diefenbaker was reminding the House that outdated laws still barred Indians from taverns, and they faced other inequalities because they were wards of the government, and did not have full citizenship rights, even though they wore the uniform of their country.

Later the same year the Hon. M.J. Coldwell questioned Crerar about the purchase of 2211 acres of land for military purposes from the Stoney Point Indian Reserve. In 1827 the reserve had comprised 12,343 acres, but through surrenders or enfranchisement of band members, 5873 acres had been disposed of, leaving only 6470 acres. Coldwell said the present sale would further reduce the reserve's size. The land was bought for the Department of National Defence at $15 per acre, and came to a total of $50,000. When the Indians were consulted on the purchase they voted 59 to 13 not to sell, stating that the treaty expressly stated that the reserve land was to be owned by the band for all time. Coldwell asked how the government could obtain the land in view of the band's negative response, and Crerar replied that "the Department of Justice expressed the opinion that the government had the right to acquire property under the War Measures Act."[53]

This action recalls a similar situation during the First World War when land was obtained for non-Indian farmers by forcing the sale of reserve lands. The action two decades later may have been handled in a completely legal manner, without any underhanded measures, but the result was still the same; the spirit of the treaties was overruled in favour of government policies that were only of importance during the war years, and had no significance for the future.

In addition during the war period, the Hon. Mr. Douglas questioned the government about its policy of withholding band trust funds, and the interest earned from these funds. Crerar once again defended the govenment, and replied that it was not necessary to secure the consent of the Indians to withhold funds, or interest on band funds, unless there was a prior understanding to the contrary. Indian agents were entrusted with the power to decide whether the Indians in question needed the funds at the time. Crerar backed this policy by presenting a hypothetical case in point:

> *If $500.00 is coming to an Indian as the result of a fur catch, and he gets that $500.00, I venture to say that in ninety-nine cases out of a hundred that the money will disappear within thirty days. I can assure my Hon. friend that it is the desire of those administering Indian affairs to deal equitably and justly, though perhaps at times it must be done firmly, with the Indians under their administration.*[54]

His statement concerning the handling of Indian finances showed that the paternalistic attitude held by the government towards natives, and their ability to control their own funds, was still firmly in place. Although it was a time of emergency, Indians had already proven they would support the war effort financially. But if government controls remained intact, the possibility of equal rights for natives would be severely limited. They would remain in an unclarified position, being wards of the government, yet expected to take the responsibilities of citizens.

Douglas replied to Crerar that if natives were to be treated as British subjects, and therefore had the responsibilities of citizens such as military conscription, then should they not also enjoy the rights of citizens? He added that the franchise should be extended to them as well as the privileges of British subjects. Indians should not be expected to pay the price and accept the responsibility without receiving some of the privileges.[55] These points, expressed by Douglas, would later develop into a serious examination of the position of Indians in Canada after the war. However, Crerar responded to Douglas' statement by saying Indians did not want the franchise at the time, though it might become compulsory in the future. He also mentioned that one of the major stumbling blocks to an agreement was the Indian idea that they were a nation, or group of nations within a nation.[56] This belief is still present today in discussions between the government and native organizations.

Like other Canadians in the service, Indian veterans were eligible for benefits under the Veteran's Land Act, which was passed by an Order-in-Council on 13 April 1945. The Director of Indian Affairs was allowed to grant up to $2320 to an Indian veteran who settled on Indian reserve lands. The money was to be used for a variety of improvements for the veteran's home. These improvements were: the purchase of essential building materials and other costs of construction; clearing and other preparation of the land for cultivation; purchase of essentials for livestock and machinery; purchase of machinery or equipment essential to forestry; purchase of commercial fishing equipment; purchase of trapping or fur farming equipment, but not breeding stock, not exceeding $850; purchase of essential household equipment not exceeding $250.

Indian veterans also would have occupational rights to lands either vacant or improved as long as they were located within the boundaries of a reserve. A merit of settlement in the amount of $6000 would be granted, and would not be required to be repaid.[57]

By August 1946, 115 Indian veterans had been located on reserves, and it was expected that 10 per cent of the Indian veterans would use the Veterans Land Act.[58] The Indian Affairs Department also assumed responsibility for the administration of all estates of deceased soldiers by helping their dependents to obtain pensions and allowances.[59]

In 1946 the government also stated that Indian veterans were entitled to the same treatment, benefits and privileges available to any other veteran. Natives living off the reserve could apply to the local District Administration Department of Veterans Affairs. Natives planning to settle on reserves would notify their Indian agent and he would contact the local Regional Supervisor of the Veterans Land Act regarding their application for government grants and loans. Handling of the payments would be done by the Indian Affairs Department.[60]

The requirement of going through the Indian agent became a point of contention. Alberta's Indian veterans claimed that they were denied war benefits because they had to deal with their Indian agent rather than directly with Veteran's Affairs. The Indian veterans also felt that Indian agents did not always pass on necessary information, and they could not find out on their own because of the law which forbade them to travel between reserves. George Monson, western regional director for veterans, said that any veterans who thought they should have received benefits should visit the Veterans Affairs office. He did not understand the confusion because Indians who settled on reserves received a grant and the low interest mortgage programme, while those who settled off the reserves received the grant formula based on individual needs. Joseph Littlechild, representing the Alberta group, replied that Indians who moved off the reserves lost their treaty rights and status.[61]

This incident demonstrates the powers and control Indian agents held over their reserves and the variety of problems that arose over treaty rights in relationship to conscription, income tax and land surrenders.

After the war, efforts were begun to clarify the Indians' position in Canada. A movement towards re-evaluating the status of Indians was mentioned by Crerar as early as 1944, when he stated that the government should examine the idea of providing means by which Indians would become self-supporting, by first instilling a desire aimed at eventual self-support.[62] A year later the government proposed setting up a study that would look into the treatment of Indians in Canada. Areas of concern included payment of old age pensions, building hospitals, day schools, nursing stations, administrative buildings and the construction or repair of Indian homes. A problem arose about what course the government should take to study the native question. The use of a royal commission would mean that commission members would have to be approved by the government, the Indians and the religious denominations that operated the schools on the reserves. Obtaining agreement from all the interested parties would prove difficult. The alternative was to set up a House of Commons committee and give each of the Indian organizations a hearing.[63] The problem with a House Committee centred upon which organizations the government should recognize as representing the opinion of Canada's natives.

By 1946 the government acknowledged that the war had helped bring natives into their own, by broadening the outlook on life for Indians who had served overseas, as well as on the home front. The government further believed that this change indicated a willingness to understand and to get to know the white man's ways better through education. It was felt that Indians did not want to be confined on their reserves any longer; they wanted to participate in the development of Canada because they had earned that right.[64] To one member the fact that the older members of the bands were the only ones who dressed in the old style while the younger members dressed "like the white men" was proof that changes had occurred. To him it was an intelligent generation of well developed youth.[65] This statement indicates that that member had missed what Indians were striving for. They did not want to simply look like white men; rather they wanted equality with white men, while retaining their Indian heritage. This view, still predominant today, fits in with the official policy that Canada is a cultural mosaic, made up of different ethnic groups, not a melting pot.

The Members of Parliament decided that Indians were entitled to more recognition in the future than they had been in the past. Mines and Resources Minister J.A. Glen stated the entire Indian question would be thoroughly studied, and their future would be brighter.[66]

The optimism of 1946 became a reality, when later that year a House Committee was set up to look into Indian Affairs. The findings were set out in a government report in 1948; based on the conclusions of this report, a new Indian Act was proposed in 1950. This new Act was totally unacceptable to Indians because they felt it gave too much power to the Minister of Indian Affairs, and with the help of the Conservatives the proposed Act was rejected. A revised Indian Act was proposed in 1951, and this version has remained virtually intact to this day.[67]

The postwar future looked bright for Canada's Indians; with most other Canadians, they avoided the expected postwar unemployment problem. Higher prices for Indian products and high employment raised the native standard of living noticeably. Life on the reserves was finally put into the hands of the band councils, a step forward in the desired native movement toward self-determination. The position of Indians improved remarkably compared to the postwar era following the Great War of 1914-1918. Hopes for self-determination were high in 1919, but never were realized. Indians in the 1920s remained caught between being government wards and Canadian citizens; the decline in their standard of living and population led the government to wonder if they would die out. A true optimism surfaced in the 1950s, and the goal of self-determination now seems more possible than ever.

NOTES

[1]Memorandum: The Record of Canadian Indians in the Two World Wars, E. St. Louis, *Archivist*, Ottawa, 27 April 1950.

[2]Canada. Department of Mines and Resources, Annual Report for 1943, p. 147.

[3]Ibid.

[4]The Indian Missionary Record, [hereafter cited as IMR], Vol. 6, No. 2, [March 1943].

[5]Canada. Department of Mines and Resources, Annual Report for 1945, p. 161.

[6]E. St. Louis, op. cit.

[7]IMR, Vol. 6, No. 2, [March 1943].

[8]Canada. Department of Mines and Resources, Annual Report for 1946, p. 195.

[9]Official Report of the Debates on the House of Commons of the Dominion of Canada, [hereafter cited as Debates], 3rd Session, 19th Parliament, 28 April 1942, p. 1960.

[10]Canada. Department of Indian Affairs, Annual Report for 1918, p. 14.

[11]Alexander Morris, *The Treaties of Canada with the Indians of Manitoba and the North-West Territories, and Kee-Wa-Tin.* [Toronto: Willing & Williamson, 1880], p. 50.

[12]Ibid., p. 69.

[13] Ibid.

[14] Debates, 4th Session, 19th Parliament, 23 July 1943, p. 5307.

[15] Ibid., p. 5308.

[16] Debates, 3rd Session, 19th Parliament, 2 July 1942, p. 3861.

[17] *Free Press*, 10 October 1940.

[18] IMR, Vol. 8, No. 5, [May 1945].

[19] IMR, Vol.3, No. 9, December 1940.

[20] IMR, Vol. 4, No. 6, [November 1941].

[21] IMR, Vol. 5, No. 4, [April 1942].

[22] Fred Gaffen, *Forgotten Soldiers*. [Penticton, British Columbia: Theytus Books, 1985], p. 131.

[23] *Edmonton Journal*, January 1940.

[24] Ibid.

[25] *Free Press*, 10 October 1940.

[26] IMR, Vol. 5, No. 8, [October 1942].

[27] IMR, Vol. 9, No. 3, [March 1946].

[28] Ibid.

[29] *Edmonton Journal*, 6 June 1940.

[30] IMR, Vol. 3, No. 6, [September 1940].

[31] Canada. Department of Mines and Resources, Annual Report for 1946, p. 196.

[32] IMR, Vol. 3, No. 6, [September 1940].

[33] IMR, Vol. 7, No. 7, [October 1944].

[34] IMR, Vol. 3, No. 9, [December 1940].

[35] IMR, Vol. 5, No. 6, [June 1942].

[36] Canada. Department of Mines and Resources, Annual Report for 1945, p. 165.

[37] IMR, Vol. 7, No. 4, [April 1944].

[38] Canada. Department of Mines and Resources, Annual Report for 1945, p. 164.

[39] Canada. Department of Mines and Resources, Annual Report for 1946.

[40] IMR, Vol. 6, No. 3, [April 1943].

[41] Interview with Mrs. Lucy Swite, February 1983.

[42] Canada. Department of Mines and Resources, Annual Report for 1945, p. 164.

[43] IMR, Vol. 5, No. 1, [January 1942].

[44] IMR, Vol. 5, No. 9, [November 1942].

[45] Canada. Department of Mines and Resources, Annual Report for 1943, p. 148.

[46] IMR, Vol. 7, No. 4, [April 1945].

[47] Canada. Department of Mines and Resources, Annual Report for 1944, p. 152.

[48] Canada. Department of Mines and Resources, Annual Report for 1944, p. 152.

[49]IMR, Vol. 5, No. 5, [May 1942].

[50]Debates, 4th Session, 19th Parliament, 23 July 1943, p. 5308.

[51]IMR, Vol. 6, No. 8, [November 1943].

[52]Debates, 3rd Session, 19th Parliament, 28 April 1942, p. 1960.

[53]Debates, 3rd Session, 19th Parliament, 2 July 1942, p. 3861.

[54]Debates, 4th Session, 19th Parliament, 23 July 1943, p. 5318.

[55]Ibid., p. 5319.

[56]Ibid.

[57]Debates, 2nd Session, 20th Parliament, 16 August 1946, p. 4914.

[58]Canada. Department of Mines and Resources, Annual Report for 1946, p. 209.

[59]Canada. Department of Mines and Resources, Annual Report for 1945, p. 161.

[60]IMR, Vol. 9, No. 4, [April 1946].

[61]*Calgary Herald*, 22 October 1981.

[62]IMR, Vol. 7, No. 7, [October 1944].

[63]IMR, Vol. 8, No. 11, [November 1945].

[64]IMR, Vol. 9, No. 1, [January 1946].

[65]IMR, Vol. 5, No. 7, [September 1942].

[66]IMR, Vol. 9, No. 1, [January 1946].

[67]In 1985 an amendment to the Act, which has become popularly known as Bill C-31, was passed. This change, while minor in relation to the overall Act, had major consequences for Canada's Indian population.

An Alberta Girl in the RCAF Women's Division

Phyllis M. Patterson

In March 1942 I joined the Royal Canadian Air Force in Edmonton and became a member of the RCAF Women's Division, or WD, as it was frequently called. After basic training in Toronto I was sent to Mossbank, Saskatchewan. After about a year at Mossbank I was then posted to London, England. Out of approximately 17,000 women in the Air Force (aside from nursing sisters and hospital staff) only about 1400 women in clerical and administrative positions in that Service ever reached England. Fewer yet went to the continent at the end of the war. Sometimes it seemed as if just joining up and getting overseas provided a sort of obstacle course requiring much of our effort and determination.

Recruitment posters attracted women to all branches of the armed forces. RCAF [WD] second from right.

Photo courtesy Government History programme, Provincial Museum of Alberta, Allen Kerr collection.

Life for most of us certainly refocused away from clothes, which even in the Great Depression had always held some importance, if only to admire and not buy. In the RCAF our thinking was gradually undergoing change, and survival and relationships became increasingly important. Relationships were particularly important, but were quickly formed and quickly lost as we were sent on various postings.

On embarkation leave to say goodbye to my grandmother and my sister Pam in Edmonton, I found a different kind of homecoming and reception than when I first turned up after Toronto and basic training, when I had been treated like a visiting celebrity. Now, I'd been away from home for some time out at No. 2 Bombing and Gunnery School in Mossbank. I was healthy and toughened up. I'd even managed to put on weight and was up to 112 pounds instead of the 96 pounds I had weighed on enlistment.

On my arrival at home I was greatly offended to find my room usurped by an Australian airman trainee. And my grandmother had no intention of moving him! The Australian would one day become a pilot. Sem was one of my grandmother's favorites. He had deep blue eyes and curly black hair. One morning when my grandmother apologized for not having bacon for him to eat, he told her it was all right because he was Jewish. She was surprised and upset because she had been feeding him pork as a matter of course, and he ate everything she put before him. All the dietary rules had been dispensed with during wartime for both Roman Catholics and Jews, and he said she should not worry. Much later after his graduation, when he was downed over Norway and taken prisoner, she pined and worried, because she felt he would be treated worse than other prisoners of war. Even now I wonder whatever happened to him.

The couch in the sitting room where I slept was uncomfortable and I felt displaced and didn't sleep well. Otherwise, we had a wonderful time together and my two weeks' leave passed all too quickly. It seemed the time to leave arrived almost as soon as I came home.

On the train bound for Halifax and overseas, I was the only girl in the car, and I believe on the entire train. The train seemed full of soldiers with no civilians in sight. At night our porter made up all the berths on the coach, except for the two or three seats at the end of the car. On the green velvet seats, facing each other at the end of my coach, soldiers sat drinking, having a party, and generally getting ribald and rowdy.

I decided to go to bed. Soon after, the soldiers sent our porter to invite me to join them, but when the porter arrived in my berth I was shocked. Usually anyone stood outside the berth curtains to speak to us, but this porter casually lifted the rough green curtains and came right into my berth. I was afraid because it was unusual for a porter to be so forward. A short time earlier newspapers had been full of reports of a woman murdered on a Chicago train by an American porter. This chap claimed he was from Chicago.

I was frightened, but on the theory that if I was going to be murdered I might as well not know about it, I rolled over and turned my back to him. At the same time I was angry at both the soldiers and the porter. I refused to go to the party. The porter was angry because the men had tipped him to get me out of bed. At the end of the journey we arrived in Halifax, a dirty, grey, wet city, in the afternoon of 9 July 1943. Here my luggage was flung off the train.

After I checked in with RCAF Headquarters, a maze of buildings and offices where I met other women who were arriving. We were assigned bunks, issued with extra gear including gas masks, and drilled on how to wear our masks. During the drill the Sergeant told us, "When I break this capsule, put on your masks as quickly as possible or you'll die, and continue walking around the room for fifteen minutes." We walked around in a circle, I felt as if I might prefer being gassed to enduring the overwhelming suffocation I felt with the mask pressing against my face. Its smell and my difficulty breathing were almost more than I could bear. The gas was either tear gas or chlorine. As soon as possible I dashed from the room and tore off my mask.

In addition to our gas masks and satchel to hold it, which weighed fifteen pounds, we were issued water flasks, small flat round metal containers. Our tin helmets hung on our gas-mask sack. We wore all this equipment slung over our shoulders, with our haversacks and purses, and in all it was quite a weight to carry on our marches. We were told we were considered as being overseas, therefore we had to swear an official oath to maintain wartime secrets. This was over and above the oath we swore when we first joined the RCAF. After this, we were issued passes to go downtown. I went out with a couple of girls, one named Griff.

Griff was extremely upset. Her boyfriend had told her that he wouldn't marry her if she went overseas, so she had decided not to go, but had decided too late. The Queen Bee at this Station put Griff in my charge to ensure that she got on the ship and didn't desert. Everywhere Griff went, there I went too. I think Griff was mainly panicking about leaving Canada.

We looked around Halifax and had dinner. Everyone claimed we would be here for weeks, until a full complement of a squadron of women was set up. Yet in the restaurant a waitress told us that we would be leaving from New York on the Queen Mary the next day. Since the other women had been waiting for weeks, we didn't believe the waitress. When we got back to barracks I washed all the clothes I'd worn on the train. At two in the morning we were wakened to pack and leave for overseas. There we were stuffing our soaking-wet clothes into our duffle bags and gas mask cases.

About four or five in the morning we boarded a troop train under British command. We were 25 airwomen, and all the rest were British airmen, with a few Canadian soldiers. The train was clearly marked as our own Canadian National, and was made up of old coaches with wooden seats, and nowhere to sleep as we headed south. We were puzzled about our destination, but decided that since the waitress's rumor had been right so far, we probably would be leaving from New York. It was an exruciatingly hot summer day, and the train windows were wide open for ventilation. We charged across the border in this puffing Canadian dragon, everyone hanging out the windows with dust and cinders flying back into our eyes and thoroughly coating us all.

Somehow the route followed by the train, and the necessary stops, allowed all the Canadian men to nose out the local liquor stores and dash across the tracks at each stop for a case or two of beer. The British Commanding Officer kept bellowing orders to stay on the train, which most of us ignored except for the British airmen. The CO complained that too many people would know we were a troop train leaving from New York. We found his worry pointless; "After all, we were on a well marked CN train weren't we?"

We arrived in New York in the late afternoon, and began boarding the Queen Mary, now being used as an American troopship. New York was in the middle of a heat wave. Of course we arrived dressed in our blue winter clothing with overcoat, wearing heavy gloves, carrying the weight of our ever-present gas masks, tin helmets, water flasks, and haversacks containing daily necessities loaded on our backs, in addition to our over-the-shoulder purses. We were supposed to hoist our large round duffle bags on our shoulders to move along more easily and quickly. This proved to be an impossibility for me. I dragged and kicked my duffle bag, which seemed to weigh a ton, full of wet clothes, ahead of me as we left the train. Policemen lined our route on either side as we walked forever, and one stepped forward and said, "Here miss I'll help you with that," and lifted my kit bag onto my shoulder. My knees buckled and I dropped the bag almost immediately, but I managed to make it as far as the Red Cross stand on the dock.

The place was swarming with American troops. The Canadian soldiers and British airmen had disappeared and there we were, 25 dusty, hot, bedraggled airwomen. The smell of the sea and the oily smell of the wooden dock was nauseating in the heat. And in the midst of this mess were the Red Cross women serving everyone lemonade and doughnuts, a job they'd been doing since six o'clock that morning. They were heaven sent. We'd had nothing to eat or drink on the train.

Nothing has ever tasted so good as that lemonade and donuts after the trying, uncomfortable trip with the dust coating us through the open windows of the train coach. We had had nothing to drink all day unless we had beer with the airmen and soldiers, and we refused to drink at all with them. This was still a time when women did not drink publicly except in certain designated places. How marvellous the Red Cross women seemed, and so quick to help. They did a magnificent job in that heat for hours on end.

We walked up the gang plank one at a time. I was so exhausted as I mounted that gang plank and saw the oily water full of bits of wood, paper and debris swirling below me, that I had the strongest temptation to drop my kit overboard, or fall into the water myself. After our draft of women, only the second to go overseas, the RCAF never required the WDs to carry their kitbags again. WDs carried everything else, but not those big, heavy blue duffle bags with the metal handles and padlocks we bought to keep our things safe.

I staggered up the gangplank onto the deck, red-faced and near fainting with heat and exhaustion, and thumped my duffle bag down onto the deck. An American officer stepped forward and picked up my bag and showed me to our room.

Our 25 women were crammed into one stateroom with thirteen double-decker brown metal bunks jammed against each other at various angles. The porthole was locked shut and the room was stifling and airless. We had army blankets over the blue-and-white striped denim-covered mattresses. I think they were stuffed with straw. They certainly were hard, but we managed to sleep on them. We had been assigned bunks so the sergeant-in-charge would know where everyone was in case of an emergency. We had to dress standing or sitting on the bed, more awkward on the bottom bunk where I would sleep because there was no floor space. We had a single lavatory for one person in our stateroom and there was no water for baths.

All the doors had been removed from the cabins and were replaced by grey army blankets. However, woodwork and brass had been left in place where it was still necessary on walls and stair rails; it was beautiful rich wood, either mahogany or oak. One of the ship's crew told me that the Queen Mary was designed to carry 700 passengers but that there were 14,000 troops aboard.

Most of the American troops slept on deck because there was not room for everyone inside, and it was probably pleasanter than inside, at least on clear sunny days.

We spent most of our time on a tiny deck which was allotted to us. There we talked with a United States Marine officer smothered in medals. He said he would take most of them off when he reached England because the British didn't think much of some of the American medals. For example one medal was for being able to shoot on target.

Sometimes we went into the lounge to watch the American officers gamble. They gambled all the way across the Atlantic. Inside we either watched or played cribbage among ourselves. One man turned to me where I stood behind him watching and said, "Here, hold this." I was surprised at the armful of money he handed me to hold. It was fascinating to see all that money changing hands, although I didn't know what game they were playing. Finally the officer turned, took his money back and left. Then some other man across the table wanted me to stand behind him, which I did but he didn't win as he had hoped, so I guess I was only lucky for one gambler.

The Queen Mary travelled alone on its way across the Atlantic because the ship travelled too fast for the slower convoy ships to keep up. We were a shipload of black American soldiers, their white officers and us. The troops were kept on the lower decks, and we women were not allowed to move about the ship without being accompanied by an officer. We seldom saw anyone else on the ship but the American officers and ourselves, except when we ate.

Helen Rothnie
Montgomerie-Bell in
the uniform of the
RCAF Women's
Division.

*Photo courtesy Glenbow
Archives, Calgary
[NA-2536-19].*

We only had two meals a day, and the kitchen crew worked around the clock to feed everyone. We were fed in 24-hour shifts. Each person had an appointed shift time for breakfast and dinner. Fortunately for us, ours were always in the daytime.

On the first day as I looked down the stairs toward the dining area, with the required officer by my side, I drew back from the steps. Below me was a mass of men such as I had never seen before and which frightened me. These were all black troops. The officer who was white, as were all the other officers, said "It's all right, the dining room is down there." So down we went. The soldiers returning from their meal stood lined up on our left side of the stairs going up as we went down on the right side.

The Captain was British but the Commanding Officer of the troops was American. The two alternated in giving news bulletins about the progress of the war, usually around eleven o'clock or noon. One day the Captain informed us that the Germans had announced their sinking of the Queen Mary that morning, so we laughed heartily and felt brave and joked about the Germans.

As if to prove the truth of the enemy claim on the following day, just as I was going down for my second meal of the day the ship lurched sharply. I fell left against a soldier who was mounting the stairs in his lineup. He promptly turned his back to me when I apologized for falling against him."What's the matter with him?" I asked the officer accompanying me. The officer said, "He did the right thing. He was told he'd be shot if he so much as spoke to you girls."

For a short time, a few hours, the Queen Mary took a zig-zag course to make sure that it had lost the submarine that was tracking us. Suddenly we all recognized our vulnerability. Everyone became very quiet. At that period of the war the North Atlantic was infested with submarines.

We headed into the South Atlantic to avoid the concentration of U-boats in the north and into still more extreme heat. However farther south we ran into rain and an overnight storm. In the morning when we leapt out of bed and headed down the hall, we found the corridor filled with sleeping soldiers. How all these men had moved inside off the deck without waking us was a marvel.

Then we ran out of food and there were no meals. We took six days to cross the Atlantic instead of the expected five. When the canteen opened on the last day all we had to eat were Hershey chocolate bars, which we bought in huge boxes.

We docked in Scotland on a dull rainy afternoon. One side of the port seemed to be called Greenoch and the other side Gouroch. As we docked we heard a thrilling sound, someone singing, lovely and clear, from the dockside. We all rushed to that side of the ship and the Captain had to order the troops to return to their allotted deck fearing the ship was in danger of tilting.

We reached a satisfactory arrangement when the singer, who turned out to be Vera Lynn, moved back where we could all see her as well as hear her. Someone gave her a microphone. She was a tiny figure in a trench coat and beret, standing on the dock in the pouring rain, singing her heart out for us. She had only a banjo to accompany her. Some of us had tears in our eyes, including the men. We were tired from the trip, from the crowding, from the inactivity and from fear. But of course this was only the beginning.

All during the war Vera Lynn sang mainly to the troops and on the radio over "Music While You Work," and between songs she gave brief sentimental messages which most of us loved. Some English hated what they called these "sappy sentimental verses," but most loved her. She seemed to be all that was hopeful and courageous. She brought out our will to survive, the best in us and in our homeland.

We disembarked slowly in the gradually darkening night and walked across the pier to a fast English train. Two English cooks tugged a copper boiler down the centre aisle of our coach, the kind most often used for washing clothes in. The boiler was full of a grey soupy stew, sloshing against its sides. One man ladled out some of this mess for us to eat while the other tugged the boiler down the aisle. "I think I won't have any," I said. Still, one of the cooks ladled out a dish full for me and said "You'd better eat luvey, you won't eat until tomorrow." I managed to eat the stew. The cook was right. We didn't eat again for almost eighteen hours.

We were wakened late at night to change trains in London, as we headed for the South Coast and Bournemouth, our English Depot. Again we were billeted in a big old house which had been converted into an English centre for airwomen. When we dumped our gear on our beds, we noticed that our mattresses were now composed of 'biscuits'. That is, three small pieces of mattress laid side by side to form a full-length mattress. Each morning we piled these biscuits on top of each other with our bedding, so we were left with bedsprings to sit on during the day when we were in barracks. However, we didn't stay inside much during the two or three days we were at that station. After our cramped quarters on the Queen Mary and the discomfort and uncertainty of the train journey, I shot out first thing in the morning to examine my surroundings.

Despite the fact that most of Bournemouth was empty, as were many of the coastal centres, it was a beautiful town full of green parks, leafy trees and many large, elegant old Tudor and Georgian houses. Many residents had been evacuated to northern England during the Battle of Britain. It seemed eerie as I walked through a town where most of the buildings were empty and the only people I saw around were in uniform. Perhaps because I was from the prairies, the first place I headed for was the sea, but I couldn't go down to the beach. I had to walk along the sea wall, while below were large cement block obstacles suggesting giant jacks, and rolls of tangled barbed wire. This was the first line of defence against a German invasion. I couldn't help but feel a bit indignant that I couldn't get to the beach for a walk.

One bright moonlit night while Griff and I were out walking, my eye was caught by a movement in a shop doorway. I stopped to find an airman and a young woman making love, taking full advantage of the blackout. Such a difference from the innocence of our unsophisticated western prairie life, where kissing in a dark corner was as far as we got.

At the Bournemouth station our bunks were located in unlocked rooms, and our kit was temporarily stored at the end of our beds rather than in locked cupboards. We knew that we soon would be posted to other stations. The English girls there stole most of our kit, including our silk stockings and sweaters. They probably hadn't seen silk stockings for years. They were welcome to my stockings but I was upset about the V-necked wool vest that my grandmother had knit for me. It was covered with souvenirs, pins, buttons, and paper flowers from chocolate boxes which both girlfriends and boyfriends had given me. They didn't

RCAF(WD) personnel at Edmonton Airport Tower, April 1944.

Photo courtesy Provincial Archives of Alberta [PAA Bl. 714/3].

steal my haversack because that was Canadian issue, although we had stuff in our backpacks as well. However, they stole the packsack that the parachute packers had made for me at Mossbank. We were annoyed, but we decided to forget about complaining. We'd be out of Bournemouth soon.

In a few days Griff left for Yorkshire because she was a Postal Clerk. Most of the girls went either to Yorkshire to the main Canadian Post Office with Griff, or to a place in London called Knightsbridge, where all the accounting for the RCAF outside of Canada was done. I was alone in Bournemouth for a day after Griff left, when I was posted to London.

I packed my gear, got myself ready, then asked where there was a phone. I was directed to an office, where I found a young, blonde British officer sitting at her desk. I saluted smartly, marched in and asked "Excuse me, do you mind if I use your phone?"

As I started across the room for the archaic phone on her desk, she floored me by replying, "I most certainly do."

"Well how am I to get a taxi if I don't phone?"

"What do you need a taxi for?"

"To get to the train. I've been posted to London and I certainly can't carry all my kit to the station, even if I knew where the station was."

"Corporal's don't use taxis," she stated, which astonished me even more.

"They don't?"

"No," she said firmly. "You don't need a taxi. Take a bus."

"I don't know which bus to take even if I knew where their stops were. I need help. I've got a lot of heavy gear." I then proceeded to tell her how much the gear weighed.

She didn't let up on the bus idea.

I thought she was crazy.

I learned that the British officers were unreasonably strong on protocol. An airwoman was not entitled to use a taxi or a car unless she was an officer, and that was that.

Finally I was assigned a Leading Aircraftsman, who reluctantly agreed to help me carry my gear and find a bus. I rode on the bus to the railway station accompanied by this airman, who then gouged me for a tip, and gladly I gave him the money. But first, I made him find me the right track and train and put my luggage on for me, which he did with little grace. And so I arrived in London in the middle of a bright and sunny day. I was ready for my assignment, and the beginning of my war service at last.

Prairie Sailor

Rodney Pike

Ed. Note: Convoy duty played a significant role during the Battle of the Atlantic. Convoys were groups of merchant ships sailing together under the protection of naval warships. The British Admiralty immediately adopted this form of protection in the fall of 1939, and it remained in effect throughout the Second World War. The Royal Canadian Navy remained an important part of the convoy system across the Atlantic for the duration. It was very dangerous duty, as the convoys were forced to travel at the speed of their slowest vessel. Early in the war, the convoys relied upon ASDIC sound-detection equipment to detect and deter U-boats on the shipping lanes. German submarine commanders soon learned ways to overcome the primitive ASDIC system, and the shipping lanes became a killing ground by June 1940. After the spring of 1943 the convoy was converted into an offensive vehicle, with its heavily armed and well informed surface escort vessels capable of destroying enemy submarines lured to their slow moving ships as they crossed the ocean.

The corvettes were small escort-patrol vessels built in Britain and Canada after 1940, and based upon a modified whaling vessel design. Over 300 little Flower Class Corvettes were built, displacing under 1000 tons, and able to make 16 knots. These were replaced in 1942 with the larger River Class, which were classed as frigates. The still larger Castle Class was developed in 1944. During the war frigates and corvettes were the main escort vessels, and served a vital function in keeping the sea lanes open despite the loss of thousands of merchant seamen and their ships.

I am not sure what prompted me, a prairie landlubber, to join the Royal Canadian Navy, or develop the desire to become the Captain of a ship. Perhaps the fact that my Newfoundlander grandfather was Captain of a square-rigged sailing vessel may have had something to do with it. However, I can relate to James Thurber's story about the hen-pecked little man Walter Mitty, who when scolded by his wife would escape by fantasizing that he was a hero bringing in a disabled bomber. Now when my wife criticizes my driving I regain my self assurance by thinking back to the time when I really was a Captain of a ship riding out a hurricane in the North Atlantic.

Joseph Conrad wrote that "[maritime] skill, like skill of all kinds, is not cultivated by the way or at chance times." In peacetime it takes years of sea-going experience and training before one can qualify for a master's ticket of an ocean-going ship; but in wartime the process has to be shortened out of necessity.

In August 1939 I was called up and appointed to the Examination Service, gaining some experience in ship handling and dead-reckoning navigation by watching the skippers of the fishermen's reserve in whose vessels we carried out our duties.

Early in 1940 I was sent on loan to the Royal Navy, and after a quick brush up on the customs of the service, officer-like qualities and celestial navigation, I was appointed in "Command" of HMS Moira, based at Freetown, Sierra Leone, in the South Atlantic Station.

HMS Moira turned out to be a converted Scottish fishing vessel, equipped with an ASDIC set and armed with depth charges. It didn't take me long to figure out, taking into consideration the depth where I patrolled and the speed of my vessel, that if I ever dropped any depth charges I would blow myself out of the water.

The crew was composed of six black *Kroomen* with big powerful shoulders from diving, who came from the Coast of West Africa. One dark night when the big diesel engine broke down, I was holding the flashlight for one who ran the engine. As the light shone on his face, his tattoo marks stood out and I could have sworn that his teeth were sharpened.

I became quite attached to my crew, and they took good care of me and taught me a basic principle about ship handling that was to stand me in good stead later on. They had a wonderful way of expressing things, and I have never forgotten "Softly, softly, catch monkey."

After a few months, I got a chance to take over a coal-burning converted Hull/ Grimsby trawler, the HMS Bengali, because the Naval Reserve Captain, a peacetime Pacific Orient Line officer, thought he had been appointed to Freetown to take over the Auxiliary Patrol. The English gentleman, accompanied by his yachtsman, didn't feel he had enough experience but said he would be my First Lieutenant if I became the Captain.

Our first patrol was a thousand miles off. It was just as well, as I had some difficulty with my celestial navigation, and filled my cabin with paper calculations. My English friend was reassuring, and said, "Don't worry, when the time comes to return to harbour you will figure it out."

Fortunately I did, because our job was to meet ships sailing independently from South America and escort them into Freetown, as well as to pick up survivors from ships that had been torpedoed.

The crew was made up of Newfoundland and English fishermen. The trawlers were coal burners, and the boiler room got very hot so we used local stokers, but we also used experienced sailors because when the alarm bells sounded the locals poured out of the engine room.

Naval parade, Edmonton, April 1943.

Photo courtesy Provincial Archives of Alberta [PAA Bl. 525/1]

When the new Flower Class Corvettes began to appear with convoys from the United Kingdom, and I learned that Canada also was building them, I put in a request to be appointed in command of one. The Captain told me I could go if I could find my own way home and the Petty Officer writer in the Admiral's office tipped me off that the HMCS Seaplane Carrier was short a watchkeeping officer, and was either going to the Pacific or a Lend-Lease refill in the USA. The Captain said that if I could command a trawler I should know enough to be a watchkeeper in a carrier.

It was quite an experience, and I learned another fundamental principle about the Navy — if you want to get something done, particularly in an emergency, just find the right Petty Officer to call.

We went to Mobile, Alabama for a refit, and I eventually got back to the Royal Canadian Navy; however, I did not get my immediate command, but was told I could apply for the Command Course, if in the interim I would serve as First Lieutenant on a new corvette, HMCS Woodstock. After a trip on the triangular run connecting Halifax, St. John's and New York, we were sent to Mid-Ocean Escort Force. After this we were back on loan to the Royal Navy, with fourteen other Canadian corvettes, to escort convoys from the UK to Gibraltar, and in the Mediterranean for Operation Torch and the landings in North Africa.

The Corvette HMCS Woodstock.

Photo courtesy Rodney Pike.

I had the benefit of learning a great deal about how to take care of a ship from our first Captain, a truly professional RN officer, Captain Denny. When we were sent to the Mediterranean he was replaced by Captain Griffin, who had retired from the Royal Navy, and also was appointed Senior Officer of the Canadian corvettes sent to Operation Torch. I learned a lot from him about naval operations. When we went back to the North Atlantic during the U-boat crisis in the spring

Crew's mess, HMCS Woodstock.

Photo courtesy Rodney Pike.

of 1943, we got a wonderful ship handler in Lieutenant Jack Watson who learned his trade in the confined locks of the Great Lakes. He let me handle the ship.

Finally in May 1943 I was appointed to the Command Course. Three of us finishing the course were promised the very latest in anti-submarine vessels, the Castle Class Corvettes built in the United Kingdom, on the condition that we would act as work-up officers, "working up" new construction at Pictou, Nova Scotia.

Finally, in January 1944 I was sent with my crew to stand by and help work up a destroyer escort being built for the RN in the Boston Navy Yard. We sailed her to the UK, and in June 1944 we commissioned a fine new Castle Class Corvette, HMCS Orangeville, in the yard of Henry Robb of Leith.

After a work up by the famous Commodore Stephenson at HMS Western Isles, Tobermory, Scotland, for the rest of the war we were part of the Canadian Close Escort Group, operating out of Londonderry escorting convoys back and forth to and from St. John's, Newfoundland.

Looking back, although it seemed fairly compressed, I did get almost five years of sea time and a lot of training before I was appointed to HMCS Orangeville.

Cmdr. Rodney Pike
[front row, fifth from
left] and crew of the
HMCS Orangeville.

*Photo courtesy Rodney
Pike.*

At a layover in St. John's, I was able to visit the home where my father was born in Carbonnear, Newfoundland, and when his sister introduced me to some of the old sea dogs in the community as "Captain Pike," I felt that I had achieved my goal and was being shown the mark of respect that only a real seaman can bestow.

From Air Training to the Defence of Britain: One Pilot's View From Tiger Moths to Mosquitoes

Stanley G. Reynolds

The Reynolds family of Wetaskiwin has always been interested in aviation. My father, Edward A. [Ted] Reynolds, was a pilot in the Royal Flying Corps during the First World War. My older brother, Byron E. [Bud] Reynolds, joined the Royal Canadian Air Force in 1940, and completed a Tour of Operations as a flight engineer on Catalina flying boats. My younger brother, Allan B. [Bert] Reynolds, joined the RCAF in 1943, and served overseas as an air-frame mechanic on Dakotas [C-47s] with 437 Squadron.

When I was sixteen years old I joined the Edmonton Fusiliers and trained with E Company at Wetaskiwin during periods that did not conflict with school hours. The two weeks' training at Sarcee Camp in Calgary during the summer months was a great experience, with sleeping in tents and target practice with Ross rifles.

In 1941 I was hired as a truck driver for MacGregor Telephone & Power Construction Co. of Edmonton during the time they were installing power lines at the RCAF stations at High River, Claresholm, De Winton, and other locations. The crews slept in tents and my job was driving and looking after MacGregor's 1928 Ford one-ton truck.

At this time a local fellow, Dallas Schmidt, home on leave from the RCAF, stopped at my father's garage. I was impressed to see him in his officer's uniform. That dapper uniform and his enviable war record probably increased my desire to join up. Dallas Schmidt received two Distinguished Flying Crosses and was promoted to the rank of Flight Lieutenant while flying Beaufighters during the Defence of Malta.

I was in the process of finishing my grade 12 education when, early in 1942, an RCAF recruiting group came to Wetaskiwin and set up a desk in the Driard Hotel. Curiosity and my desire to learn how to fly prompted me to visit the recruiting officer. I was told that I could enlist in the "Pilots and Observers" category, and if I passed the required tests I would be selected for training as a Pilot or Observer. The recruiting officer was quite persuasive and before I left the hotel I had enlisted.

On 15 April 1942 I was called to Edmonton to start training at RCAF No. 3 Manning Depot. I was assigned living quarters in a barracks which housed about fifty airmen, and we slept in two-tier bunks. Except for a few technicians we all started with the rank of AC2 [Aircraftsman second class]. We were issued uniforms, mess kits, sewing kits called "housewives," brass button polishers, shoe shiners, and other gear. We received medical and dental checkups, inoculations, physical training, marching drill, and lessons in airmanship. Each airman made his own bed, polished his buttons, badges and shoes and the entire group received periodic inspections. Everything had to be kept neat and clean, strict discipline was enforced and every man did his stint on guard duty.

When a group of about forty Australian airmen arrived at the Manning Depot they decided to take in some Edmonton city night life, even though they did not have permission to leave the base. They elected to leave the base when I was on guard duty, and when I was near the farthest end of my beat they made a hole in the fence big enough for a man to crawl through. When I turned around at the end of my beat I saw a long lineup of men in their dark blue Australian uniforms, in single file, crawling hurriedly through the hole in the fence. I was carrying a .303 Enfield rifle with fixed bayonet, but no ammunition was allowed for anyone on guard duty. Being quite confident that I would not be able to stop these Australians, I began running towards them, mostly running on the spot, waving my rifle and shouting "Halt in the name of the King." They did not pay any attention to me and when I arrived at the hole in the fence the last Australian was a few feet too far away for me to reach him with the bayonet. Someone else was on guard duty when the Australians returned [probably during the early hours the next morning]. I heard no more about it so I presumed they got back without incident.

During passes I would hop on my 1928 Harley Davidson motorcycle and head for Wetaskiwin, where I spent most of the time building a Model T Ford race car from parts at my father's auto wreckage. The category "Pilots and Observers" was discontinued and all airmen in that category were remustered to "Aircrew." This meant that any airman could be selected for training as a pilot, navigator, bomb aimer, wireless air gunner or air gunner.

On 19 July 1942, I was posted to No. 7 Initial Training School at Saskatoon. There were 42 airmen in Course #58 and we received classes and tests in mathematics, wireless, navigation, meteorology, armament, anti-gas measures, airmanship, drill, administration, and aircraft recognition. White cloth flashes were placed in the front of our wedge caps to signify that we were aircrew trainees. My Link trainer instructor was a Flying Officer Elder. I passed the Link trainer portion of the course with the grade of 89 per cent which, I was told, was the highest mark in the class. After the final exams each graduate was interviewed individually by the selection committee which, after considering the airman's abilities, decided which members of air crew should receive training. I wanted to be a pilot and was pleased to be selected for pilot training. All graduates of the course were promoted to LAC [Leading Aircraftsman] and were given cloth propellers which were sewn on the sleeves of their clothing to indicate their rank. Squadron Leader Fred McCall of Calgary, the famous First World War ace, was one of the officials in the picture when the class photograph was taken. Thirteen of the aircrew in this class were killed on active service.

The graduates were authorized to have a pass the following weekend in early October. The Model T Ford races were being held in Edmonton on Thanksgiving day, 12 October. I had my car entered in the races, and consequently I made an arrangement with the Station Warrant Officer by which I would stay on the station the weekend of 3 October and would receive my pass the following weekend. I was put to work in the station hospital and spent the entire weekend doing undesirable jobs, mostly cleaning washrooms and toilets. I did what I was told to do, I did a good job and I did not complain about anything. When the following weekend arrived I was told all passes were cancelled. Considering that it had taken nearly all of my leave periods during the past five months to complete the assembly of the race car, that it was painted with RCAF lettering and roundels on both sides, that the Edmonton and other newspapers had published writeups and photographs promoting me and my car in the races, that I had been promised leave to attend the races, and that I had already paid the consideration by working the previous weekend in the hospital, I believed I was entitled to leave to attend the races. When I left the station that weekend without a pass I was considered to be AWL [away without leave]. I proudly raced my car and won second prize in the second race. When I returned to Saskatoon, Squadon Leader Bawlf, the Chief Ground Instructor, announced to other classes that I had gone AWL and was therefore washed out of aircrew. I believe this announcement was to emphasize to other students the consequences before they considered going AWL.

As I was now ground crew I was put to work in the camp kitchen where I washed dishes, pots and pans, dished out meals in the mess hall, and scrubbed tables and floors. Once again I did what I was told to do, I did a good job and I did not complain about anything. After two weeks of kitchen duty I was called into the office of Wing Commander Russell, the Commanding Officer. He told me that I was being put back into aircrew and was being sent to No. 6 Elementary Flying Training School at Prince Albert for pilot training. It appeared he had received good reports of my work and discipline while I was on kitchen duty; however, he never asked me why I had gone AWL and I believe he never was fully aware of the reasons.

On 25 October I was posted to EFTS, where I was one of 45 students in Course #67. We were issued flying suits and other items needed for our flying training and ground classes. My first flight in a Tiger Moth biplane was on 28 October; my first solo flight was on 9 November, after receiving eight hours and 45 minutes of dual-flying training. Most of the flying instructors were civilians, and during flights they talked to the students through speaking tubes called Gosports. On 23 November I was given a 30-hour check by Ernie Boffa, a well known bush pilot who was the Assistant Chief Flying Instructor. During the test I was required to do various manoeuvres, including slow rolls, blind flying [flying by instruments while under a hood], practice forced landings, cross-wind landings, steep turns, tail spins, side slipping, and other exercises. While practising aerobatics during a solo flight on 28 November, an oil line ruptured and I flew back to base with oil spraying on the windscreen. I flew 29 different Tiger Moths at EFTS; my last flight there was on 18 December by which time I had logged 73 hours and 25 minutes flying time on Tiger Moths. In my log book endorsement in the space allocated for "Instructor's remarks on pupil's weakness" was written "no particular faults." My flying grade was 74 per cent, and my assessment was "above average." At least 14 pupils from Course 67 were "washed out," which means their pilot training was terminated. Ten of the students in this course were killed on active service overseas.

Pilot student Stan Reynolds at No. 6 EFTS, Prince Albert, Saskatchewan, December 1942. The Tiger Moth is equipped with skis. A Gosport hearing-tube needed for in-flight conversation between instructor and student hangs from his helmet.

Photo courtesy Stanley G. Reynolds.

After completing my elementary training in December, I went home on leave. A US pilot flying a Bell Airacobra fighter experienced engine trouble during a flight to Alaska, baled out and the plane crashed nose first into the ground near Wetaskiwin. Personnel from the US air base at Namao picked up all the parts they could locate, but they left the engine which was buried about 17 feet down in the ground. I took it upon myself to dig out the Allison V12 engine, the 37 mm cannon that was buried under the engine, live ammunition, propeller, and other gear. When I was digging out the engine a spectator standing nearby threw a cigarette into the hole, causing an explosion of the gas fumes. I came out of the hole so fast I don't know whether I jumped out or was blown out. Not knowing of any useful purpose for the articles, my father notified US officials who sent an army truck to pick up the remains of the Airacobra.

On 10 January 1943 I was posted to No. 4 Service Flying Training School at Saskatoon, where I was placed in Course #72 with 61 other student pilots. We were learning to fly twin-engine Cessna Cranes, and my flying instructor was Pilot Officer MacIntyre. My first solo in a Crane was on 24 January, after receiving eight hours and 40 minutes dual-training. During a solo flight on 7 April the fuel pump quit in the starboard engine. I flew back to base on one engine and made a successful single engine landing. My last flight in a Crane was 22 April, by which date I had logged 166 hours and 40 minutes twin-engine day-and-night flying time. By then I also had logged 35 hours in the Link trainer, not including my Link time at ITS. At least 14 pupils in Course 72 were washed out.

Not every pilot received his wings on the parade square. A day or two before this important occasion I was stricken with appendicitis and taken to the base hospital where I received an appendectomy. As I was not allowed to leave the hospital bed, my pilot wings were pinned on my pyjamas by an officiating officer from high command. In attendance were my instructor, other graduating pilots from my course, the doctor and nurse, various officials from the base and my very proud father. This was one of the most thrilling experiences in my air force career. I had graduated from SFTS flying twin-engine Cessna Cranes, and was now a full-fledged pilot. In my log book endorsement in the space allocated for "Instructors remarks on pupil's weakness" was written "High average student, should do well in all future flying." I was promoted to the rank of Sergeant. Fifteen of the students in this class were killed on active service overseas.

LAC Stan Reynolds readies himself for a solo flight in a Cessna Crane at No. 4 SFTS, Saskatoon, during April 1943. Note the quick release fastener at the front of the parachute harness and the ripcord on his left side.

Photo courtesy Stanley G. Reynolds.

I went home on embarkation leave prior to leaving for overseas. I boarded a train with other airmen, and arrived at No. 1 "Y" Depot, Halifax, Nova Scotia, on 21 June. A few days later we boarded the troop ship "Louis Pasteur," joined a convoy and headed for England. The ships travelled in a zig-zag path to lessen the chances of being hit by a torpedo from an enemy submarine. We were told that some submarines were picked up in the ships' sonar, although no ships were torpedoed in this convoy.

On Dominion Day I was posted with other pilots to No. 3 Personnel Receiving Centre at Bournemouth, on the south coast of England. This city had been the target of a low-level attack by enemy aircraft and a number of buildings showed mute evidence of the strafing and bombing. At Bournemouth we were given training in parachute-harness releasing over land and water, use of the life preservers called "Mae Wests," jumping into a pool of water from a high platform, and lots of physical exercise which included routinely swimming several lengths of the swimming pool. We also received instruction on the use of firearms, and did target practice with revolvers. As part of our emergency kit, our photographs were taken in civilian clothes, to be used by the underground for forged passports if we were forced down in enemy territory. We received training and tests on wireless, aircraft recognition, link theory, armament, ship recognition, and naval theory. On 26 and 27 August, at the Empire Central Flying School at Hullavington, I took flight tests in a Miles Master and an Airspeed Oxford. From Bournemouth the pilots were posted to various bases for further flight training, depending upon their qualifications and capabilities. I was fortunate to have good night vision, good aircraft recognition and my ability as a pilot was satisfactory so it was decided my further flying training should be as a night fighter pilot.

On 22 September I was posted to No. 12 Advanced Flying Unit at Grantham, Lincolnshire, where I was one of 51 pilots in Course #17. In this course were servicemen from around the world: 33 RAF, six RCAF, four RAAF [Royal Australian Air Force], two RNZAF [Royal New Zealand Air Force], two SAAF [South African Air Force], an airman from Poland, one from Java, one from Scotland and one from USA. One of the pilots in this course was S/L George Edwards, who was the Chief Flying Instructor during the time I was training at No. 4 SFTS Saskatoon. We were flying twin-engine Bristol Blenheim Mark Vs, known in England as Bisleys. I received 4 $^1/_2$ hours dual-instruction before my first solo flight on 8 October, and was promoted to Flight Sergeant on 30 October. Shortly before Christmas a group of about half a dozen airmen in my barrack block got together to play carols using a group of bottles partially filled with water. Each bottle was filled to a different level to produce a different musical note when an airman blew over the top of the bottle. Each of us controlled several bottles and after hours of practice we became quite proficient in playing "Good King Wenceslas." During a solo cross-country flight on 24 February 1944, the ceiling, 10/10th overcast, came down and I was forced down to under 300 feet to fly below the low ceiling. Endeavouring to map read at such a low height while flying over territory containing numerous roads and railways crisscrossing and running all directions, often having to read the aircraft instruments and look ahead for obstructions, I became lost. I flew with 15 degrees of flap to maintain safe control at a slower speed, but I was unable to pinpoint my location on the map. I still had a reasonable fuel supply when I flew over an air base where the planes were all grounded because of the bad weather. I made a quick circuit, landed and taxied up to the control tower. The control officer said that if I shut off the engines I would have to stay. Therefore I left the engines idling at 1000 rpm, set the brakes, and walked into the control tower where I was told I had landed at Polebrook, a United States Air Force base. I drew a line on my map from Polebrook to Grantham, took off and map-read my way back to my base, landed and parked the plane in its proper place. When I landed at Grantham I was over two hours late; however nobody asked me why I was overdue. Flying Officer Osborne, RAF, was one of the pilots killed during the flying training of Course #17. Ground school classes were Morse code, wireless, navigation, meteorology, aircraft recognition, armament, and engines.

During a pass I went to London and spent the night at a servicemen's hostel at Earls Court. That night the air raid sirens began wailing and the German planes dropped their bombs. Instead of going to an air raid shelter as most cautious people would do, I stayed in my room which was on an upper floor. I could not quite muster the urge to leave the hostel bed and traverse four flights of stairs for a sojourn in a bomb shelter. Next morning I looked out the window and noticed that the street was barricaded. A large bomb had dropped in the street in front of the building but had failed to explode. Being a born collector I picked up from the streets of London about twenty pieces of shrapnel which I still have.

On 29 February I was posted to No. 51 Operational Training Unit at Cranfield, Buckinghamshire. Here we had to learn to fly twin-engine Bristol Beaufighters, an airplane which had a gross weight of over twelve tons, and a top speed of over

300 mph. This was a plane on which we could not receive dual instruction because it had only one front seat and no provision for a second pilot. I was in Course #31 which had 25 pilots and 24 radio navigators. Six of the pilots held the rank of Flight Lieutenant or higher. One of the pilots was a Technical Sergeant in the United States Army Air Corps.

An RAF Sergeant, who was not a member of aircrew, gave each pilot instruction while he was sitting in the pilot's seat of a Beaufighter cockpit section called a "dummy fuselage." We had to learn the readings and all the operations of the instruments, gauges, switches, controls, and radio. We had to be proficient in going through the sequences of operations needed by a pilot during takeoff, climb, flight, gliding, and landing. This would include adjustment of the propellers, engine coolers, retracting the landing gear, operation of the flaps, and radio operation. When the ground instructor was satisfied that the pilot knew what to do in the cockpit, he would approve the pilot to fly the Beaufighter. I received nine hours and 40 minutes dual day-and-night flying, and instrument flying in a Bristol Beaufort. On 19 March I made my first solo flight in a Beaufighter. After 5 $^1/_2$ hours of solo flying I was assigned a radio-navigator, Sergeant Donald MacNicol from Winnipeg. The call sign allocated to me was "Jungle three niner," used mostly during radio communications. During time off we often chummed around with another crew in the same course, Sergeant Robert S. Walker, a pilot, and Sergeant George R. Fawcett, his radio navigator. During a landing on 23 April the port tire blew out and the drag was too great to keep the Beaufighter on the runway. The wheel tore a deep groove in the sod, although the plane was undamaged. There was another pilot coming in to land behind me, and after I got stopped I heard his voice on the radio saying "good show three niner!"

During a night flight in April, I was flying near London when several flights of German aircraft began dropping bombs. I could see the German planes coned in the searchlights with numerous anti-aircraft shells exploding around them. There was nothing I could do because on training flights we carried no ammunition for the guns. During night flights we were directed by ground control which gave us messages by radio. The Germans had jammed our radio frequencies during the raid so I could not be vectored back to base. Also the lights were shut off at the air fields to prevent them from becoming a target, so I was unable to land during the raid. After the raid was over and the radio jamming was lifted I was directed back to my base. On 30 April, after 32 hours and 55 minutes day-and-night flying training in a Mark I Beaufighter plus numerous hours in ground classes I finished my course at No. 51 OTU.

On 1 May Don MacNicol and I were posted to RAF Station Winfield on the east coast of Scotland. We were the only RCAF crew in "A" Flight. All the rest of the fifteen crews were RAF. Robert Walker and George Fawcett also were posted to Winfield and were one of sixteen crews in "B" Flight. From this base most of our flights were over the North Sea in Mark VI Beaufighters, with two Bristol Hercules 1650 horsepower engines, four 20 mm cannons, six .303 machine guns and radar in the nose. We flew Mark II Beaufighters with Rolls

F/S Stan Reynolds wearing "battle dress" beside his Mark II Beaufighter at RAF Station Winfield, Scotland in May 1944. A radar antenna is fastened to the port wing behind him.

Photo courtesy Stanley G. Reynolds.

Royce Merlin engines during air-to-ground firing, and when firing at target drogues being pulled by Fairey Battles. One of the first things we noticed was the number of WAAF [Women's Auxiliary Air Force] working on airplane engines. With my folding camera, which I could carry in my pocket, I took some photographs of these women at work. On 6 June 1944 [D-Day], the supercharger in the starboard engine was unserviceable so we flew back to base after a short flight. We were not informed about the invasion until the next day. On 11 June we flew back to base after a short flight for the reason "weapons bent," meaning our guns wouldn't fire.

Quite often the night flying aircrew received carrots with their meals as the vitamins in carrots were said to be of benefit to our night vision. Everyone had brussels sprouts with most meals, and periodically a chicken egg was allocated to each flyer. We had to stand in a single-file queue, and when we got to the front of the line we signed our name on a dotted line to receive our single egg. Each airman took his own egg to the mess kitchen and told the cook how he wanted it cooked; we would then eat the egg with the rest of the meal that was dished out to us. Don MacNicol received comfort parcels from home which contained cans of Spork, Spam, jam, peanut butter, and margarine. He would take a can of jam or peanut butter to the mess hall and put it on the table in front of us. After a few minutes RAF ground crew would come over to our table with a slice of bread in their hand and meekly ask if they could have a little bit of the jam or peanut butter. Don never refused anyone, and soon the can was empty. My twenty-first birthday was on 17 May, and on this day I spent an hour and ten minutes flying a Mark II Beaufighter, firing 20 mm cannons at a target drogue being pulled by a Fairey Battle.

Don became quite friendly with Robert Walker, and asked if I would mind if he crewed up with Walker, in which event George Fawcett would become my R/N [radio navigator]. George and I had no objection, so MacNicol became Walker's R/N and Fawcett became my R/N. Late at night on 19 June George and I were "scrambled" [took off] and vectored to intercept two "bogies" [enemy aircraft] flying high over the North Sea towards Edinburgh. We had climbed to 16,000 feet when the bogies had completed their reconnaissance mission and were heading back towards Norway. During their flight they descended, at the same time giving them a greater speed. Because we were on an interception course we were able to get fairly close to one of the bogies, but not close enough to be able to see the plane visually, which would enable us to fire our guns. When our height was down to about 100 feet above the North Sea waves, we had to level out and the German planes, being faster than our Beaufighter, pulled away from us. Later we were told that they were probably Messerschmitt 21Os based in Norway. On 21 June, after 31 day-and-night flights in Beaufighters, I was posted with my R/N to 410 Cougar Squadron RCAF based at Zeals, Wiltshire. At this time 410 Squadron was assigned to the Defence of Britain. It was a night fighter squadron equipped with Mark XIII and Mark XXX DeHavilland Mosquitoes fitted with four Hispano Suiza 20 mm cannons in the belly and radar equipment in the nose. They had two Rolls Royce Merlin 1650-horsepower engines, and a top speed of 420 miles per hour. There were instruments, gauges and controls on both sides as well as in the front of the cockpit, and the radio had 32 channels. There also was one Mark III Mosquito that had dual controls. On 23 June, with F/0 Edwards at the controls and me in the other seat, he flew one circuit, then told me to fly a circuit. After I landed he told me to continue flying circuits and left me alone in the plane. I took off on my first solo flight in a Mosquito, and practised takeoffs and landings for an hour and 25 minutes. I thought to myself at the time how much nicer and easier it was to fly the Mosquito than the Beaufighter.

We were using a grass airfield without runways, smaller than most other bases. We slept in tents on folding cots at that time. When we took a shower we used a hand-pumper fire extinguisher filled with water, and took turns spraying water on each other. W/C Abner Hiltz was our Commanding Officer, and George Fawcett and I were one of sixteen crews in "B" Flight. S/L J.D. "Red" Somerville was our Flight Commander, and F/L Walter Dinsdale was the Assistant Flight Commander. During a night flight in a Mark XIII Mosquito on 9 July, the starboard engine burst into flame. I shut off the fuel line and switches for this engine, feathered the propeller and activated the fire extinguisher which put out the fire. I flew back to base on one engine, arriving about 2:30 AM. When a twin-engine airplane flying on one engine slows below a certain air speed, there is not enough rudder control to keep the aircraft in a safe attitude if too much power is used on the operating engine. The increased pull from the operating engine causes the plane to become uncontrollable and crash. Consequently pilots are trained to approach the landing field at a greater height than is usual; if there is an overshoot or undershoot during landing, it is safer to hit the far fence at a slower speed than it is to hit the near fence at flying speed. When I was certain I would reach the landing field, I activated the flap and undercarriage controls. There is a hydraulic pump on each engine; as one engine was inoperative the hydraulic pump connected to that engine was not working. The hydraulic pressure from the single pump operated the flaps and undercarriage so slowly that they were only partially down, and I could not get the plane stopped before I ran out of landing space. As soon as I was aware that the plane was not slowing down fast enough and the undercarriage was only part way down, I returned the landing gear control to the retract position and the plane skidded on its belly into a coulee adjacent to the landing field. The plane could not be stopped while it was skidding down the slope on the near side of the coulee; however, it came to a sudden stop when it went across a small creek and hit the bottom of the ascending slope on the other side. My head hit the instrument panel and I received facial lacerations while George's jaw was broken. The port engine caught fire, and in order to save time I disconnected my parachute and threw off my helmet with earphones and oxygen mask, rather than disconnect them. When I attempted to leave the plane I found my left foot was caught under the damaged rudder bar. After twisting around and spraining my ankle in the process, my foot became dislodged. By this time the fire was burning up the left side of the fuselage singeing the left side of my clothing and the hair on the left side of my head. We crawled out a hole on the right side of the fuselage, and while we were crawling away on our hands and knees the port fuel tanks exploded. A few seconds later the ammunition also started exploding. After we had crawled about 100 yards away we sat on the ground getting our bearings and watching the burning plane. After another ten minutes we got up on our feet, I put one arm over George's shoulders to take some of the weight off my sprained ankle, and we walked about a quarter mile to a house. George knocked on the door and an elderly lady in her night gown opened the door. She was quite startled when she saw us with blood running down our faces and the front of our uniforms. She let us in the house and after we told her what happened she telephoned the base and a short time later we were picked up by an ambulance-hearse, and taken to the base hospital. Lacking any anaesthetic, the doctor stitched the lacerations in my face without benefit of painkillers.

RCAF 410 Squadron Mosquito night fighters stationed at Colerne, Wiltshire, in August 1944. Black and white striping was painted on the underside of the aircraft shortly before D-Day. Facial scars on pilot Stan Reynolds resulted from crash landing his partially disabled Mosquito during a night flight in July 1944.

Photo courtesy Stanley G. Reynolds.

Later we were strapped on stretchers in an Oxford ambulance plane piloted by F/0 Snowden. With F/L Rogers, the Medical Officer, in attendance, we were taken to Gatwick airport. From Gatwick we were taken to the Queen Victoria Hospital at East Grinstead, Sussex. Soon after we were placed in hospital beds and official photographs were taken of our head wounds for the hospital records. I was visited by Wing Commander Ross Tilley, the doctor in charge of the Canadian wing of the hospital. He took a quick look at me, ripped the scabs off my face, talked to me for a few minutes, then left to attend other airmen whose injuries were more severe than mine. Many of the patients were burn victims and were receiving plastic surgery from Dr. Tilley. Because this type of surgery was in its infancy, and was somewhat experimental, these patients became known as Guinea Pigs. A Club was formed and all patients who were in the Queen Victoria Hospital became official members of the Guinea Pig Club.

German V 1 flying bombs, called "buzz bombs" or "doodlebugs," flew over quite often on their way from France to London.

During my recovery at the Queen Victoria hospital the patients were visited by an entertainment group from the Women's Division of the RCAF, called the "All Clear" group. The lady in charge was Flight Officer Alice Fahrenholtz, who later married Brigadier General William F. Newson, a member of Canada's Aviation Hall of Fame. Some of the airmen who were not confined to their beds were honoured by having their photograph taken with the young ladies. I was one of six airmen who had their picture taken with four smiling ladies in their RCAF uniforms; the pretty redhead with her hand resting on my left shoulder was LAW [Leading Airwoman] Maureen Harrington from Edmonton.

When I left the hospital to return to the squadron I was picked up by F/0 Sexsmith in an Airspeed Oxford. He was accompanied by W/O Jones and W/O Gregory, who slept in the same tent as George and I. George was not released from the hospital until later because his jaw had not yet healed. On 5 August I was given a flight test in an Oxford by F/0 Green, to check that the accident had not affected my flying ability. On 8 August, being anxious to get back into the air, I took the Squadron utility airplane, a Miles Magister, for an hour's flight. Many of the ground crew wanted to get into the air whenever they had a chance, so I took LAC Coffin, from Edmonton, as my passenger on this flight. On 11 August I was back flying a Mark XIII Mosquito, and made three flights that day. In August the squadron was moved from Zeals to Colerne, Wiltshire, an airfield with paved runways.

We were given RCAF Form R60, which was a Will, and were urged to complete it. On 16 August I completed my Will, and another air crew signed as witnesses. These were F/L Ben E. Plumer, pilot, from Bassano, Alberta and his N/R F/0 Evans.

I flew a number of practice intercepts in which my Mossie was the target and a crew in another Mossie would track me with their radar and endeavour to catch

F/S Stan Reynolds in the cockpit of a Mosquito Mark XXX Night Fighter in August 1944.

Photo courtesy Stanley G. Reynolds.

or intercept me. During these exercises, both aircraft carried loaded guns in the event either one or both planes were diverted to intercept a bandit or buzz bomb.

After 35 day-and-night flights in Mosquitoes, I flew a Magister to an airport near London. From there I was sent to the Repatriation Depot at Manchester, and received a promotion to Warrant Officer second class effective 30 April. On 10 October my first R/N Don MacNicol was killed while he was serving with 406 Mosquito night-fighter squadron. On 14 October I was awarded a Wound Stripe for injuries received on active service, and on 30 October was promoted to WO 1 [Warrant Officer first class]. I left Manchester on the ocean liner Queen Elizabeth, which was filled with troops, and several days later docked in New York harbour. From there I travelled to eastern Canada, and then back to Alberta by train.

I was very disappointed when I was discharged in 1945, as I liked to fly and would have been happy to stay in the air force as a pilot. In January 1947 I received a letter from No. 2 Air Command, RCAF Winnipeg, stating that a Mosquito Squadron was to be formed for overseas service, and offering me a five-year commission with the rank of Flight Lieutenant. Later it was learned that this squadron was sent to China where the Canadians taught Nationalist Chinese to fly and maintain Mosquitos obtained in Canada for use against the Communists. By this date I had built a garage, owned a car sales lot and had a business that was progressing successfully. I therefore did not go back into the air force; however, if I had done so it is probable that my future would have been significantly different.

When God Shakes the Dice

David J. Lewis with Catherine J. Lewis

Fate places man unpredictably in strange predicaments. His response can bring death or distinction, as would the casting of dice. How he handles his chances may however determine the outcome of his task. This is the story of a fortunate cast of fate, exploited brilliantly by Major Peter Young, a dashing and talented soldier, in the face of many difficulties and hazards.

Dieppe 1942 has become a synonym for blood-soaked disaster, an intensity of shot and shell which gave Canada its worst casualty list of any single day in the Second World War. It left wounded men drowning helplessly as the Channel tide came in. The Navy sometimes took soldiers to the wrong beach and had to torpedo one of its own bombed destroyers.

Yet one single landing craft broke away from a furious initial sea fight, landed 20 men who did the work of 23 other boat loads, inactivated a coastal force battery for the duration of the battle and returned to England with no serious injuries, its whole party intact.

A Landing Craft Infantry (Large), R-Boat, 36' length, at speed, 9-11 knots fully loaded in the Solent. Eight cans of petrol are strapped on each side deck to add range. A smoke canister is mounted aft, with boating poles and a ramp on the tarpaulin struts. No. 3 Commando embarked in these plywood craft for Beaches Yellow One and Two.

Photo courtesy David J. Lewis.

It was my good fortune to have been switched into this fortunate vessel by a die cast on high the previous day. Sub-Lieutenant Cliff Wallace RCNVR, my replacement in the doomed vessel I left, was killed outright by a shot to the head in the third hour of the morning. He was the first to be killed in the operation.

His death was followed by the death or capture of all those with whom I would, but for that cast die, have shared the Dieppe venture. This was a difficult personal burden to bear, as others too would find out.

How to describe that venture of a calm August night 52 years ago? For my companions and me, several of us Albertans at the time or now, it all started in the candlelit drawing room of the commander of our training base. It was a request for volunteers for "hazardous, secret, overseas duty." Those with family ties were discouraged but not refused. Our ratings had responded to a similar invitation posted on barrack and ship notice boards. We were all volunteers to a man.

We had crossed the ocean, having run aground on one occasion, and on another witnessed the loss with all hands of an escorting destroyer. We arrived in what seemed a rather puzzled and erratic British Combined Operations Command. Yet "Combined Ops" had already known success in dozens of little clandestine raids and was well on its way to the amazing, though bloody, success of St. Nazaire in which an Albertan, Sub-Lieutenant John O'Rourke RCNVR, had participated.

Landing Craft Personnel (Large)s in line ahead leaving Newhaven Harbour. The mast and boom of a sunken freighter show above the water to right.

Photo courtesy David J. Lewis.

But Combined Ops was still a johnny-come-lately enterprise, not to be taken seriously by the power train of military planners and poohbahs. The Canadian blood spilt on the sands, water and sidewalks of Dieppe was to change all that. Some 400 officially recognized lessons were learned at Dieppe, one for every two or three of Canada's fatalities. The Canadian losses did change all that but the changes were not yet for us, the 71 RCN and RCNVR personnel of the Canadian Naval Combined Ops recognized as having participated.

For the second time that summer we of the Canadian Naval Combined Ops had come south from our usual training and biding bases in Scotland. We were split up amongst Royal Navy landing craft flotillas, and were now afloat making towards Yellow Beach One [Berneval] and Yellow Beach Three [Belleville-sur-Mer] on the French coast on a dark, calm summer night. This was not to be one of those sea-sick trips. My boat had been LCP(L) 42'; now it was No.15 of the 24th Flotilla. Most were asleep at 03:47 when a star shell lit up the scene into a ghostly simulacrum of daylight reality. Twenty-three plywood landing craft in four columns followed our mother ship, H.M. Steam Gunboat 5 (SGB), for me auspiciously christened the "Grey Owl." All SGBs were christened Grey Something or Other. I felt good because I remembered the Englishman Archie Belaney, self-named Grey Owl, who masqueraded as a Cree Indian, with a real native wife and his famous tame beavers, back in Canada during my boyhood.

We were scheduled to be defended by two new destroyers allocated to us, but they had disappeared on a private cruise of their own and were not in attendance for what was soon to come. Motor Launch 346 was more faithful. A Landing Craft Gun vessel also was reportedly laid on, but again I did not see it. It was a time, we found out, when the degree of participation in Combined Ops was still seen as optional. This apparently applied to heavy bombers and battleships as well.

What we had got into was like all the fireworks I had ever seen compacted into a few minutes. Only this time it was live ammunition. Heavy machine guns fired tracer ammunition and light artillery. The Steam Gunboat being larger, absorbed most of the fire; her engine room was riddled and her speed was limited to five knots, and half her crew was wounded. We had run into a convoy of five enemy ships guarded by three E-Boats. Both German and English commanders now became essentially isolated because they had shot away each other's radio telegraphic apparatus.

It was later reported that the senior officer of our "protective" destroyers had noted the nightime flak in our direction but decided that whatever had occasioned the flak would be over and done soon and therefore they did not come to our rescue. Later reports also indicated the results of this tragic event and that the crew of LCP(L)42 were all killed or fatally wounded, including Lt. Cdr. Corke, the flotilla officer. The coxswain was replaced at the wheel by a commando.

Excitement was rife within our own landing craft. Were 20 highly-trained commandos to tolerate being fired upon by an enemy of any kind without replying hot and heavy with every weapon they had? However, Major Peter Young, their commander, ordered that they hold their fire or "You will have to deal with me!" It sounded a bit like "HMS Pinafore" which had fascinated me during my recent boyhood.

Lt. H.L. Buckee, the naval commander for Yellow Beach Two, was in command of our vessel LCP(L)15. He was leading the starboard column of landing craft, the opposite one from an approaching German convoy and its

E-Boats. Buckee seized his opportunity and broke out of the melee at full speed. It was not long before we were all by ourselves with the fireworks behind us. Here we were, approaching the French coast with 23 men in an unarmoured 36-foot plywood pleasure-boat whose deck was festooned with sixteen tin cans of petrol for the trip home, or more probably to the sky. We were not in a position to engage the Kriegsmarine, but what were we to do now ?

There followed a council of war in the lightening morning darkness. Many suggestions were offered: go and report our catastrophe to the high command before Dieppe — then we could receive further orders; return to Newhaven; seek out the other 22 after the battle cooled off; look for the other four boats that were to land with us at Yellow Beach Two.

Then an interesting thing happened. A voice was heard, something like the voice speaking in Sir Henry Newbolt's poem "Vitaï Lampada," a stirring relic of the British Imperial days.

> *The River of Death has brimmed his banks,*
>
> *And England's far, and Honour a name,*
>
> *But the voice of a schoolboy rallies the ranks:*
>
> *"Play up! play! and play the game!"*

What the voice in fact said was, "Our orders are to land at all cost." Whoever said it did rally the ranks; it was like the crack of a whip to a team of good horses and the game was on. Before the shooting started Major Young had revealed our destination to his commandos and said: "It's something you've got to do even if all you've left is a jackknife." His momentarily forgotten words were to be well-nigh fulfilled by what followed.

In short order Lieutenant Buckee spotted the silhouette of our beach, Belleville-sur-Mer, and we made for it. Whether for death or glory, history was pointing the finger at us.

We made the beach five minutes before H-Hour, unnoticed by the enemy. A trench dug on the beach by them was empty. I saw a sign to the right of it announcing "Achtung! Minen!" [Attention! Minefield!]. What confronted us was a gully with steep banks over a hundred feet high filled with rolls of barbed wire and secured in place with rabbit wire.

The passengers we carried represented the No. 3 Commando headquarters' party. It was revealed that they had not brought aboard LCP(L)15 any Bangalore torpedoes, the usual way vast quantities of wire are blown away. The Bangalore torpedoes were out there on La Manche somewhere, either on or under the water. No wire clippers either.

The dip in the coastline is Yellow Beach Two, Belleville. The Goebbels Coastal Defence Battery was situated inland and to left of the left border of this photo.

Photo courtesy David J. Lewis.

What you cannot penetrate you must surmount. Here the commando training was called upon. First the east and then the west side of the gully were tried, and the west side chosen. Major Young, going first as was the commando practice, managed to scale their height utilizing the pegs carefully applied by the Germans to hold the wire in place. We could bless German thoughtfulness. Young apparently had left his gloves at home, but still made the passage bare-handed as did his soldiers.

The story of Young's miraculous victory over the Goebbels Coastal Battery, which possessed the heaviest guns in the battle, has been well reported by himself, reporters and historians. He was able to cow the hundred men of the Goebbel's battery. He got them so rattled that they fired their 5.9-inch big guns at our soldiers, knowing the German gun barrels could not be depressed low enough to hit them. But the noise was very impressive. The shells burst somewhere off in France in a plowed field. By sniping off their opponents the commandos were able to hush up the battery and prevent them from causing damage to the ships lying off the main Dieppe beaches. Fortunately, Young had had the forethought to cut the phone lines to town.

Our commando troops had been abashed by their relative lack of weaponry and defences; but the ever-ready Young gave them a formula that fifteen feet of ripe corn was the equivalent of three layers of bricks as a protection against enemy fire power. Their response was immediate.

As the ammunition began to run low for his Tommy guns, Bren gun and 2-inch mortar, Young sent Captain Selwyn and his file back to see if LCP(L)15 was ready and waiting, or whether he "would have to retreat toward the main beaches of Dieppe," ten miles away up the coast. If we were there Selwyn was to fire three white Very lights.

The boat was there in fact, having attracted the attention of a Dornier-17 bomber which had dropped two sticks of bombs on us before being deterred by our Stripped-Lewis fire.

Then followed a wild scene in which the commandos had to descend the cliff and its wire, pursued by their former targets from the Paul Joseph Goebbels gun sites. One commando kicked over a land mine, which oddly enough did not take his foot. We were able to keep the Germans' heads down by firing along the cliff top; our on-site theory was that a diet of dirt and stones and chalk and bullets would not be easily accepted by our enemy. We had wild time trying to de-beach the boat in the face of the falling tide, the increasing load of our human cargo meanwhile pulling those still splashing around in the water back on board. There was a horrible moment when we found that we had been dragging two of them actually under water a good way, and we had to slow the boat down to haul them back over the gunwales.

Motor Launch 346 steams out to meet Landing Craft Personnel (Large)15 waiting for the Commandos to return from their engagement with the Battery. We had speeded up to dodge the attacks of a Dornier Bomber.

Photo courtesy David J. Lewis.

Meanwhile the commandos took over the Lewis guns and kept the Germans at bay. A German bullet did pierce the thigh of one of our seamen but fortunately did not damage bone, nerve or artery. One of the commandos was found to have a bandaged ear; he had been struck by a shell fragment fired by Motor Launch 346, which now came to assist us. At that time Lt. Fear, the captain, had been trying to support the Yellow Beach One landing, which had gone ahead to a brave but complete disaster. Shattered, burned and sunken boats, dead and wounded men, and four years of prison, part of it spent in shackles, were the result of this tragic endeavour. It was a tragic story so similar to what went on in the majority of other beaches. Our own vessel had several petrol-tank holes, but this was the extent of our gunfire damage.

The motor launch came alongside us as we beat our retreat. After having recovered every man jack of our passengers we were sorry to see them transfer to ML 346. However, we did not have the supplies of spirits available that Lt. Fear possessed. So our soldiers and our wounded seamen made off at more speed than LCP(L)15 could muster towards England, Home and Beauty. I remember how the White Cliffs of Beachy Head sparkled warmly in the afternoon sun. We had unfortunately missed out on a survivor of the early morning fight, Lieutenant Smale of 3 Commando, as he floated down the Channel to be picked up by Germans coming out from the now-silent Dieppe beaches.

Flat out for Newhaven. Our troops are aboard Motor Launch 246. When she entered harbour in England bystanders observed Major Young in high spirits on deck. The interested reader can identify the Very pistol, Stripped - Lewis gun, and an old-fashioned, air-cooled, double-mounted Lewis gun pair which peer out below our tin-helmeted Motor Mechanic. Harness, ropes, spent cartridges, and all kinds of gash objects litter every flat surface. Commandos lived in lodgings ashore and so could always depend on others to tidy up after them.

Photo courtesy David J. Lewis.

I don't remember a word being spoken by Buckee on the way home. One Canadian historian in an otherwise admirable book on the Dieppe raid renamed him "Duckee" throughout. It was an error in more than one sense. Recent trans-atlantic conversation with Captain Selwyn indicates that while Buckee attended Combined Operations anniversary celebrations over the years, he had very little to say on those occasions too. He returned to legal work following the war and finished his career as an Essex County Judge, dying early in this decade. Major Young continued to climb the military ladder, attaining the level of Brigadier. For a while he commanded a regiment of the Arab Legion and lectured on this experience in Canada. Like Julius Caesar, he has written up his own wars, and also other historical subjects of note.* He died in the course of the last five years, and I am sorry not to have met them both again before their recall came.

Both Buckee and Young were awarded the DSO for their achievement, as were the captains of our aberrant destroyers, while Captain Selwyn received the Military Cross. The author also was happy to be mentioned in dispatches.

Captain Hughes-Hallett, the naval commander, saluted Young's achievement as probably the most outstanding individual achievement of Dieppe. The story goes in Young's book, *Storm From the Sea*, that when he was rushed off to London to present his account to the chiefs of staff the following day, he was still in his battle-worn uniform. When he apologized, Lord Louis Mountbatten, who was present amongst the assembled brass hats, graciously accepted his apology with the comment, "What the hell, there is a war on!"

Captain and later Admiral and Member of Parliament, Hughes-Hallett must have had some explaining to do as to why he had not informed Grey Owl (SGB-5) of the approaching German convoy. But one could argue as to what the result might have been if he had passed on that information.

Seventy-one Canadian Naval Combined Operations personnel participated in the Dieppe engagement. A Roll of their names was officially presented to the Mayor of Dieppe in 1992 on the occasion of the 50th Anniversary. Those returning could all add to the history of those times. Certainly one of the hazards of Combined Operations was that of falling between the three stools of the three services. Accounts of Canadian Naval Combined Ops in the Second World War, and the difficult tasks it performed under the most dangerous circumstances, are only now slowly gaining the recognition and appreciation they deserve.

*See Lt. Peter Young, *Storm From the Sea* [London: William Kimber, 1958].

Alberta Women Join Up

Donna Alexander Zwicker

At the outbreak of the Second World War nurses volunteered for service in the Royal Canadian Army Medical Corps, building on the military tradition of the previous half century. At the same time, other women struggled for recognition beyond the role of nursing, eventually becoming part of a new military structure. Admission requirements had to be established, training centres opened and recruiting campaigns launched in order to facilitate the transition of women into skilled and unskilled positions formerly held by men. Young women were relocated near and far, some even overseas, in the line of duty. An active media campaign encouraged the general public to accept and support the new women's service.

Canadian nurses have a history of caring for soldiers in both domestic and international confrontations. They were first called upon for the purpose of nursing military wounded during the Northwest Rebellion in May 1885. In June 1899 nurses were officially affiliated with the Canadian Army and were assigned duties in Imperial Hospitals in Canada. By 1902 Canadian Army nurses had served in the Boer War and were considered an essential part of the Canadian Army Medical Corps. During the First World War the nursing service was again mobilized, and 2000 nurses served at home and abroad, with nearly 600 receiving decorations.[1]

Although the active nursing service was demobilized at the end of the Great War, a few nurses were kept on staff to work at military hospitals. At the outbreak of the Second World War one matron and ten nursing sisters were serving in the Permanent Force, and 331 were on a reserve list.[2] The Canadian Nurses' Association, in cooperation with the Red Cross Society, maintained a National Enrollment list of nurses in each province who were ready for service in case of war or disaster. However, nurses volunteered in such numbers during the Second World War that there was no need to recruit from the National Enrollment list.

As Canada mobilized in 1939, Nursing Sisters were included in the initial plans for proposed military hospitals and medical units.[3] In September 1939, the first two divisions of the army corps were quickly organized and provisions were made for nurses to be included in eight medical units. The nursing volunteers were sent either to Toronto or Winnipeg to receive two weeks' training before they were posted to duty at a hospital, or later to a medical unit.[4] In April 1940, Nursing Sisters were sent overseas as part of the Royal Canadian Medical Corps and by the end of that year there were 227 nurses stationed at Canadian installations in Great Britain.[5] The first Alberta unit of nurses left for England on 8 September 1941, although a number of nurses had already been sent overseas with other units.

While Canadian nurses were enlisting and many were being sent overseas, other women were lobbying for admission into the forces in a non-combat support role. The idea of women caring for the sick and wounded was consistent with the accepted social values of the times, although it was an untried experiment to view women, even temporarily, as something other than caregivers, homemakers or mothers. Western women, including those from Alberta, were partly responsible for changing such views within federal government circles. They organized themselves into like-minded groups preparing for service in the war effort, and they pressed the government to consider their value in the military.

More than eighteen women's paramilitary organizations registered under the War Charities Act as women's corps.[6] The Canadian Auxiliary Territorial Service, the Canadian Women's Service Force and the Canadian Women's Service Corps were the three primary paramilitary organizations in Canada that challenged the status quo. Each was involved in the recruiting and training of women. Although units of many of the organizations were formed in Alberta, the strongest support went to the Canadian Women's Service Corps, an offshoot of the British Columbia-based group under the leadership of Mrs. Joan Kennedy. Nearly two years after the Corps had been established in British Columbia the Alberta branch was founded in Edmonton in July 1940, under the leadership of Mrs. E.C. Pardee.[7]

The Women's Service Corps organization and structure were typical of most service corps across the country. The members underwent a three-month training course, wore uniforms and were trained in military and stretcher drills, air raid precautions and first aid. The women paid dues to maintain a building with lecture rooms and a drill hall, and they pledged to be on call for war work, patriotic drives and civilian emergencies.[8] In addition to volunteer work and drill training, some of the women learned map-reading skills, motor mechanics and aircraft recognition techniques.

Groups such as the Women's Service Corps were overjoyed when an announcement was made by the government in February 1941, stating that women would be incorporated into the military forces. A severe manpower shortage had developed due to declining male enlistment, and the inclusion of women would relieve some of the shortfall in enlistment.[9] A precedent was set in Great Britain where women were being recruited into the regular forces and the Canadian government realized that it had at hand a similarly eager and available replacement work force.[10] As a result of both the public pressure and the increasing need, the Royal Canadian Air Force, Women's Division [RCAF(WD)] was formed by an Order-in-Council on 2 July 1941, and the Canadian Women's Army Corps [CWAC] was established by another Order-in-Council on 13 August 1941. The Royal Canadian Navy, however, did not begin recruiting women into the force until 31 July 1942, nearly a year after the RCAF(WD) and CWAC were organized.

The administrative core of the three forces was drawn from Canada's patriotic and educated women. The CWAC, the largest of the women's forces, first recruited its administrative personnel solely from the many women's military organizations. Whereas the RCAF(WD) and the Women's Royal Canadian Naval

Service [Wrens] recruited women with a higher education from the general public. The new administrators did not have any formal military background, yet they were thrust into responsible positions as leaders of the newly formed military services.

The CWAC borrowed Matron-in-Chief Miss Elizabeth Smellie of the Royal Canadian Army Medical Corps as overseer of the new corps until the newly appointed administrator, Mrs. Joan B. Kennedy, and eleven Military District officers could take charge on their own. The Headquarters Staff of the Department of National Defence organized the framework of eleven Military Districts for the service, which was to coincide with the army recruiting districts already in operation.

The district officers were drawn from among 1000 recruits in an administrative training drive, and the women selected were recruited from the many women's paramilitary units. From Alberta's quota of 94 recruits, Mary Dover and three other women were chosen as officers for Military District No. 13, Alberta. Mrs. Dover, the daughter of A.E. Cross and the granddaughter of Colonel James F. Macleod, was active in Calgary clubs and city affairs. She carried these leadership skills from civilian life, along with her membership in the Women's Service Corps, into her career as a CWAC officer. From her entry position as senior staff officer she rose through the ranks to command the largest training centre for women in Canada at No. 3 CWAC in Kitchener, Ontario with the rank of Lieutenant-Colonel.[11]

Mrs. Dover's Alberta Women's Service Corps counterparts also attained a high level of involvement in the CWAC. By the summer of 1942 Mrs. Ethel English, who had been commandant of the Calgary unit of the Women's Service

Captain Mary Dover [at left] swearing in Canadian Women's Army Corps recruits, 1941. Lieutenant McIlevena stands to her left.

Photo courtesy Glenbow Archives, Calgary [NA-2624-5].

Corps, was transferred east and promoted to Captain.[12] Mrs. McIlevena of Lethbridge was transferred to the west coast becoming staff officer of Military District No. 11, and Miss Pearl Brent of Calgary was also appointed to the position of Captain.[13] By 1943, 75 per cent of the Women's Service Corps girls who enlisted held commissions or were noncommissioned officers, a remarkable display of energy and determination.[14]

The RCAF(WD) was modelled on the British Women's Air Auxiliary Force. In the first year of operation, the administration of the Canadian organization was entrusted to British WAAF officers, and this affiliation to the British force undoubtedly enhanced the image of the new corps. Strong support for the corps also was shown by the appointment of Princess Alice, wife of the Governor General of Canada, as honourary commandant. The princess made inspections and commemorative appearances.

RCAF(WD) administrative officers were selected from across the country. After completing the five-week administrative course in Toronto, the women were sent, where possible, to their home provinces. It was expected that local women would be better equipped to encourage other members of the community to enlist.

Alberta women were anxious to be part of the officers' corps. Approximately 200 applicants for the administrative positions were received prior to the application deadline of 15 September 1941. A screening process was conducted by a traveling board composed of members of the national war services department. Fourteen candidates were chosen.[15] The successful candidates had three things in common: they all had a higher education, were currently employed or in training, and they were single. Since most of these women held well paying positions in civilian life, it is unlikely that they joined up for monetary reasons. Rather, it was their patriotism and their desire for adventure and prestige that brought them into the force.

Similarly, the Women's Royal Canadian Naval Service borrowed leaders and organizers from their British counterparts and chose administrative personnel with a higher education or administrative experience. Wrens had to be willing to relocate, especially those in landlocked Alberta. The main Wren sites were located in Halifax and St. John's, although there were Wrens in Toronto, Ottawa and Vancouver.[16] As with the other women's forces, over 800 applications were received for only 70 positions.[17] Five candidates were chosen from Alberta; two from Calgary and three from Edmonton. The first quota of recruits from Alberta consisted mainly of teachers. For many teachers, especially those from the prairies, the navy proved to be a great alternative to their profession in which poor pay and working conditions had developed during the Great Depression, and had not greatly improved throughout the war.

General recruitment in the women's services was not as successful as the campaign for the officers. The number of female recruits increased greatly as the war continued but still fell short of government projections. Enlistment quotas for training facilities, jobs and recruiting techniques varied among the three forces, but the results were disappointing in each case. Women seemed to be more willing to support the service from the outside than to actually enlist.

The admission requirements were basically the same for the three forces. The recruits were signed on for the duration of the war and, if necessary, for twelve months after. Applicants in the CWAC, for example, had to be between ages 18 and 45, British subjects, have grade eight education, and place in an acceptable medical category. Officers, however, had to be 21 years of age and have university entrance. Women were allowed to be married but were not allowed to have dependent children. Those who became pregnant while in the forces were immediately dismissed from service.[18]

Once admitted, new recruits in the three forces were sent to a basic training centre in central Canada. The Wren training centre, located in Galt, Ontario, was capable of accommodating 400 Wrens-in-training at one time, and provincial quotas were set accordingly.[19] Alberta quotas were relatively low, beginning with five women per quota and rising to about twenty by the fall of 1943.[20] The upsurge in the number of recruits from Alberta was part of a national drive for more women, not only in the navy but in the other services as well. In all, 565 Wrens from Alberta trained in Ontario; they were part of a group of over 6500 Canadian women who enlisted in the navy.[21]

New RCAF(WD) recruits were sent to No. 6 Manning Depot, Havergal College, Toronto, or No. 7 Manning Depot, Rockcliffe, near Ottawa for basic training. National recruitment quotas fluctuated from 400 to 1000 recruits per month, reaching more than 16,000 female personnel in the air force by war's end. 1,848 of the recruits were from Alberta.[22]

Alberta hosted a number of air force locations. Calgary was home to No. 2 Wireless Training School and No. 11 Equipment Depot. Currie Barracks served as the main field for the Calgary region of the British Commonwealth Air Training Plan. In July 1942 approximately 100 airwomen arrived to replace men in such basic duties as transport drivers or cooks.[23] No. 4 Command Technical Detachment was located in Edmonton, as well as No. 2 Air Observer School. Other air force sites included No. 7 Service Flying Training School [SFTS] at Fort Macleod, No. 8 Bombing and Gunnery School, Lethbridge, No. 15 SFTS, Claresholm and No. 2 Flying Instructor School at Vulcan.

No. 7 SFTS Macleod, for example, received 106 airwomen in February 1942. Women were trained in radio operations, a few with Morse code training, while others worked as telephone operators, bus drivers, stenographers, clerks and maintenance workers. Bombing and Gunnery schools and Air Observer schools on average had 100 female personnel. As early as 1942 over 1000 women were at work at the many RCAF facilities in Alberta.[24] Incorporating women into the system was not a simple task, since most schools or air bases were not equipped for female personnel. Living quarters had to be modified and adequate hospital and recreation facilities had to be provided for the WDs.

At first CWAC recruits were sent to Ste. Anne de Bellevue, Quebec for basic training. Due to Canada's increased commitment to the European war during 1942, the government turned to Canadian women to further ease the demand on men at home, freeing more men for overseas duty. As a result, CWAC recruitment numbers were increased, and rumours of adding a second training base abounded. On 14 July 1942 Major Joan Kennedy ended the speculation with the announcement that a new training centre would be opened at Vermilion Agricultural College, in Vermilion, Alberta.[25] The western location was chosen to save the time and expense of transporting western trainees east and then to their posts. The college had good access by train to other areas of the West, and was large enough to accommodate 300, and possibly up to 500 new trainees without too much renovation.

A staff of 150 officers and general personnel were assigned to Vermilion College in July, to prepare the institution for the first group of recruits. Just prior to the opening of the Vermilion facility there were 3500 women in the force, and of that number 335 were from Alberta.[26] A great deal of faith was put in Vermilion. National reports relayed this sentiment, claiming that with the new centre 1000 recruits per month were to be trained for CWAC duties, with a goal of 10,000 recruits by December 1942.[27]

Government officials believed that by placing the training centre in the heart of the West, and by adding an active recruiting campaign, there would be thousands of western women drawn into the CWAC in a few short months. However, such an overwhelming response was not seen in the West, and by 1943 Vermilion was averaging 300 recruits per month, although expectations ran as high as 500 per month.[28] It is interesting to note that Alberta did not lead the prairies in enlistment, in spite of the location of the training centre at Vermilion; in fact, it had the lowest actual enlistment. In addition, the location of the centre in the West did not significantly increase the enrollment of the CWAC over the RCAF(WD) in the three provinces.[29] The opportunity to train at Vermilion did not prove to be a significant motivating factor for local girls.

The women's service experienced the same recruiting problems in 1942 as did the men's service during 1941. The employment available to women who enlisted as general recruits was a factor, since most of the jobs available to female recruits lacked the glamour or excitement that was so often connected with the military service by the media. After the small administrative quota of recruits was filled, thousands of women were needed to perform menial tasks. The types of recruits that were needed were primarily Category C and B tradeswomen, the least skilled workers.

The most general of the jobs were included in Class C, consisting of such work as orderly room clerks, A and B helpers, storeroom workers, drivers, mechanics and cooks.[30] Class B trades were employed in assistant roles, including assistants to trade work, A category jobs, specialized clerks, stenographers, signal and telephone operators, tailors, motor mechanics, class 2 cooks and dental assistants. Throughout the war, the call for these women continued to dominate recruiting quotas.

Recruits leaving for training centre in Vermilion, Alberta, 1943.

Photo courtesy Glenbow Archives, Calgary [NA-2624-9].

Category A recruits included supervisory clerks, certified radiographers, draughtsmen with experience in architecture, class one hospital cooks and laboratory assistants. In 1942 a request was issued for more women with special skills and university degrees: "We are particularly anxious to get university students and graduates," said Major Kennedy, "and we need girls who have studied commercial art. We cannot begin to meet the demands for draughtsmen."[31] This plea coincided with the massive expansion in the CWAC, which naturally required additional administrators, and the decision to gradually phase women into a wider range of trades.

The Canadian Women's Army Corps adopted a scheme to provide a limited amount of training in the trades to interested recruits. The three main courses offered to women considering entering the CWAC were clerical, cooking and driver courses.[32] Private Lillian Alberta Sachwell, from Strathmore, Alberta, the only female instructor in mechanics in Western Canada, conducted instruction in motor mechanics for female recruits at Currie Barracks.[33] In August 1942, the first 22 women completed a two-month course in motor mechanics, and then were qualified as transport drivers. The graduates remained "feminine," despite their training, and were not tomboys, according to a newspaper account.[34] Later, civilian schools, such as the Edmonton Technical High School, offered cooking and clerical courses transferable to the CWAC.[35] On completion of their course the skilled recruits were sent to Vermilion for basic training. As an incentive to enlistment the trade pay for women was raised from two-thirds of men's salary to the full-scale pay of men in similar positions, beginning in July 1943.[36]

Opportunities were similar in the RCAF(WD). Throughout the war, women in Alberta were told that there was an urgent need for cooks and messwomen in the

RCAF. However, after the administrative positions were filled, "most applicants interviewed at Calgary indicated they wished to become transport drivers."[37] Alberta recruits went into all areas open to them, but they were most often signed on as clerks, general-duties women, equipment assistants and drivers.

Until 1942 most women were required to be trained personnel upon their enlistment, saving the government time and money, although in May of that year training in new trades became available to members of the RCAF(WD). One new trade was in the operations room, where operations clerks were given confidential work involving mapping and plotting aircraft on operational flights.[38] The service also was compelled to add a training dimension to its programme as the pace of recruitment was stepped up. Cooking recruits, for example, were eligible for a six-week course in Guelph, Ontario after completing basic training. As a severe shortage of clerical help developed in 1943, women were also offered a five-month stenography course prior to enlistment under the Wartime Emergency Training Plan. In Calgary, this training was available at Western Canada High School.[39]

As with the other two forces, the RCN most required cooks, domestics and clerks. Calgary was the focal point for the Navy's Alberta campaign, where interested cooking recruits were told that Wrens would train in the officers' mess before transfer to shore establishments for the duration of the war. It was stressed that they were needed to release men for active sea duty, and that enlistment in the most needed categories best served the war effort.

One aspect of service which was given a great deal of publicity was the notion that female recruits could travel abroad. In reality only selected women with the most seniority and best record were given an opportunity to serve overseas. Work opportunities outside Canada became available in February 1942, when a number of women, all of them highly skilled in clerical and business matters, became part of the Canadian Legation in Washington.[40] Beginning in May, CWAC tradeswomen went to England, followed shortly by a group of laundresses.[41] A total of 2000 Canadian Women's Army Corps personnel saw service in the United Kingdom by the war's end. Some of these were sent to Europe in May 1944 to serve in the rear stations connected with the invasion of Italy, France and Germany.[42]

It was August 1942 when the RCAF began sending women out of the country to Newfoundland. Jobs there were mainly clerical, including work as typists, switchboard operators, and hospital assistants.[43] A total of 740 RCAF(WD) women served on the island during the war. In 1942 six airwomen, including J. Allerton of Calgary, also were posted to Washington, D.C. to work with the US Army Air Corps.[44]

The first airwomen to be sent overseas were well educated, usually with a university degree, and often with clerical and operations-room training. About 40 women, three of whom were Albertans, were the first to be stationed overseas under the command of Section Officer Patsy Griffin of Winnipeg and Section Officer

Nancy Smith of Calgary.[45] In total, over 1300 girls served overseas with the RCAF by the end of the conflict.[46]

The Wrens began sending women out of Canada in July 1943 to fill such positions as pay writers, typists, stenographers, and clerks; 503 Wrens were stationed in Great Britain at Londonderry, HMCS Niobe in Scotland, at London, with a few in Plymouth as well. Five hundred and sixty eight members of the WRCNS also were sent to Newfoundland, and about 50 to New York and Washington.[47] In all, over 17 per cent of the Wrens saw active service outside Canada, while only between ten and thirteen per cent of the women in the other two forces were sent abroad.[48] Overseas service was unlikely for most eager recruits no matter in which of the forces they enlisted, although their odds were a bit higher with the Navy.

In contrast, there were ample opportunities for travel abroad as Nursing Sisters, especially with the Army. The Royal Canadian Army Medical Corps [RCAMC] sent nurses to Newfoundland and Hong Kong, as well as the European and Mediterranean theatres of war. One special recruiting campaign sent 300 nurses to South Africa for duty in the South African Military Nursing Service. In fact, two-thirds of the 3656 army nurses that were in the service during the war spent some time overseas.[49]

The RCN and RCAF required fewer nurses in their operations. By December 1942 there were 1500 nurses in the combined military forces serving at home and abroad, with approximately 1400 of them in the RCAMC.[50] Some nurses were stationed at RCAF hospitals, and at the British Commonwealth Air Training Plan [BCATP] flying schools. As Canada's commitment to the BCATP increased, so did the number of nurses, rising to a total of 395 women by 1945.[51]

As the demand for nurses grew the government began to allocate funds to encourage more young, single women to enter into this respectable occupation. On 23 July 1942, there was a war appropriation of $115,000 to be expended on promotional campaigns, new nursing facilities at existing schools, and student scholarships.[52] Alberta's eleven nursing schools benefitted from the government's commitment to nursing, since many of these qualified as acceptable training institutions.

Recruitment drives were primarily focused on schools, since the 18-year-old girls proved to be the best target age group. Funds were made available for students who could not afford the three-year course but were otherwise interested. A total of $100 per student was available: $50 for initial expenses and $50 after the first term. The grant was restricted to "those who sign an agreement that they will give their services to the armed forces or war industries."[53]

Members of the Canadian Nurses' Association in Alberta cooperated with the government scheme. They held meetings with other organizations to create an awareness of the nursing courses in the community. At one such meeting representatives of thirteen affiliated organizations were present at the Edmonton Local Council of Women to hear Margaret Frazer, superintendent of nurses at the Royal Alexandra Hospital, give an address on "Nursing and National Service," in which she suggested that the public should encourage young women to enter the nursing profession.[54]

Members of the Alberta Chapter of the Canadian Nurses' Association organized publicity tours and recruiting drives. In April 1942, Miss Jean Davidson went on a publicity tour of Alberta to recruit young student nurses, and addressed community groups and high schools in an attempt to increase interest in nursing. However, the head of the Alberta Registered Nurses' Association told the press that while 11,200 nurses were enrolled in the programme, only about 3000 graduated, and of these 30 per cent married within two years and were no longer active nurses.[55]

Canadian nurses showed an exemplary patriotic spirit in the war. Both the government scheme to encourage women to enter the nursing programme, and the eager support of the community, indicated that nurses were highly valued, although the enthusiastic response to military nursing led to a shortage of nursing personnel in the civilian population. The number of nurses who were available at this time for work in hospitals, homes, public health clinics, schools and factories declined in Alberta, as it did across the country.[56]

Recruiting tours also were organized by the regular forces. At first the recruiting tours in Alberta were held almost entirely in Edmonton and Calgary. However, by 1942 they were being conducted throughout the province. The tours put the officers in touch with the young women of the community, and included talks to high schools encouraging young women to consider enlistment upon graduation.

Wren recruiting tours went into full swing at the beginning of 1943. By the spring of that year, recruiting officers were stationed in both Calgary and Edmonton, and rural recruiting tours were added to the campaign. Quotas from the prairies were easily met throughout the war. On a national recruiting trip, Third Officer Rich observed that there was a greater interest in the Wrens in the prairie provinces than in the Maritimes.[57] The chance to travel out of landlocked Alberta, and the novelty provided by the Navy, may have helped to make it popular with potential recruits. Quotas were set much lower for Alberta than for the eastern centres as well.

Unlike the Royal Canadian Navy, the Army and RCAF had a great number of female recruits stationed in prairie cities, towns and isolated bases, creating a greater impact on the local communities. Officers of the two forces reached out to groups in their communities, requesting they supply friendship and support for the enlisted women in their area. Women's clubs responded by organizing teas, dances, special events, and by opening their homes to girls on leave. Nevertheless, it appears that such club endeavours frequently were met with little appreciation or interest by the enlisted women, and quite often a liaison officer was required to smooth things over. Small problems tended to mar the reputation

WREN'S recruitment.

*Photo courtesy
Provincial Archives of
Alberta [PAA Bl. 619].*

of the forces and interfere with support from the general public, while it seems that the acts of kindness shown to the enlisted girls were often inappropriately matched with actual needs or desires.

Both the CWAC and the RCAF(WD) tried hard to establish good public relations. In September 1942 newspaper women were taken on a tour of No. 8 B and G School, Lethbridge, and No. 3 SFTF, Calgary, and broadcasts were made over CFAC radio from No. 3 SFTF by members of the women's forces. The Imperial Order of the Daughters of the Empire [IODE] held fashion shows which featured women's service uniforms and included a fifteen-minute speech by recruiting officers. Over 3000 women attended the two evening shows.[58] In February and April 1943, the two services held public inspections for interested civilians. Currie Barracks, which housed RCAF(WD) and CWAC members, was thrown open for inspection. Later that year the RCAF provided a tour for 150 civilians through No. 3 SFTS, Currie Field, showing spectators the variety of tasks performed by women. Similarly, Assistant Section Officer Ivie Summers made an appeal for support of their recruitment efforts to the Business and Professional Club meeting at Knox United Church in Calgary.[59]

The CWAC also began to use women's organizations as civilian advisors in recruitment drives in Alberta. In June 1943, a two-day conference of civilian advisors was held at the Palliser Hotel in Calgary, with 125 delegates from 82 cities and towns in Alberta in attendance.[60] Further attempts were made at improving community relations through the use of precision squads, parades, bands, public booths and displays. The CWAC and the RCAF(WD) demonstrated the marching skills of its female recruits through such precision squads. The RCAF(WD)'s first precision squad was organized at the Rockcliffe

Manning Depot in Ottawa. In November 1942, this squad went on a western Canadian tour in aid of the Victory Loan Campaign, demonstrating their routines in Calgary, Edmonton and Medicine Hat. Precision squads were later formed in Calgary and Edmonton. At the Calgary Horse Show in April 1943, the squads were pitted against each other in an effort to strike up an inter-city rivalry.

CWAC demonstrating marching and drills on stage, 1943.

Photo courtesy Glenbow Archives, Calgary [NA-4784-8].

Parades were organized in Edmonton in the autumn of 1942 to celebrate the graduation of CWAC recruits from the Vermilion training centre. On 5 October 1942, the second graduation parade was scheduled; new recruits marched through the streets of Edmonton with thousands witnessing the parade.[61] In April 1943, drill squads from Calgary and Edmonton, with more than 400 CWAC members, paraded through the downtown areas as part of an intensive recruiting campaign.[62] A 30-piece brass band was assembled and trained in Calgary at Currie Barracks, and then posted to Vermilion. In October 1943, during a Victory Loan Campaign, the Vermilion band and the Ste. Anne de Bellevue pipe band conducted a cross-country tour. While in Calgary the band put on a concert and took part in a church parade.[63]

The CWAC was the most aggressive in organizing public displays, although they were not all effective. In July 1942, a booth was set up in the Calgary Stampede Fair Grounds, but the display was hardly successful, attracting only 56 women to sign up for interviews. The results at the Edmonton Exhibition booth also were disappointingly shy of the expected 500 interviews.

Department store window-displays in downtown Calgary and Edmonton were used as yet another device to attract attention to the services. In April 1943, the CWAC had a special week to show their women at work. In Edmonton, the Hudson's Bay Company provided an actual barracks room scene showing all the kit equipment in one window and a group doing some cooking for the onlookers in another window. The T. Eaton Company displayed uniforms and showed photos of the jobs women performed. Woodwards Department Store showed women at work, highlighting those who were motor transport drivers and workers.[64]

The RCAF(WD) and the Wrens also provided displays to attract women into the service. The RCAF established an information booth on the second floor in the Hudson's Bay Company department store in Edmonton. Similarly, the Navy organized a mobile exhibit that toured across Canada, which was set up in the Eaton's store in Edmonton during July, and again in October 1943.[65]

Typical department store window display promoting the CWAC.

Photo courtesy Glenbow Archives, Calgary [NA-4784-5].

All three forces simultaneously undertook a major advertising campaign for women in the summer of 1943. The federal government announced that "recruitment methods would include newspaper advertisements, radio programmes and other methods which would stimulate interest."[66] Walter MacDonald, manager of the *Edmonton Journal*, at a meeting of officials with national publishers, stated that "the most authoritative and effective way to distribute government information was by paid advertisements in the daily newspapers."[67] This new recruiting technique encouraged businesses to aid the war effort by sponsoring local advertisements in print or on the air. Despite the support shown by the media and the business community, the women's forces continued to fall short of recruitment objectives.

WRENS at the Navy
Show in Eaton's,
Edmonton, July 1943.

*Photo courtesy
Provincial Archives of
Alberta [PAA Bl. 595/1].*

Canadian Nursing Sisters were the first women to answer the call to serve in the military during the Second World War. With a strong tradition of patriotic duty which included service in the Boer War and First World War, they were viewed as a great asset to the military in the Second World War as well. Key administrative personnel were recalled from the reserves, which had continued to function during peacetime, and new recruits were quickly raised from civilian hospitals and schools. In fact, nurses left their old positions for military service in such large numbers that civilian nursing shortages soon developed. The government was forced to increase the output of nursing schools in order to ensure adequate care for civilian and military personnel. Both the military and society in general saw the value of the dedicated girls who were willing to treat the sick and wounded, in Canada and abroad.

Other areas of military service were not as readily accessible to women. Although paramilitary groups were formed at the outbreak of the war, it took nearly two years for them to press the government into accepting women into the ranks of the Army, Navy and Air Force. The Canadian Women's Army Corps, the Women's Royal Canadian Naval Service and the Royal Canadian Air Force, Women's Division first brought women into the officer ranks, and later began general recruitment. Thousands of Alberta girls joined the three women's forces as ordinary servicewomen, performing ordinary tasks like cooking and office work. Western women travelled to training facilities, and many to work locations far from home. Alberta hosted a number of recruiting centres, bases and training facilities that maintained female personnel.

Reasons for enlistment were reviewed at a reunion of RCAF(WD) veterans in 1983:

> *'Joining up' provided a legitimate opportunity for women to become independent of family. Women came from the security of home, school, shop, office, farm and factory. Some were teachers and some were already involved in the war effort.... Many were being patriotic.... Some had family in Nazi-occupied Europe. Others...had loved ones who were POWs and joining up might bring them home sooner.*[68]

From this response it is clear that, in the final analysis, women enlisted for a variety of reasons, but ultimately they responded to a personal call to serve.

The V-J Day parade held in Edmonton on 15 August 1945 passes the Cenotaph.

Photo courtesy Provincial Archives of Alberta [PAA Bl. 965/5].

NOTES

[1]*Edmonton Journal*, 23 January 1943.

[2]W.R. Feasby, *Official History of the Canadian Medical Services 1939-1945, Vol. 1* [Ottawa: Queen's Printers and Controller of Stationery, 1956], p. 310.

[3]Ibid., Chapter 2, passim. Staffed military hospitals were proposed for locations in Halifax, Montreal, Toronto, Kingston, London, Winnipeg, Regina, Calgary, Edmonton and Vancouver. It was decided that casualties should be hospitalized in their region of enlistment whenever possible for the benefit of the patient, family and friends.

[4]G. W. L. Nicholson, *Canada's Nursing Sisters* [Toronto: Samuel Stevens Hakkert and Company, 1975], pp. 116-118.

[5]Feasby, *Canadian Medical Services*, p. 312.

[6]Charlotte Whitton, *Canadian Women in the War Effort*, [Toronto: The Macmillan Company of Canada Ltd., 1942], p. 52.

[7]*Public Archives of Canada, Records of the Governor General's Office, 1774-1966* [hereinafter cited PAC RG 7, G21] second series, Vol. 679, file 328A. Letter dated 26 December 1940 to Lady-in-Waiting to Her Royal Highness the Princess Alice, Ariel Baird from Joan B. Kennedy.

[8]*PAC, RG 7, G21*, second series, Vol. 679, file 328A. Letter dated 1 October 1940 to Colonel O'Conner from Lt. Gov. G.W. Hamber.

[9]Margaret Eaton, "Canadian Women's Army Corps," *Canadian Geographical Journal*, 27, No. 6 [1943], p. 279.

[10]*PAC, RG 7, G21*, second series, Vol. 679, file 328A. Letter of 25 September 1940 to Lt. Gov. of British Columbia, G.W. Hamber from Joan B. Kennedy.

[11]*Edmonton Journal*, 8 May 1943; *Calgary Albertan*, 13 July 1943.

[12]*Calgary Albertan*, 26 August 1942.

[13]Ibid., 18 July 942.

[14]*Edmonton Journal*, 11 January 1943.

[15]*Calgary Albertan*, 16 September 1941; *Edmonton Journal*, 11 September 1941; 28 November 1941.

[16]Rosamond 'Fiddy' Greer, *The Girls of the King's Navy* [Victoria, British Columbia: Sono Nis Press, 1983], p. 15.

[17]*Calgary Albertan*, 18 May1 942, p. 6.

[18]Whitton, *Canadian Women*, p. 15.

[19]Adelaide Sinclair, "Women's Royal Canadian Naval Service," *Canadian Geographical Journal*, 26, No. 6 [1943], p. 288. A quota was an admission number set to meet projected needs in the service. Each province was given a monthly number of recruits to enlist for basic training.

[20]*Calgary Albertan*, 20 August 1943.

[21]There was a total of 5893 in the service at its peak. Greer, *The Girls*, pp. 17-18.

[22]Ruth Roach Pierson, "Canadian Women and the Second World War," *The Canadian Historical Association, Historical Booklet No. 37*, Ottawa, 1983, p. 8.

[23]*Calgary Herald*, 18 December 1942; *Calgary Albertan*, 5 July 1942.

[24]*Calgary Albertan*, 6 August 1942; 18 November 1942; 9 November 1942; 21 April 1942.

[25]Ibid., 15 July 1942.

[26]*Edmonton Journal*, 15 July 1942.

[27]Ibid., 12 August 1942.

[28]Ibid., 9 June 1943.

[29]Vernon Fowke, "Effects of the War on the Prairie Economy," *Canadian Journal of Economic and Political Science*, 11, No. 3 [1975], p. 384.

[30]*Calgary Albertan*, 28 November 1941.

[31]*Calgary Albertan*, 18 July 1942.

[32]Ruth Roach Pierson, "'Jill Canuck': CWAC of All Trades, But No 'Pistol Packing Momma'," *Historical Papers*, [1978], p. 118.

[33]*Calgary Albertan*, 4 November 1942.

[34]*Edmonton Journal*, 26 August 1942.

[35]Ibid., 31 July 1943.

[36]Ibid., 29 July 1943.

[37]*Calgary Albertan*, 1 October 1941.

[38]*Edmonton Journal*, 24 September 1942.

[39]*Calgary Albertan*, 10 March 1943.

[40]Ibid., 16 February 1943; 23 February 1942.

[41]Ibid., 7 August 1942.

[42]Pierson, *Canadian Women*, p. 8.

[43]*Edmonton Journal*, 22 August 1942; *Calgary Albertan*, 24 August 1942; 26 August 1942.

[44]*Edmonton Journal*, 23 December 1942; *Calgary Albertan*, 9 September 1942.

[45]Ibid., *Edmonton Journal*, 1 August 1942.

[46]Pierson, *Canadian Women*, p. 8.

[47]Greer, *The Girls*, p. 18.

[48]The CWAC had a total enlistment of 20,497 with over 2,000 serving outside Canada, the RCAF(WD) 16,221 with over 2000 serving outside Canada, the Wrens 6665 with 1121 serving outside Canada. The information is based on Pierson, *Canadian Women*, p. 8. and Greer, *The Girls*, p. 18. These figures do not include the 4439 Nursing Sisters of the three forces.

[49]Nicholson, *Nursing Sisters*, p. 195.

[50]*Edmonton Journal*, 12 December 1942; 23 January 1943.

[51]Nicholson, *Nursing Sisters*, p. 190; and Feasby, *Canadian Medical Services*, Chapter 24.

[52]*Calgary Albertan*, July 24, 1942. The monetary division was $15,000 to the Nursing Association for promotional campaigns, $75,000 for facilities to help deal with new increased enrollment of students, $25,000 for graduate nurses' scholarships for those nurses who would make good teachers, supervisors and administrators.

[53]*Calgary Herald*, 27 April 1943.

[54]*Edmonton Journal*, 26 March 1943.

[55]*Calgary Albertan*, 4 August 1942.

[56]Feasby, *Canadian Medical Services*, pp. 311-312.

[57]Greer, *The Girls*, p. 17.

[58]*PAC, RG 7, G21*, second series, Vol. 679, file 328-C.

[59]*Calgary Albertan*, 8 January 1943.

[60]*Edmonton Journal*, 9 June 1943.

[61]*Calgary Albertan*, 1 September 1942; *Edmonton Journal*, 1 September 1942; 5 October 1942.

[62]*Calgary Herald*, 9 April 1943; *Calgary Albertan*, 9 April 1943.

[63]*Calgary Albertan*, 29 October 1943; *Edmonton Journal*, 25 October 1943.

[64]*Edmonton Journal*, 17 April 1943, p. 9; 19 August 1943, p. 12.

[65]Ibid., 17 July 1943, p. 12; 21 July 1943, p. 12.

[66]Ibid., 8 June 1943, p. 18.

[67]*PAC, RG 36*, series 31, Vol. 13, file 8-10-D. Report of conversations with newspaper publishers, 25 March 1943. See also *PAC, RG 44, Records of the National War Services, 1939-1954*, Vol. 8, file S-8.

[68]Patricia J. W. Daine, "Doing Their Bit—Canada's Air Women of the Second World War," *The Atlantic Advocate*, 74, No. 6 [February 1984], p. 52.

Albertans on the Home Front

DON'T LET THIS HAPPEN!

*I*T is time for action - - -
Right now, enemy bombers lurk closer to Edmonton than ever before. Don't wait for your home . . . your business to be blasted to destruction . . . do your part to hold and drive back these threatening monsters by lending more and more money to supply our fighting men with more ships . . . more guns and more planes.

Buy
WAR SAVINGS CERTIFICATES
Regularly!

Western Canada During the Second World War

Reginald H. Roy

Someone once said that Canada has too much geography and not enough history. One can take that with a grain of salt, perhaps, since European settlement on the Atlantic coast of Canada and the United States began within a few years of each other. It would be more apt to say that we have too much geography and not enough people.

In September 1939, when Canada declared war against Germany, our population was estimated at 11,295,000. Of this number, about sixty per cent lived in Ontario and Quebec, while Manitoba, Saskatchewan, Alberta, and British Columbia, had a combined population of only 3,239,766. To look at it another way, under half the population of New York City occupied an area of 1,124,940 square miles.

Aside from its sparse population, there are one or two other things that should be kept in mind before we take a closer look at Western Canada and the Second World War. The area was basically a producer of primary products whose economic health depended on exports of such material as grain, cattle, timber, pulp and paper, and fish. The West had been severely hit by the decade-long Depression that started in 1929. Added to that, as with the Western United States, the drought had increased the economic woes of the prairie farmers. When war did come, there is little doubt that thousands of young men joined the services to get off the relief rolls as well as to fight for king and country. But as the war dragged on and the demands for wheat and timber increased, there were many who resented being called to the colours, especially when for the first time in at least a decade the family farm or ranch began to show a profit.

There is one other aspect about Western Canada at the beginning of the war that should be remembered — one that it shared with the nation as a whole. This was our complete unpreparedness for war, either on the sea, on the land, or in the sky. In the post-"Great War" period, Canada like most other nations, had reduced its armed forces to a minimum. With a friendly country to the south, the Arctic wastes in the north, and the oceans to the east and west, Canadians saw no threat to their security. In the 1930s when the Germans, Italians, and Japanese began to flex their military muscles, Canada was caught up in an economic depression that severely limited and then reduced even the minuscule defence budget. For example, in fiscal year 1930-1931, the total expenditure of the Department of National Defence was $23,732,151. Two years later, in 1932-1933, this had been slashed to $14,145,361. Although more funds were given for defence as the decade wore on, nevertheless two decades of neglect had its impact. At the outbreak of the war, to use the army as an example, there were only 4,261 in all ranks in the regular force and a little over 51,000 in the reserves. Poorly trained and ill-equipped, this force offered no means for rapid intervention in an overseas theatre of operation.

Naval parade in
Edmonton, April 1943.

*Photo courtesy
Provincial Archives of
Alberta (PAA Bl. 525/3).*

Despite this low base, to look forward for a moment, by the end of the war
Canada had raised a force of 1,029,510 servicemen and 45,423 servicewomen.
Of these, Western Canada was to provide 325,728 of the total, of whom two-
thirds went into the army, the remainder into the Royal Canadian Navy [33,539]
and the Royal Canadian Air Force [82,251]. Although it is beyond the scope of
this article to deal with the overseas exploits of Western Canadian units, it is
interesting to note that when the 1st Canadian Infantry Division went overseas in
December 1939, it included a "Western" brigade made up of the Princess
Patricia's Canadian Light Infantry, the Seaforth Highlanders of Canada, and the
Edmonton Regiment. It was one of the formations that landed in Sicily in July
1943. Similarly, the 3rd Canadian Division called the 7th Brigade its "Western"
formation. It was made up of the Royal Winnipeg Rifles, the Regina Rifle
Regiment, and the Canadian Scottish Regiment. It, too, was used as an assault
formation on the beaches of Normandy on 6 June 1944.

The outbreak of the war brought about the implementation of the War
Measures Act, which gave the federal government immense powers over almost
every aspect of the nation's activities. Since Canada had permitted its defences to
wither to a dangerously low level, there was a great deal to be done. The surge of
young men to enlist resulted in a large and immediate demand for barracks,
uniforms, mess halls, warehouses, hangars, drill halls, armaments, dockyards,
aerodromes, training areas, and weapon ranges, as well as a wide variety of
vehicles and equipment.

The demand for material and facilities of all kinds was far greater than the
supply, particularly as Canada had almost no armaments industry. Everything
had to be built from scratch. Moreover, Western Canadian defences did not have
the priorities of Eastern Canada. The threat of German submarines in the

Atlantic, to say nothing of German surface vessels, had to be balanced until the end of 1941 against the lack of any threat in the Pacific. Canada's only naval base in the West was at Esquimalt, British Columbia. Well situated at the tip of Vancouver Island to protect the major seaport of Vancouver, its location also guarded the entrance of the Juan de Fuca Strait and the sea approaches to Puget Sound and Seattle. There were four destroyers at Esquimalt when the war broke out, and half of these were sent immediately to Halifax. Steps were taken to improve and enlarge the naval base, which would serve not only Canadian naval vessels but units from the Royal Navy as well. New oil depots, wharves and jetties, machine shops, warehouses, barracks, ammunition bunkers, and a host of other needs began to receive long-overdue attention as did the coastal fortifications of the main harbours. The largest ship to enter Esquimalt during the war was HMT Queen Elizabeth, 85,000 tons, and extensive dredging operations had to be carried out in the harbour before it could enter the drydock.

Although a great deal of work was done to improve Esquimalt as a naval base, it never became as important as Halifax. No great convoys were assembled in the harbours of Vancouver or Victoria to be escorted across the Pacific or south to the Panama Canal. The small fleet of corvettes and minesweepers stationed at the naval base were not intended to take part in any great sea battles, but instead were used for offshore duties. The long coastline of British Columbia needed surveillance, but this could be done by the Fishermen's Reserve. Throughout the war, their small, lightly armed vessels poked into the innumerable bays, coves, and inlets but found nothing alarming.

The greatest scare of the war occurred on 20 June 1942, when a British vessel was torpedoed in the Strait of Juan de Fuca. On the same day, a Japanese submarine shelled the lighthouse at Point Estevan, a remote spot on the west coast of Vancouver Island. This was the only recorded instance during the Second World War of an attack from the sea on the West Coast of the Dominion.

Gas attack precautions demonstration for Calgarians.

Photo courtesy Provincial Archives of Alberta [PAA P5876].

What the threat might be, of course, could only be estimated while the war was in progress. This was reflected in the number of naval vessels based at Esquimalt which varied from a low of twelve to its greatest strength of 31 in June 1942. The danger to Canada's Western shores was determined by fleet actions far out in the Pacific, well beyond the range of even the long-distance RCAF aircraft based in British Columbia.

British Commonwealth Air Training Plan No. 2 Wireless School, Calgary.

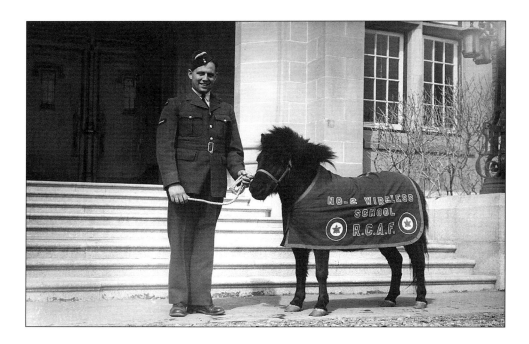

Photo courtesy Provincial Archives of Alberta [PAA P6487].

Even before the declaration of war, there had been a considerable amount of discussion between Canada and Great Britain respecting the establishment of what came to be known as the British Commonwealth Air Training Plan [BCATP]. It was realized that thousands of pilots, navigators, and other aircrew would need to be trained. Britain, with its limited available space for aerodromes, looked to Canada for assistance. As one writer put it:

> *The plan's large scale training commitments required a great many airfields, and clear skies, free from the threat of enemy air activity. Training had to take place within reasonable distance of the likeliest operational theatre, Western Europe, and in close proximity to an industrial base with significant potential for expansion....*[1]

The idea and practice of training RAF pilots in Canada was not new. During the Great War of 1914-1918, British authorities had conducted flying training schemes in Canada; but this time Canada, once the BCATP was negotiated, insisted on far greater control over the entire operation.

It was to be a tremendous effort. At the outset of the war, the RCAF was straining all its resources to establish a programme to train some 125 pilots a year. Under the new plan it was now asked to produce 1,460 trained aircrew every four weeks, or roughly 18,000 a year. Western Canada, with its clear skies and open prairies, was to provide the largest number of bases for the pilot training portion of the Training Plan and somewhat less than half for other aircrew. There were Initial Training Schools, Service Training Flying Schools, Air Navigation Schools, Wireless Schools, Bombing and Gunnery Schools, and a host of others. Almost all of them had to be created from scratch; and in every case, there was great pressure to have the landing runways, hangars, barracks, classrooms, and other facilities completed in a great hurry for the thousands of Canadian, British, Australian, New Zealand, and other Allied forces who would use them. The German blitzkrieg victories of the spring and summer of 1940 put even more pressure on the training facilities. The RCAF official historian, for example, noted that

> *Course No. 53, . . . which began training at Moose Jaw on 12
> April 1942, included eighteen Norwegians, fourteen Canadians,
> eight Britons, four Americans, three Czechoslovakians, three
> Free French, one Pole and one Belgian.*[2]

By the autumn in 1940, the skies over Western Canada were buzzing with aircraft of all sizes, ranging from Tiger Moths and Harvards to Ansons and Yales. The results of the BCATP were prodigious, far exceeding the expectations of those who had originated the scheme. By the end of the war, some 131,553 aircrew had been trained, of whom 72,835 were Canadians.

The German blitzkrieg in the spring of 1940 had met with great success. Norway, The Netherlands, Belgium, and then France were overrun and occupied. The British were able to evacuate most of their forces from the Continent but lost massive quantities of warlike stores and material. Up to that time, during the

Commonwealth servicemen on parade float represent No. 2 Wireless School, Calgary.

Photo courtesy Provincial Archives of Alberta [PAA P 6488].

so-called Phoney War, Canada had pursued its rearmament with vigour. Now there was a sense of urgency, and with it the realization that much more had to be done. For the first time conscription was imposed, initially for Home Defence only. Army enlistments jumped initially from a monthly average of about 6,000 in April and May 1940 to over 30,000 in June and July. In Western Canada this meant that the various district military camps had to be enlarged and new ones created; more weapons, equipment, and ammunition had to be manufactured and a more stringent war-time economy imposed.

Equally important, when Britain's fall seemed a possibility, was the initiation of secret and informal talks between Canadian and American senior military officers. President Franklin D. Roosevelt had to keep in mind the deep-rooted desire of the United States to remain neutral. However, the German victories and the growing concern about Britain's fate as the Battle of Britain was being fought led to a change in American opinion. In mid-August 1940, the Canadian Prime Minister and the American President met at Ogdensburg, New York. There they decided to create the Permanent Joint Board on Defence. This Board, which still functions, considered continental defence problems and made recommendations for their resolution to Ottawa and Washington. It was the first of several American-Canadian bodies and agencies formed to consider all aspects of joint measures for defence. Some of the Board's recommendations, most notably the one that launched the Alaska Highway, were to have considerable impact on Western Canada.

For over two years after war broke out, Western Canada provided bases where Canadians could be recruited and trained for service overseas. Following Japan's attack on Pearl Harbor, however, there was the possibility that British Columbia might be subjected to raids from the sea. In the province itself, there was considerable alarm not only over the possibility of Japanese attacks but also because of the very limited number of troops available to defend the coast. Intense political pressure was put on Ottawa for greater defence while at the same time British Columbians demanded the removal of some 23,000 men, women, and children of Japanese ancestry from the coastal regions of the province. Although this process, which began in February 1942, has been condemned by a later generation, one must remember the fear of the coastal population at the time as Japan's military forces swept all before them as they reached toward the fringes of Australia and the borders of India.

With the United States now in the war, there was far greater liaison and cooperation between Canadian and American forces. The coastal defences of the Strait of Juan de Fuca were closely coordinated. Prince Rupert, which was to become a major supply base for American forces going to Alaska, was provided with two eight-inch railway guns from the United States to bolster its defences. A month or two later, Canadian army and air force units moved into the Alaskan Panhandle. Two RCAF fighter squadrons were sent to help defend the site against possible attack. The US naval commander in Seattle was told that Canadian naval vessels and port facilities in British Columbia would be placed at his disposal should the need arise. Should there be an attack on American territory, Canada would "provide every possible assistance." In May 1942, for example, American Intelligence learned about a Japanese attack on Midway with a subsidiary attack on Alaska. General De Witt, of the US Western Defence Command, asked for two RCAF squadrons to help meet this threat. Two squadrons were sent to an American air base on Yakutat, north of Juneau, and two more squadrons were made ready to reinforce them should they be needed.

A few days later, the Battle of Midway was fought and Japanese forces landed on Attu and Kiska, both islands in the western reaches of the Aleutians. This brought RCAF squadrons deeper into Alaska where, in the months to come, they were involved in the bombing of the Japanese-held islands.

Meanwhile, Canada was bolstering its own Western defences. There was over a thousand miles of coastline to defend and innumerable inlets and bays where an enemy submarine or naval vessel might hide. Although the Fishermen's Reserve would patrol some of the shoreline, their vessels would be unable to cope with an enemy ship even if they found one. The best that could be done would be for them to send information to headquarters where the quickest reaction would be the dispatch of RCAF bomber squadrons.

Another force that was organized in 1942 was the Pacific Coast Militia Rangers. It was made up of rangers, trappers, miners, loggers, and others and was organized into 137 companies scattered over British Columbia. Its composition and role reflected the rather primitive transportation network in the province.

Many smaller communities were difficult to reach from the main centres. To provide them with some measure of protection, it was decided to form and arm a body of "irregulars" or "home guard" units composed of men who were familiar with their area and accustomed to the climate and conditions of the mountains and bush country. Like the American Minutemen, they could be called upon at very short notice to leave their civilian jobs to defend their localities. Their role was to provide local defence against minor raids, to gather intelligence, and to operate, either by themselves or in conjunction with active units, to repel a major attack.[3] The Manitoba Volunteer Reserve, Saskatchewan Veterans' Civil Security Corps, and Veterans Volunteer Reserve in Alberta served a similar role on the prairies.

The major impact of Canada's declaration of war against Japan was the decision to increase the army's presence in British Columbia. Before Pearl Harbor, Army Headquarters had created Pacific Command, which encompassed British Columbia, Alberta, the Yukon, and the District of Mackenzie. Before Japan's attack, the vast area of British Columbia had only six battalions ready for an instant counterattack role. More were needed, and during 1942 Pacific Command's strength was increased until there were two full divisions in the province, one to defend Vancouver Island and the other the mainland. It was considered, quite rightly that there were only limited areas along the rugged coast where the Japanese might attack; and it was there that most of the battalions were located.

But the attack never came. Searchlights swept the skies, coastal gunners strained their eyes, and reconnaissance aircraft and radar stations were on alert for the approach of any enemy vessels or airplanes. An estimated 35,000 Canadian soldiers stood on guard in Pacific Command waiting for the enemy to come from the northern mists, but only the RCAF — weather permitting — had the occasional chance to strike at the Japanese.

Transportation, particularly by road, was quite limited in the interior of British Columbia. For the United States, more worrisome was the complete lack of any highway leading into Alaska. As early as 14 November 1940, the Permanent Joint Board on Defence made a recommendation that suitable landing fields should be provided on a route across Canada between the United States and Alaska. In July 1941, the Board noted that the completion of both the Canadian and American sections was now "of extreme importance." Early in 1942 the Board urged that "a highway to Alaska be constructed following the general line of the existing airway." The recommendations were brief, but implementing them was to involve the efforts of tens of thousands of men and women and the expenditure of millions of dollars by both countries.

An overland route to Alaska had been suggested several decades earlier; in fact, the idea can be traced back to the days of the Klondike gold rush. The easiest and least expensive means of supplying Alaska was by sea; but with the US Navy's losses at Pearl Harbor, there was some doubt that this route could be guaranteed free from attack. It was with this in mind that the project was approved by both the American and Canadian governments; and within a remarkably short time, six regiments of US Army Engineers and thousands of civilian road builders were working on the road. Most of the 1,500-mile route ran through Canadian territory, but most of the cost and labour was provided by the United States since Canada's resources were already strained by her war effort. It was a huge task accomplished through areas that had never been properly mapped. In a remarkable feat of engineering and careful planning, the road was open for traffic in November 1942. There was much to be done to improve the road, but at least Whitehorse received its first truckloads of supplies from Fort St. John well before even the most optimistic estimate for completion when work on the highway started.

The highway tied together two other war-time projects in Western Canada and the US Northwest. One was the Northwest Staging Route, which was made up of a series of airports from Edmonton through Fort Nelson, Whitehorse, and on to Fairbanks in Alaska. Eleven of the thirteen airfields on the route were Canadian; and in time, the highway connected almost all of them. The route had opened in 1941, and further work, with American help, was done to allow for the ferrying of aircraft to Russia when that country was reeling under German attacks. At the same time, the CANOL Project was undertaken. This was an oil pipeline from Norman Wells in the Northwest Territories to Whitehorse in the Yukon, where the oil was refined and used to serve both the airfields and the vehicular traffic along the highway. All three projects required a great deal of cooperation from both Canada and the United States, and under the pressure of war-time necessity, all were completed in a remarkably short time.

The tremendous construction work going on in Western Canada by both Americans and Canadians was primarily defensive in nature, since the likelihood of Japan's launching any sizable attack on the mainland of North America was remote. But small " spoiling" raids remained a possibility. The Japanese shelling of a lighthouse on the coast of British Columbia in June 1942, and their occupation of Attu and Kiska, had resulted in Canada's increasing its military strength in British Columbia to two divisions. These forces protected an area stretching from Victoria to Whitehorse and represented a massive overreaction to a modest threat. It was many months before even part of this force was involved in an operation against the enemy.

Western Canadian troops, however, were among the first to fight the Japanese face to face. Late in 1941, Canada had agreed to send two infantry battalions to Hong Kong to help strengthen the British garrison there. One of these was the Winnipeg Grenadiers from Manitoba. These troops arrived in Hong Kong on 16 November 1941, just three weeks before the colony was attacked. By Christmas, following three weeks of vicious fighting, Hong Kong was forced to surrender. Many of the Grenadiers had been killed or wounded, while the remainder faced over three and a half years as prisoners of the Japanese.

It was this enemy success combined with the perceived savagery of the Japanese that had led to the large number of Canadian soldiers being stationed in British Columbia. But they did not have the means to attack the Japanese in the Aleutians, and when the Americans launched their assault on Attu in May 1943, they were cheered by their Canadian allies who were anxious to join them in their next assault.

Even before the "thoroughly nasty little campaign" was over, plans were being laid for an attack on Kiska. This time Canada was to be involved. The 13th Canadian Infantry Brigade from Pacific Command was selected and during the summer trained in combined operations on Vancouver Island.[4] When the American-Canadian assault on Kiska went in on 16 August 1943, there was no defence; the Japanese had evacuated the island about two weeks earlier. They had given up their last foothold in the North American zone without a fight, and in all probability they were as pleased to go as the Canadians were three months later when they, too, began their withdrawal from that cold, bleak, windswept island to the milder climate of southern British Columbia.

With the Japanese gone from the Aleutians and the tide of war pushing them back from their bases in the South Pacific, there was a reduction of Canadian servicemen in Western Canada. The last indirect attempt by Japan to harass Western Canada was in November 1944 when they began to release hydrogen-filled balloons from the island of Honshu. Relying on the prevailing winds to take them to North America, the balloons carried high explosive and incendiary bombs timed to be released by automatic devices. Some reached beyond Manitoba, but the only deaths from them occurred in Oregon.

It is almost impossible to give a statistical account of the contribution of Western Canada to the war-time effort of the nation. The highest formation where battalions from any one region were grouped was in a brigade or, to use the American equivalent, a regiment. Western Canadian units fought in Hong Kong, the Mediterranean, and Northwest Europe. Western sailors and airmen, sometimes fighting with the Royal Navy and Royal Air Force as well as with the Royal Canadian Navy and RCAF, fought on almost every continent and on the high seas. Fortunately Western Canada itself was never a battleground, but it provided tens of thousands of men and women who were willing to serve wherever they were needed.

A veteran returning from overseas, 26 October 1945.

Photo courtesy
Provincial Archives of
Alberta [PAA Bl. 1009].

NOTES

This article was first published in *Journal of the West* [October 1993] and is reprinted with the kind permission of the author and Kansas State University Press.

[1] W. A. B. Douglas, The Official History of the Royal Canadian Air Force, Vol. 2 [Toronto: University of Toronto Press, 1986], p.191.

[2] Ibid., p.236.

[3] R. H. Roy, *For Most Conspicuous Bravery* [Vancouver: University of British Columbia Press, 1977], p.178. The Militia Rangers were to reach a strength of about 15,000 officers and men during the war.

[4] Two of its four battalions were from Western Canada - the Rocky Mountain Rangers and the Winnipeg Grenadiers. The latter were reconstituted in Canada after the original unit was lost in Hong Kong.

Community in Transition: Red Deer in the Second World War

Michael Dawe

In the twenty years following the end of the Great War of 1914-1918, central Alberta experienced a long series of troubles. The immediate post-war period was marked by high inflation and the widespread 'flu epidemic. Then came a deep depression and an extensive drought. While the late 1920s brought a brief promise of prosperity, the community soon found itself in the depths of another great depression. Only as the 1930s drew to a close did the long siege of economic hardships finally seem to be lifting.

Ironically, as the hard times came to an end the era of peace drew to a close as well. In the newspapers and on the radio, the people learned of the gathering storm clouds of war in Europe. On 3 September 1939 the expected and feared event finally happened. Great Britain declared war on Germany after the latter invaded Poland, and one week later Canada joined the hostilities. For the second time in 25 years another terrible global conflict had broken out. Red Deer would never be the same again.

A flurry of activity followed the declaration of war as the military authorities ordered a complete mobilization of the Canadian Army Active Force. Almost immediately, a dozen men from the militia's 78th Field Battery Royal Canadian Artillery [RCA] left Red Deer for Esquimalt, British Columbia, where they joined the coastal defence artillery.

It was decided not to bring the local 78th Battery RCA up to full war strength. Instead recruitment commenced at the Red Deer Armoury for an Edmonton unit, the 92nd Battery RCA. As had been the case at the start of the First World War, the local men quickly responded to the new call to arms. On 11 September 1939, the day after war was officially declared by Canada, thirty men left Red Deer to train with the 92nd Battery RCA. A week later, another 24 followed them to Edmonton. A number of others also left to enlist with Calgary units such as the 23rd Battery RCA and the Calgary Highlanders.

As the military got its plans of action under way, work was also begun to organize the "home front." On 21 September 1939 more than 130 people turned out to reorganize the moribund Red Deer Branch of the Canadian Red Cross. A fund-raising drive was initiated and more than fifteen hundred dollars was soon raised. In a community which had suffered years of economic hardships, the pocket books had been quickly opened.

By mid-October the pace of recruitment began to slacken. Most of the units which were to make up the First Canadian Division had met their quotas, and the military authorities had no immediate plans to mobilize new units. In a speech made in Red Deer, Brigadier George Pearkes explained that the intention was to train troops in Canada thoroughly before sending them overseas. He added that the authorities felt it was more efficient to handle the recruits in batches rather than in a continual stream.[1]

This apparent lack of urgency was reinforced by the unusual quiet along the several fronts during the "phoney war." There were a few skirmishes, air raids and submarine attacks. However, most military leaders expected the same static style of warfare as had existed in the First World War. They consequently directed most of their attention to preparing defences and building the strengths of their fighting forces rather than launching offensives.

During the lull political conflicts moved to the forefront. By early 1940 there was growing criticism of the Federal Government's conduct of the war. As a result, Prime Minister Mackenzie King called a federal election to secure a new mandate. Alberta's Premier Aberhart cunningly called a provincial election for the same time. The Liberals and Conservatives who had joined forces in the anti-Social Credit "Unity" movement now found themselves in the awkward position of campaigning against the Aberhart government in the provincial contest and against each other in the federal election.

Across the province, Premier Aberhart's strategy worked well. The Social Credit government was returned, albeit with a much-reduced majority. In Red Deer, however, anti-Social Credit feelings were strong. Alfred Speakman, the former United Farmers of Alberta [UFA] Member of Parliament, and now an Independent, was elected by a comfortable margin. In the federal election five days later the Social Credit candidate F.D. Shaw won the riding. Nevertheless, in the City of Red Deer, Shaw finished third behind the Liberals and Conservatives.

Ironically, two weeks after Prime Minister Mackenzie King received the electoral endorsement of his policies of caution and restraint, the war changed dramatically. The Germans launched their stunning "Blitzkrieg" offensive, and the great defences of the Western Front collapsed. By the late spring of 1940 Great Britain and its Commonwealth allies were left to fight on alone against the victorious German forces.

Almost immediately, new enlistment drives were commenced across Canada. The 78th Battery RCA was ordered to mobilize at once as part of a new active service unit with the 22nd Battery RCA from Gleichen, Alberta. In two days, more than forty recruits reported at the Red Deer Armoury. Within two weeks 150 men had enlisted in the artillery.

Shortly thereafter, the military authorities announced that a company of the Calgary Regiment [Tank] would be raised in Red Deer. In one day, more than seventy men volunteered to join the unit. The company quickly met its quota of 150 men.

Manpower was not only needed for military service. Crews were hired to start work on an expansion of the Penhold airport, which had been built south of Red Deer in the late 1930s. The airfield had been chosen as a training base under the British Commonwealth Air Training Plan, a joint programme of Canada, Great Britain, Australia and New Zealand. With the crisis in Europe deepening each day, plans were accelerated and the construction work was pushed forward at a frenetic pace.

First arrivals at Penhold, 16 November 1940.

Sid Wardle. Photo courtesy Red Deer and District Archives [P 186 489].

Despite these initiatives there was a widespread feeling that not enough was being done for the war. The Red Deer Board of Trade held a special meeting in June 1940, and passed five resolutions demanding more speed and vigour in the war effort, the internment of all subversives, registration of foreigners, conscription of manpower and wealth, and more stringent regulations in the sale of firearms and explosives. Plans were also made to hold a massive public meeting which would demand more action from the government.[2]

While the Board of Trade was voicing its concerns and opinions, the Federal Government passed the National Resources Mobilization Act which authorized compulsory selective service for home defence and civil employment. With the adoption of these new measures, the Board of Trade's mass meeting was changed into a "Stop Hitler" rally which sought to marshal public support for the war effort rather than to express grievances against the government.

The rally was an outstanding success and reflected the enormous readiness of the townspeople to "do their bit" for the war effort. A special appeal for funds to buy an ambulance for the Red Cross had a strong response, and nearly $2,000 was soon raised for the project. Service clubs such as the Kinsmen undertook to promote the sale of war-savings certificates, while the Rotary Club decided to raise funds for refugee relief.

One special community endeavour began in early July 1940, when Red Deer welcomed the first of its "war guests." These were usually young children, sometimes accompanied by their mothers, who were being evacuated from England as the great Battle of Britain was about the erupt. On one occasion, a ship carrying some children bound for central Alberta was torpedoed by a German submarine. Fortunately, all of the young passengers were rescued.

As the summer progressed, the 78th Battery was reorganized as a unit of the Non-Permanent Active Militia and another round of recruitment began. A decision also was made to form a Red Deer Battalion of the Veterans Volunteer Reserve. Within a brief period of time, a number of First World War veterans joined this home guard unit.

On 7 August 1940 the Federal Government announced the construction of a militia training centre in Red Deer. For the 2500 residents of the city, the scope of this facility was staggering. More than 30 buildings were to be constructed on a 20-hectare site northeast of 55th Street and Waskasoo [45th] Avenue. Thirty-two officers and another 150 non-commissioned officers and men were to be stationed at the camp. As well, up to one thousand men were to be accommodated during a four-week training period.

Work on the camp began almost immediately. Soon nearly two hundred tradesmen were employed on the site. With an even larger number of men working on the Penhold airport, and others employed on such civilian projects as the new wing of the Municipal Hospital and the new public Intermediate School, a critical shortage of labour developed.

Train carrying military equipment along CPR main line, Penhold, 1943.

Sid Wardle.
Photo courtesy Red Deer and District Archives [93.15.1].

Moreover, the new militia centre meant that the city had to provide extensive sewer, water and electrical-power hookups. With the cost of these utility installations exceeding $15,000, the city was forced to borrow money from the banks to meet current expenses for the first time since 1924.

Throughout the fall, the community hastily prepared for the imminent onslaught of soldiers. A coordinating committee of fifteen organizations was formed to arrange for the soldiers' entertainment. The Citizens' Band was resurrected after being dormant for over two years. The Public School Board, after some debate, agreed to let the soldiers use the gymnasium in the Intermediate School on one night a week. A member of the Board of Trade suggested that with the large numbers of newcomers expected in Red Deer shortly, perhaps the time had come to have all the streets and avenues clearly marked and the houses numbered. The aldermen decided, however, that with all the extraordinary expenses they were currently facing, this would be one extra project that they could not afford.

Despite all the activity engendered by the new militia training centre, the community continued to busy itself with such home-front efforts as the National Victory Loan campaign. The city and military officials decided that with the new reports of the bombing raids on England, Red Deer should be "bombed" with leaflets promoting the bond drive. Unfortunately, the scheme was not a great success. Most of the pamphlets were blown well north of the city by the wind and only a few fell on their intended targets.

In early October 1940, the militia training centre was finally ready to be opened. However, as often happens with well planned and rehearsed events, there was chaos when 200 men showed up one day earlier than expected. The military authorities spent a frantic evening trying to find bunks for all of the men and enough rations to feed them supper. Eventually, all of the snags were straightened out. The next day, the first group of 900 men received their medical examinations and began their one-month period of training.[3]

As the militia camp became fully operational, its impact was felt throughout the City and the Village of North Red Deer. Restaurants found it necessary to expand their premises and the local hotels enlarged their beer parlours. A number of the officers and permanent staff at the camp decided to bring their families to Red Deer to live. As a result, although several new residences were built, there was a growing shortage of housing. School enrolment also rose sharply, and the Public School Board found itself with full classrooms despite the opening of the new Intermediate School.

In the second week of November, the first class of soldiers at the militia centre finished their prescribed period of training with an air raid drill. A few days later the next group of 1000 trainees started their stint at the camp. Their arrival in Red Deer coincided with the sudden appearance of winter; several centimetres of snow fell and temperatures plunged to -30° C. While the cold weather allowed the City's staff to flood three open-air skating rinks, it also made life miserable for many of the soldiers. A round of 'flu swept through the camp and several dozen men were laid up in the camp hospital, which did not yet have all of its furnaces hooked up.

Disease was not the only unsettling occurrence at the camp. In December 1940, four men were charged under the Criminal Code with pilfering $5 worth of "regimental necessities" from the camp kitchen. Their haul included two kilograms of halibut, a five-kilogram pail of drippings and a hard old piece of cheese. The defence lawyer agreed that the food was unfit for human consumption, but the prosecutor contended that the cheese at least could have been used with macaroni. The men were convicted and given heavy fines.[4]

In another case, a young soldier on leave got too boisterous on a local bus and was ordered to take another bus. He took the suggestion literally and was caught driving the borrowed vehicle near Ponoka. He, too, was convicted, given a $100 fine and deprived of the rest of his leave.[5]

Early in 1941, the third group of trainees arrived at the militia training camp, and a new round of recruiting was conducted for the 2-78th Field Battery at the Armoury. In February the Calgary Regiment [Tank] was mobilized and became the 14th Army Tank Battalion [Calgary Regiment]. Nearly 130 local men enlisted in this unit. In March a huge crowd saw them off in Calgary when they left for further training at Camp Borden in Ontario.

Meanwhile, the Federal Government announced that the training period for men called up under the National Service Act would be extended to four months from thirty days. Consequently, in March 1941, the military authorities announced that the militia training centre would be changed into an eight-week advanced training camp for the Royal Canadian Army Service Corps. The new centre, which was named A-20, was to include 100 officers, 550 instructors, 500 active service men and 500 recruits in training. Work began on a number of new buildings, and large quantities of equipment and vehicles were transferred to Red Deer from other military installations.

Main gate, A-20 Army Camp, Red Deer, 1942.

Ernest Wells.
Photo courtesy Red Deer and District Archives [80.L60.6].

While the new construction work got under way at the A-20 Camp, the work at the Penhold airport had progressed sufficiently that the military authorities were able to turn the base temporarily into No. 2A Manning Depot for the RCAF. As such, the facility was used for the initial training of fresh recruits prior to their being assigned to flying, wireless, or other training centres.

As the number of men and women on active service continued to mount, a decision was made by the federal authorities to have one coordinated national charity drive to raise funds for personal comforts and services. In March 1941, a joint appeal on behalf of the Salvation Army, YMCA, YWCA, Knights of Columbus, Royal Canadian Legion and IODE was launched with a nation-wide objective of $5,500,000. Organizers in Red Deer and the surrounding area expected to raise between $3,000 and $3,500. To their surprise, more than $8,000 in contributions and pledges were received.

Immediately after the end of this War Services Drive, the Federal Government began its Victory Loan Campaign to sell bonds to finance the war effort. The Red Deer and District quota was set at $177,000. In order to get the appeal off to a strong and emotional start, the local officials organized the largest parade of military personnel and equipment in Red Deer's history. More than three thousand people turned out for the event. Within a month, the local organizers proudly reported that 132 per cent of the quota had been raised.

The great successes of the Victory Loan, War Services and other fund-raising campaigns reflected the tremendous increase in prosperity in the community since the start of the war. In contrast to the situation of only a few years before, jobs were now plentiful, wages were rising, business profits were increasing and local farmers were enjoying both abundant harvests and good prices for their produce. Instead of economic hardship and suffering, the war had engendered the best boom for Red Deer in thirty years.

Victory Loan parade, Royal Army Service Corps, Red Deer, 31 May 1941.

Sid Wardle.
Photo courtesy Red Deer and District Archives
[P 348 871].

The signs of the boom were everywhere. The Central Alberta Dairy Pool, which had been losing a great deal of money in the late 1930s, was now making a sizable profit. It consequently built a large addition onto its milk condensery. A new creamery was constructed on Ross Street by United Dairies, while Red Deer Bottling began building a new soft-drink works on Gaetz Avenue South. Throughout the city, several new houses were built.

The wartime economy had some serious detriments. By the summer of 1941 there were growing shortages of several essential products. Sales of gasoline were cut off in Red Deer in the evenings and on Sundays. Inflation began to reappear. However, unlike the situation during the First World War, the Federal Government took strong corrective measures. In October 1941, the powers of the Wartime Prices and Trade Board were expanded. Stringent wage and price controls were imposed, and plans were set to implement a system of rationing.

The war also brought personal grief and suffering. In August 1940, the first man in Red Deer to have enlisted, Ben Long, became the first to be lost when he was killed in an accident in Manitoba. Three other men died of illness while on active service. In July 1941, a pilot in the RCAF, Matt Dunham, became the first local resident to be killed in action. The tragedy of war was starting to strike home.

During the summer of 1941 Red Deer was honoured by the Royal Canadian Navy when a new Bangor Class minesweeper was named after the city. While only two central Albertans ever served on the ship, a sense of camaraderie developed between the townspeople and the sailors. Letters and gifts were continually exchanged, and the local newspaper carefully followed the ship's activities and adventures.

In August 1941, construction work on the Penhold airport was finally completed. The RCAF discontinued the use of the facility as a manning depot and turned it over to the RAF for its new use as a Service Flying Training School. On 20 August 1941, the first contingent of 600 airmen arrived at the base. Unfortunately, actual flight training was slow in getting started; there was a critical shortage of qualified instructors and, initially, only twenty planes on hand.

Despite these handicaps, the pressures of the war made it imperative to use all resources to the utmost and to continue the recruitment and training of personnel. The military authorities began construction of another flying training school south of the Penhold air base near the Village of Bowden. Meanwhile, the Canadian Women's Army Corps recruited and stationed three companies in Red Deer for clerical, motor transport and commissariat duties.

With the hundreds of airmen at Penhold and the hundreds of soldiers and other personnel at the A-20 Camp, the problem of providing adequate recreation and entertainment facilities became more pressing. A private dance hall was built in North Red Deer to meet the need, while the YMCA built a large new recreation hut at the A-20 Camp. However, many people felt that there should be a public recreation centre in the city as well.

Canadian Women's Army Corps parade on Ross Street, Red Deer, Army Week, July 1942.

Ernest Wells. Photo courtesy Red Deer and District Archives [80.L60.6].

There was great consternation in the community when the Auxiliary War Services Board in Ottawa vetoed a proposal to build a new hall despite the offer of City Council to pay one-half of the costs. After the public protests went unheeded, the aldermen decided to proceed on their own initiative. An old furniture store on First Street South [49th Street] was purchased and $3,000 was spent on the necessary renovations. City Council then leased the building for $70 per month to the Knights of Columbus, who had agreed to act as the facility's operators. Despite the ad-hoc nature of the project, it proved to be a great success. Within a short period of time the management reported as many as 1000 visitors a day and an average of 3700 a week.

The success of the K of C Hut and the return of unseasonably mild weather to central Alberta may have brought some joy to the community. However, such feelings were more than offset by the grim news from overseas. In December 1941, Hong Kong was captured by the Japanese, and Horace Gerard became the first local man to be taken prisoner of war. Shortly thereafter, word was received that three local young men serving in the air force had been killed, and that

Knights of Columbus War Services Recreation Building, Red Deer, 1942.

Ernest Wells. Photo courtesy Red Deer and District Archives [80.L60.6].

another serving in the navy had been lost at sea. In a small city where people generally knew one another, the sense of loss and anguish was widespread.

There were also tragedies close to home. In late December 1941, LAC D.A. Phillips died from injuries sustained in a plane crash. He was the first of twenty young airmen stationed at Penhold to be killed in flying accidents in central Alberta. Military funerals were to become almost a monthly occurrence in the city.

Early in 1942, members of the various war auxiliaries met to form the Red Deer Home Comforts Fund. There was a concern in the community that some who were serving their country were being missed or neglected. There was also a desire to ensure that the provision of comforts and services was handled as expeditiously and efficiently as possible. Work began immediately on a comprehensive list of those on active service. A number of fund-raising projects were organized, including Saturday night dances at the Armoury.[6]

RCAF training plane after crash near Penhold, 1943.

Sid Wardle.
Photo courtesy Red Deer and District Archives [93.15.1].

In February 1942, the Federal Government commenced its Second Victory Loan canvass and set Red Deer's quota at $137,000. The bond drive was to be kicked off with a "Beacon Fire of Freedom" on Ross Street, by the City Hall, but cold weather forced the cancellation of the ceremonial bonfire. Ironically, a few hours before the event was to take place a blaze caused several thousands of dollars worth of damage to a downtown business block. Nevertheless, the loan campaign proceeded smoothly. Within a brief period of time, the Red Deer organizers had reached 128% of their goal.

The Victory Loan drive received a big boost when City Council decided to buy several thousands of dollars' worth of bonds with surplus City funds. After the brief disruption caused by the construction of the militia training centre in 1940,

Ross Street, Red
Deer, 28 June 1942.

Ernest Wells.
Photo courtesy Red Deer
and District Archives
[80.L60.6].

the municipal coffers had begun to swell again, despite further cuts in property and business tax rates. The financial conditions of previous years had been completely reversed.

Not all of the City's extra funds were invested in the government's war bonds. An extension was built on City Hall, and Gaetz Avenue was paved. After much cajoling from the Chief of Police, City Council finally agreed to buy a second-hand police car. The aldermen also reversed their decision on house numbering and agreed to spend several hundred dollars to buy metal letters for all of the houses and business blocks in Red Deer.

The letters which they bought were made of zinc because supplies of other metals such as aluminum, iron and steel were scarce. The problem had become so acute that a proposal by Northwestern Utilities to provide the City with natural gas service had to be scrubbed because the company was unable to secure a sufficient quantity of steel pipe.

In order to help alleviate these shortages of metal, a national "Scrap Hitler With Scrap" campaign was organized. The Red Deer Salvage Committee was able to collect several tons of cast iron and steel. City Council even contributed to the cause the First World War field guns which had been displayed on the City Square since 1919. The demands of the war were so great, however, that these efforts made little obvious impact on the problem.

There were also serious and growing shortages of a number of other goods and materials. In the late spring of 1942 ration cards were distributed for such items as sugar. Special permits had to be obtained to purchase rubber tires. A few months later, the government announced that ration books for sugar, tea, coffee and other staples would soon be issued.

As the demands and restrictions on the civilian population grew, there was an increasingly strident call on the Federal Government to institute conscription for overseas military service. Because of the divisiveness of the 1917 conscription crisis, the Prime Minister wanted to avoid such a measure. Finally he was forced to relent, and he called a national plebiscite on the question for 27 April 1942. Red Deer voted "yes" to the new conscription plan by a tally of 1300 to 141. Most of the rest of the country agreed by almost as strong a margin.

Ironically, the demand for overseas conscription came at a time when the Canadian Army had seen little actual fighting. Canadian airmen and sailors had been embroiled in the Battle of Britain and the Battle of the Atlantic, but most of the Canadian soldiers were still in training in either Great Britain or Canada.

The situation changed on 19 August 1942, when 5000 men, including those in the Calgary Tank Regiment, landed on the coast of France in a raid on the port of Dieppe. The losses were horrendous. More than 900 men were killed and nearly 2000 were taken prisoners of war. For nearly a month, the townspeople of Red Deer were left wondering about the fate of several local men. Eventually the word came that 21 were being held as POWs.

While the community was still anxiously awaiting the awful news about the losses at Dieppe, the townspeople were thrown into a tumult by an incident on the south side of the city. The crew of a freight train very nearly ran over a soldier from the A-20 Camp who was lying bound and gagged on the tracks. The badly shaken fellow told the trainmen that he had been kidnapped by two German-speaking strangers who demanded that he provide them with information on local munitions supplies and troop movements. He claimed that when he had been unable to answer their questions, he had been left on the tracks to die.

After two days of interrogation and no sign of the alleged assailants, the police began to suspect the soldier's story. They finally concluded that he had tied himself up and had gone into shock when he was unable to release himself before the train reached him. The soldier was charged with attempted suicide. The local citizens were relieved to learn that "enemy agents" were not lurking about the city.[7]

In mid-October 1942 local authorities decided to stage some dramatics of their own to publicize the launch of the Third Victory Loan. They organized a "black-out" and mock air-raid, and a week later simulated an occupation of the city by "enemy" soldiers. The theatrics went well, and once again the residents of Red Deer contributed far more than had been expected.

On 15 and 16 November 1942, the worst storm since late December 1924 struck central Alberta. Although the temperatures did not initially drop too severely, there was a very heavy snowfall which made Red Deer's streets impassable. Moreover, the severity of the storm presaged the brutal conditions of the coming winter.

The harshness of the weather was compounded by an acute shortage of coal throughout the district. By January 1943, fuel had become so scarce that the Public School Board was forced to shut down the schools periodically. Many public meetings were moved from the large halls and auditoriums into smaller, warmer rooms. Even City Council decided to move its meetings from the Council Chamber into the cosier City Office.

RAF Airmen buying lingerie at Osborne's Ladies Wear, Red Deer, Christmas 1942.

Photo courtesy Red Deer and District Archives [P 348 871].

The military did its best to help out in the crisis. Convoys of soldiers were dispatched to mine emergency supplies of coal. This was not an easy task when temperatures plunged to as low as -45° C. The trucks got stuck in snowdrifts or slipped into the ditches. All too often vehicles used up their meagre supplies of gasoline before the soldiers made it back to Red Deer.

Some people managed to keep their sense of humour through the adversity. One popular story held that a local man had been so busy during the cold snap carrying coal in the front door while his wife was carrying the ashes out the back door, that they did not see each other until the weather finally warmed up.[8]

While the return of balmier temperatures eased the fuel crisis, shortages of other goods and materials continued. In February 1943, the government issued a second set of ration books with more than 8000 distributed in Red Deer and district. The government also imposed stiff reductions in the allowable sales of beer and liquor. The *Red Deer Advocate* reported that some outlets used up their daily quotas in as little as half an hour. One journalist expressed relief that the liquor store was next door to the newspaper office.

Troop train at CPR station, Red Deer, 1943.

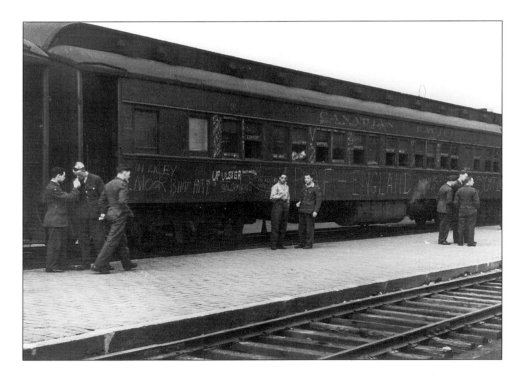

Photo courtesy Red Deer and District Archives [P 348 871].

While alcohol was becoming scarce, there was also a growing shortage of recruits for the city police force. Finally, the aldermen decided to phase out the local constabulary and to sign a policing agreement with the RCMP. The Mounties had manpower problems of their own, but their greater resources allowed them to establish a Red Deer detachment on 1 April 1943.

Spring break-up began in early April. Although the end of the hard winter was welcomed by central Albertans, the quick thaw brought a new set of problems. An ice jam formed on the Red Deer river and within a few hours, the water levels rose nearly seven metres. A local feed lot operator lost over one hundred animals, and several homes were flooded. Ironically, there was a shortage of domestic water in the city as the water treatment plant was washed out of commission. The army agreed to dynamite the jam, but before they finished their preparations the ice gave way on its own.

As the weather continued to improve and the land began to dry up, the local farmers resumed the threshing which had come to an abrupt halt with the heavy snows of the previous fall. Unfortunately, the wet conditions and an epidemic of mice severely reduced the quality of the harvest.

If the local farmers had suffered a setback, it did not seem to affect the Fourth Victory Loan campaign, which was launched on 1 May 1943 with a mass military parade. Twelve days later there was a spectacular fireworks display to celebrate the fact that Red Deer had raised $83,000 more than the $340,000 objective which had been set by the campaign organizers.

The immense success of the latest war-bond drive did not seem to impair the local Elks Club's efforts to raise funds for a wading pool on the City Square. By late June construction work had started. Seven weeks later, a large number of children turned out for the official opening ceremonies, proving that dedication to the war effort had not reduced support for community projects.

In the early summer of 1943, the long wait of the Canadian Army for combat duty came to an end when the First Infantry Division joined in the successful invasion of Sicily. Among the troops deployed were several Red Deer and area men who had enlisted in such artillery units as the 92nd Battery.

On the home front during the first week of August, the annual Red Deer Fair was held. The 92nd Women's Auxiliary received a big boost in their fund-raising efforts when the Wallace Forbes family lent their pet beaver Mickey as a special attraction. Mickey had been found as an orphan kit in 1939 and had quickly become so famous that several thousand people were eager to pay a small fee to see him.

During the fall of 1943 Red Deer began to take measures to avoid repeating the previous winter's fuel crisis. More than 100 cords of firewood and 150 tons of coal were purchased as emergency supplies. The community also began to plan for the eventual end of the war; in November, the Central Alberta Post-War Reconstruction and Rehabilitation Committee was formed. There was a proposal to build a special housing development for veterans, and the idea of constructing a memorial community hall was also discussed and debated.

While people were looking forward to a future of peace, there were continual reminders that the war was far from over. The RCAF was conducting massive nighttime bombing raids over Germany, and the Canadian Army was embroiled in the invasion of Italy. The Red Deer Advocate reported that six more local residents had lost their lives in the service of their country, and a number of others had been wounded. On the home front, Tuesdays and Fridays were designated as meatless days. The newspaper had to suspend all new subscriptions because of a scarcity of newsprint.

As the year drew to a close, politics again became a burning issue in the community. Red Deer's Independent Member of the Legislative Assembly, Alfred Speakman, died suddenly and a by-election was called for 16 December 1943. In contrast to the bitter contest of 1940, Social Credit had become somewhat more popular during the following war years. Fewer people viewed it as a radical and dangerous movement. Moreover, Premier Aberhart had died earlier in the year and had been replaced by the young Ernest Manning. The by-election results confirmed that the partisan tides had turned; the Social Credit candidate, David Ure, was elected by a margin of 185 votes.

There was also a major change in the realm of municipal government. On 31 December 1943, the five rural municipalities in central Alberta were amalgamated into a new, larger district known as the Municipal District of

Penhold. Early in 1944, the new councillors decided that the MD of Red Deer was a more appropriate name and voted to locate their administrative offices in the city. A problem of finding affordable office space was solved when Red Deer City Council agreed to turn a corner of the building into a public women's washroom and to pay the MD's Council $40 a month rent for the convenience.

In the early spring of 1944, the community was caught up in the excitement of some of the best hockey in the history of central Alberta. Red Deer's A-20 Wheelers included two former members of the National Hockey League and others from national championship teams. The opposing clubs in the Central Alberta Garrison Hockey League were of equal calibre, and the play off games in March 1944 were closely contested and superbly played matches. Unfortunately, the Wheelers lost their last game to the Calgary Currie team by a score of only 2-1. The men were still local heroes, and the Red Deer Board of Trade subsequently held a lavish banquet to honour them.[9]

In the late spring, the Federal Government decided that the need for the British Commonwealth Air Training Plan had diminished. It announced that 28 flying training schools, including the one at Penhold, would be closed by December 1944. However, for the residents of central Alberta the toll of war continued to rise. Six young airmen from the district were killed in action as were two others serving in the artillery and the navy. Eight RAF trainees from Penhold also lost their lives in crashes during the first five months of the year.

The financial costs of the war remained high, and in May 1944 the Sixth Victory loan appeal commenced. As in the five earlier efforts, Red Deer's contributions greatly surpassed expectations, and a record $365,000 was raised.

On 6 June 1944, a date now remembered as D-Day, the Allied Forces launched the long awaited assault on the coast of Normandy in France, and opened up the second front against the Germans. Over the next several weeks the Canadian, American and British forces were generally victorious, but at a terrible cost. Seven young men from Red Deer and area lost their lives. The Canadian forces as a whole suffered more than 18,000 casualties.

The new successes in France and the continuing victories in Italy gave hope to central Albertans that war would soon be over. The annual Red Deer Fair in August 1944 was dubbed the Victory Year Fair. That September a committee was formed to make the necessary arrangements for Armistice Day celebrations. The hopes for peace proved to be premature, and in December 1944 the German Army launched a major counteroffensive. While the attack was eventually stemmed, it slowed the Allied advance and demonstrated that the Germans were not about to surrender.

As yet another wartime Christmas approached, the volunteers with the war auxiliaries, the Home Comforts Fund and the Red Cross pressed on with their work of sending Christmas parcels to the troops overseas and to those in the prisoner-of-war camps. The official farewells were held for the departing RAF men from Penhold. The personnel at the A-20 Camp held an elaborate Christmas party for 200 children with the highlight being the arrival of Santa Claus in a jeep laden with gifts.

Tragically, in the days leading up to Christmas, word was received that five more local lives had been lost overseas. The *Advocate* reported that while the usual holiday parties and gatherings were still held, there was a decidedly sombre note to the normally festive events.[10]

Unfortunately, the first few weeks of the New Year brought little relief from the heart-breaking news. Nine men were killed in battle, three lost their lives in plane crashes and another was taken prisoner of war. Some people recalled the old saying that the outlook is often the blackest just before the dawn.

RAF airmen singing around the piano at Bill and Elsie Brown's, Red Deer, 1942.

RCAF Official Photograph. Photo courtesy Red Deer and District Archives [P 348 8210].

In late February, there was a reminder that the war was indeed coming to an end. The military authorities announced that the A-20 Camp would soon be closed and that the facility would be turned into a rehabilitation centre for returned servicemen under the Vocational Training programme. As the operations at the Camp wound down, and the RCASC personnel departed, the need for the Knights of Columbus Hut quickly diminished. It too was soon closed and the building was sold to the Red Deer Elks Club.

Throughout the spring of 1945 increasing numbers of veterans returned to their families and friends in central Alberta; at the same time there was the welcome news that some of the POWs had been released. The Federal Government launched yet another Victory Bond drive and cajoled the people to help provide the means to finish the war.

By early May 1945 people realized that the fighting in Europe would be ending very shortly. Plans were renewed for the Victory Day celebrations, and early on Monday, 7 May, the long-awaited news finally arrived. Germany had surrendered.

School children arrived for class only to be dismissed for a three-day holiday. Some businesses opened for a brief time, but many remained closed. The authorities also had the government liquor store and the beer parlours shut down for two days.

Everywhere there was great jubilation. Many people gathered on the streets and large numbers flocked to their churches for services of thanksgiving. On 8 May 1945, the official V-E Day [Victory in Europe Day], civic celebrations were held. A large parade proceeded down Ross Street to the City Square where, despite a bitterly cold wind, a crowd of more than a thousand people had gathered to hear the speeches of local dignitaries.

Although the hostilities in Europe had ceased, the fight against Japan continued. A number of soldiers and airmen returned to Red Deer on thirty-day leaves pending re-assignments to new stations in the Pacific theatre of war. At the same time, demobilization work also continued. The CWAC canvassed for more recruits to help with the enormous load of paperwork generated by mass demobilization. The old A-20 Camp officially became the Canadian Vocational Training Centre No. 8 on 14 May 1945, and preparations were made to start on trades instruction for recently discharged men. In July, the Federal Government began building 25 houses, each on one-half hectare lots, for the returned servicemen.

On 8 August 1945, the *Red Deer Advocate* reported that on the preceding Sunday, a new awesome weapon had been used on the Japanese city of Hiroshima. While the nature of this new "atomic" bomb was not yet clearly understood, the editor of the paper predicted that "a new epoch in both war and peace is at hand."[11]

On 14 August 1945, word was received that Japan had surrendered. Across the city, the municipal siren, the CPR train whistles, and countless automobile horns broke out in a din of celebration. People gathered in the downtown area and City officials quickly organized a special street dance on Gaetz Avenue. On the evening of 15 August, the official V-J Day, a service of thanksgiving was held on the City Square. Afterwards, another outdoor public dance was held. For those who were more sedentary, the Capital Theatre showed the movie *Brother Rat* which starred an actor named Ronald Reagan and his wife Jane Wyman.

For the rest of the summer and into the fall, the transition from wartime to peacetime continued. Special gatherings were held to welcome and honour the returning veterans. New fund-raising and clothing drives were held to provide emergency relief supplies to the war-torn regions of Europe. In Mid-October the Ninth Victory Loan campaign commenced and a new record of $770,000 was raised.

The military authorities began holding huge auction sales to dispose of the massive quantities of surplus materials. After the closure of the RCAF's No. 2 Technical Signals Unit which had been repairing and rebuilding radio instruments at Penhold, there were widespread reports of the destruction of hundreds of thousands of dollars worth of equipment. The air force replied that only material which was "no longer valuable" was being destroyed.[12]

Meanwhile, the proposal to install natural gas service was revived, and on 24 September 1945 the local ratepayers overwhelmingly approved a new by-law granting the franchise to Northwestern Utilities. A proposal by the Councillors of North Red Deer that the Village be amalgamated with the City did not meet with as easy a response. There was general agreement on the desirability of such a move, but there were serious reservations about the costs of installing utility services north of the river and about who would be responsible for paying for them.

There was also great concern throughout the community about the worsening housing situation. Accommodations had been scarce throughout most of the war, but with the return of the servicemen and the arrival of a number of newcomers, the situation was becoming desperate. Twenty suites were created in the old barracks huts at the Canadian Vocational Training Centre. However, this was a stop-gap measure which only slightly alleviated the crisis.

The housing situation reflected the paradox of the war for Red Deer. Prosperity and progress had returned to the community, and there had been the first significant increase in population in more than thirty years. Although the city's residents had dreamed of such a development for a very long time, the wartime shortages and restrictions actually had hampered the ability of the community to absorb the growth. Hardships had come with the long-sought boom.

The benefits of the wartime economy had also been accompanied by considerable dislocation and grief. More than a thousand men and women from Red Deer and district had disrupted their lives to go and serve their country. Tragically, 52 of them had lost their lives, and many more had been wounded. The human costs of the war had been heavy.

In retrospect, the Second World War was a major turning point in Red Deer's history. While the First Great War had been the bench mark between the pioneer boom years and the troubles of the inter-war era, the Second World War marked the transition from a small, quiet parkland community to a burgeoning modern centre. Old Red Deer was fading into the past, and a new city was taking its place.

NOTES

[1]*Red Deer Advocate*, 27 September 1939.

[2]*Red Deer Advocate*, 17 June 1940.

[3]*Red Deer Advocate*, 23 October 1940.

[4]*Red Deer Advocate*, 18 December 1940.

[5]*Red Deer Advocate*, 1 January 1941.

[6]Red Deer and District Archives, M 305-762 [Home Comforts Fund Fonds].

[7]*Red Deer Advocate*, 2 September 1942.

[8]*Red Deer Advocate*, 17 February 1943.

[9]See David Grove, *The Puck and I in Red Deer.* [Red Deer: Adviser Publications, n.d.].

[10]*Red Deer Advocate*, 20 December 1944.

[11]*Red Deer Advocate*, 8 August 1945.

[12]*Red Deer Advocate*, 24 August 1945.

"A Name if Necessary, But Not Necessarily a Name": Why There was No HMCS Edmonton

Bruce Ibsen

During the Second World War more than 7360 men and women from the land-locked province of Alberta served in the Royal Canadian Navy. Along with this contribution of personnel, towns and cities throughout Alberta had various types of vessels named in their honour. Scanning a list of names for His Majesty's Canadian Navy vessles one finds ships named for Blairmore, Calgary, Camrose, Drumheller, Lethbridge, Medicine Hat, Red Deer, Stettler, Vegreville and Wetaskiwin.

Noticeably absent from this list is Edmonton. This absence was made more unusual considering that Edmonton had a naval presence since 1923, when the HMCS Nonsuch Naval Reserve was established. During the Second World War alone this vibrant and active reserve unit trained over 114 officers and 3,582 ratings.

On 10 September 1942 it appeared that this oversight would be remedied when R.A. Pennington, Secretary for the Naval Board, Department of National Defence, Naval Services, wrote to City Council explaining that "[in] view of the relative importance of your City, in the Dominion of Canada, it is considered that one of the vessels of the R.C.N. should be named after it."[1] However, Pennington went on to describe a problem impeding the provision of this honour: "It is regretted, however that 'Edmundston,' one of the H.M.C. Ships already bears a name so similar to the name 'Edmonton' that it will be impossible to apply the name of your City to any of the ships of the Royal Canadian Navy."[2] Pennington concluded by asking the Edmonton City Council to provide him with three alternative names of "local significance in order of preference."[3]

This letter was brought up on 14 September during a session of City Council. Following some discussion, Alderman Harry Ainlay moved a motion to "request citizens to submit names, and the Commissioners [to] select the three best." Council also decided that the Commissioners should "write to find out if it is possible to make the change suggested, namely, giving Edmonton preference over Edmundston."[4] The following day a contest was announced in both the *Edmonton Journal* and the *Edmonton Bulletin*.

Meanwhile Mayor John Fry wrote to Pennington expressing some surprise and indignation over the fact that

> *the small City of Edmundston had been given precedence over a*
> *City such as Edmonton with a population of 100,000, the Capital*
> *of the Province of Alberta, and the 8th City in Canada. A year*
> *ago the smaller City of Calgary, Alberta was honored by having*
> *a Corvette named after it.*[5]

Mayor John W. Fry.

Photo courtesy City of Edmonton Archives [EA-10-1537].

Mayor Fry then proposed a solution to this predicament, asking the Naval Board to name the new ship "The City of Edmonton."

The second salvo of this skirmish opened on 21 September 1942, when R.A. Pennington replied to Council's letter of 15 September 1942 explaining that:

> *H.M.C.S. Edmundston was one of the first Canadian Corvettes and was so named at the request of the City of Edmundston. At the time the number of requests from Cities was small enough to allow most requests....Unfortunately, the name "The City of Edmonton" is too long to be practical. Among other things it is too long to appear on cap ribbons....*[6]

Pennington then asked Mayor Fry once again to provide him with three alternative names of local significance.

It is interesting to note that Mr. Pennington's reason for disqualifying the name, "The City of Edmonton," was his view that it was too long to be practical. Yet it was only one letter longer than that for the Navy Corvette HMCS Cap de la Madeleine, and if the definite article is dropped from the name it actually became shorter than Cap de la Madeleine and one letter longer than the HMCS Charlottetown. However it appeared to some that the wartime rationing taking place all over Canada included cap ribbon lettering as well.

Back in Edmonton contest entries flooded into City Hall. The minutes from the Council meeting of 28 September noted that "[the] subject seemed to create considerable interest and we were pleased to receive numerous suggestions from our citizens." Like most contests of this kind a variety of suggestions were received, from the practical and meaningful to the bizarre and unusual.

Some thought the ship should honour a notable dignitary, so names like the Aberhart, Fighting Joe [after former mayor Joseph Clarke], Frank Oliver, Lord Strathcona, Riel and the Grads were suggested. Others wanted a descriptive name like Alberta Capital, Bloodhound, Conquest of Edmonton, Friendly City, Edmonton Belle, or the Unique, while others opted for amalgams like Capalta, Edmonscona, Edmonstrath, Edalta, Noralta, Sconaton, and Sol-Nav-Air.

After examining the entries Council found that "[the] suggestion which appeals to most of us is the name 'Fort Edmonton'." So it was moved by Alderman Guy Patterson that the first selection [Fort Edmonton] be approved. There was some discussion as to the possibility of making Strathcona the second alternative; however, when it was brought up as a motion in Council this suggestion was defeated. Therefore, the City decided that if it could not choose "Edmonton" or "The City of Edmonton" it would graciously accept "Fort Edmonton" as an appropriate name.

On 30 September 1942 Mayor Fry once again wrote to Pennington, suggesting that the ship be named the "Fort Edmonton." Fry explained that "[we] would have liked to have complied with your request for another two alternatives, but none of the names suggested appealed to members of City Council as they all lacked local significance." [7]

The growing frustration of this situation was beginning to become apparent. In his response on 12 October Pennington appears somewhat testy.

> *[It] is regretted that the prefix "Fort" is reserved exclusively for ships building under the programme of Wartime Merchant Shipping Limited....It is regretted therefore that it will not be possible to apply this name to one of H.M.C. Ships. I am accordingly directed to request once more that three alternative names, having some local significance, may be supplied to this Department.* [8]

Apparently Pennington was unaware that, contrary to what he had informed City Council, it was and had been possible to name one of His Majesty's Canadian Ships after a fort. The HMCS Fort William, a Bangor Class minesweeper, was commissioned on 25 August 1942. Later the HMCS Fort Erie, a River Class frigate, would be commissioned on 27 October 1944, while the HMCS Fort Francis, another Bangor Class minesweeper, would be commissioned on 28 October 1944.

These naval manoeuvres seemed to be wearing down Council, and during the regular meeting of 26 October, Commissioners' Report Number 26 recommended that "the matter had better be dropped unless some name of real local significance [can] be suggested." [9] However during this same meeting Alderman Harry Ainlay made an interesting recommendation, suggesting "that this ship be called 'Stettler' after the Town of Stettler." [10] The suggestion was put to a vote and subsequently agreed to by Council.

Why Stettler? A letter dated 28 October 1942, from Mayor John Fry to F.J. Kirby, the Mayor of Stettler, offers some insight into this recommendation. After summarizing Council's recent experience with the Naval Board and the difficulty they were having with Ottawa, he explained why Council had suggested the Town of Stettler as an alternative name.

> *It was pointed out that your Town had been always among the forefront of Towns in respect to Victory Loan Campaigns, and also that many of your brave sons honoured Alberta and Canada by their actions at Dieppe. We hope that you will accept this action as an expression of goodwill toward one of the most progressive towns in Alberta.* [11]

In Ottawa, Edmonton MP James MacKinnon had been lobbying on behalf of the City. However, it seems he encountered the same problem that City Council had. On 29 October 1942 the Minister of National Defence for Naval Services, the Honourable Angus L. MacDonald, wrote to MacKinnon informing him that "the Admiralty will not approve the name H.M.C.S. 'Edmonton'."[12] However, he indicated that "[if] the citizens of Edmonton are particularly anxious to have the name 'Edmonton' given to a ship, I have no doubt that Wartime Merchant Shipping, Limited, would name one of their ships Fort Edmonton'."[13]

The Mayor also received a letter of the same date from Merchant Shipping Limited of Montreal, explaining this point in further detail.

> *We have been naming the 10,000 ton cargo ships built under our programme after historical forts in Canada....The only reason we have not yet allocated the name "Fort Edmonton" to one of our ships is that we were under the impression that the Naval Service were going to name a corvette the "H.M.C.S. Edmonton" and we wished to avoid any confusion.... If you wish to do so, we will be only too pleased to have one of the ships building in a Pacific Coast yard named the SS. "Fort Edmonton."*[14]

On 30 October 1942 City Council received a letter from a grateful Mayor F.J. Kirby of the Town of Stettler expressing his surprise and enthusiasm at Edmonton's decision to have a ship named in their honour. Mayor Kirby complimented Edmonton's action, describing it as "a humble tribute to the gallant men of Stettler who fought and died at Dieppe...."[15]

A few days later, on 3 November, Mayor John Fry wrote to Senator James MacKinnon informing him of Council's decision to name the Corvette "Stettler." He also mentioned the offer from Wartime Merchant Shipping to name a 10,000 ton cargo ship "Fort Edmonton." Fry told MacKinnon that Council would be pleased with this offer and he was preparing to send a brief history of Fort Edmonton to be placed on a plaque on the cargo ship.

Fry wrote to E.L. Harrison the next day explaining that Council would "expect to avail ourselves of your offer but first we would like to hear from the Secretary of the Naval Board as to the final disposition of our name in regard to a Warship."[16]

Almost a year passed before the matter of naming the ship surfaced again. On 4 August 1943 Wartime Merchant Shipping wrote the City asking for information concerning Fort Edmonton: "We are considering naming one the S.S. 'Fort Edmonton'....Could you help us in obtaining an authentic history of Fort Edmonton."[17]

The Mayor responded to this request with a brief history and a promotional brochure. Eight days later John J. Connolly, Executive Assistant to Angus L. MacDonald, wrote inviting Mayor Fry to the launching of the HMCS Stettler. On 18 August 1943 City Commissioner John Hodgson replied that Mayor Fry was away at a conference in the United States and would not be able to attend the ceremony. However, James MacKinnon attended the event to represent the City of Edmonton.

Upon his return, Mayor Fry wrote to MacKinnon not only to thank him for going to the launch ceremony but to explain that Edmonton had "always regretted that no ship could have been named after our own City but Council felt that any other name than Edmonton would have no local significance and could not be a source of any special pride to our City."[18]

In replying to Mayor Fry, Senator MacKinnon mentioned Mayor Kirby's public expression of gratitude toward Edmonton which had been made during the event. Also rather interestingly he closed by saying that he was making further inquiries as to the possibility of a government ship being named after Edmonton. Was this over or not?

Invitation card to HMCS Stettler launch.

Courtesy City of Edmonton Archives, RG11, Class 111, File 2.

After the dust apparently had settled on the naming issue, Angus L. MacDonald wrote to City Council on 13 December 1943, requesting that Edmonton adopt the HMCS Stettler. He stated that "[many] communities which have had ships named after them have undertaken to supply the crew of the ship comforts which are not supplied by the Department...."[19] He closed by writing that "I would be glad if you would let me know if your community or some organization in the community would consider adopting the Frigate HMCS 'Stettler'." [20]

Even though it was not named 'Edmonton', Ottawa still considered the Stettler as Edmonton's ship. John Fry's reaction was positive and quick; he sought out an agency that was willing to carry out this work. This agency turned out to be the Edmonton Civic Opera Society, and with organizations in Stettler helping, the relative comforts of home were soon reaching sailors through their combined efforts.

The final page in this interesting story began on 15 March 1944, when the City Commissioner wrote Pennington with a familiar request.

> *You will remember that we had some correspondence last year in the matter of naming a corvette after the City of Edmonton, but were unable to arrive at a name that was satisfactory to your department. It has been recently suggested that such a boat might be named "Edmontonia," and we would like to hear from you whether this would be in order or not.[21]*

One can only imagine Pennington's thoughts when he read this letter. His eyes must have rolled like the deck of the Stettler in the North Atlantic in November. He had his Secretary draft a reply reminding the City of their recommendation that the ship be named the "Stettler."

> *The name "Stettler" was subsequently approved and allotted to a frigate which is due to be commissioned shortly and of which your Council has been advised in recent correspondence. Moreover, as names have now been approved for all ships presently building under our programme, it is regretted that no provision can be contemplated for the use of the name "Edmontonia."*[22]

Thus concluded the Battle of the Atlantic, Edmonton-style.

As for the Stettler, she received her commission on 7 May 1944 at Montreal. Her first commander, Lieutenant Commander D.G. King RCNVR, remained at the helm until the end of hostilities. She undertook her first convoy duty on 7 March 1945, and patrolled the waters around the United Kingdom until the end of hostilities. She has the distinction of being the last Canadian warship to leave Londonderry at the end of the war and continued to serve as an active ship until 1966.

The fate of the "SS Fort Edmonton" is unclear. It does appear as though Wartime Merchant Shipping were constructing a cargo ship to be named the "Fort Edmonton," but any further mention of her, like an invitation to an official launching, does not appear in Edmonton Council minutes. In 1976 Canadian Pacific Shipping launched a "Fort Edmonton," but according to the Canadian Pacific archives there is no record of an earlier Fort Edmonton in their fleet.

Throughout this episode it appeared that Admiralty had it in for Edmonton, but the city was not alone. During the war there were a total of 37 municipalities whose names could not be applied to naval vessels. Two examples among those were Victoria's ship named "Beacon Hill" because there already was a HMS Victorious, and Portage La Prairie's vessel, which because of the length of the name was known as HMCS Portage.

Students of history sometimes recognize a cyclical nature to our past. This certainly appears to be evident in the naming of ships for Canada's navy. Recently Ottawa announced the names for twelve new Canadian frigates. All major centres in the country were honoured, with one notable exception; the country's fifth largest metropolitan area, Edmonton, was once again not included.

NOTES

[1-3] Edmonton City Archives [EA], Record Group [RG] 11[City Commissioners Department], Class 111, File 1.

[4] EA, City Council Minutes, 14 September 1942.

[5-13] EA, RG 11/111/1.

[14-22] EA, RG 11, Class 111, File 2.

Morale and Morality on the Alberta Home Front

Jeff Keshen

Like their fellow Canadians, Albertans responded in myriad ways to back the campaign against Nazism. "Beautiful Co-eds" at the provincial university sold tags on behalf of Finnish relief; in Millet, a small rural town just south of Leduc, one resident recalled her mother spending every spare moment knitting "sweaters, gloves and balaclavas for the boys"; war gardens abounded in Calgary and Edmonton so more food could be sent abroad; and when it came to Victory Bonds or salvage drives, Albertans rightfully claimed that they were second to none.[1]

"Send Milk to Britain" campaign.

Photo courtesy Provincial Archives of Alberta [PAA Ks.42].

Patriotism was also on display when it came to the treatment extended to those in uniform, particularly men from across Canada and the Empire stationed at the seventeen British Commonwealth Air Training Plan [BCATP] bases opened up across the province. For example, in the *Penhold Log*, the magazine printed for those stationed at the No. 2 Service Flight Training School [SFTS] just southwest of Red Deer, one British airman joked that though newcomers might at first despair over a posting "akin to Siberia," soon the "great hospitality shown by the people" would ease their despondency.[2] Thousands of Albertans extended dinner invitations to ease the loneliness of men who were distant from loved ones, helped auxiliary services like the YMCA or the Salvation Army by organizing dances, or if in business, by providing troops with special discounts [such as the owner of Calgary's Uptown Theatre who, on every night except Thursday, allowed those in uniform and their dates to watch a movie for twenty-five rather than thirty-five cents].[3]

Locations of BCATP
Flying Training
Schools in Alberta.

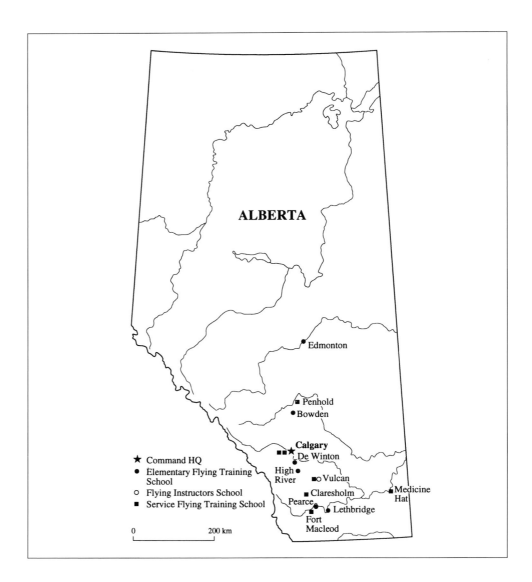

*Originally compiled and
drawn by the
Department of National
Defence, Directorate of
History.*

The appearance of soldiers from so many places, as well as the presence of
smartly attired local regiments, provided for considerable excitement. After all,
even major centres like Edmonton and Calgary were still rather quiet
communities whose populations in 1939 had not reached 100,000. In the latter,
for example, even after three years of war, thousands turned out regularly at local
parks and golf courses to watch troops drill.[4] Meanwhile, in Lethbridge, then a
town of approximately 25,000, more than a quarter of the population came to
Kenyon Field in late 1941 to witness the opening of an addition to the Bombing
and Gunnery School, during which the Royal Canadian Air Force put on some
precision flying.[5] Good feelings between the military and civilians also were
forged through inter-battalion sporting contests to which the public frequently
were invited, like that in March 1941 at Edmonton's Clarke Stadium. There were
many friendly games between base and community teams as well, such as the
regular softball games where the Calgary Tigers faced competition from the
nearby No. 2 Wireless and No. 3 Flying Training Schools.[6]

Beyond such patriotism and enhanced social activity, however, the warm welcome extended to those in uniform in more than a few cases related to economic self-interest as well, especially in a province that had been so devastated by the Great Depression. Anywhere troops were stationed, nearby businesses prospered. In fact, it became easy for all military bases in the province to sustain their own newspaper because practically all costs were covered by firms eager to advertise. Hotels in Banff not only took out space in such publications across Alberta, but also in sources like the *Moth Monthly*, distributed at the No. 33 Elementary Flying Training School in Caron, Saskatchewan.[7] In Red Deer, the 5¢ to $1 store "cordially invited" readers of the *Penhold Log* to examine its "well-stocked shelves," while those perusing the pages of the *Slipstream* at the No. 7 SFTS in Fort Macleod, were informed by the local photography shop that it had colour film and "special RCAF frames."[8]

BCATP bases also provided civilian jobs related to the construction of hangars, barracks, and airfields, as well in provisioning supplies and other forms of support — such as at Edmonton's Aircraft Repair Limited which by April 1941 employed more than a thousand. Recognizing the immense benefits furnished by the bases, not only in the short-term but also by creating permanent infrastructure critical for long-term growth, Edmonton politicians griped to Ottawa about the fact that all but two of the training centres were located south of Red Deer. Perhaps this fact was more attributable to the treeless terrain of the southern foothills, but it was only accepted to a degree by this northern community during early 1942 when its economy was booming due to the arrival of thousands of Americans to construct theAlaska Highway. Almost overnight at the Municipal Airport "brush disappeared...and massive hangars began blotting out the horizon." In less than a year the Americans spent over $3.5 million on the critical upgrading of facilities; in order to adequately service their Army Engineering Corps farther north, the level of outgoing air traffic by November 1942 reached a peak of five flights per minute.[9]

Yet, for Albertans, there was far more to the war years than patriotic demonstrations and a stronger economy. Besides the worry many a resident harboured for loved ones overseas, trends on the home front also accounted for considerable and painful upheaval. While the rural sector faced a record demand for food, military recruitment and war jobs reduced the availability of labour, and hence the ability of numerous farmers to seize this opportunity. Even with women taking on more responsibilities, as well as the help sometimes provided by students during their summer vacation, many farms could not survive — especially given the lack of new machinery coming on the market and the imposition of government price controls over most produce by late 1941. Only the more efficient enterprises flourished, and in fact started to enlarge their holdings and become more capital-intensive by buying up land and usable machinery from those forced to pull up roots. Between 1941 and 1946, Alberta's rural population dropped from 61.5 per cent [489,600] to 55.9 per cent [448,900] of the total, while the average size of farms expanded from 433.9 to 462.9 acres, and their total value climbed from $711 million to $958.1 million. These patterns were evident throughout Canada as a whole where, during the first four years of the war, the agricultural population plunged by 25 per cent and gross output soared by 60 per cent.[10]

Those who relinquished farm life usually headed for larger cities where, though employment was available, decent accommodation soon became rare. In Edmonton, into which approximately 20,000 new residents poured by the end of 1942, municipal surveys taken two years earlier classified 22.2 per cent of accommodation as "overcrowded" and 46 per cent as "substandard."[11] And in Calgary, where during the first three years of the war construction firms managed to acquire only enough material to build 300 homes, the vacancy rate hit an all-time low of 0.09 per cent.[12] In 1941, Ottawa established the Wartime Housing Corporation to construct prefabricated temporary shelter for war workers in the most crowded areas, but shortages of building supplies, along with opposition in the Finance Department towards large-scale publicly-owned accommodation, kept the programme to a fraction of needs.[13]

Wartime housing.

*Photo courtesy
Provincial Archives of
Alberta [PAA Bl.720].*

As a result of these conditions newcomers were forced to accept all types of lodgings, such as garages or cellars whose ceilings barely reached six feet. Aware of such desperation, a number of Alberta homeowners, like Canadians elsewhere, grasped at the chance to make some tax-free cash. For those who could move to the countryside, windfall profits were available. After the arrival of the Americans in Edmonton, with their numerous civilian advisers, talk circulated about 300 per cent profits on house sales.[14] Because most people could not leave the city, excessive rents became far more common. It did not surprise municipal officials in Edmonton to find a family of three paying $30 monthly for an 81 square foot room with no running water, a price which before the war could have secured a small bungalow.[15] To control such behaviour, in late 1941 the Wartime Prices and Trade Board [WPTB] imposed nationwide rent controls and a service to evaluate the worth of accommodation. It slowed, but by no means stopped the abuses — which also included demands for "key money" and the forced purchase of furniture — because numerous landlords realized that only a minority of tenants would report illegal charges for fear of finding themselves on the street.

Whenever opportunity beckoned on the underground war economy, plenty of Albertans proved willing to ignore government entreaties for loyal conduct. With the appearance of gas rationing in April 1942, not only did one find, as in the rest of the country, the appearance of forged coupons, but also a substantial number of farmers selling extra consignments of coloured gasoline authorized to them by Ottawa to help increase food output. Meanwhile, in Edmonton a particularly active black market emerged in cigarettes, as some civilians created an organized network with American soldiers who received a large excess of subsidized smokes.[16]

Of all black market activities, however, that most specifically related to Alberta concerned beef. Ranchers not only resented Ottawa's demand that they produce more food with less help, but also felt that after years of low returns during the Depression, the WPTB price ceiling established over meat in November 1941 was far too low. Moreover, throughout much of 1942 the United States did not impose a ceiling on beef, and when one was created it was higher than that in Canada, thus prompting record shipments of cattle south until the federal government imposed strict export controls.[17]

Feeding the resentment of ranchers was the former Premier of Saskatchewan, and now federal Agricultural Minister, Jimmy Gardiner, an ambitious politician who realized that rural voters constituted his power base. In cabinet, he argued for a price hike on all agricultural commodities, particularly beef, and justified the decision of some ranchers to hold back cattle from the marketplace in protest.[18] By late 1942, shortages of meat selling at the official ceiling price appeared in butcher shops across Canada, admittedly a situation primarily due to rising demand from overseas, but also made worse by the actions of ranchers. Besides some who held back stock, others smuggled steers to the United States, or slaughtered the product themselves and sold at an illegal price to anyone passing by. Moreover, transactions flourished between ranchers and black market dealers who passed on the untagged meat to slaughterhouses. One report submitted before parliament in early 1943 estimated that over the previous year, the number of uninspected killings had doubled.[19]

With complaints mounting from citizens, restaurants and supermarkets about shortages and price gouging, Ottawa responded with coupon meat rationing on 27 May 1943, permitting each person two pounds per week made up of various quality cuts.[20] Distribution improved, but by no means did black marketing disappear. For instance, under the scheme ranchers were permitted to keep back enough beef for slaughter to feed their family. However, there were few government inspectors to see that this was not exceeded; and with the grievances of ranchers over prices still not addressed satisfactorily, under-the-table operations continued, thus providing those consumers possessing extra cash with more than their fair share.

In addition to such unsavoury conduct, the war, with its generally heightened level of activity, also brought to Alberta many "big city'" trappings which some residents, despite their loyalty to the cause, voiced reservations over. In Calgary, for example, a number of people complained to those in charge of nearby BCATP bases about excessive noise and asked that planes not fly over the city after dusk.[21] Such nuisances, however, were minor compared to those relating to soldiers on leave. Troops continually poured into the nearest towns, whose facilities usually were quite limited, making it impossible, said many residents, for them to eat out, see a movie, or in the larger centres, to find a seat on a bus or get a taxicab. It even became necessary for regiments like the Edmonton Fusiliers to threaten its members with fines if they did not stop hassling citizens for free car rides.[22]

Moreover, many soldiers felt a strong desire while on leave to let loose after enduring the rigours and petty rules of training; this was especially true, as one might expect, in those prairie camps where signs of civilian life seemed absent. For example, one contributor to the *Foothills Flier*, the BCATP magazine at Airdrie, described that town as a "runway, a garbage dump, half a hangar, [and] a building in which...personnel sleep, eat, lounge, and are administered unto," but provided solace to readers by pointing out that the "beer parlours of Calgary lay only 30 minutes down the road."[23]

To help soldiers steer clear of trouble, military publications, as well as auxiliary services, advised them on places to lodge, eat, and seek entertainment. Those arriving in Edmonton were told about cheap accommodation at the 'Y', canteen services provided by the Salvation Army, a "good Chinese menu slung up at the Green Lantern," and should they have "some extra change," the Macdonald Hotel was recommended as having the "best pub and dancing...."[24] Most behaved, but with every lot came a portion intent on throwing caution to the wind, perhaps believing it best to experience life to the fullest during these precarious times. For instance, records for both the Calgary-based Strathconas and Edmonton Fusiliers contain numerous entries referring to drunk and disorderly conduct, something for which first-time offenders usually received a few days' forfeited pay, but was known to bring repeaters several weeks' fine or time in the stockade, or both.[25]

More serious from the standpoint of local citizens was the tendency of those in uniform to develop [in the words of one U.S. army psychologist] a rather "direct view towards sex," seeing it as a way to relieve tension, prove their manliness, or obtain a modicum of intimacy before heading towards an uncertain future.[26] Military publications printed in Alberta, as elsewhere, not only carried racy cartoons such as Milton Caniff's widely syndicated "Male Call," but also joked about women desperate for men in uniform.[27] Bearing such attitudes, more than a few soldiers, in defiance of regimental orders, loitered on streets whistling at

young women, or even blocked the way of some in a persistent search for dates
— one such gauntlet being along Calgary's 8th Avenue. In both the Strathconas
and Fusiliers it became necessary to bar soldiers from hanging around high
schools after it was reported that some "annoyed" and even "molested" girls
during their lunch hour.[28]

ALCOHOL REDUCES SELF-DISCIPLINE, LEADS TO V.D.

THE FACILITATOR

Sketches from
*Venereal Disease,
What You Should
Know*, [n.d.].

*Information Services
Division, Department of
National Health and
Welfare, Ottawa.*

Besides soldiers too eager for action, communities fretted over lonely wives
and fiancés, as well as women of low morality, all of whom were presumed as
willing to satisfy. Therefore, police regularly patrolled near military bases to
keep watch over camp followers who, as one Calgary law enforcement official
contended, were mostly made up of "sexual delinquents," rather than, as a
majority of the women themselves claimed, people simply desiring to be close to
their loved ones for as long as possible before they got posted abroad.[29]

Providing apparent legitimacy to such accusations was the rising wartime
illegitimacy rate. Whereas the number of fatherless babies reported in Alberta
stood at 617 in 1939, this climbed to 720 in 1941 and reached 886 two years
later.[30] Some social workers claimed that many of the women planned to marry
the fathers of these babies, but that these men were shipped overseas before it
was realized that a baby was on the way. This explanation, as in other parts of
Canada, did not convince provincial officials to extend Mothers' Allowances lest
promiscuity be condoned — thus forcing many women to send their child to a
foster home or put it up for adoption.

Another disturbing trend related to venereal disease; nationwide, between 1939 and 1940, reported cases among civilians climbed from 7,826 to 10,356.[31] For the military the grief was even greater, as just within Canada 35,036 soldiers were stricken between 1 January 1940 and 20 June 1943, accounting for a total of 697,259 hospital days at a cost of $7.955 million — a rate which far exceeded any other illness among those in uniform.[32] While major depots like Montreal and Halifax produced VD rates reaching 50 per 1,000 in uniform, the prairies remained a concern, with Edmonton and Calgary attaining wartime peaks of approximately 30 per 1,000.[33] In communities across Alberta, police forces launched major offensives against houses of prostitution, with encouragement from military officials. Indicative of what was to come, arrests of those working at Calgary brothels went from 44 in 1938 to 75 the next year.[34] Alberta also increased its budget to fight VD, as did other parts of the country, reversing a trend established in 1932 when, in order to save money during the Depression, Ottawa cut off funding provided to the provinces in this area since 1919. By 1942 lectures on VD sponsored by the Provincial Board of Health reached 25,000 people — a figure more than triple that in 1939 — including about 7,000 high school students.[35] By 1944 the Alberta Teachers' Association [ATA], reflecting thinking by their counterparts elsewhere in Canada, formally recommended that a prominent place be given to sex education within health classes, first established by the province in 1928.[36] Beginning in earnest following a 1942 conference among Western Canadian Health officials in Edmonton, new and comprehensive standardized forms were developed for doctors to help them glean enough information from their VD patients to enable authorities to locate so-called facilitators. This approach was re-emphasized the next year at a national conference in Ottawa which also saw the federal government re-establish VD funding for the provinces and coordinate its efforts more fully with the military to find those guilty of infecting Johnny Canuck.[37]

On the one hand, all these initiatives increased public awareness of matters not usually discussed, and with improved treatment facilities began bringing VD rates down by 1944.[38] It was also a campaign that ended up infringing upon the freedom of women once it was shown that more than half of infected soldiers claimed that those from whom they contracted the disease were first encountered in a restaurant, dance-hall, or on the street.[39] Believing that prostitutes had taken their trade from bawdy houses to such locations, the military often declared "out of bounds" those establishments which were named as a contact place by more than one soldier with VD — locations which in Edmonton included the very popular International, Blue Willow, Regal and Arrow cafes.[40] To avoid losing business, a number of such establishments, if warned by the military or police, were known to ask unaccompanied women to leave their premises. The same was true in dance halls and hotels, and even some taxi drivers refused to give a ride to young women on their own at night for fear of losing their licences if it was proven that they had knowingly transported a prostitute to an illicit rendezvous.[41]

Complaints came from some women's groups who said that those who joined the workforce, especially as a patriotic gesture to free up more men for military service, had a right to enjoy themselves in the evening. Widespread sympathy was not generated, however; in addition to convictions about protecting Canada's fighting men from disease, many citizens, while willing to accept large-scale female labour as a wartime necessity, nevertheless believed it important to retain some restraints over their conduct lest they develop too much independence and lose attachment to their first priority — the family. Fearing such disintegration, Calgary's Chief of Police went so far as to accuse "working girls" of being the cause of much VD, especially those who worked late and then, he intimated, galavanted around with their extra cash.[42]

Although considerable criticism was expressed over this position even in Alberta, where industrial war jobs for women were relatively limited, some "troubling" trends became evident to those concerned about family stability. Edmonton's Local Council of Women, in demonstrating a realization that females were more than capable of performing traditional male jobs, spoke out in favour of equal pay for equal work; when dismissed from well paid positions at places like Aircraft Repair Limited, the Local Council insisted that the Liberal government live up to its election pledge of June 1945 to secure full employment by creating more jobs for everyone, as opposed to "forcing Jill back into the kitchen."[43]

No doubt countless women, after years of strain and loneliness, as well as the double bind of home and outside work, gladly chose marriage, children, and sole custody of the domestic sphere after the war. But clearly the stress upon traditional family life in the 1950s was also a societal reaction against perceived threats to its sanctity during the conflict. When married women began re-entering the workforce in substantial numbers during that decade, not only was it principally in pink collar jobs such as the retail sector, but also usually on a part-time basis and only after their children reached school age. For hand-in-hand with the new wartime roles for women came what many perceived as unsettling attitudes and the inadequate care of youth; in order to correct this situation governments supported the return of mothers to the home rather than sanction facilities which held out the possibility of making their full-time employment a permanent feature of Canadian society.

This certainly became evident with the issue of day nurseries and day care, which Alberta was considering implementing in late 1943 on a 50-50 shared cost basis with Ottawa under the provisions of a federal act passed the previous year. Even in Ontario and Quebec, where the concentration of war industry forced approximately thirty such centres to open, the supply of space fell far short of demand; officials insisted upon interpreting the term "war worker" [for whose children eighty per cent of space was reserved] narrowly in order to keep the number of applicants down and prevent women from regarding the measure as anything more than a temporary expedient. In Alberta the government proved more hard-headed; despite the wartime employment of thousands of women, it simply maintained that state-financed day care was unjustifiable since most jobs did not relate directly to the conflict, thus ignoring the fact that private creches already were near the breaking point. At the single downtown facility in Edmonton in 1942, 118 children aged two to thirteen attended at different times of the day, in buildings which according to the owners could perhaps accommodate another ten at the most. In Edmonton and Calgary committees were formed to lobby for government day care, as well as for after-hours and lunch-time supervision for those at school, the availability of which depended upon the decision of the individual institution. Some businesses which depended upon women workers were supportive, such as Edmonton's Great Western Garment Company, which manufactured uniforms; the GWG president reported that from May to July 1943, his female staff fell from 470 to 377 due to an inability of mothers to find acceptable child care services.[44]

Still, the provincial government resisted, only agreeing in late 1943 to place some newspaper advertisements asking people to write in if favouring such a programme. It was an approach denounced by day care advocates. Many female workers, they pointed out, only read Ukrainian. Moreover, the advertisements failed to cite the subsidized fees of state-supported centres and strongly suggested that only the children of those directly involved with war work would qualify, thus guaranteeing a less than overwhelming response.[45]

Not only did the determination to protect the traditional family structure scuttle day care, but also, somewhat ironically, drew strength from one of the consequences of that policy — children were too often left without adequate supervision. Newspapers and magazines across the land bemoaned so-called "car babies" left all day in parking lots while the mother worked, or if older, the "latchkey child" who returned home at lunch or after school to an empty house. This neglect, it was said, was producing a generation of maladjusted youth and juvenile delinquents.

Indeed, whereas convictions for crimes of those under sixteen in Alberta stood at 58 per 1000 at the outset of the war, this climbed to 111 three years later; this rate was lower than Quebec [120] and Ontario [114], but above the national average of 101.[46] Horror stories of wayward youth were cited by the Edmonton Family Welfare Bureau in one annual report which told of "a 12 year old boy approaching a group of soldiers with a contraceptive device...and a 13 year old newsboy...who was picked up at 12:20 a.m. in a cafe where he had been winning money from a drunken man by matching pennies."[47]

The fact that delinquency statistics peaked in 1942, the year Ottawa authorized the recruitment of mothers into war work, confirmed to many the fundamental cause; ignored, however, was the fact that over the next two years, before "Jill returned to the kitchen," national rates dropped by 5.5 and then 15.5 per cent. Although a mother's care in some households might have prevented some juvenile crime, especially in cases where the father was overseas, arrest patterns indicate other factors at work. During the war an increasing proportion of offences committed by youth were minor infractions such as breaking curfew. What this trend suggests is that even though police forces nationwide shrank from 1.30 officers per 1000 citizens in 1940 to 1.11 in 1944 the fact that they no longer had to concern themselves so much with 18-30 year old males, traditionally the most troublesome crime group, meant that in fact more effort could be devoted to prosecuting such petty offences.[48] Arrests of juveniles for committing minor infractions began declining significantly in 1944, at a time when wounded veterans began returning home in increasing numbers and leave to Canada was introduced for those overseas; both these factors perhaps caused the reallocation of police resources to combat a rising number of major crimes within the population as a whole.[49]

Focusing upon the patriotic activities of countless children in wartime, a number of people dismissed the delinquency scare. Considering "all the confusion and tension [produced by the war]," said Fred Gardiner, the Superintendent of the Calgary Children's Aid Department, "youth has maintained a remarkably high standard of integrity."[50] In Edmonton high schools, for instance, students purchased $516.75 in War Savings Certificates in November 1940, a figure which climbed to $1,145 during the same month the following year. Girls also took Red Cross training while boys made model aircraft for RCAF recognition classes, or if between the ages of twelve and seventeen, joined the air, sea, or land cadets, whose ranks in Edmonton by January 1943 had grown to around 750.[51] Praise was also accorded to thousands of adolescents for giving up part of their summer vacation to help bring in harvests, an activity encouraged by several Alberta school boards during the final three years of the war by changing the dates of this holiday to August through mid-October.[52]

No doubt, as one Edmonton teacher concluded, there was much "panic" in the reaction to wartime delinquency; still, this does not mean that no reason existed for concern over the lack of guidance and structure in many children's lives during these years.[53] Particularly in places like Alberta, the war brought an upheaval from tranquil rural settings to the bustling streets, overcrowded homes, and larger schools of the urban sphere, a disruption which two-income families,

Victoria Composite High School cadets in Edmonton, May 1942.

Photo courtesy Provincial Archives of Alberta [PAA Bl.387].

Cadet graduation
dance, No. 4 Initial
Training School, June
1943.

*Photo courtesy
Provincial Archives of
Alberta [PAA Bl.584/4].*

sometimes coupled with absent parents, only served to exacerbate. Even when parents were home it was noted that some had no time for their children, such as night shift workers who, in order to get some sleep, often forced youngsters outside during the day to play. Organizations such as the Big Brothers argued that some children turned to gangs as a replacement for their disrupted families; their presence increased not only in Montreal and Toronto but also in Edmonton and Calgary.[54] Lack of parental supervision was sometimes cited as the chief reason why girls were increasingly found on streets late at night; in Edmonton the number arrested for breaking the 10 p.m. curfew doubled during the first two years of the war, though the total figure still remained under fifty.[55]

Prosecutions under curfew regulations and compulsory education laws increased further as more young people worked full-time and in late-night jobs. In Alberta, as in schools across Canada, the war years witnessed a significant rise in non-attendance — 50 per cent in Edmonton between 1941 and 1944 ![56] After having watched their parents endure the Great Depression, numerous teenagers seized upon the new opportunities in the war economy to make money. Many left classes with the approval of their parents as schools received a record number of requests for permits to allow children to work full-time before reaching the age of sixteen; this was true particularly in cases where the father was overseas and the mother said she could not survive on a dependent's allowance. More widespread, according to school officials, were those parents just too busy to realize that their children, if not missing class to work long hours, were falling behind in their studies due to fatigue. To control such trends, Alberta schools appointed more attendance officers to track down truants, and with the help of the police warned a number of employers in sectors thought to be hiring minors [such as bowling alleys, pool halls and cafes] about the possibility of suffering hefty fines.[57]

Coupled with threats, curfews, and the condemnation of parental neglect was the conclusion reached by a growing number that the tendency of youth to choose menial jobs over school meant that the education system needed major modifications, particularly if Canada hoped to thrive in a presumably more complex postwar world. What the war did was help highlight some basic problems, many of which unsurprisingly were related to funding. At the outset of hostilities, public education in Alberta, as elsewhere in Canada, was overwhelmingly financed through local property taxes. With minimal help from the provincial government, a number of school districts, primarily but not exclusively in underpopulated rural areas, found themselves starved for money. This fact was reflected in the salary of teachers; their average pay in Alberta in 1940 stood at $860 per annum, roughly equivalent to the national mean in that occupation, but about $500 less than an industrial worker. As late as 1944 some

Buddies celebrate
graduation from No. 4
ITS, June 1943.

*Photo courtesy
Provincial Archives of
Alberta [PAA Bl.584/2.*

instructors in one-room country schoolhouses brought home, after taxes, $58 monthly.[58] Of course the war created other employment opportunities of which numerous teachers promptly took advantage. By the end of 1943, the year in which Ottawa finally froze teachers in their jobs except for military service, the exodus of instructors was blamed for the closure of 449 Alberta schools, most of which were located in rural districts and forced children to bus long distances.[59]

Fewer teachers, as well as a general rural-to-urban migration, accounted for a greater number of congested classrooms. In September 1942, 120 of 204 Calgary classrooms assigned to grades one through six had 35 or more children, despite a school board policy limiting the number to thirty.[60] Concern also grew over the quality of instruction as school boards found themselves under tremendous pressure to quickly hire replacements. While many married women called back into service were of high calibre, some retirees were not physically up to the task, while at the other end of the age scale was an increasing number who were placed in classrooms before having completed their required course of study.

Yet the wartime teacher shortage, when combined with the rise in truancy and delinquency, also focused more attention on schooling and the need for improvements. "A surge of interest" is how the *A.T.A. Magazine* characterized the trend in 1944 after surveying several magazines and newspapers over the past year.[61] By 1945, in order to keep people in the profession and re-attract former teachers returning from the war, the Alberta government, following the lead of Ontario and Saskatchewan, promised a minimum salary of $1,000. The provincial government and ATA followed the national trend by making greater efforts to encourage professionalization. This process was seen as serving both groups by creating a system not only more academically effective, but whose teachers would have a stronger case for better pay, and consequently more loyalty to the job. In this spirit the Alberta government in 1944 underwrote costs for a record number of summer upgrading courses for teachers, and centralized training for high school level instruction at the provincial university.[62]

Helping to make such initiatives possible were changes in both the quantity and source of education funding. Although the ATA was disappointed that Ottawa, as part of its wartime expansion into social welfare, balked at taking a constitutional foray into this area to raise and equalize educational services across the country, still it saw reason to express optimism over the school of the future. Between 1939 and 1946 Alberta reflected a general trend when it increased its total educational expenditures from $10.2 million to $14.9 million, with the provincial contribution rising from approximately 18 to 30 per cent.[63] Moreover, greater centralized direction sped the move to enlarge school districts, which had proceeded rather slowly before the war. One-room schoolhouses, most provincial officials seemed to agree, were not cost-effective, offered inadequate services, often injected unproductive local idiosyncrasies into the curriculum, and, according to a 1944 ATA study which endorsed centralization, produced students who scored about ten per cent lower on standardized mathematics, social studies, language and science tests.[64]

In larger rural institutions, as well as a number of urban schools to which additions were planned, not only were superior facilities promised in areas such as science, but also decent gymnasiums, industrial arts courses formerly often available only at technical schools, as well as music and art classes. Educational strategy also called for the expansion of vocational guidance services which it was hoped would link high school students with a course of training to which they were both suited and where jobs existed. A rudimentary version of this service was inaugurated in Calgary's Western High School in 1934, although it was not until the 1941-42 academic year that the programme began to expand. By the end of the war both Calgary and Edmonton had guidance directors for their school systems.[65] The idea was to make the modern educational facility a more dynamic and relevant place, especially for adolescent students. Those undecided about whether to take a vocational or academic course of studies could experiment with both in these new and larger institutions; it was predicted that this new postwar system would produce fewer truants as well as a better trained and more content work force.

The wartime focus upon truancy and delinquency also appears to have rekindled an early twentieth-century campaign inspired by the Progressives, which faded by the 1920s, that called for a comprehensive and compassionate system of dealing with juvenile offenders. In 1908 Ottawa had passed a Juvenile Delinquents Act setting down guidelines for municipalities to establish separate youth courts. By 1914, Winnipeg, Halifax, Charlottetown, Montreal, Ottawa, Toronto, Vancouver, and Victoria had responded, and three years later, Alberta came on board, technically applying the legislation throughout the province.[66]

Still, at the outset of the Second World War, only Canada's largest urban centres had juvenile courts, according to a 1943 Alberta report, thus frequently leaving youth to be tried as adults. It also noted that judges were often regular magistrates with no special training to deal with children; psychologists were, at best, used sparingly; parole officers were few in number and poorly trained; and inadequate detention facilities for youth often existed, such as in Edmonton where boys stayed in an adjunct of the local adult jail.

Recognizing the present system as inadequate to deal with wartime delinquency, and fearful of yet higher levels during the early postwar period which many feared would be plagued with high unemployment, Alberta established a committee that year to examine juvenile crime. After hearing from 35 people or groups working in the area, its formal recommendations included: an increase in the number of courts; the appointment of judges clearly familiar with current psychological theories about deviant youth; the creation of special observation facilities where before a trail a child might be examined by a psychologist; the establishment of more detention facilities keeping youth separate from adults and placing rehabilitation over punitive measures; and better training, perhaps at universities, for parole officers, as well as their appointment on the basis of one per 5000 people.[67]

Change did not occur overnight, but by the time the war ended some improvement was evident. Part-time psychologists were assigned to courts in Edmonton and Calgary; pre-trial observation centres were created in both jurisdictions; the provincial government publicly committed itself to improving the calibre of its judicial and parole services; and in 1945 Edmonton and the Alberta government both contributed a total of $40,000 for a new South Side detention centre. At this centre the plan was to segregate boys according to age and the seriousness of their crime, assign them to a house leader to approximate a family environment, and in addition to academic lessons, to provide them with training in either industrial arts or farming.[68]

The Second World War brought much excitement and opportunity, as well as commotion and anxiety, to the Alberta home front. In addition to countless citizens whose actions reflected their patriotism, there were those who bemoaned the turmoil which came to their once-tranquil setting; in addition to those businesses which legitimately prospered by serving a new military clientele were those individuals who grew rich on the black market; accompanying the thrill of meeting soldiers from around the world were concerns about growing moral laxity; and counterbalancing the new roles and ambitions of some women was apprehension over family stability which played a fundamental role in producing a postwar conservative backlash. Although evident throughout Canada, such conditions were perhaps more profoundly felt in places like Alberta where practically overnight communities were thrust into a pace of life and confronted with social problems on a scale usually associated with big cities. What these exciting and unsettling experiences also suggest is that the Second World War proved to be a national experience for Alberta, beyond its common resolve with the rest of Canada to defeat the Axis powers, perhaps due to the fact that its residents met so many people from different parts of the country. In being opened up to a wider world so quickly and on such a grand scale, and then in taking a number of initiatives both to employ the potential and contain the negative manifestations of what rapidly became an increasingly complex socio-economic environment, Alberta demonstrated its growing sense of identification in common with a generally modernizing nation.

NOTES

[1]*Gateway*, 23 Feb. 1940, 1; Interview with Laura Hamilton, Edmonton, Alberta, 20 May 1993.

[2]Directorate of History, National Defence Headquarters [D. Hist.], 77/658, *Penhold Log*, April 1943, 6-7.

[3]Glenbow Institute [GL], Manuscript Group [MG] 1961, Department of National Defence Collection [DND], Regimental Orders & Notices, 2 Oct. 1940.

[4]GL, MG 1951, Records of the Calgary Highlanders, Clipping from the *Calgary Herald*, 23 March 1943.

[5]*Canada Year Book*, 1942, 88; D. Hist, 77/648, *Lethbridge Herald*, 19 Nov. 1941, 1.

[6]GL, MG 1961, DND, 29 March 1941; City of Calgary Archives [CC], Record Group [RG] 26, Records of the City Clerk, File 2102, Corporal D.R. Lynes to Major Davidson, 30 April 1941.

[7]D. Hist., 77/633, *Moth Monthly*, Dec. 1942, 31.

[8]D. Hist., 77/658, Dec. 1941, 11; D. Hist, 77/650, *Slipstream*, June 1941, 2.

[9]*Maclean's*, 1 November 1942, 19.

[10]*Canada Year Book*, 1948-49, 163; *Canadian Affairs*, 15 Feb. 1944, 10.

[11]National Archives of Canada [NAC] MG26 J2, William Lyon Mackenzie King papers [WLMK], Vol. 372, File W-310, Undated memorandum entitled "Urban Areas - More than 20,000 Population."

[12]*Maclean's*, 15 July 1942, 15; GL, MG 5841, Calgary Local Council of Women, *1943 Yearbook*, 37.

[13]John Bacher, *Keeping to the Marketplace: The Evolution of Canadian Housing Policy*. [Montreal-Kingston: McGill-Queen's University Press,1993], p. 87.

[14]City of Edmonton Archives [CE], RG 11, Records of City Clerk, Class 210, File 35, M. Mills to Mayor Fry, 26 May 1944.

[15]Ibid, file 29, Memorandum in Support of our Application for Increased Quotas for Goods for Edmonton and Northern Alberta, Submitted by the Wholesale and Retail Divisions, Edmonton Chamber of Commerce, 7 April 1943.

[16]Royal Canadian Mounted Police, *Annual Report*, 1945, 32-3; Interview with Laura Hamilton.

[17]NAC, MG26 J4, WLMK, Vol. 372, undated resolution of Kent County Council; Ibid, C.G. Rutter to King, 8 Jan. 1943.

[18]*Canadian Business*, March 1943, 61; Joseph Schull, *The Great Scot: A Biography of Donald Gordon* [Montreal-Kingston: McGill-Queen's University Press, 1979], p.70.

[19]House of Commons, Debates, 18 Feb 1943, 547.

[20]NAC, RG 36, Records of the Wartime Prices and Trade Board, Vol. 1547, Memo to Local Ration Boards, 27 April 1943.

[21]CC, RG 26, Mrs. C.J. Orman to J.M. Miller, 26 Jan. 1941.

[22]GL, MG 1961, 17 July 1941.

[23]D. Hist. 77/636, 1 July 1944, 4-5.

[24]*Khaki*, Vol.2, No. 19, 7.

[25]Lord Strathcona Archives [LS], Regimental Orders, 4 Oct. 1939, 16 Oct. 1939.

[26]Henry Elkins, "Aggressive and Erotic Tendencies in Army Life," *American Journal of Sociology*, Vol. 51, 5 [March 1946], pp. 408-13.

[27]D. Hist. 77/650, June 1941, 5.

[28]GL, MG 1961, 10 March, 1941, 6 June 1941.

[29]NAC, MG 28 I 10, Young Men's Christian Association papers, Vol. 82, File 1944, "Report for the Committee on Morale - Research on Rumours," n.d.

[30]PAA, Accession Number 68.145, Department of Public Health, 1944 Report, 39.

[31]Statistics Canada, *Incidence of Notifiable Diseases by Province, Number of Cases and Rates, 1924-1968* (Ottawa: 1970) 86-7.

[32]*Canadian School Journal*, Vol. 23, No. 2 (Feb. 1945) 48.

[33]D. Hist. 112.21009 (D20), V.D. Rates among the Army in Canada by Districts, 1942.

[34]Margaret Gilkes and Marilyn Symons, *Calgary's Finest: A History of the City Police Force.* [Calgary: Century Calgary Publications, n.d.], p. 88.

[35]PAA, 68.145, *1939 Report*, 19; 1942 Report, 39.

[36]Ibid, *1944 Report*, 40-1.

[37]Ibid, *1942 Report*, 21; Department of National Health and Welfare, *1945 Report*, 54-60.

[38]NAC, RG 24, Records of the Department of National Defence, Vol. 12216, File 218-4, Venereal Disease in the Canadian Army in Canada, 31 Dec. 1945.

[39]PAA, 68.145, *1943 Report*, 97.

[40]LS, Regimental Orders, 19 Sept. 1940.

[41]PAA, 68.145, *1943 Report*, 91-2.

[42]Calgary Police Archives, Records of the Police Commission, File 42-12, Undated clipping from Calgary *Albertan.*

[43]GL, MG 5841, *1944 Yearbook*, 19; *1946 Yearbook*, 37-8.

[44]CE, RG 11, Class 32, File 7, Brief submitted to City Council from Council of Social Agencies, Summer 1943; F.D. Sutcliffe to Council of Social Agencies, 21 Sept. 1943.

[45]Ibid, Information Regarding the Wartime Day Nursery Situation in Edmonton Presented to the City Council of Edmonton by the Day Care Committee of the Edmonton Council of Social Agencies, 12 June 1944.

[46]NAC, MG30 E256, Charlotte Whitton papers, Vol. 31, File "Juv-Del 1943," A Statement on Juvenile Delinquency Prepared by a Committee of the Toronto Assistant Masters' Association, 1943.

[47]PAA, Accession Number 83.192/754, Records of the Department of Public Welfare, Memo of the Edmonton Family Welfare Bureau, July 1943.

[48]*Canada Year Book*, 1946, 1116.

[49]Ibid, 1947, 260.

[50]CC, Records of the Board of Commissioners, Series 3, Box 2, File 15, Report of the Children's Aid Department, 12 April 1945.

[51]Edmonton Public School Board Archives [EPSB], Board Minutes, 2 Dec. 1941, 26 Jan. 1943.

[52]*A.T.A. Magazine*, May 1944, 30.

[53]Ibid, March 1944, 8.

[54]Ibid, Nov. 1945, 54-5.

[55]Edmonton Police Archives, *Annual Reports*, 1939, 1940, 1941.

[56]EPSB, *Annual Report*, 1946, 35.

[57]NAC, RG 27, Records of the Department of Labour, Vol. 988, File 1-1-4, undated memorandum.

[58]Historical Statistics of Canada 2nd edition, Series E41-48; *A.T.A. Magazine*, Feb. 1944, 12-3.

[59]Ibid, Jan. 1944, 8.

[60]GL, MG 5841, 1943 Yearbook, 31.

[61]*A.T.A. Magazine*, Jan. 1945, 9.

[62]Ibid, May 1944, 33-4, Jan. 1945, 15.

[63]*Canada Yearbook*, 1948-49, 316-7.

[64]*A.T.A. Magazine*, Jan. 1945, 6.

[65]John Abram Ross Wilson, *The Counsellor in Canadian Secondary Schools*, Education Doctorate, Oregon State College, 1951, 22-3.

[66]Neil Sutherland, *Children in English-Canadian Society: Framing the Twentieth Century Consensus.* [Toronto: University of Toronto Press, 1976], pp. 125-6.

[67]PAA, Accession Number 70.414/2147, Records of Department of Social Services, Report of the Child Welfare Committee as Appointed by Orders in Council Nos. 913/43 and 1256/43.

[68]CE, RG 11, Class 32, File 9, Mayor Fry to City Council, 12 March 1945.

Popular Culture in Edmonton During the Second World War

David Leonard

On the morning of 2 June 1939, the people of Edmonton were abuzz with excitement. Rumors of war in Europe and the lingering effects of the Great Depression were, momentarily, secondary news items, for the City was about to experience the first-ever visit of its Monarch. King George VI and Queen Elizabeth were about to arrive, in the third week of their North American tour, intended to foster greater Commonwealth solidarity and encourage closer ties between Great Britain and the United States. In Europe, the power and military threat of Germany dominated public attention, and although the British Prime Minister was outwardly optimistic about "peace in our time," politicians of all colours in Britain and throughout the Commonwealth were apprehensive about the designs of Adolf Hitler and the capacity of Britain to withstand another major war.

King George VI and Queen Elizabeth on their way down Portage [Kingsway] Avenue, 2 June 1939.

Photo courtesy Provincial Archives of Alberta [Bl.473/4a].

The city which greeted the Monarch when he stepped down from the train at the Canadian National Railway station was one of great cultural diversity. It had risen as a northern metropolis in the wake of the Klondike gold rush; between 1900 and 1914 its population, including that of Strathcona, had zoomed from 2,321 to 72,516. During the First World War, however, Edmonton experienced a massive recession. Over-extension of credit and rapid depopulation brought economic hardship to thousands of people, and the physical face of the city became stratified into an Edwardian motif which lasted into the late 1930s. For Edmonton, and indeed much of the rest of Alberta, the Depression had really begun with "the Great War," with brief respites occurring just after the Armistice and during the late 1920s. Vacancy rates remained high as businesses stagnated, while many people relocated their homes to outlying communities such as St. Albert, Jasper Place and Beverly to avoid high taxes.

During the late 1930s, however, the physical appearance of the city began to change. In 1938, the value of building permits soared from $865,560 to $2,806,340.[1] That same year, both the T. Eaton Company and the Hudson's Bay Company completed new "department stores" in the downtown core, bringing a new style of shopping to many people. With many art deco elements, they, and the recently completed Birks Building, were bringing a sense of modernity to the city centre. Fluorescent lighting and block glass were now being used, while the huge neon sign on the Agency Building a short while earlier had initiated a wave of such advertising along Jasper Avenue. The Roxy Theatre was built in 1938, while the Capital was extensively renovated the same year. Construction of the Varscona, Garneau and Odeon were soon to follow.

In front of the Empress Theatre, 1936.

Photo courtesy Provincial Archives of Alberta [A.291c].

In sports, the Edmonton Eskimos commenced playing football in the recently built Clarke Stadium in 1938. Golf, cricket, baseball and lawn bowling also were popular in the summer, as were curling, skiing and hockey in the winter. All sports were non-professional, and there were no "leagues." In the arts, the Art Museum and famous Edmonton photographer Ernest Brown's Birth of the West Museum had survived the Depression, while the Civic Opera was now three years old.

By 1939 the worst of the Depression was over, although the economy was far from healthy. While tax assessment was lower than at any other time since the 1920s, $924,806 would be in arrears to the city at the end of the year. Crops in the surrounding rural areas had been good in recent years, and in 1939 they were described as the best in a decade.[2] Wheat prices that year rose to 54 cents a bushel, up 20 cents from the low of 1932. However, the capacity of people to purchase was still limited.

During the late 1930s there had been several hopeful signs of growth in the city as well. In 1936, Canada Packers had brought some encouragement with its major new packing plant in the east end. It was obvious that use of air transportation also was greater than ever. By 1937, 42 planes were operating out of three hangars at Blatchford Field. Two years later Trans-Canada Airlines was established, providing regularly scheduled Dominion-wide air service to and from Edmonton. The first trolly bus also appeared on the city's streets in 1939, marking the beginning of the end to the old "radial" street railway system.

In 1939 the political scene in Edmonton was still dominated by the economic mores of the Depression. In the 1935 provincial election Social Credit had swept the polls, bringing radical and confusing new monetary theories to the attention of Albertans. The following years saw Edmontonians, and other Albertans, caught up in the swell of controversy over the viability of Social Credit and its chief proponent, Premier William Aberhart. Two of Edmonton's six Members of the Legislative Assembly were Social Crediters. Although Aberhart had his local supporters, he was intensely disliked by many others, and much vilified in the press. *The Edmonton Journal* was scathing in its attack on the Premier, so much so that Aberhart attempted, unsuccessfully, to impose a censorship law over the province's newspapers.

In Parliament, Edmonton East was represented by the Social Crediter Orvis Kennedy, while a Liberal, James MacKinnon, sat for Edmonton West. In civic politics, the three year reign of the radical "fighting Joe" Clarke was brought to an end in 1938 with the election of the more conservative, business oriented John Fry as mayor.

Edmonton remained characterised by extreme cultural diversity. The federal census of 1941 would disclose that while most people [62,775] claimed British ancestry, eight other nationalities numbered over one thousand or more: 6070 Ukrainians, 4997 French, 4658 Germans, 3967 Scandinavians, 2923 Poles, 1512 Dutch, 1449 Jewish, and 1256 Austrians.[3] A host of other nationalities totalled 4,210. In Edmonton's 133 places of worship, services were conducted in the English, French, German, Ukrainian, Russian, Danish, Swedish, Lebanese and Chinese languages. Among the social clubs at the time were the Hungarian Cultural Club, the Ukrainian Institute, the Chinese Benevolent Society, and L'Association Canadienne Française d'Alberta. This international mix was augmented by the great ethnic diversity of the communities which were located close to Edmonton. To the north were the francophone centres of St. Albert, Bon Accord, Legal, Villeneuve, Morinville and Rivière Qui Barre. To the northeast, a strong German presence was found around Bruderheim. Farther to the northeast and east, in communities like Smoky Lake, Willingdon, Mundare and Vegreville,

The war brought
prosperity to
Edmonton
businesses.

Photo courtesy
Provincial Archives of
Alberta [PA.610/1].

the predominant culture was Ukrainian. At Neerlandia, a Dutch community
flourished, while other ethnic groups dotted the countryside as well.

Diversity aside, the "upper crust" of Edmonton society had always been
British. Although a number of francophones and a few others of non-British
ancestry had become powerful financial and community leaders, Edmonton's
politics and public affairs were conducted with a distinctly British flavour.
The leading newspapers carried extensive British news coverage, while the
society columns invariably reflected British upper class tastes. This situation also
was usually reflected in local politics. Elected to City Council in 1938 were Mayor
Fry and Aldermen J.H. Macdonald, M.B. McColl, J.H. Ogilvie, S. Parsons and
A.B. Paterson. The Chamber of Commerce featured similar representation, while
the incorporated social clubs also were predominantly of British origin. The
political stability and relative prosperity of Alberta no doubt did much to secure
the concurrance, albeit passive, of the non-British peoples with this circumstance,
in particular the migrants from the devastated regions of eastern Europe.

The ideals of Edmonton were greatly wrapped up in the ethos of the British
Commonwealth, and therefore the Canadian Crown. It had come to represent
fairness, tolerance and harmony among diverse peoples seldom witnessed in
other parts of the world. Hence the enthusiasm which greeted George VI in June
1939. Though he stayed in Edmonton only six hours, he and Queen Elizabeth
took the city by storm. Over 68,000 people, in a city of 90,419, flocked to see his
motorcade as it rolled down Portage Avenue, shortly to be renamed Kingsway.[4]
Many had travelled miles in special trains and motor caravans to witness the
great event.

Despite this satisfaction with British ties, the early 20th century also had witnessed the gradual, but inexorable, invasion of American popular culture. In many respects, the city which greeted King George was an Americanized city. Itself a "melting pot of nations," the United States had for some time been in the process of cultivating distinctive art forms, architecture, literature, wearing apparel and culinary trends which by 1939 were reflected around the world. Aided by immense wealth, large worldwide immigration, and turn-of-the-century technology which developed the gramophone, cinema, radio and rapid transportation, the United States was well on its way towards setting international trends in 20th century popular culture, at least in the western world.

When King George arrived in Edmonton, there were ten motion picture theatres in operation. The movies then playing had all been made in Hollywood. They included *Broadway Serenade, Return of the Cisco Kid, Stage Coach, East Side of Heaven, Man of Conquest, The Desert Song, A Man to Remember, Home on the Prairie, The Lady Vanishes, Spring Madness, Vacation From Love, Young Heart*, and *There's That Woman Again*. Among the five radio stations Edmontonians were listening to were NBC from Denver and CBS from Salt Lake City. In the evenings, a host of other American stations could be picked up. CFRN was the Canadian Broadcasting Corporation station, and therefore presented extensive eastern Canadian broadcasting, while CKUA, operated from the University of Alberta, featured mostly classical music. CJCA, however, presented the "pop music" of the day, which was predominantly American big band music. Other programmes on CJCA on 2 June 1939 included *Eddie Allen, Doc Salera True Stories, Road of Life, Mary Martin, Ma Perkins, Pepper Young Family, The Guiding Light, Curly, The Yodelling Cowboy* and *Campbell's Playhouse*.

Mike's News Stand, 10 August 1945.

Photo courtesy Provincial Archives of Alberta [Bl.964/2].

On the newsstands of Edmonton were many of the same American magazines which were widely read in later years, with *The Saturday Evening Post*, *Life*, *Time* and *Newsweek* among the most familiar. American pocket books were prevalent, while at the juvenile level, comic books featuring a host of American heros such as Superman, Ozark Ike and Dick Tracy were becoming popular. Cartoons in the local newspapers were largely from American syndicates. In June 1939, these included *Little Orphan Annie, Moon Mullins, Gasoline Alley, Dick Tracy* and *Alley Oop*.

Non-American trends in popular culture did not disappear; except for British cultural influences, however, they were not pervasive. Newspapers like *The Ukrainian News* and journals like *La Survivance* continued to be read, but not outside their respective ethnic groups. On radio, programmes like *The Ukrainian Hour*, which could later be heard by all, were not a feature in 1939. Public socializing along ethnic lines was very common, and Edmonton was far more a cultural mosaic in 1939 than it would be ten years later.

Three months after the Royal Visit, Germany invaded Poland and the series of cataclysmic events known as the Second World War began to unfold. Like most of Canada, Edmonton became emotionally committed to the cause of Great Britain. In particular during the summer of 1940, when Britain stood virtually alone against Hitler's aerial onslaught, the Edmonton papers were filled with stories and photos about the valiant defence of the island nation. Within a week of the invasion, Prime Minister Mackenzie King announced Canada's active participation in opposition to Hitler and Mussolini. The country was at war, and so was Edmonton. On the day of the invasion, the Edmonton Regiment was put on a war footing under Colonel Stillman and began to sign up recruits. The City began to brace itself for combat.

Unlike the First World War, the Second was to bring Edmonton instantly out of a depression, and to a great extent would mould the economy and physical face of the city. The character of Edmonton also would be greatly affected by the war, which would see a greater blend of its ethnic communities. The city which would gasp spellbound at the news of Hiroshima in 1945 was vastly changed from that which gleefully cheered the arrival of King George a little more than six years earlier.

Unlike many wars, the Second World War provided most people in the Allied camp with a clear sense of direction. In the public mind, there was no doubt as to who was the aggressor and who was the defender. There was also little doubt as to the just cause of the peoples attacked and the valour of those who fought back. Germany, Italy and later Japan, were clearly wrong and must be stopped. The battle for survival was also a battle for justice. The justice of the Allies and the evil of the Axis were concepts firmly implanted in the public mind for the duration of the war. As a result, a clear sense of purpose took hold over many communities in the western world, including Edmonton. The despondency and empty solutions spawned by the Depression were now over. Something more alarming, but more identifiable and therefore more combatable, now faced the people, civilian as well as political and military.

The war soon brought economic rewards for Edmonton. Demands were made on local industry, and people began to flock to the city. Although many Edmonton men and women were sent overseas or to eastern Canada, the city increased its population by 3398 in two years. Many of these newcomers came from Britain and other parts of the Commonwealth when Edmonton was chosen as a major centre for the British Commonwealth Air Training Plan. Early in 1942, however, the emphasis began to shift when the Japanese attack on Pearl Harbor jolted the United States instantly into the war. As one of the most compelling early concerns was a possible invasion of Alaska, plans were immediately put in place for the defence of this remote territory. Edmonton, as Canada's "Gateway to the North," was chosen to be the Canadian administrative centre for the Northwest Staging Route, the Canol Project, and especially for the construction of the Alaska Highway. Before long, thousands of Americans began to flood into the city to fill various war-related administrative and industrial jobs. By late 1942, they exceeded 15,000 in number.[5] Accommodation was at a premium, and many Americans had to board with local families. The fact that they blended in as well as they did with the resident population attested to the unity of purpose felt by Canadians and Americans alike. It also attested to the extent to which Edmonton, a city over three hundred miles from the United States border, had become acclimatized to the American way of life.

It is in the popular culture of the time that so much of what people felt during the war years was given expression. Fear, anger, hatred, longing, heartbreak, patriotism, determination and exuberance were all engendered by the war, and were all reflected in the movies, radio programmes, music, novels and magazines of the day. Wartime controls generally kept prices in check. However, with rationing people did not have access to many of the commodities which they had enjoyed before the war. Nevertheless, with increased purchasing power, they were better able to entertain themselves. The disruption of family life, with fathers, mothers, sons and daughters frequently serving in distant locations, compelled many people to seek solace outside the home. During the Depression, economic restraint and the widespread popularity of radio had served to keep families together at home. Now people ventured out more into the open, to cinemas, restaurants, dance halls, night clubs, canteens, bars, or simply to the homes of other people.

During the war people in Edmonton did not often travel very far, due to gasoline and rubber rationing, but they did move about more energetically within their own community. Indeed, Edmonton was a city distinctly on the move, with soldiers marching, office workers scurrying in the streets, and blue collar workers and labourers alike evincing an earnestness seldom displayed before. During 1942, Blatchford Field became the busiest airport on the North American continent. In Edmonton, unemployment practically came to an end, as virtually anyone who wanted a job had one. All employment was regarded as a contribution to the national cause; hardly anyone wished to convey the impression that he or she was not doing their utmost, albeit indirectly, for the purpose of the war. "Don't you know there's a war going on?" became the most common cliche of the day whenever an excuse was needed or a price questioned.

The intensity of the work-a-day world created a lively social scene. In fact, the night life of Edmonton was never livelier. Night clubs like The Barn, the Danceland Ballroom, the Tivoli Ballroom, the Night Owl Cabaret, the Trocadero and the Army, Navy and Airforce Club did a roaring business, featuring performers like Gaby Haas, King Gannam and Tipp's Orchestra. Edmonton now had twelve cinemas, and they were almost always full; several began operating in the early hours of the morning to satisfy shift workers. Sports continued to draw much attention, especially in the summer. A city baseball league was formed consisting of the Hornets, Arrows, Dodgers and Yanks, the latter comprised entirely of Americans. On 4 July 1943, Renfrew Park saw its largest attendance ever. The renewed ability of people to enjoy themselves was coupled with a desire to escape temporarily from the overwhelming public preoccupation with the war. Even then, escape was difficult as so much of the popular entertainment was wrapped up in wartime themes.

In the canteens, restaurants, night clubs and dance halls of Edmonton, people were exposed to American popular music as never before. In general, the sentiments expressed in most American popular songs of the day were sufficiently in tune with Canadian sentiments to make them acceptable locally. The fact that popular band leaders like Glenn Miller and Artie Shaw joined the service no doubt made their music even more acceptable. Those songs directly addressing war situations nonetheless did so from an American perspective. Songs like *Remember Pearl Harbor, He Wears a Pair of Silver Wings* and *I Left My Heart at the Stage Door Canteen* all made the hit parade and were much heard in Edmonton. On the country side, *There's a Star Spangled Banner Waving Somewhere, Silver Dew on the Bluegrass Tonight,* and *Stars and Stripes on Iwo Jima Isle* were all popular in the city, but were not songs to which the average Edmontonian could directly relate. The most popular songs about the war appear to have been those which addressed the conflict indirectly, such as *I'll Be Seeing You* and *White Christmas*, easily the most popular song of the war.[6]

Certain British popular songs not on the American hit parade were quite popular in Alberta, particularly ones popularized by Vera Lynn. *We'll Meet Again* and *Run Rabbit, Run* were popular in Edmonton, but only marginally so in the United States. *White Cliffs of Dover* was the most popular British song in America during the war years; in fact, on 13 December 1941 it became the first war song to make the American hit parade. It rose to "number one" on 10 January and remained at or near the top for ten weeks. This was the only British song to be extremely popular in the United States during the war, although *When the Lights Go On Again All Over the World* was made popular by British as well as American vocalists.

From December 1941 until the end of 1942, at least one song speaking directly about the war was on the American, and therefore the Canadian, hit parade each week. Some, such as *Johnny Doughboy, Praise the Lord and Pass the Ammunition* and *This is Worth Fighting For* spoke directly of war activity and patriotic concerns. Most, however, concerned a girl's loneliness at a lover's departure; *Miss You* and *Don't Sit Under the Apple Tree* were the most popular of these.

As the war continued it brought a subtle change to the nature of American popular music. The disruption of family life encouraged greater nostalgia, and the more driving music of the early big band era gradually gave way to greater sentimentality. In addition, a musicians' strike from October 1942 to March 1944 brought about a scarcity of big band music in general. January 1943 saw virtually no lively music on the hit parade at all, aside from *Praise the Lord and Pass the Ammunition.* The most popular songs of this period were *White Christmas, Moonlight Becomes You* and *There Are Such Things..*

During 1943 war songs became fewer. During the entire month of March not one song on the hit parade spoke of the war, although *You'd be so Nice to Come Home To* indirectly implied a circumstance of the war. Of the war songs released that summer and fall, the most popular were *Coming In on a Wing and a Prayer* and *They're Either Too Young or Too Old.* It was as though people were growing tired of the war occupying their leisure time and reminding them of the actual or possible death, injury or imprisonment of a loved one. Over the winter of 1943-44, the songs from the musical Oklahoma, evoking a nostalgia for the innocence and simple ideals of the romantic American West, dominated the hit parade. During 1944, nostalgia and sentimentality continued to be the order, with *I'll Be Seeing You* and *Long Ago and Far Away* topping the charts that summer. During that fall, *I'll Walk Alone* was easily the most popular song on the continent.

Over the winter of 1944-45, it gradually became apparent that the Allies were winning the war, and in popular music a more positive note came to the fore. *The Trolley Song, Accentuate the Positive* and *Don't Fence Me In* topped the charts that winter. During the spring, the positive tone continued as *I'm Beginning to See the Light, Candy* and *My Dreams Are Getting Better All the Time* were the most popular. Sentimentality was not dead, for families were still fragmented and separated, and casualties on the battlefield still a reality. The summer of 1945 saw *Dream* and *Sentimental Journey* top the charts. When the war finally ended, however, the number one song was *It's Been a Long, Long Time.*

In the popular country songs of the time, similar expressions were presented throughout the war. There were hardly any female country vocalists recording so the perspective was usually male, and in general on the theme of the young soldier eagerly off to war, such as in *So Long Pal, Goodby Mama, I'm off to Yokohama* and *You'll Never Be Blue in a Blue Uniform.* The tragedies of the war also were expressed by country performers in songs such as *Searching for a Soldier's Grave* and *Soldier's Last Letter.* Frequently, extreme patriotism was evinced, in songs such as *There's A Star Spangled Banner Waving Somewhere,* the most popular country song of the war, as well as in *The Last Page of Mein Kampf* and *Smoke on the Water,* which contained such lines as:

There will be an end to Axis,

they must answer with their lives

and

There'll be nothing left but vultures

to inhabit on that land

when our modern ships and bombers

make a graveyard of Japan

While hatred for the enemy occasionally made its way into the popular hit parade as well, with songs such as *Der Fuhrer's Face* and *Remember Pearl Harbor*, it was in motion pictures that the greatest patriotism, xenophobia and racism were expressed. It was also in the movies that the greatest doses of "Americana" were administered in Edmonton, and the strongest propaganda attacks leveled against the enemy. The United States' government was intent on having Hollywood carry the American national banner, and in the spring of 1942, a Co-ordinator of Motion Pictures was appointed to ensure that goal.[7] Later that year a Government Information Manual for Motion Pictures was circulated to the various studios.

There were many movies made at this time in which the circumstance of the war was intertwined with another plot. *Casablanca* and *In Which We Serve* were two of the better of these. Many other movies were directly about combat, the gallantry of the Allies and the evil of the enemy. In Hollywood, the enemy was easily recognizable, being either the dull-witted, subservient German thrall, or the cunning, cruel Japanese. It was not difficult for the directors to portray the foe along these lines, for this was only reinforcing stereotypes already in place. "Japs" and "Krauts" were common terms in the movies as well as the rest of North American society.

The first war movies following the invasion of Pearl Harbor depicted the confusion and anger of ordinary citizens. Spy and sabotage movies such as *Joe Smith, American, Saboteur* and *Nazi Agent* all came out early in 1942, and all eventually played in Edmonton. Films like *Hitler's Children, The Hitler Gang* and *The Seventh Cross* depicted German people in general as racial perverts, while *Yellow Peril, Behind the Rising Sun* and *Dragon Seed* did the same for the Japanese. Of course, in virtually all of the early war movies, the fighting American soldier was depicted as brave, honest and capable. Respect for the cause of other Allies was common also, as with the British in *Mrs. Miniver*, the French in *This Land is Mine*, the Norwegians in *Edge of Darkness*, the Czechs in *Hangmen also Die*, the Chinese in *Dragon Seed*, and even the Russians in *Mission to Moscow* and *Song of Russia*. In *Captains of the Clouds*, James Cagney joined the Royal Canadian Air Force. Alfred Hitchcock's *Lifeboat* told of a variety of Allied nationals valiantly holding together in a highly symbolic rescue craft. Among them is a Nazi who initially takes charge of the situation, but whose treachery eventually becomes obvious; he is bludgeoned to death by the other survivors after he kills an innocent member of the party. Certain American popular songs spoke approvingly of other nationals. *My Sister and I* told of the gallantry of the Dutch resistance, while the most popular country song of 1945 was *Filipino Baby.*

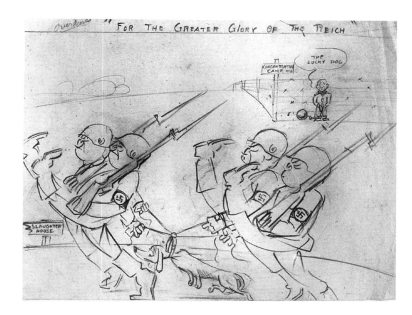

Stewart Cameron sketches for wartime cartoons prepared for *Calgary Albertan.*

Photos courtesy Provincial Archives of Alberta [78.63/99 and 78.43/249].

The later war films often told of actual circumstances, such as important battles. *Bataan, Wake Island* and *Action in the North Atlantic* were three of these. The later war films were also grimmer; too many real casualties and too many newsreels showing the realities of war no doubt caused filmmakers to recraft their stories. Films like *The Purple Heart* and *Thirty Seconds Over Tokyo* concentrated on the barbarous treatment of American prisoners of war; in these, the cruelty of the enemy is brought to the fore. In *Objective Burma*, the protagonist cries out against the Japanese, "Degenerate, immoral idiots! Wipe them off the face of the earth!"

Public attitudes during the war were even reflected off-screen, as many actors and actresses publicly promoted the war cause, mainly by advertising the sale of Victory Bonds. Movies such as *Stagedoor Canteen* and *Hollywood Canteen* were made specifically for popular entertainers to demonstrate their appreciation for the people in the services. Of course, many major Hollywood personalities also joined the service themselves.

During the war, colour cartoons were used for purposes of propaganda, particularly those of Walt Disney, as Donald Duck and others joined the fray.[8] This was also the case in syndicated cartoons and comic books. Ozark Ike, Joe Palooka, Dick Tracy and a host of other cartoon characters joined the service, while Terry and the Pirates began taking on the Japanese navy. The enduring figures of G.I. Joe and Captain America were born at this time. Lesser known figures such as Wash Tubbs and Tillie helped the cause on the home front by volunteer work or in seeking out enemy spies.[9] As in the movies, stereotyping of the enemy was common. In the Classical comic *Marco Polo*, purportedly an authentic account, Marco is made to express his admiration of all peoples of the Orient "except the sneaky people of Japan."

On radio during the war, many of the regular programmes such as *Ma Perkins, The Aldrich Family, Green Hornet* and *I Love A Mystery* would address the war in some way. Other programmes such as *People on the March, Soldier's Wife* and *These Make History* were created specifically to speak about the war. The musical variety shows would invariably send prayers and messages to "the boys overseas" and appeal for the purchase of Victory Bonds.

"For the Cause,"
15 August 1943.

Photo courtesy
Provincial Archives of
Alberta [Bl.616/1].

In Edmonton, the American-oriented movies, radio programmes, music, magazines, comics and cartoons were, of course, made even more abundant by the fact that over 33,000 American military personnel would reside in or near the city.[10] They also were made popular by virtue of the unity of purpose shared by Canadians and Americans, and their common attitude towards the enemy. The war served not only to disseminate American popular culture, but also to break down cultural barriers among Edmontonians; war industries did not hire along ethnic lines, and many women were brought into the labour force at this time. People worked and enjoyed themselves together as never before, and the popular entertainment of the day, in so many ways, spoke of the one subject that occupied every adult's mind and kept them unified, the war. The city collectively took pride in news stories about the exploits of local heroes no matter what their ancestry. It also was collectively saddened by stories of those local men and women who became casualties, and at the never-ending casualty lists which appeared regularly in the daily papers. American popular culture provided a conduit for all people to escape from the horrors of the war, to reflect on war circumstances, or to vent their anger towards the enemy. It also resulted in less attention paid to folkways brought over from other nations.

Many of the local German population, along with residents from eastern Europe and a number of Japanese immigrants and naturalized citizens, were to endure many indignities and suffer much abuse during the war, and for several years thereafter. Hutterites and Mennonites in particular were singled out for their pacificism, while the Japanese were forbidden to travel more than twelve miles from their homes. Most of the city, however, was socially in harmony and politically stable during the war. Provincially, Social Credit settled into being another conservative party on its way to 36 consecutive years in office. In Edmonton, Mayor Fry would remain in office until after the war.

101 Street north of Jasper Avenue, 13 August 1945.

Photo courtesy Provincial Archives of Alberta [Bl.965/2].

When the war was finally over and the Americans departed, Edmonton was a much changed city. Its physical appearance was only slightly altered, for there had been few permanent buildings constructed during the war, aside from those located at the airport, and a host of Quonset huts at various locations. The character of Edmonton, however, was much different. The feeling of urgency created by the war continued as people bustled to get reacquainted with a civilian way of life. New night clubs like the Silver Glade and the Skyland were opened, while the Edmonton Eskimos and Edmonton Flyers were soon engaged in semi-professional baseball and hockey. A new Community Theatre Society was added to the arts scene in 1946. The local press reflected the new sense of economic optimism which was in the air; there was a distinct feeling that the wartime boom would continue. In 1946, the population of Edmonton had grown to 111,745, exclusive of the adjacent towns of Beverly and Jasper Place. In 1947 the Leduc oil strike would lend further credence to this postwar faith in the future.

At the end of the war the emergence of members of ethnic minorities into positions of social and political prominence became more noticeable, with names like Gariepy, Bisset, Tomyn, Holowach and Hawrelak being returned at civic and provincial elections. Edmonton would remain culturally diverse, although the intermingling of peoples initiated by the war would not slacken. The significant and irreversible transition caused by the wartime boom economy, and a forward-looking optimistic approach to the postwar years, continued to bring people together more, as the war had done. Socially, there were simply more things unrelated to various ethnic communities for people to do than ever before. Canadian popular culture, and with it Edmonton's, continued in a state of rapid evolution, although largely along lines developed south of the American border.

Notes

[1]*Henderson's Directory* for Edmonton, 1938, p. 14.

[2]*Edmonton Journal*, 5 July 1939.

[3]Canadian Census for 1939, vol.6 [population], p. 273.

[4]*Edmonton Bulletin*, 3 June 1939.

[5]Sean Moir and Steve Boddington, *"The Friendly Invasion": The American Presence in Edmonton 1942-1945*, in this volume.

[6]All conclusions regarding the popularity of particular songs are based on the weekly listings for *Your Hit Parade*, which was compiled from surveys of record and sheet music sales, and the volume of requests made to national disk jockies. The surveys were undertaken by the advertising agency, Batton, Barton, Durstine and Osborne. See John R. Williams, *This Was Your Hit Parade* [Rockland, Maine: Courier-Gazette, 1973]. See also Nat Shiparo, *Popular Music*, Vol. 2 (The 1940's), [New York: Adrian Press, 1965].

[7]Norman Kagan, *The War Films* [New York: A Hornet Book,1974], p. 26.

[8]Richard Sale, *Donald Duck Joins Up* [Washington, D.C.: UMI Research Press 1976].

[9]See, for example, the *Edmonton Bulletin*, 4 May 1944.

[10]See Sean Moir and Steve Boddington, op. cit., p. 1.

"The Friendly Invasion": The American Presence in Edmonton, 1942-1945

Steven Boddington and Sean Moir

Japan's aggressive expansionary activities throughout the Pacific rim during the late 1930s and early 1940s, and the attack on the United States naval base at Pearl Harbor on 7 December 1941, jump-started the Canadian and American governments to follow through with the development of plans for the defence of mainland North America. Their strategy called for the fortification of Alaska and the construction of the Alaska Highway, the Canol Pipeline and a series of landing strips known as the Northwest Staging Route. Prior to Pearl Harbor, almost all North American defence activities had been oriented towards the east coast.[1] In some cases existing air bases such as Edmonton's Municipal Airport were expanded to meet wartime demands, while other projects were undertaken in remote regions of the continental Northwest. During the construction of the airstrip, highway and pipeline throughout 1942-1943, and for the next few years, thousands of American soldiers, civilian contractors and government officials were stationed throughout the Canadian northwest [central and northwestern Alberta, northeastern British Columbia, and the Yukon and Northwest Territories]. American military strength in north-west Canada surpassed 15,000 by late 1942. By mid-1943 the total number of American military and civilian personnel exceeded 33,000 individuals.[2] Edmonton served as the administrative centre, as well as the transportation and supply staging area for these projects and thus was "home" to a very large contingent of Americans between 1942 and 1946.

On 18 August 1940, at Ogdensburg, New York, Prime Minister Mackenzie King of Canada and President Franklin D. Roosevelt of the United States issued the following statement.

> *The Prime Minister and the President have discussed the mutual problems of defence in relation to the safety of Canada and the United States. It has been agreed that a Permanent Joint Board on Defence shall be set up at once by the 2 countries. This Permanent Joint Board on Defence shall commence immediate studies relating to sea, land and air problems including personnel and material. It will consider in the broad sense defence of the north half of the Western Hemisphere. The Permanent Joint Board on Defence will consist of 4 or 5 members from each country, most of them from the services. It will meet shortly.[3]*

This was the first serious attempt at joint Canadian-American cooperation in the field of military affairs.[4]

Talk of constructing a land route through Canadian territory from the continental United States to Alaska had been a matter of discussion for some time. After much debate, it was decided at the Permanent Joint Board on

Defence's [PJBD] Vancouver meeting in late 1940 that when the road was built, it would be used to link the airports of the Northwest Staging Route.[5] Approximately 1500 miles in length, stretching from Dawson Creek, British Columbia to Fairbanks, Alaska, the completion of the pioneer road in just nine months [February-November 1942] was an amazing engineering feat. The project involved seven engineering regiments, 77 contractors, 14,000 men and 11,000 pieces of equipment. Work by civilian contractors was called off in October 1943, at which time the worst hills and turns had been eliminated and the route had been improved beyond the initial pioneer road stage. As C.P. Stacey has pointed out, however, despite the enormity of the undertaking "as a military route carrying supplies to Alaska, the highway was completely insignificant," and "apart from its utility in connection with the airway, there was no real military requirement whatever for the Alaska Highway."[6] Although a great deal of traffic passed over the road during 1942-1943, it served primarily for the supply of the military and civilian construction forces, and the airfields and other installations along the route.[7]

The Canol Pipeline project linked the oil fields of Norman Wells and a refinery in Whitehorse, Yukon Territory. The project was undertaken by US Army Engineers without intergovernmental approval, and has been called by some an ill-conceived, $34-million afterthought that left US tax-payers on the hook. The line and oil supply both proved to be unreliable, and the project was the most debated and controversial of those undertaken in the Canadian Northwest during the war.[8]

The Northwest Staging Route, a series of air strips linking Edmonton and Fairbanks, Alaska, had two main functions: first, to provide insufficiently supplied American bases in Alaska, including those on the Aleutian Islands, with the materials and manpower necessary to defend themselves and launch

This view of the Edmonton Municipal Airport during the Second World War shows numerous aircraft and newly constructed buildings. The airport was a vital part of the Northwest Staging Route, and was expanded rapidly to accommodate the large numbers of aircraft being shuttled north as part of the Lend-Lease Programme.

Photo courtesy Provincial Archives of Alberta [PAA A 5291].

operations. Second, it was to serve American and Canadian pilots who were shuttling Lend-Lease aircraft to Fairbanks, where they were turned over to Russian crews. These planes were used against Germany's army on the Eastern Front in Europe. The Northwest Staging Route was the only one of the three projects that was developed using proper government channels in Canada and the United States.[9] The Alberta-based air strips of the staging route were located at Edmonton and Grande Prairie. Other airstrips were constructed throughout the north, and the supplies and manpower required to complete these projects funnelled through Edmonton.[10]

This February 1945 view of the "Redwood Building," 114 Street and Jasper Avenue, Edmonton, housed the offices of the Bechtel, Price Callahan Engineering firm, and components of the Northwest Service Command. It was turned over to the Federal Department of Veterans Affairs at the end of the war. Its name was derived from the expensive redwood lumber imported from California which was used to refurbish the building.

Photo courtesy Provincial Archives of Alberta [PAA Bl. 875].

In addition to the military, two large American contracting companies, Bechtel, Price and Callahan, and the Kansas City Bridge Company [KCB Co.], set up operations in Edmonton. Major-General W.W. Foster, who was appointed Special Commissioner for Defence Projects in the North West by Prime Minister King, also made Edmonton his base of operations. Bechtel held a $500-million contract for road construction, while the KCB Co. was hired to build more than 250 bridges along the highway. Bechtel occupied the Jesuit College, also known as the "Redwood Building," on Jasper Avenue, and the KCB Co. established its offices in the converted Empire Theatre. The moniker "Redwood Building" was applied to the College after it was refurbished with expensive, imported, California redwood panelling rather than locally available products.[11]

General Foster, who was given the assignment of asserting Canadian sovereignty throughout the northwest, established his headquarters in Edmonton during May 1943. His headquarters were located at "Oliver House," 9937-103

Street, the former home of Frank Oliver, founder of the *Edmonton Bulletin* and Minister of the Interior from 1905-1911.[12] Upon his appointment, Prime Minister King wrote to Foster and noted the following,

> *The Northwest possesses valuable natural resources and is an area of strategic importance in the event of conflict between the United States and any Asiatic nation. The Canadian Government desires to ensure that the natural resources of the area shall be utilized to provide the maximum benefit for the Canadian people and to ensure that no commitments are made and no situation allowed to develop as a result of which the full Canadian control of the area would be in any way prejudiced or endangered.*[13]

Foster's role was not only that of "watch-dog," but he also was given the task of simplifying intergovernmental relations. Anything having to do with the US presence in Canada passed through Foster's office, whether these were broad-based policy issues, or specific matters such as security for dignitaries or press relations with the local media. King also wrote Premier Ernest Manning regarding Foster's appointment, requesting the Alberta government's cooperation, and to reassure Manning that Ottawa was not foregoing Canadian sovereignty.[14] In addition to appointing Foster, the Canadian government opted to pay for all construction undertaken on Canadian soil, thereby negating any future, postwar claims the Americans may have contemplated.[15]

Foster's appointment stemmed from two sources. First, Prime Minister King had growing concerns over American activities in the area. Near the end of 1942, King was genuinely worried about US designs on Canada during the postwar period. He believed that they would attempt "to bring Canada out of the orbit of the British Commonwealth of nations and into their own orbit. I am strongly opposed to anything of the kind," he wrote. "I want to see Canada continue to develop as a nation, to be, in time, as our country certainly will, the greatest of nations of the British Commonwealth."[16]

Second, Prime Minister King received a letter from the Hon. Malcolm MacDonald, British High Commissioner to Canada. MacDonald happened to be associated with a small, informal, Ottawa-based clique known as the "Northern Nationalists" which was devoted to the preservation of the North and Canadian sovereignty. The Northern Nationalists wished to ensure that American activities on Canadian soil did not continue unsupervised.[17] During the period 1941-1943 the US army command in northwestern Canada operated almost autonomously from both Washington and Ottawa, a situation which has been described by military historian J.L. Granatstein as Canada's "fit of absence of mind." Other historians such as Donald Creighton have chastised the government to an even greater extent, noting that Canada's failure to take charge and to command American respect was an inexcusable failure to protect the nation's assets. Creighton argues that with the exception of the Northwest Staging Route, "they [Americans] forced Canadian consent, paid little heed to Canadian Sovereignty and generally acted as if they had a right to be on Canadian soil as if it were a separate but tributary part of the Empire of the United States."[18]

Foster initially interpreted the US Army Engineers' attitude towards the projects on Canadian soil as "cavalier."[19] Communication was strained at first, and this was indicative of the early scepticism most Canadians harboured about American intentions in the Northwest. Prime Minister King noted in his Diary:

> *It was not without some concern that...I viewed the Alaskan [sic]*
> *Highway and some other things growing out of the war, which*
> *was clear to my mind that America has had as her policy, a*
> *western hemisphere control which would mean hemispheric*
> *immunity, if possible, from future wars but [with] increasing*
> *control by the U.S.*[20]

It is apparent from Foster's reports, however, that relations between US personnel and Canadian authorities relaxed with the passage of time, and Foster came to admire the enthusiasm displayed by the Americans, and their ability to "get the job done."[21]

This large influx of soldiers, in addition to the establishment of command and company offices, and US government agency project headquarters, such as the Public Roads Administration, had a significant impact on daily life in Edmonton, which was then a community of not yet 100,000 people.[22] The most apparent impact was the creation of thousands of jobs that gave the city's struggling economy and war-weary morale a much needed boost. The construction undertaken to upgrade facilities and transport systems, and the leasing of all available space for residential and office use, provided local workers, businesses and land owners with opportunities previously unattainable. Local firms prospered as American government money and individual pay cheques were spent in the city.

On a social level United States servicemen and civilian workers quickly became part of the wartime fabric of the community, but Edmontonians reserved judgement as to whether this would prove to be beneficial for their city. Officially, all levels of government went to great lengths to praise one another, in the hope of maintaining a harmonious relationship. However, not everyone agreed, and some Americans had little positive to say about Edmonton. One individual was quoted as saying that "there isn't much doing in town," and New York Mayor Fiorello LaGuardia, a member of the Canadian-American Permanent Joint Board on Defence, "observed somewhat slyly during a visit that Edmonton was 'a most attractive city from the air'."[23] After the appearance of several critical articles in American newspapers describing conditions in Canada, US officials ordered workers on the Canol project not to make any further inflammatory statements. One New York journalist wrote what was supposed to be a flattering piece on the city for the *Edmonton Bulletin*, hoping to appeal to an apparent age-old desire among Canadians to be just like Americans. After stating that he saw little difference between his host community and his home town of New York, he observed that

"You have all the things we have in New York, street cars, automobiles, raids, juke boxes, and even hamburger emporiums."[24] Despite these disparaging comments, the fact that most Edmontonians welcomed the American "invasion" with open arms supported the official view. Cases of local families inviting soldiers and civilian workers into their homes and families were not uncommon.

Relations between US servicemen and the locals never were completely free of friction, and some "residents of the city complained a good deal about the dislocations of the wartime activities — the housing shortages, the labour shortages caused by the generous pay offered by the Americans, the dust and noise of the construction equipment, the raffish ways of the soldiers."[25] At times, local displeasure with the American presence even manifested itself in some merchants and suppliers taking advantage of the city's "guests."

Given the relatively small size and quiet nature of Edmonton at the time, the somewhat mixed reaction to the "invading army" was to be expected. The nature of the North West Service Command's projects in Edmonton alone were staggering. As of 1943 the US Government had requested land for over 1200 projects in the Edmonton vicinity alone.[26] The construction undertaken by the North West Service Command at the Edmonton Airport included quarters for 528 officers and 1920 enlisted men, two hangars, 66,000 square yards of warm-up apron, 39,750 square feet of storage space, and miscellaneous other buildings.[27] The Namao project, just outside the city, was equally impressive, and was built entirely under the supervision of the US Forces.[28]

The greatest problem faced by all was the lack of residential, office, and industrial space to house personnel and equipment. Those Edmontonians in need of shelter found the housing situation the most disturbing, feeling shut out in their own community. This situation remained unchanged until 1945 when the American army began withdrawing large numbers of men. In 1943 one observer wrote that there were often so many requests for hotel accommodation in Edmonton that single cots were placed in banquet and meeting halls. Another factor exacerbating the constraints on space was that many American civilian workers and some US servicemen were accompanied by their families. According to the Edmonton Emergency Accommodation Bureau:

> *We are still looking for 1000 suites.... We would have no difficulty filling them. We have hundreds of people living in temporary quarters just waiting until a two or three room suite is vacant. Many of these people are Americans working for U.S. concerns in the city, and their families.*[29]

Despite offers from many Edmontonians to house servicemen and employees of private contractors in spare bedrooms, the resulting strain upon the city's housing was such that in 1943 a plan for the repatriation of American families by their government was considered. Although this was not carried through, it was sufficient to cause considerable anxiety among these families.[30]

Bechtel Price Callahan surveyed its employees about the housing situation and found that nearly one-half expressed profound displeasure.[31] Despite massive undertakings by the military and private contractors to construct new residences, the classified sections of the city's newspapers were full of pleas from Americans looking for "well furnished" houses or apartments for short- or long-term lease. They guaranteed care of the properties, and were willing to pay almost anything for a suitable home. At the end of 1942 the *Edmonton Journal* reported that

> *...more than 100 people are putting up with temporary accommodation—three or four of them living in one room....[We] could use a thousand suites. We could rent them in about a week. Long-time residents of the city, living in large homes, don't seem to realize the seriousness of the situation. Surely some of them have one or two rooms they are not using."*[32]

A letter from two Americans revealed that some landlords took advantage of the housing shortage.

> *...the two of us have been charged $25 to $40 for a basement suite or attic room, and $10 for a heated garage! At one place, the tenants...sublet to us a tiny upstairs room with no door for $25.... Another time we paid $22.50 for 18 days in an 8' X 10' room containing only a chiffonier and double bed, sublet to us by tenants who were paying only $52.50 per month for the completely new 4-room apartment....*[33]

The war years in Edmonton saw many people living in marginal and substandard housing. There was little regard for building regulations and zoning laws as old houses, basements and second floors of houses, and even garages, were converted to apartments or suites. By mid-1943 the Edmonton Emergency Accommodation Bureau had 1350 names on its waiting list.[34]

Almost any available space was leased, purchased or, in the case of vacant land, built upon for the purpose of housing, offices and storage facilities. Office space was also at a premium during this period. Every square foot left untouched by Canadian military services was leased by the Americans.[35] The extensive renovations undertaken by Bechtel at the site of the Jesuit College not only included sixteen residences, each capable of housing 32 people, but also a mess hall with seating capacity for 450, a two-storey office structure, and a number of shops and buildings to store supplies.[36] Further examples of American leasing and building activity in Edmonton included the following: the Kansas City Bridge Company and several other businesses joined forces to lease and renovate the Empire Theatre office structure; the Kansas City Bridge Company also sought to lease the Old Glenora School for residential purposes; and the US Public Roads Administration undertook the construction of residences at 114th Street and Jasper Avenue.[37] The Americans leased a total of 59 office buildings in Edmonton during 1943, to headquarter the staffs of the various businesses and agencies that were involved in various local and regional projects. This new-found rental revenue helped the City of Edmonton collect the highest taxes in its history up to that time.[38]

The Department of Public Works for the Province of Alberta also reported these economic changes in its *Annual Report of 1942-43*, in which it was recorded that many wholesale warehouses in the northern part of the province had been leased to the military authorities or to firms engaged on the Alaska Highway Project. Another notable change was the increase in personnel in the catering industry, in which employment had more than doubled.[39]

The future economic potential of the highway was certainly not lost among civic boosters, even in the northwestern states. A representative from the Great Falls, Montana Chamber of Commerce pointed out in a letter to the Alberta Government:

> *The greatest share of what is known as tourist travel after the war is over would, in our estimation be through Montana and Alberta and that is something we are working ahead for, so that when this comes about our state and your province would, in a way, have this motor tourist travel properly linked up. It seems that practically "everybody" is figuring on a trip to Alaska when the War is over now the highway is completed.*[40]

When the Americans pulled out in 1946, and the Canadian government took control of the Alaska Highway, the city inherited many facilities built by the US military. Many of the existing buildings adjacent to the Municipal Airport still serve as a lasting reminder of this period. Several examples of the judicious use of war surplus facilities include the use made by the Edmonton Public School Board of two army huts as "temporary" classrooms during the postwar "baby boom." This was known as the R.J. Scott School Annex, and was still being used in 1970.[41] The Jesuit College, which had served as the Northern Command Headquarters for the US Engineers, was converted into a temporary veterans' hospital, and the many huts at "Camp 550" in the Calder area were transformed into 80 postwar housing units. Administered by the National Housing Administration, these former US Army residences helped alleviate the severe housing shortage faced by the city after the war.[42]

Many Edmontonians were able to benefit from the presence of the American military and civilian contractors as they were presented with opportunities for more work and better wages, previously unimaginable. According to former employee Mary Waldal:

> *In early 1943 I was employed as a clerk-typist at the Royal Alexandra Hospital. My wages were $55 and $6 cost of living allowance per month. After hearing that the Americans were hiring, I went over and got a job with the Alaskan Division for $100 to $110 per month for the same job.*[43]

Mary's husband also found better pay working for the United States Army Air Force as an aircraft parts assembler at Aircraft Repair Ltd., on the northwest corner of Edmonton Airport. This facility was later to become known as Northwest Industries.[44]

So many were leaving to work for the American military and civilian contracting companies, that concern was voiced in the House of Commons. It was pointed out that "alien" contractors were ignoring the existing wage rate imposed by the Canadian War Labour Board, and that this was causing great distress to Canadian employers, who could not compete either economically or legally.[45] The *Edmonton Bulletin* reported in 1943 that four constables had resigned their posts on an already war-depleted Edmonton Police Department, after having "secured work on northern war development projects."[46] One Edmontonian employed by the American military remembered that he had been told by a lawyer who worked in the McLeod building that, "early in 1943, an American officer began knocking on doors on the top floor and worked his way down recruiting typists and secretaries," presumably with offers of better wages.[47]

Given the expediency required during wartime and the legendary abundance which seemed to accompany a visit by the United States military, advantage was sometimes taken by those contracted as suppliers. According to one former Edmonton clothier:

> *Lots of people took the Americans for what they could get. They over-paid for everything. People thought they were nuts. They were big tippers - twenty-five cents wasn't good enough, they had to tip a buck! I was contracted as an outfitter, to provide them with northern clothing. They often paid far too much - but I warned 'em. I used to go to the 'Redwood Building' to get my orders for where to send stuff.... American clothing was lousy, they needed good Canadian stuff!*[48]

This attitude seemed to reflect an opinion voiced by some local residents that American servicemen and civilian workers were pampered. They usually pointed to such "soft touches" as the abundance of food, cigarettes, liquor and recreational supplies, the more comfortable material and attractive cut of American uniforms, and the superior wages American civilians earned for the same job as their Canadian counterparts. One particularly irksome perquisite, according to these locals, was the so-called "service abroad bonus," which amounted to some 35 per cent on top of their regular pay. Another American practice held up for public ridicule was that of giving decorations for "foreign service" in Canada.[49]

Upon closer examination, it is clear that these sentiments had much deeper roots. This was, after all, the first "foreign army" on Canadian soil since Confederation, Allied or not, and the event perhaps challenged some long-held perceptions Canadians had about Americans and about themselves. The notion

American soldiers enjoying a steak dinner at an Edmonton cafe. US Army personnel were encouraged to patronize local businesses and to take an active role in the community.

Photo courtesy Provincial Archives of Alberta [PAA Bl. 696].

that the American soldiers were pampered and soft was probably an extension of the military myth that one's own army was the finest and all others were somehow below par. Another belief which may have been challenged was the notion that rugged Canadians were "masters of the north." Americans had done, with their overwhelming resources and technology, what many Canadians had not thought possible; cut a road to Alaska, linking the Canadian North to a source of supply previously only available, intermittently, by air. This achievement was balanced, of course, by substantial Canadian contributions to the construction of these projects. Critics of the Americans were not only quick to point out these contributions, but they extracted great joy from the many anecdotes that revolved around the theme of the naive Americans who, due to their own ignorance of the North, regularly called upon experienced Canadians for advice and assistance. Many members of Alberta's provincial government shared this view. According to General Foster:

> *It was rather amusing to find Mr. Aberhart's colleagues scandalized by the prodigality of the Americans both as regards governmental expenditures and as regards the propensity of the military and civilian personnel to spend wages as soon as they got them. This may be a natural reaction of a community whose standards are naturally rural, but it seems a little out of keeping with the political propaganda of Social Credit.*[50]

Nevertheless, these attitudes did not represent the majority opinion. As Harold Morrison, a former Canadian employee of the Americans put it, "there was some friction...but it was all blown out of proportion."[51]

Close cooperation between Canadians and Americans was the norm, but not at the expense of expediency. Although the Americans adopted a policy of employing as many Canadians as possible, partially to placate their hosts, at times their good will was stretched to the limit by shortages of manpower and supplies that extended deadlines beyond reasonable delays. To be fair, some of these delays were the fault of the US Army Engineers, and American regulations that required fingerprinting and medical examinations for all employees, even those provided through the Canadian Selective Service Board.[52] Of course this did not change the opinion of those who felt that Canadian sensibilities were less important than completing the projects as soon as possible, and these sentiments are apparent in some of General Foster's reports:

> *The feeling still exists in certain circles that U.S. contractors and labour should have been given the work in the Edmonton area. It is also reasonably apparent that due to delays in commencing the work...together with the present labour shortage, the contracts in the Edmonton area will not be completed within the time limit set by U.S. authorities.*[53]

On a social level, relations between Americans and Edmontonians seemed to be extremely cordial. US Consul General John Randolph kept a high profile in the community, visiting dignitaries such as the Premier, the Mayor, business, community and university leaders, and law enforcement officials, on a regular basis. Randolph also joined the Edmonton Club in order to keep in touch with civic leaders, and participated in a number of local social events, such as attendance at the opening night of Edmonton's Little Theatre production of *Dirty Work At The Crossroads*.[54] For the most part Edmontonians appeared willing to overlook what they viewed as American indiscretions. The American Ambassador to Ottawa, Pierrepont Moffat, expressed alarm at both what he viewed as a lack of discipline among US Army personnel, and the fact that few officers had made courtesy visits to Canadian civilian authorities. Edmonton's Mayor and Chief of Police brushed these concerns aside, arguing that what problems had arisen were insignificant, and that the behaviour of most servicemen had been exemplary. The Americans made a conscious effort to improve their image and fit into the community by supporting local businesses, activities, and causes, and those that brought their families with them enrolled their children in local schools. Senior officers took Moffat's message to heart and more than 100 US Army Engineers joined local politicians and business leaders at the annual banquet of the Alberta and Northwest Chamber of Mines and Resources, held in the Macdonald Hotel in January 1943, while others joined the local Shrine Club in reaching its fundraising goals.[55]

A.G. Shute, Edmonton's Chief of Police, stated that relations between Americans and the local population generally had been excellent, and problems encountered by law enforcement officials were usually the result of civilian wrong-doing. The Edmonton Police Force was decimated by resignations, from among those who left to serve overseas and those who took higher-paying jobs with the US military or contractors, and consequently it was ill-prepared to

Edmonton City Police and American Military Police, August 1943. The Edmonton Police Department was assisted by American MPs from 1942 to 1946. American MPs were authorized to investigate and arrest both Canadian and American military personnel and civilians.

Photo courtesy Provincial Archives of Alberta [PAA Bl. 625/1].

handle the increased workload. The Americans brought with them their own MPs [Military Police] who were given a great deal of latitude in enforcing military law as well as civil and criminal legislation. With the Edmonton Police Department desperately short of manpower, local authorities welcomed their assistance. US MPs soon were patrolling the streets of Edmonton with local officers, and in some cases on their own, and they were given the authority to detain Canadian civilians until the police arrived. Anne Coltman, whose father was a member of the Edmonton Police Force, and worked alongside the MPs as part of a coordinated patrol system, later confirmed that relations between Edmontonians and American servicemen were surprisingly cordial. It is very difficult to determine just how many serious violations were committed by US military personnel, as records are not easily accessible, and Canadian and American authorities were quick to "hush up" such transgressions so as not to raise concern among the local population.[56]

Anne Coltman describes how Americans went out of their way to maintain good relations with the residents of Edmonton. When a local trolley turned over on its side one night in downtown Edmonton, US Army personnel and employees of Bechtel Price Callahan cleared the road, despite the fact that it was bitterly cold.[57]

> *The real turning point in the way the Americans were thought of came during the winter of 1942. There was a big storm and they used their equipment to help clear the roads. They also helped transport emergency patients to the hospital. From that point on they were considered our friends and they were respected. Some stayed in town with families for the odd meal, although I don't think they were billeted here. They had Quonset huts over by the old Jesuit College and, eventually out at Namao.[58]*

Americans did not find it difficult to mix socially with Edmontonians, either "officially" and "unofficially."[59] Mrs. Shelah Davis later recalled that the most popular night spots for Americans included the former "Danceland Ballroom" on Jasper Avenue, Edmonton's main street, between 96th and 97th streets, the "Barn," which was on 102nd Street and Jasper, or any of the movie theatres that lined Jasper Avenue.[60] Social clubs, such as the Army, Navy and Air Force Club also counted many Americans among their membership.[61] In addition to these activities, parties and other social events were hosted and sponsored by the military, and by Edmonton's business sector and community organizations on a regular basis. The new relationships that were formed at these and other activities sometimes blossomed into lifetime friendships and even marriages. A fair number of Edmonton and Alberta women married American servicemen stationed throughout the northwest, and despite the fact that US officials frowned on this type of "fraternization," wedding announcements appeared regularly in the newspapers during this time.[62]

Amateur athletics provided another means by which Americans and Edmontonians could mingle. In additon to baseball at Renfrew ball park, located next to the Rossdale Power Station, a glance at the local sports pages reveals that the Edmonton Senior Basketball League listed the US Engineers, Air Transport Civilians and Bechtel, Price Callahan along with local teams such as Police, Varsity, Alcans, Latter Day Saints, and the YMCA.[63] The Edmonton Athletic Club even boasted a former member of the Green Bay Packers as their football coach. According to the *Edmonton Journal*:

> *Bill Starr, former fullback with the Green Bay Packers, famous*
> *United States Professional Football [sic] club, ... is helping*
> *coach the Edmonton Athletic Club in the Edmonton Junior*
> *Rugby Football League. Bill will be on the bench tonight when*

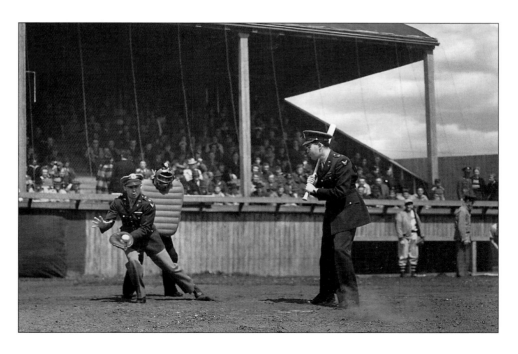

Victoria Day opening for a baseball series at Renfrew Park, 24 May 1943. Many celebrities passed through Edmonton during the war. Here World Heavyweight champion Joe Louis is seen at bat. The Americans participated regularly in community activities and sporting events.

Photo courtesy Provincial Archives of Alberta [PAA Bl. 542/1].

the E.A.C. go into action against No. 3 Manning Pool at Clarke Stadium...under the flood lights. He has provided the team with some razzle dazzle plays which, if they are properly executed, will guarantee trouble for the young airmen.[64]

Social and economic aspects of the American military presence in Edmonton between 1942 and 1945 were significant. Edmonton became the initial staging area for much of the defence-related construction activity carried out by the United States and Canada in the North West. The logistical facilities required by the United States created a much needed boost to Edmonton's economy, and the massive influx of military and civilian personnel provided a vital increase in morale to an already war-weary city. These construction projects provided employment, and prosperity for local retailers and suppliers. On a social level, United States servicemen and civilian workers quickly became part of the wartime fabric of the community. While friction between American soldiers and civilian contractors, and the people of Edmonton became apparent at times, most local residents welcomed the American "invasion."

NOTES

[1]Stanley W. Dzuiban, *Military Relations Between the United States and Canada, 1939-1945.* [Washington, D.C.: Office of the Chief of Military History, 1959], p. 199.

[2]Ibid.; National Archives of Canada [NAC] *Reports of the Special Commissioner for Defence Projects in North West Canada*, Record Group [RG] 36/7, Vol. 5, Nineteenth Report, Foster to Heeney, 1 February 1994.

[3]J.C. Arnell, "The Development of Joint North American Defence," *Queen's Quarterly*, Vol. 77, [Summer 1970], p. 198.

[4]William R. Willoughby, *The Joint Organizations of Canada and the United States.* [Toronto: University of Toronto Press, 1979], p. 104.

[5]*Maclean's Magazine*, 15 November 1939, p. 13; Hugh L. Keenleyside, *Memoirs of Hugh L. Keenleyside: On the Bridge of Time, Vol 2.* [Toronto: McClelland and Stewart, 1982], p. 69.

[6]Dzuiban, *op. cit.*, p. 383.

[7]Ibid.

[8]Ibid., p. 180; Keenleyside, *op. cit.*, p. 72, and; P.S. Barry, *The Canol Project: An Adventure of the U.S. War Department in Canada's Northwest*, unpublished manuscript, 1985, p. iv.

[9]Edwin R. Carr, *Great Falls to Nome: The Inland Air Route to Alaska, 1940-1945.* [Ph.D. Dissertation, University of Minnesota, 1946], pp. 14, 52; Dzuiban, *op. cit.*, p. 199.

[10]See map entitled "Northern Development During World War Two," in K.S. Coates and W.R. Morrison, *The Alaska Highway in World War II: The U.S. Army of Occupation in Canada's Northwest.* [Norman, Oklahoma: The University of Oklahoma, 1992], p. 39.

[11]*Edmonton Telephones Directory, 1943*; W. Evard Edmonds, *Edmonton Past and Present: A Brief History*, [Edmonton: Historical Society of Alberta, 1943], p. 21; *Edmonton Journal*, 12 January 1943, "Three Firms to Join Theatre Lease"; Coates and Morrison, op. cit., p. 160.

[12]NAC, *Special Commissioner's Report*, RG 36/7, Vol. 3, part 1, Correspondence, Foster to Heeney, 20 October 1943.

[13]Curtis R. Nordman, "The Army of Occupation: Malcolm MacDonald and the U.S. Military Involvement in the Canadian Northwest," pp. 83-94, in Kenneth Coates [ed], *The Alaska Highway Papers of the 40th Anniversary Symposium*, [Vancouver: University of British Columbia Press, 1985], p. 91.

[14]C.P. Stacey, *Arms, Men and Government: The War Policies of Canada, 1939-1945*, [Ottawa: Department of National Defence, 1970], pp. 386-387; NAC, *Special Commissioner's Report*, RG 36/7, Vol. 4, part 3, King to Manning, 10 July 1943.

[15]J.L. Granatstein, *Canada's War: The Politics of the Mackenzie King Government, 1939-1945*, [Toronto: Oxford University Press, 1975], pp. 322-323.

[16]Jack W. Pickersgill, ed., *The Mackenzie King Record, Volume I: 1939-1944*, [Toronto: University of Toronto Press, 1960], p. 436.

[17]Nordman, op. cit., pp. 84-85.

[18]Ibid., p. 100; Granatstein, op. cit., p. 323; Donald Creighton, *The Forked Road: Canada, 1939-1957*, [Toronto: McClelland and Stewart Limited, 1976], p. 73.

[19]NAC, *Special Commissioner's Report*, RG 36/7, vol 3, part 1, Correspondence, Foster to Heeney, 20 October 1943.

[20]NAC, *Mackenzie King Diaries*, 18 March 1942, p. 243.

[21]NAC, *Special Commissioner's Report*, RG 36/7, Vol. 3, part 1, Correspondence, Foster to Heeney, 20 October 1943; compare for example, Vol. 3, part 2A, Correspondence, Foster to Heeney, 31 July 1943 to Vol. 4, part 3, Correspondence, Foster to Heeney, 12 July 1945.

[22]*Edmonton Journal*, 8 January 1943. According to the Dominion Census of 1941, Edmonton's population was 93,817. It had grown to 103,000 by the beginning of 1943, an increase of 10,000, or more than ten per cent in ten years, and further growth was expected.

[23]Coates and Morrison, op. cit., p. 162; *Edmonton Journal*, 13 July 1943.

[24]*Edmonton Bulletin*, 16 November 1942.

[25]Coates and Morrison, op. cit., p. 162.

[26]*Special Commissioner's Report*, NAC, RG 36/7, Vol. 4, F. Thomas to the Deputy Minister, 3 November 1943.

[27]*United States Air Force Official History of the Air Transport Command, Alaskan Division*, [Washington, D.C.: 1952], p. 67.

[28]Ibid., pp. 67-68.

[29]*Edmonton Journal*, 13 January 1943.

[30]Ibid., 7 January 1943.

[31]Ibid., 13 January 1943; Coates and Morrison, op. cit., p. 161.

[32]*Edmonton Journal*, 28 December 1942.

[33]Ibid., 11 November 1943.

[34]Ibid., 21 June 1992.

[35]Edmonds, op. cit., p. 21.

[36]*Edmonton Journal*, 7 January 1943.

[37]Ibid., 8 and 11 January 1943.

[38]Edmonds, op. cit., p. 21.

[39]Provincial Archives of Alberta [PAA], Alberta Department of Public Works, *Annual Report, 1942-43*, p. 30.

[40]PAA *Premier's Papers*, A.J. Breitenstein, Secretary, Great Falls Chamber of Commerce to G.H.N. Monkman, 23 November 1942.

[41]Edmonton Public School Board Archives [EPSBA], Department of School Facilities, *Design and Construction Files 1940-1970*, acc. no. 85.227.237, Correspondence. L.C. Hubick to G.H. Luck, 20 October 1970.

[42]NAC, *Special Commissioner's Report*, RG 36/7, Vol. 4, Foster to Heeney, 31 October 1944.

[43]Interview with Mary Waldal, by Steven Boddington, 5 March 1987.

[44]Ibid., Shelah Davis, a former employee, recalled that the bus to the American Air Base "stopped in front of the Shasta Cafe on 99th Street and Jasper Avenue, just west of the Macdonald Hotel."

[45]*Debates*, House of Commons, 8 June 1942, Humphrey Mitchell, Minister of Labour, p. 3127, in answer to a question asked by Yukon MP George Black, 3 June 1942, pp. 3016-3017.

[46]*Edmonton Bulletin*, 2 February 1943, "4 Constables Quit Posts on Police Force."

[47]Interview with Harold Morrison, by Steven Boddington, 26 May 1992. Mr. Morrison worked for the Americans on the Namao and the Edmonton airport projects as a teenager.

[48]*Edmonton Journal*, 5 January 1943; and interview with Cal Pickles, by Steven Boddington, 17 December 1991.

[49]NAC, *Special Commissioner's Report*, RG 36/7, Vol. 4, part 3, Memorandum for Mr. Robertson from Foster. This was a communication sent by Foster shortly after his arrival in Edmonton entitled "Confidential Note of the General Impressions."

[50]Ibid.

[51]Interview with Harold Morrison, by Steven Boddington, 26 May 1992.

[52]NAC, *Special Commissioner's Report*, RG 36/7, Vol. 3, part 1, Foster to Heeney, 2 September 1943.

[53]Ibid.

[54]Coates and Morrison, op. cit., p. 163; and *Edmonton Journal*, 6 January 1943.

[55]Coates and Morrison, op. cit., pp. 163-164; *Edmonton Journal*, 8 January and 15 January 1943; NAC, *Mackenzie King Diaries*, Lucien Maynard, Alberta Attorney General to Prime Minister Mackenzie King, 14 September 1943.

[56]Coates and Morrison, op. cit., pp. 103-104, 165; *Edmonton Journal*, 21 June 1992; and interview with Shelah Davis, by Steven Boddington, 18 December 1991.

[57]*Edmonton Journal*, 15 January 1943.

[58]Interview with Anne Coltman, by Steven Boddington, 31 May 1991.

[59]The newspapers reported many of these functions. As well as being "newsworthy," they also served to foster good relations.

[60]Interview with Shelah Davis, by Steven Boddington, 18 December 1991.

[61]PAA, Alberta Liquor Control Board, *Inspector's Reports*, acc. no. 74.412, Box 5, "Army, Navy and Air Force Club (1940-1945)."

[62]See for example the *Edmonton Journal*, 31 October 1942, and 12 January 1943. See also the newspapers over the period February 1942 through 1946.

[63]*Edmonton Bulletin*, 13 January 1943.

[64]*Edmonton Journal*, 13 September 1942, "Giving E.A.C. New Football Plays."

Working For the Yankee Dollar in Edmonton During the War

Bob Oliphant

After studying art and design in Victoria, British Columbia from an early age, I went into business for myself during 1930. When George Sweeny came to Victoria in early 1936 and offered me a job in the Vancouver art department of Neon Products of Western Canada, I quickly accepted the opportunity.

Unfortunately, when I left for Vancouver as a young bachelor, at the beginning of March 1936, I took nothing with me other than a suitcase and my box of oil paints. When I got to Vancouver, I thought my life-long romance with poster design was a thing of the past, because for the next several months I spent every day designing neon displays. The temptress which had distracted me from "serious" art studies soon got hold of me again, as I was transferred to our outdoor billboard company to learn the details of the poster and bulletin business. My instructor was Reg Stevens, who was then famous all over North America for winning an unbelievable number of national and international awards for 24-sheet and bulletin designs.

Later I was transferred to Calgary to open an art department in Alberta, where we had not yet begun to market outdoor boards. I once again thought my poster designing days were over, for even though I did a lot of freelance work in my spare time, it consisted mostly of designing houses and a few apartments for contractors, or painting murals for various customers such as Canadian Pacific Railways.

Shortly after the start of the Second World War, and probably because of two or three of my own innovations, I got a letter from the Wartime Bureau of Technical Personnel, stating that my services would be required shortly, and instructing me to remain in place until summoned. While similar letters arrived every few months, actual orders to report anywhere never arrived. By the end of 1942 I was completely frustrated, as very few signs were being sold and I could not obtain a legal permit to work elsewhere.

After obtaining a leave of absence from the company, I went to Edmonton where, by showing some questionable documents and bribing a civil servant with two dozen golf balls, I obtained a permit that enabled me to get a job with Bechtel Price and Callaghan, one of the largest American firms working on the Alcan Highway project. Having been tipped off, I knew that the only way to avoid income-freezing interference by federal bureaucrats was to hire on as a tradesman, all of whom were obtaining hourly union wages for an 84-hour week. So I hired on as a house painter, though my only experience in that field was that I had once painted my mother's porch when I was a kid. However, it must have compared well with many of the guys from Utah and Texas, as I was promoted to Painter Foreman after two or three months.

Shortly after that promotion, the general superintendant mentioned that he was having trouble ordering a part from the machine shop because people there could not understand his sketches. Because I liked the guy, I made an isometric drawing of the part after work that night, and solved his problem for him. He asked if I could make plans for buildings, and when I told him I had done a few, he sent me into Edmonton to buy a drawing table with suitable instruments.

During the next few months I made drawings for numerous buildings including sleeping quarters, mess halls and nose hangars, which were to be built in sectional prefabricated form for shipping to the North. During those same months the Canadian Wartime Prices and Trade Board's beancounters discovered my name in payroll records and ordered that I be cut to a 48-hour shift, as I apparently was making too much for a Canadian. Each time that happened, the boss reclassified me to jobs such as "Glazer Foreman" or "Steam-shovel Operator Foreman," assuring me that it would be months before the nosey parkers might discover me under such classification.

Bechtel's contract was finished at the end of the year and everyone sent home, except for me. I got a little slip to state that I was terminated as of midnight 31 December, but was rehired by Metcalf Hamilton Kansas City Bridge Company at 12.01 AM, on New Year's Day. That firm had a sign shop in Edmonton which employed six or seven sign painters, one photographer and two carpenters. It also had the latest in silk screen equipment, and wanted an illustrator to design and produce patriotic and safety posters for both the firm itself and the Northwest Division of United States Engineers. How the heck they knew about me, I never found out; I certainly had never previously heard of them.

Safety posters produced for construction crews building the Alaska Highway.

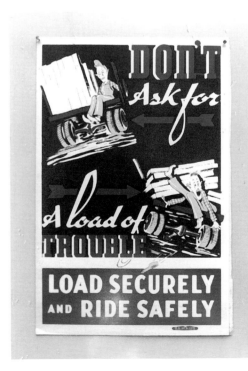 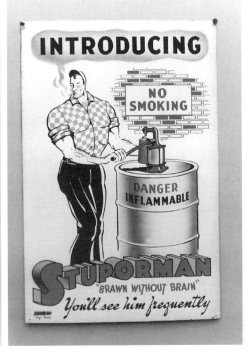

Posters courtesy Bob Oliphant.

Though that job continued at the same grueling 84-hour week, I spent one of the happiest years in a lifetime of work that was almost always so much fun that I couldn't wait to get to work in the morning. The first thing I was asked to do was design and produce 400 patriotic posters, to be distributed throughout the North where there was a heavy turnover of civilian workers who were homesick for Omaha or wherever. I borrowed some pictures from a nearby newspaper office and did a Victory Poster featuring the four world leaders who were still allies at that time.

From the time that first poster was finished, I was kept busy by both the company and government safety engineers, who watched all accident reports and would request a poster when some type of accident happened two or three times. Though we had the new Sensitone photo capability available, I did the large majority of my jobs by hand, cutting profilm and producing mostly flat-coloured posters. I did use the photo technique for a series of multi-panel funny papers that evolved from the character "Stuperman" used in a couple of hand cut jobs. I used the same technique to produce 1200 runs of monthly menu covers for the company's northern mess halls.

Patriotic poster produced by Bob Oliphant for Bechtel Price and Callaghan.

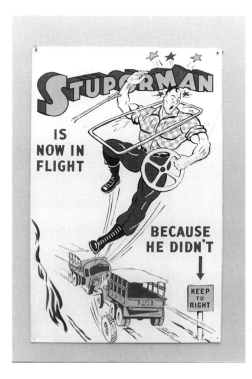

"Stuporman" strips designed to promote safety awareness among northern workers on Alaska Highway.

Posters courtesy Bob Oliphant.

Stuporman is cautioned to keep his mind on his work.

The Metcalf Hamilton Kansas City Bridge project in Edmonton wound up around the end of 1944, and I was again transferred without being consulted, to the Calder base of the Northwest Division, United States Engineers, under Brigadier General L.D. Worsham, though I reported to a Major Riley.

I never found out why they wanted me, as in the three or four months I was there I designed absolutely nothing, painted a few signs on wood for bathrooms or parking areas, and enjoyed only one fascinating experience. General Worsham's gorgeous secretary came into my shop one day, announced that they were having an officers' dance and asked if I could paint realistic, staight seams on the backs of her painted legs. Once more, inventiveness rather than art work was required. Stealing a technique from the carpenters, I darkened some of her leg paint, soaked a piece of twine in it, then shyly suggesting that she hold the top of the cord, I held the bottom end on her achilles tendon and used it like a snap line. The results were incredible; not only were the seams absolutely straight, but the twist in the twine sort of dotted the lines like stitches.

Unfortunately, that secretary was a blabbermouth and I had a parade of girls through my shop all afternoon, requesting my services (an unfortunate choice of words, but it does have a dreamlike quality). Soon after a well-known Hollywood

Some posters appealed to the patriotism of American workers on the Northern Wartime Projects.

Posters courtesy Bob Oliphant.

star and her entourage, imported by Uncle Sam to entertain the troops, entered my shop requesting a paint job. Any hope that I might have been rewarded for my efforts was completely frustrated by the fact that half the U S Army was gawking through my windows throughout the exercise.

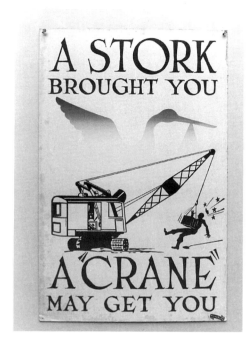

The dangers of the construction camps threatened vital wartime manpower.

Posters courtesy Bob Oliphant.

A couple of days after that memorable experience, I was called to Major Riley's office, to be told by that worthy that the Canadian beancounters had again located me, and had ordered that my hourly pay be cut and my week reduced from 84 to 48 hours. When I told him I would quit, Riley replied: "You cannot do that; your Queen, or somebody, has passed a law that Canadians may not leave a war job without giving two weeks notice." I told him to tell the Queen, or whoever, that the much older laws of equity would also require that the same Canadian be given two weeks notice of any change in remuneration.

While he was digesting that suggestion, I went to the payroll shack, told them I had been terminated, without telling them I had done the terminating, collected my money and left. My family and I took the train to Vancouver the next day.

The Japanese Balloon Bomb Assault on North America: An Alberta Perspective

N. Frank Chiovelli

Japan's surprise attack on Pearl Harbor early on the Sunday morning of 7 December 1941 shocked the world and drew the United States of America into the Second World War. Simultaneous attacks arcing across the Pacific Ocean through Midway, Guam, Wake Island, Hong Kong, the Philippines, Malaya and Thailand soon resulted in victory over this huge area by Japan's armed forces. Coupled with huge losses meted out by Nazi Germany and her Axis partners in Europe and North Africa, the population of the Allied countries was thunderstruck. The series of military defeats on all fronts was a serious blow to their morale; an Allied military success was needed quickly to restore confidence.

The United States Navy and the US Army Air Force cooperated in training a squadron of B-25 bomber crews to fly from aircraft carriers. This squadron was put aboard the USS Hornet and sailed for the South Pacific. Off the coast of Japan, being discovered by Japanese picket boats, the Hornet launched her B-25s under the command of Lieutenant Colonel James A. Doolittle on 8 April 1942, successfully carrying out the first air raid on the Japanese home islands. News of this air raid immediately raised morale throughout all of the Allied nations.

Shock reverberated throughout Japan. The Imperial Japanese Navy understood the severe threat to their supply lines caused by the Doolittle Raid and sought out the US Fleet. This action ultimately led to the pivotal battle of Midway. When the US Fleet won the Battle of Midway it began a chain of military reversals that led to the final defeat of Japan on 14 August 1945, and the formal surrender on 2 September 1945.[1]

The Japanese military were forced to seek alternative ways to bolster the morale of its civilian population. It did not have long-range bombers that were capable of reaching the continental United States. Aircraft that could make such a one-way flight were still on the drawing board. The 9th Military Technical Research Institute [MTRI], after conferring with meteorologist Mr. H. Arakawa, decided that using balloons to mount a bombing attack on the North American continent could accomplish its goal and provide an immediate face-saving opportunity for the military. Arakawa had access to wind current information from civilian forecasting agencies, and from balloon experiments initiated in 1933 by the 9th MTRI [Tokyo], and the infamous Unit 731 in Manchuko [Manchuria]. Established during the Sino-Japanese War, Unit 731 had carried out medical experiments using imprisoned civilians and POWs as guinea pigs. This unit also had conducted experiments using balloons as delivery vehicles for biological warfare agents, and even as a possible method of transporting foot soldiers behind Chinese lines. Balloons used by both establishments were small, having a diameter of 4 metres [13.1 feet], and were designed to fly at a constant altitude for a distance of about seventy miles. Timing fuses were designed to release the bomb loads. However, work on these projects was never completed, and they were stopped in 1935.[2]

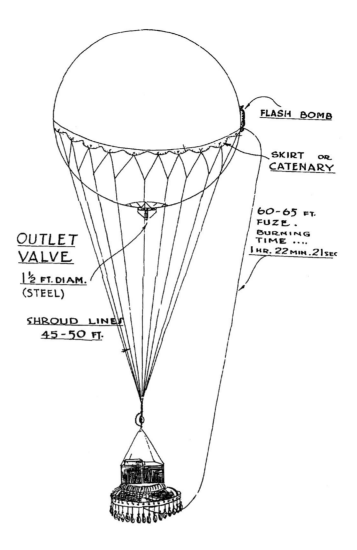

FLASH BOMB

SKIRT OR CATENARY

60-65 FT. FUZE. BURNING TIME .... 1 HR. 22 MIN. 21 SEC

OUTLET VALVE
1½ FT. DIAM. (STEEL)

SHROUD LINES
45-50 FT.

Diagram of balloon bomb.

Illustration taken from Pacific Coast Militia Rangers Instruction Chart.

Japan trained an elite parachute force at this time, and the tactical advantage of that fighting unit far outweighed the helter-skelter performance of balloons. Low-altitude balloon experiments for propaganda leaflet drops or the transport of infantry soldiers remained in progress, but were transferred back to the 9th MTRI in Tokyo. The degree of importance given to this research is difficult to determine, although after the Doolittle Raid it was given higher priority. Balloon size was increased to six metres [19.6 feet] in diameter, which also increased its range. Two submarines, I-34 and I-35, had modifications made to their hatches to facilitate the launch of these new balloons off of the west coast of North America. This would never happen, as both subs were reassigned to the Guadalcanal operation. The new six-metre balloons had a range of about three thousand kilometres and could remain airborne for thirty hours at an altitude of 26,200 feet.[3]

When the Japanese Army took full control of the project it meant that launches would have to be made from the home islands. The balloon diameter was increased further to ten metres [32.8 feet], while instrumentation was developed to work at higher altitudes and bomb payloads were recalculated. The 5th Army Technical Research Institute developed a high-altitude battery and instrumentation that allowed test units to be tracked as far as 130 degrees west longitude. Project engineers were exuberant over the trial results and decided to go ahead with offensive operations, choosing the period of November 1944 to March 1945 for their launch envelope.

The Imperial Navy started a balloon programme that paralleled the Army's in 1942, using a rubberized silk fabric for their envelopes. Known as the "Internal Pressure Type," the production model had a gas-release valve that would vent hydrogen when it reached a pressure of 50mm Hg [by mercury barometer]. The valve system allowed this model to fly at a steady altitude. Brought into the

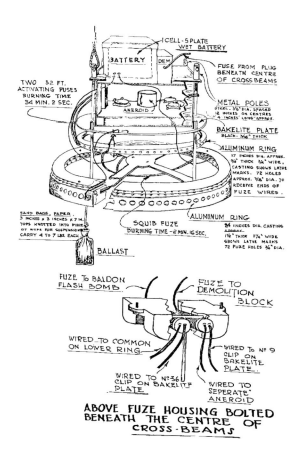

Diagram of bomb component of balloon bomb.

Illustration taken from Pacific Coast Militia Rangers Instruction Chart.

RELEASE ARRANGEMENT.

Army programme as Balloon Type B, it was noted that the payload of the rubberized silk envelope was less than that of the paper balloons. Therefore the Type B was employed to carry radio-tracking transmitters, one being launched with each group of bomb-carrying paper balloons. When it was decided that development had progressed to the point that the Balloon Offensive could begin, contracts were let out for the production of 10,000 balloons to be ready for the November-March period of 1944-1945.[4]

The production models which carried armaments were characterized by spherical 33-foot diameter paper envelopes. A rope-reinforced catenary curtain horizontally surrounded the envelope slightly below its midsection. Nineteen suspension lines 45 feet in length were attached to the catenary curtain. These lines were then loop-spliced through a steel load-ring which was slung vertically. Attached to the load ring were four double ropes that were eye-spliced through cap nuts on top of the gondola, or "chandelier." A rubber shock-cord was installed between the load-ring and a point where the double ropes attached to the chandelier forming a pyramid. The base of the envelope had a small appendix used to fill the balloon with hydrogen gas, and to carry the gas-relief valve. This valve was set to bleed excess pressure of expanded hydrogen when a force of approximately one-half ounce per square inch was exerted, a force well below the bursting strength of the paper.[5]

Japanese balloon bomb "chandelier."

Photo courtesy Government History collection, Provincial Museum of Alberta.

The chandelier itself consisted of two aluminum rings held, one above the other, by four pillar-bolts mounted on a cross-brace attached to the inside of the larger lower ring. The large ring had 72 holes drilled into its horizontal edge, which were numbered in pairs 1 through 36. The bottom face of the ring had a thin channel cut through the entire circumference with a depth surpassing the horizontal holes. Rectangular suspension links with one hole drilled on each end were placed into the channel, and pinned in place by inserting explosive blow-plugs through the horizontal holes. "S" hooks were then used to sling ballast bags or bombs from the suspension links.

The small ring had holes drilled horizontally, and these also were numbered in pairs from 1 through 36. These holes contained spring switches which were connected to matching pairs of blow-plugs in the lower ring by a safety fuse. Centred over the small ring, and attached by the pillar-bolts, was a bakelite disc with a rotating contact-switch which was controlled by four aeronoid barometers mounted in the false bottom of a wooden box. Attached to the top of the box was a celluloid container with a waterproof compartment containing a battery. Surrounding that was a space to contain water that served as a solar-heating device, which enabled the battery to function at the low temperatures encountered at high altitudes.

Two 33-foot safety fuses were wound around the wooden box and connected to blow-out plugs in position on the small ring. These fuses were ignited by friction igniters when the balloons were launched. Burning for about three-quarters of an hour, they gave the balloon time to gain altitude. At this time the blow-out plugs were fired, releasing a spring-switch which in turn activated an automatic-switching device.

Set to fly at an altitude of 30,000 feet, the balloon vented gas during the warm daylight hours. During the cooler night hours when losing altitude, the barometers would fire the blow-plugs, in turn dropping the ballast bags,

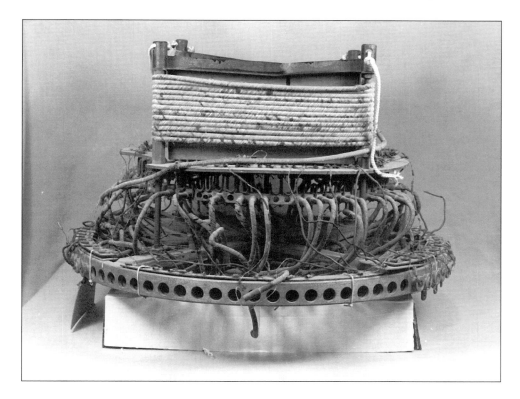

Japanese balloon bomb assembly from Canadian War Museum.

Photo courtesy Government History collection, Provincial Museum of Alberta.

providing lift to a now lighter craft. Calculated to give an estimated flight time of between three and five days, bomb loads were sequenced to drop near the end of the estimated flight paths.

Two "self destruct" charges were attached to many of the balloons. One of these was placed in a pocket near the catenary curtain. Sixty feet of fuse connected this charge to a casting attached to the cross-brace in the large ring. A T-hook in that casting was held in place by two blow-plugs; generally a 32-kilogram high-explosive bomb was slung on this hook. When this bomb was dropped, the blow-plugs were designed to ignite the fuse leading to the envelope charge. A burn time of about one hour was required for this. When the envelope was destroyed, the automatic switches on the chandelier would then close as the mass dropped to 15,000 feet, setting off the second charge which was placed beside the battery box.[6]

Hardware and instruments for the balloon bombs were manufactured in Japanese factories. The paper balloon envelopes were made in large theatres and sumo wrestling halls, which allowed assembly and inflation-testing of the finished product on-site. Construction of the balloon envelopes was a labour-intensive operation in which large numbers of high school students were employed.[7]

As the manufacture of balloons started, a new Army unit designated the "Special Balloon Regiment" was created. Comprised of three battalions, it was commanded by Colonel Inone. This regiment was to select and prepare three bases suitable as launch sites, to coordinate radio tracking duties with the Army Weather Bureau, to set up gas-production facilities, and to train its personnel for launch duties.

When this project had reached its final stages, the Japanese government began to publicize the effort in an attempt to stiffen public support for the war. However, the military took great pains to erase any markings that could identify the balloon equipment as Japanese. There does not appear to have been any attempt to remove markings from the bomb load. This probably was a deliberate ploy to confuse victims and investigators regarding the means by which attacks were carried out. Of course this would be valid only if the self-destruct devices functioned as planned, which in fact they did not.[8]

After the attack on Pearl Harbor, the Canadian and US governments put together a joint defence plan using knowledge acquired from British and Canadian experience in the defence of the British Isles. Factored into these plans was secret work on chemical and bacteriological warfare that Canada and Britain had been conducting since the First World War. A defence strategy was put in place, based upon the premise that "if we have it - they have it." Directives to top-level officers and civilian personnel outlined military and civil defence measures, and imposed censorship regulations for the media. The entire North American west coast was prepared for an air attack from carrier-borne air raids.

Preparations were made to defend the population against chemical or bacteriological attacks. Protection of the huge timber stands along the Pacific Coast was a major concern and was singled out as a priority item.[9]

T.F. Blefgen, Director of Forestry for the Province of Alberta, stated in a memorandum of 20 April 1942:

> *In connection with the fast approaching fire season and its relation to the entry of the Japanese into the world war, it is noted that the Forestry Branch of our neighboring Province to the West is extremely apprehensive of the possibility of "calling cards" in the form of inflammable leaflets being dropped in some of the west coast forests, and have warned their personnel to be on the lookout for any eventuality along these lines.*

Blefgen went on to describe a raid of this type carried out by the RAF over the Black Forest in Germany, using small incendiary bombs, during the summer of 1941. He further stated that if such a campaign were initiated, a possible danger zone lay in the area of northern British Columbia and along the corridor of the Alaska Highway.[10]

The vulnerability of the northern forests during a time of increased wartime air traffic was underlined in the preamble to The New Prairie and Forest Fire Act given assent on 8 April 1941:

> *A great number of aircraft flying in the northern part of the province was, perhaps, the cause of at least some of the fires fought in outlying districts. Of nine fires that occurred in the Athabasca Valley, north and west of Whitecourt, seven were directly on the beam used between Edmonton and Fort St. John, B.C., and two of these were only a short distance on either side. Whilst being unable to definitely state that the fires referred to were caused by lighted cigars or cigarette butts being thrown from planes, a thorough investigation into all other possible causes was made and the conclusion was therefore arrived at that these fires were caused in this manner. It is definitely known that a large percentage of lighted cigars or cigarette butts dropped from as high as 6000 feet are capable of starting fires....*[11]

Another factor in the defensive measures being developed at this time was the "Free Balloon Barrage" [FBB], an anti-aircraft defence system put forward by a Commander Fraser RN, a member of the Boom Defence Organization. The Royal Navy Department of Miscellaneous Weapon Development [DMWD], headed by Captain G.O.C. Davies RN, was quick to assign Canadian-born Commander Charles Goodeve RNVR to implement the idea. He in turn arranged for Commander F.D. Richardson RNVR to head the development team.

The Free Balloon Barrage, as Fraser envisioned it, would consist of large groups of individual rubber balloons launched in the flight path of incoming enemy aircraft. Designed to operate at altitudes of 14,000 to 18,000 feet, each balloon would carry an explosive device suspended from it, and hanging below that would be a 2000-foot length of thin piano wire with a parachute attached to its free flowing end. An aircraft coming into contact with the wire would create drag, thus deploying the parachute. This in turn would cause the wire to pull the bomb onto the surface of the aircraft. A spring-type pressure-plate surrounding the bomb casing then would be tilted, setting off the powerful explosive. Enemy aircraft were destroyed or damaged by this system, and their pilots did have concern when over British targets.

The FBB was assigned to the RAF Balloon Barrage Organization for operational deployment, while the DMWD continued to improve the system until it reached a dependability factor of 80 per cent. However, in early 1941 large bombing raids over Britain ceased and the system was withdrawn from service. While employed the FBB System was treated as Top Secret, and only people directly involved were given instruction as to how it worked. The general public were not told of it, but merely asked to stay away from any suspicious objects with which they came in contact and to inform the authorities immediately.[12]

These developments parallel defence planning in Canada and the United States from 7 December 1941 until the end of the war. Instructions were given to top-level officials warning of air raids, troop landings, and naval attack; all of these were considered capable of employing high-explosive, incendiary, or chemical warfare agents.[13]

Canada and the United States were generally in complete harmony on defensive and security measures. Both worked hard to deny the Japanese any knowledge of the effects of enemy activities, and at the same time to prevent alarm among the civilian population. This was effectively accomplished when the press and radio of both countries voluntarily observed a complete blackout on matters relating to the balloon offensive.[14]

However, this purely negative form of security measure failed to promote public safety or popular co-operation with the authorities. It was perhaps inevitable that Col. J.H. Jenkins, OBE, ED, with the Directorate of Military Operations and Planning, would have incidents such as the following to report:

> *Experience with the Minton [Saskatchewan] incident [which involved an unexploded 15-kg bomb and two incendiary devices recovered on 12 January 1945]; and the recent Alberta incident [near Rocky Mountain House, Alberta] where boys used a red hot poker to unsolder connections from the brass demolition charge attached to the instrument pack, indicates the advisability of discreet publicity. The O.C. [Officer Commanding] K - Division R.C.M.P... considers it essential for the proper*

detection and collection of balloon material that the general
public be put in the picture.[15]

This legitimate and practical concern led to the practice of informing people on a "need-to-know" basis. Some rural Postmasters, ranchers, trappers and Hudson's Bay Company trading-post factors were asked to assist in passing along word of sightings and findings.[16]

The military already had formed the Interservice Bomb Disposal Unit [IBDU] commanded by Lt. Cdr. E.L. Borradaile RCNVR, with headquarters in Ottawa. Members of this unit attended a special course conducted at A-5 Canadian Engineer Training Centre at Camp Petawawa, near Pembroke, Ontario, prior to being posted to bases near likely balloon-intercept zones in western Canada.

Military District No. 13, headquartered at Calgary, Alberta, had a detachment of four who maintained and operated two sets of bomb disposal equipment. They were Lieutenants B.G. Day and R.H. Neame, and Sergeants G.A. Hart and A.W.H. Ivens. Their area of responsibility was the province of Alberta and the District of MacKenzie. They were to be kept busy with twenty definite balloon bomb recoveries in Alberta and four in the District of MacKenzie, both during the war and shortly thereafter.[17]

It was critical to defence planners to recover and analyze the characteristics of this weapon delivery system. Radar and Radio Detection Systems would enable the Royal Canadian Air Force to intercept and destroy incoming balloons while still over the Pacific, or away from populated areas when over land. Analysis of sand in the ballast bags would help identify probable launch sites and render them vulnerable to air attack. At the time the fear that Japan might attempt to use these craft to spread chemical or bacteriological warfare agents was very strong. Therefore scientists and B/D crew carried out routine tests to determine if this was indeed happening.[18]

An example of problems that could arise from an overly strict security programme occurred when a balloon came down about five miles north of Delburne, Alberta on the evening of 20 March 1945. Souvenir hunters removed most of the debris before the RCMP arrived. This made it difficult to determine if the envelope self-destruct charge had in fact functioned.[19]

Retired RCMP Staff Sergeant Ed E. Buchanan, now living in Edmonton, recalled that while he was stationed in Lethbridge during the war he coordinated the recovery of a few balloons. The lack of knowledge by the general population and the need for security led to several close calls, endangering life and limb in Alberta locations. Mr. Buchanan cannot now recall the date; however, one day about noon a Japanese balloon flew over the centre of Lethbridge, and Red Flight, two Mosquito Bombers stationed at the local airport on intercept duties, were scrambled. The eager pilots took off at high speed in a shallow climb that rattled windows and shook many houses in their flight path. A local grocer, startled by the noise and vibrations, lost his temper as he watched his goods shaken off their shelves and onto the floor. Having demonstrated to the citizens of Lethbridge that they had the best air force squadron in the Dominion, the two pilots gained altitude and pursued the balloon to an open range between Turin and Vauxhall where they shot it down. Mr. Buchanan, having seen the balloon with the aircraft in pursuit, gauged the direction of its flight and notified Constable Simbalist at Picture Butte to track the balloon and render any assistance required.

About late February or early March, 1945 a balloon came down in a field of grazing cattle. The rancher living nearby heard the cattle bawling, went to investigate and saw a few cows tangled in the rigging of what he thought was a weather balloon. Working quickly, he freed the cows and draped the balloon and lines over the nearest fence. He then removed what he assumed was a recording

Locations of recoveries of balloon bombs in Alberta.

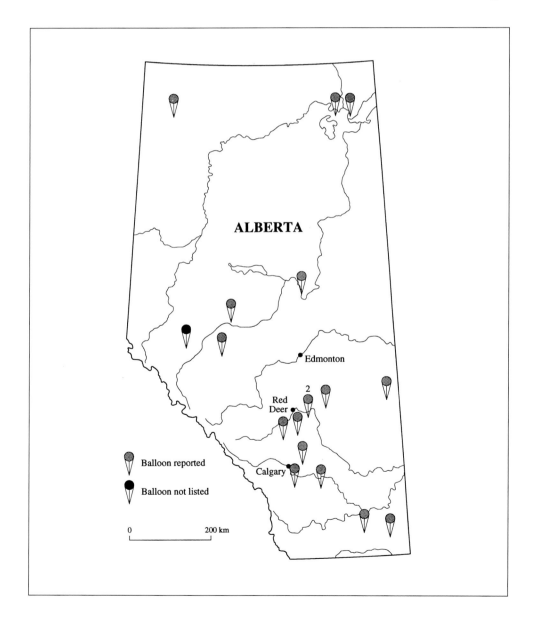

device and threw it in the tool box of his truck. A week or two later while in Foremost shopping he paid a visit to the local RCMP Detachment. Storming into Cpl. John Wilson's office, he banged the brass box down on Wilson's desk, telling Wilson what he and the Weather Office could do with their scientific apparatus. After finishing his flowery list of instructions the rancher then left. A somewhat confused Wilson phoned S/Sgt Buchanan at Lethbridge with a description of the brass box and requested instructions. Buchanan very diplomatically informed Wilson that he was holding a demolition charge which, if it exploded, probably would level the detachment office. Buchanan also observed, with tongue in cheek, that it might also damage the phone. He asked Wilson to put the box in a secure place until the B/D team could remove it. Buchanan and the B/D Team arrived shortly and placed the demolition charge in their bomb-disposal trailer, then with Wilson paid the rancher a visit to recover the balloon. This recovery was recorded

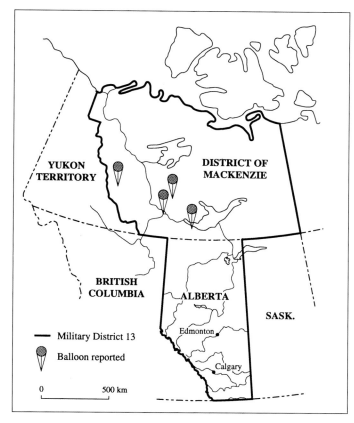

Locations of balloon bomb recoveries in the District of Mackenzie.

as Foremost 20 March 1945. While there were no bombs attached to this balloon, about two weeks prior to the Foremost incident a sheep herder moving his flock to a new location heard a loud explosion around noon. Returning to his shack that evening he was startled to find it demolished. Mr. Buchanan believes that the explosion and destruction of the sheep herder's line cabin were caused by a high-explosive bomb dropped by the balloon recovered at Foremost.[20]

Eric Huestis, Alberta's Acting Director of Forestry in 1945, recalled that during the war there were only seven full-time Forest Rangers to patrol the entire province. Nonetheless, when the balloon attacks started his department gave whatever assistance that was requested by the military. Rangers helped when a balloon landed outside Edson on 11 March 1945. Shortly thereafter, when a summer camp was being set up in the Jarvis Creek area near Hinton, the Forestry Crew were surprised to find that a balloon had landed in the creek valley. Mr. Huestis was informed that after the war his department could dispose of any balloon-related material in their possession. A disarmed high-explosive bomb was put on display in the Edson Forestry Office and remained there for some years. Between three and five chandeliers from balloons that landed in the Edson-Coal Branch area were taken to the dump.[21]

The last balloons were launched on 20 April 1945. The Japanese stated that this was due to erratic wind conditions, although it would seem more likely that the effects of Allied bombing raids on factories and launch sites made it a wiser choice to devote war materials to more conventional uses.[22]

During the entire campaign the total production of about 9300 balloons was launched. However, only six fatalities were caused by the balloon bomb offensive. A woman and five children detonated a bomb while dragging a balloon out of a treed area near Bly, Oregon on 5 May 1945. Another near-disaster was averted when the fail-safe mechanism kicked in at the Hanford Engineering Works during a power outage on 10 May 1945. A Japanese balloon, flying low over the Yakima Valley, shorted power lines of the Bonneville generating station. Interestingly, this was the power source for the Hanford plant which was manufacturing heavy water for the Manhattan Project. The production of atomic bombs for use against Japan was delayed a few weeks because of this.[23]

Since the balloon bomb offensive against North America was carried out in the winter and spring months, snow and an extremely wet spring prevented the anticipated severe fire damage.[24] Specialized personnel were trained to defend against this new weapon. However in the main both military and civilian establishments simply added one more chore to their duties. Thus the Japanese failed to drain vast amounts of manpower from the war front, as they had hoped, or for that matter to disrupt the flow of material to the Allied war effort. In fact shortages of food and material in Japan itself resulted in the employment of extra manpower to watch the students assembling the balloons, as they had to be prevented from eating the vegetable-based glue being used on this project. This anticlimactic situation coupled with other more telling reversals soon led to the Japanese surrender.[25]

At the war's end it was estimated by some that there might have been as many as 1000 undetected balloons or bombs in remote areas of North America. In fact some have been found as recently as 1972. Many without a doubt have caused forest fires by self-detonation, or when triggered by animals which may have been trying to eat the rotting mulberry paper. Many balloons or their payloads also must have been destroyed by forest fires caused by other natural means such as lightning strikes.[26]

During the months following the Japanese attack on the US Fleet at Pearl Harbor, fear and concern regarding the vulnerability of the North American continent to enemy attack grew to a peak. By mid-1942 this virtual hysteria had abated on the home front, where most Albertans simply got on with the business of supporting the war effort. Many of the rumours regarding saboteurs, fifth columnists, and even the feared Japanese attack on the continental mainland which appeared to have been heralded by the brief invasions of the Aleutian Islands, were no longer a concern. The irony is that at the end of the war, when most Albertans felt most confident, the most dangerous and direct assault did occur. Even more ironic is the fact that few knew about the balloon bombs which were sometimes landing near their communities. Due to wartime media blackouts, it would be decades before the facts of the Japanese balloon bomb assault would begin to come to the attention of Albertans, for whom the war was an increasingly distant memory.

NOTES

[1]For an account of the Doolittle Raid, see Carroll V. Glines, *The Doolittle Raid* [New York: Orion Books, 1988].

[2]Robert C. Mikesh, *Japan's World War II Bomb Attacks on North America* [Washington: Smithsonian Institute Press, 1973; Number 9 Smithsonian Annals of Flight]; Peter Williams and David Wallace, *Unit 731* [Hodder and Stoughton, 1989].

[3]Robert C. Mikesh, op. cit.

[4]Ibid.

[5]R.W. McKay, "Japanese Paper Balloons," *The Engineering Journal*, September 1945. McKay prepared this article for the Canadian Army Operational Research Group, Department of National Defence.

[6]Ibid.; most of the technical information regarding the balloon bombs is taken from the McKay article.

[7]Robert C. Mikesh, op. cit.

[8]Ibid.; Mikesh provides an excellent historical overview of the development of the balloon bomb campaign.

[9]John Bryden, *Deadly Allies Canada's Secret War 1937-1947* [McClelland & Stewart, 1988].

[10]T.F. Blefgen, Director of Forestry, Province of Alberta, Memorandum dated: 20 April 1942; papers and other information regarding wartime forestry concerns were provided to the author by Peter J. Murphy, Associate Dean of Forestry, Faculty of Agriculture and Forestry, University of Alberta, on 21 August 1984.

[11]Alberta, *The Prairie and Forest Fire Act, 8 April 1941*; Peter J. Murphy materials.

[12]The history of the Free Balloon Barrage, and the Royal Navy Department of Miscellaneous Weapon Development, are described in Gerald Pawle, *Secret Weapons of World War II* [Ballantine Books, 1968]. See especially pp. 23, 122-123, 132-134.

[13]Canadian Army Headquarters, Historical Section [GS], Report No. 28, 15 October 1949.

[14]Ibid.; Canadian Army Headquarters, Historical Section, Press Note 1-0-9-2, 8 February 1946, p.7.

[15]Canadian Army Headquarters, Historical Section, op. cit.; C.P. Stacey, *Six War Years The Army in Canada, Britain, and The Pacific* [Ottawa: Queens Printer, Department of National Defence, 1955].

[16]Canadian Army Headquarters, Historical Section, op. cit.

[17]National Defence Headquarters, General Staff Directorate of Military Operations and Planning, *General Summary Japanese Balloons in Canada, 15 March 1945*. This report provides the best account of the Interservice Bomb Disposal Unit.

[18]Ibid.; also see HQ 11th US Air Force, Report No. 46 Re: 13 BALLOONS SIGHTED. This report of radar and radio signal statistics is not dated.

[19]National Defence Headquarters, General Staff Directorate of Military Operations and Planning, op. cit.

[20]Ed E. Buchanan, Interview with author, October 1994; this interview provided a unique opportunity to research previously unknown details of the balloon bomb recoveries in southern Alberta.

[21]Eric Huestis, Interview with the author, April 1984.

[22]Canadian Army Headquarters, Historical Section, op. cit.

[23]Robert C. Mikesh, op. cit.; Randall A. Johnson, "Japanese Balloons Bombed West," *The Pacific Northwesterner*, Vol. 20, No. 3 [Summer 1976]; Carmine A. Prioli, Banzai Balloons a Bust," *American Heritage*.

[24]Weather Records: Edmonton Municipal A [3012208] January-December, 1944, January-December, 1945; Rocky Mountain House [3015530] January-December, 1944, January - December, 1945; Kelowna BC [1123930] 1944-1945; Vancouver International A [1108447] 1944-1945; Prince Rupert BC [1066480] 1944-1945; Prince George BC A [1096450] 1944-1945; Victoria International A [1018620] 1944-1945.

[25]Randall A. Johnson, op. cit.; the following sources also provide useful information: HQS 8872-2 Vol 4 [Oprs 206-0], Restricted Extracts From A Preliminary Report Of A U.S. Army Field Organization Concerning Japanese Balloons, 15 November, 1945; Restricted Copy, General Headquarters United States Army Forces, Pacific Scientific and Technical Advisory Section, Scientific and Technical Advisory Section, 25 September 1945; Text of Joint Army and Navy Press Release Re: Japanese Balloons Fm. Bissell AD G-2, Washington DC To: Military Attache, American Embassy, Ottawa, Canada.

The author wishes to thank the following people who aided in the preparation of this paper: Robert C. Mikesh, Curator of Aircraft, Aeronautics, National Air and Space Museum, Smithsonian Institution, Washington, DC; Peter J. Murphy, Associate Dean-Forestry, Faculty of Agriculture and Forestry, University of Alberta; D.E. Adderly, Manager, Public Affairs, Ministry of Forests and Lands, Province of British Columbia; Lt S. Brown, CFB Dockyard, Victoria, BC; William Beahen, RCMP Staff Historian, Ottawa; Eric Huestis, former Deputy Minister of Forestry, Province of Alberta; and especially RCMP S/Sgt Ed Buchanan [Retired]. Also Stefano Chiovelli and Bill Galloway for their assistance.

The Northwest Staging Route: A Story of Canadian-American Wartime Co-operation

Carl A. Christie

One of Canada's lesser known contributions to the war effort came in the form of a string of airfields in the northwestern part of North America, stretching from the United States to Alaska through Alberta, northern British Columbia, and the Yukon Territory. Many people know something about the Alaska Highway; few have heard of the Northwest Staging Route, developed during the war as an airway over which military aircraft and supplies could be sent to Alaska. In fact, the Canada-United States Permanent Joint Board on Defence [PJBD], when it proposed the ground route, simply called for a road to link the airfields between Alberta and Alaska.[1]

Early in the war, as the Japanese threat in the Pacific intensified, the officially neutral US military gained free use of the Northwest Staging Route from Edmonton to Fairbanks, Alaska, an air distance of about 1700 miles, or 2210 miles overall between the two US terminal bases at Great Falls, Montana and Anchorage, Alaska.[2] The principal staging points were Grande Prairie, Alberta; Fort St. John and Fort Nelson in British Columbia; and Watson Lake and Whitehorse in the Yukon. Intermediate landing strips were located at Dawson Creek, Beatton River and Smith River, British Columbia, and Teslin, Aishihik, and Snag in the Yukon Territory.[3]

The history of the Northwest Staging Route dates from pioneering flights by bush pilots, surveys undertaken by the Canadian Department of Transport in 1935, and the start of aviation modernization before the war. However, by 1940 it was still little more than a string of primitive landing strips usable only in daylight and good weather. In November 1940 the PJBD recommended that the plans to improve the route be enlarged to accommodate American needs and pushed forward as quickly as possible.[4] The United States agreed to pay for all facilities required beyond those planned by the Canadian government.

While American interest in the route as a strategic air connection with Alaska predated the war, little use was made of it until just before the Japanese attack on Pearl Harbor. As tensions increased in 1941, even before the United States entered the war, the United States Army Air Corps checked out the route and stored gasoline at the various airfields in case it had to be used as an emergency supply route to Alaska. In September 1941, J.A. Wilson, Director of Air Services with the Department of Transport in Ottawa and one of the key figures in the development of aviation in Canada, toured the route and reported, perhaps a trifle optimistically, that the airway would be in full operation, complete with radio ranges, and able to handle any type of aircraft in a few weeks. As the work progressed, a small American presence was built up around Alberta airfields that served as links in the chain connecting Montana and Alaska. Those who arrived from south of the 49th parallel viewed Alberta as a virtual frontier; those who came from the North reportedly found the provincial capital a real treat. One group of airmen from Alaska toured facilities on the route and were "quite excited at getting into civilization again even for a short time," when they reached Edmonton.[5]

After 7 December 1941, work was pushed ahead with renewed vigour, amidst fears that the Japanese had designs on Alaska. Despite the accelerated pace of construction, the principal user, the United States Army Air Forces [as the Air Corps was renamed in June 1941], found the route unsuitable for the volume of air traffic following Pearl Harbor. Early in January 1942, for instance, thirteen Martin B-26 Marauder twin-engine bombers, accompanied by 25 single-engine Curtiss P-40 Warhawk fighters, set out for Anchorage. Seven of the P-40s crashed en route and five were still on the way a month later, delayed by mechanical failures and other problems. Five of the B-26s also crashed, four coming down between Edmonton and Whitehorse in an isolated spot subsequently known as "Million Dollar Valley."[6] Lieutenant-Colonel R.W. Hale, Officer Commanding, 2nd Battalion, Edmonton Regiment, reported on 16 February 1942:

> *Some forty-five large U.S.A. aircraft have used this route since it was completed. They, however, did not find it as easy as it looked, losing nearly a million dollars' worth of aircraft, and incurring injury to a number of Aircrews, some of them seriously.*[7]

Mechanical problems and inexperienced pilots were two factors involved in the mishaps, but on the whole the operation pointed to the undeveloped state of the airfields and the lack of navigation facilities, proper communication systems, and reliable meteorological services. Authorities stepped up their efforts to upgrade the airway.[8]

In January 1943, Air Force Headquarters [AFHQ] in Ottawa summarized the progress:

> *All main Staging units, viz; Edmonton, Grande Prairie, Fort St. John, Fort Nelson and Watson Lake and Whitehorse, are now in use. Accommodation is available for personnel and refuelling facilities are provided by the United States Army Air Force. Radio Ranges are installed and point-to-point communication has been set up. The intermediate staging units are not fully serviceable. They are located at Beatton River, Smith River, Teslin, Aishihik and Snag. Landings can be made in an emergency at Teslin, Aishihik and Snag.*[9]

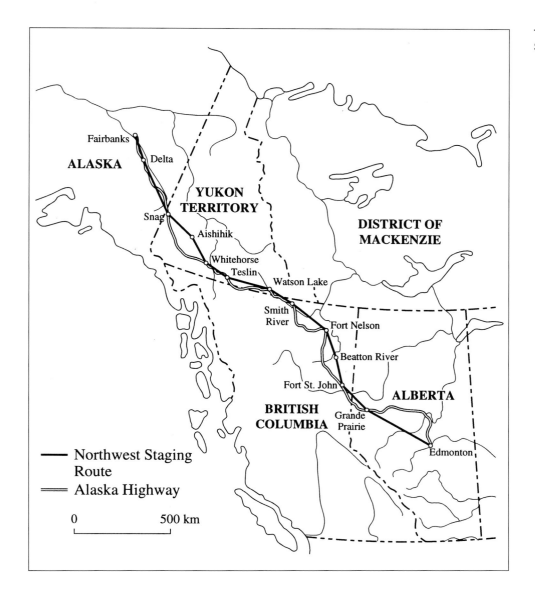

The Northwest Staging Route.

Throughout 1942 the Canadian government clung to its plan to develop the route as a national project. However, the improvements required by the United States and the limited supply of domestic labour brought about the reluctant conclusion to accept American assistance. After February 1943 the two countries developed the northern airway as a joint venture. Frequent meetings took place between Canadian and American officials with the aim of upgrading the facilities on the crucial connection between the continental United States and Alaska.[10]

For lack of better machinery, the work was co-ordinated through the Permanent Joint Board on Defence and, eventually, by the Special Commissioner for Defence Projects in Northwestern Canada, Major-General W.W. Foster, who reported to the Cabinet War Committee.[11] With responsibility for supervising and co-ordinating the expanded construction programme, he succeeded in introducing a degree of harmony and order.

While the contractors managed to make the airway usable fairly quickly, it was not until the end of August 1943 that the monthly Progress Report on Canada-United States Joint Projects was able finally to report:

> *The initial building programme, representing the minimum requirements at main staging units, has been completed with the exception of a few minor items. This initial plan of development ... has been carried out by Canadian contractors. A considerable expansion of existing facilities ... is now being initiated. This further development will be undertaken by United States contractors and is designed to provide additional facilities to meet the requirements of the United States staging programme. Any additional construction which may be required specifically for R.C.A.F. will, however, be carried out by the R.C.A.F. Construction Unit.*[12]

The dominant feature of the Northwest Staging Route was the preponderance of American aircraft and American personnel, civilian and military, referred to only half in jest as the "American Army of Occupation." It seemed to many Canadian observers, as it did to Vincent Massey, the Canadian High Commissioner to the United Kingdom, that the Americans "have apparently walked in and taken possession in many cases as if Canada were unclaimed territory inhabited by a docile race of aborigines."[13]

By June 1942 the USAAF had a detachment established at Edmonton's municipal airport. Air Transport Command planes passed through each day with men and materials for points north. This created a housing problem.[14] Near the end of August 1942, the Canadian Army Area Commandant reported: "Six hundred, all ranks, have arrived and all have been accommodated in tents on the airport. Permanent hutments are being erected for the U.S. army personnel."[15] In 1944, the reduced intake of trainees at No. 2 Air Observers School permitted a number of men working on or passing through the route to be housed there.[16]

Six civilian airlines supported US operations in Canada and Alaska, giving some indication of the scale of American air activity. By contrast, Canadian Pacific Airlines was the only Canadian company operating over the Northwest Staging Route. It prospered on war-priority orders and apparently enjoyed a good relationship with the Americans who made it possible for CPA to obtain transport aircraft.[17]

In granting authority for the US companies to use Canadian facilities, the government specified that the arrangement was strictly a war measure that would be terminated at the end of hostilities and refused permission for the aircraft to carry fare-paying passengers or otherwise engage in commercial enterprises. Only one, Northwest Airlines, caused any real concern.

The trouble began at the end of February 1942 when Northwest, recently contracted to the USAAF's Air Transport Command to carry men and materials to Alaska, made its first flight before the Canadian government had granted official approval. Lieutenant-Colonel E. Brown, Area Commandant, wrote from Prince of Wales Armoury in Edmonton:

> *Some excitement caused over week-end when large American plane grounded here on authority Director of Civil Aviation, Ottawa. Plane had fourteen civilians who claimed to have authority to proceed over route from Washington.*[18]

Even the American Consul had been unaware that the C-47 was on its way.[19] C.D. Howe, the Minister of Munitions and Supply, who happened to be going to Washington, made personal inquiries to find out "what this was all about." Subsequently, he was able to report to the House of Commons that the difficulty was no more than a misunderstanding:

> *I found that everybody there had assumed that someone had asked Canada for permission for this plane to fly, and it was explained that the army wished to engage this airline to do certain transport work. The necessary permission was given that very day. I telephoned back to Ottawa and was able to convey full permission to the army to use this civilian transport company.*[20]

This verbal authorization, reflecting the dominant role played by Howe in the formulation and administration of Canadian policy, was followed by a letter to Major-General Robert Olds of the USAAF's Air Transport Command in which Howe requested that Northwest Airlines and other civilian carriers involved in military projects in Canada be brought completely under military control. Their pilots should either be enlisted in the service or replaced by air force personnel.[21]

For the next year little attention was paid to this part of the bargain either by Air Transport Command, preoccupied with the rapid expansion of its operations in Canada and Alaska, or by Northwest Airlines, whose president believed that the United States should get its airlines firmly established in Canada. Periodic concerned memoranda, letters, and signals appear in Canadian Army and Air Force files about American personnel and aircraft passing through the Northwest Staging Route.[22] Stanley Dziuban, in the American official history of Second World War Canada-United States defence relations, admits:

> *Northwest Airlines employees apparently deliberately emphasized and flaunted the civilian complexion of their operations. Personnel, aircraft, and facilities bore company identifications, and the employees identified their work as a company rather than U.S. Army task ... The situation displeased Canadians who saw the Northwest Airlines' actions as designed to create and advertise a privileged position that could be*

> *exploited after the war in commercial operations ... Reports that*
> *Northwest Airlines was carrying passengers for hire were*
> *circulated and did not improve the atmosphere.*[23]

Protests against the attitude of Northwest Airlines were made through the
PJBD, the RCAF, and regular diplomatic channels. Complaints were also made
directly to the president of the company, with whom Howe reportedly had
several clashes. Under pressure of these representations the Air Transport
Command finally gave assurances of its intention to bring all its contract carriers
into line. By the spring of 1943 most of the grievances had been satisfactorily
resolved.[24] Even so, the high-handed methods of Northwest Airlines, which
ironically had taken over the residence of the Lieutenant-Governor of Alberta for
office space, had a damaging effect on Canadian-American relations.

Canadians found it easy to believe that their American neighbours sought to
entrench themselves permanently on the Northwest Staging Route. The behaviour of
Northwest Airlines seemed to confirm this fear. Vincent Massey, who from his
distant post in London kept his own watch on events in Canada, confided to his diary:

> *The American government clearly have in mind the use of the air*
> *routes for commercial purposes. All they have to do is to repaint*
> *their planes and change the clothes of their crews and they will*
> *have their civil routes in being directly peace is declared.*[25]

In an attempt to allay Canadian fears of US expansionist ambitions, Prime
Minister William Lyon Mackenzie King made a brief statement in the House of
Commons on 1 February 1943 on the status of American military undertakings in
Canada. He emphasized that they were part of an authorized programme of
wartime co-operation and did not give the United States "any continuing rights in
Canada after the conclusion of the war. Indeed, in regard to most of the projects
... agreements have already been made which make the post-war position
completely clear."[26]

An exchange of notes between the two governments provided that Canada
reimburse the United States for all permanent improvements to airfields in the
northwest. The agreement was later extended to all airfields in the Dominion, as
well as to Goose Bay in Labrador.[27] In referring to the agreement C.D. Howe
placed the cost of the Northwest Staging Route, up to the end of 1943, at
$46,000,000 and estimated the total wartime cost of developing airways in the
northwest at $58,500,000. He told the House of Commons:

> *In brief, the Northwest Staging Route is Canadian property,*
> *owned and operated by the Canadian government. It was built*
> *and developed by Canada, with the co-operation of the United*
> *States army engineers and workmen. The cost of the project is to*
> *be borne wholly by the Government of Canada.*[28]

The United States willingly ended its air operations in Canada as quickly as possible after the war.[29] Still, Canadians worried that their big neighbour would press for new concessions. The war suggested that long-range aviation would loom large in the Canadian-American defence relationship. The Arctic air approaches to Canada were also air approaches to the United States. Airfields in the North, such as those along the Northwest Staging Route, Goose Bay in Labrador, and the Crimson [or Northeast Staging] Route across the barren lands of the Arctic, carried a special strategic importance to the Americans. In January 1945, the Advisory Committee on Post Hostilities Problems reported to the Cabinet War Committee: "The possibility ... of the United States being moved to exert undue pressure on Canada, particularly as respects matters of defence, should not be overlooked."[30]

Notwithstanding his public pronouncements, Mackenzie King may have felt uneasy about the future air relationship with the United States. About a year after assuring the country that an exchange of notes made the postwar position "completely clear," he confessed some personal concerns to Vincent Massey. The Prime Minister, the distinguished diplomat recalled,

> *raised the subject of future relations between the USA and Canada and spoke apprehensively of the process of disentanglement which must follow when the Americans must withdraw and leave us in full control of our own bases and their wartime installations. The P.M. showed that he had grave doubts as to whether the international agreements on this which Canada had secured from the United States provide any practical guarantee against the United States' claims and pretensions. When I suggested that the Americans although undoubtedly friends, did not take us seriously enough as a nation, King said that Canadians were looked upon by Americans as a lot of Eskimos. This was a striking observation made by a man who had been so often accused of being subservient to American policy.*[31]

Mackenzie King may have been playing to the anglophile inclinations of Massey. There can be little doubt, however, that the scale of American air activity in Canada concerned him deeply.

A more positive development growing out of the proliferation of American planes in Canadian skies was the standardization of rules and regulations on matters essential to the orderly movement of aircraft. When large numbers of aircraft were involved, most of them flown by newly trained pilots, the differences between American and Canadian procedures could be confusing and hazardous. The effort to co-ordinate this military traffic appears to have been tackled first in the West. The PJBD encouraged US and Canadian regional commanders on the Pacific coast, *to effect by mutual agreement any arrangements they deemed necessary ... for the common defense including but not limited to, the installations of accessory equipment in the territory of either, the transit of armed forces, equipment or defence materials into or through the territory of either, and the utilization by either nation of the base and military facilities of the other.*[32]

Local and regional co-operation gradually increased[33] until, on 1 February 1943, Western Air Command of the RCAF, Northwest Sea Frontier of the USN, the US Army's Western Defense Command, and Air Transport Command of the USAAF signed the comprehensive JAN-CAN [Joint Army, Navy-Canadian] Agreement, "with one purpose - to give the Canadian Western Air Command advance notice for identification of U.S. and Canadian flights across their Defense Zone."[34]

Strangely, the agreement applied to the route through the BC interior to Prince George but not to the Northwest Staging Route, which came under the jurisdiction of No. 4 Training Command of the RCAF.[35] Both these routes were used extensively by American aircraft. The anomaly reflects the problems that were developing in the control of Canadian airways and airports. There is little doubt that the Northwest Staging Route was the main trouble spot. Flight plans were not always properly filed, aircraft en route frequently went unreported, and when reported could not be identified.[36] All the interested parties understood the urgent need for improvement. The Canadians, however, wanted to avoid the embarrassment of asking the Americans to take over control of the airways, even as an interim measure.

The JAN-CAN Agreement was improved in June 1943 and its overseeing committee called for better communications and for "clarification of the organization of the Northwest Staging Route to make one formation responsible

Aircraft Repair Ltd. hangar, Blatchford Field, Edmonton. Bell P-39 Airacobras, Lend-Lease to Russia; also RCAF Ansons and Harvards from the British Commonwealth Air Training Plan, are repaired and receive time checks.

Photo courtesy of Alberta Aviation Museum.

for proper control of enroute flights, and for the timely passage of information concerning the flights."[37] Air Vice-Marshal L.F. Stevenson, Air Officer Commanding Western Air Command, wrote from Vancouver expressing concern about,

> *a lack of control along the North West Staging Route and between points on it and Western Air Command. This lack of control of aircraft in flight, coupled with the density of the traffic, and the need and practice of some of the operating agencies doing instrument flights has created a potentially dangerous operation. This danger will increase with the arrival of fall and winter instrument weather.*[38]

Air Force Headquarters quickly developed a plan that was essentially an enlargement of the JAN-CAN Agreement, with the RCAF assuming control over airways in Western Air Command as well as the Northwest Staging Route.[39] The scheme was adopted and soon expanded. In August 1943 a committee, composed of Canadian and American air force personnel and Department of Transport officials, decided, in part,

> *That Canada be responsible for the control, maintenance and defence of the following airports: Feeder: Prince George, Kamloops, B.C.; Lethbridge and Calgary, Alta.; Regina, Sask. Main: Edmonton, Alta.; Grande Prairie, Alta; Fort St. John and Fort Nelson, B.C.; Watson Lake and Whitehorse, Y.T. Intermediate: Beatton River and Smith River, B.C.; Teslin, Aishihik and Snag, Y.T.; [Whitecourt, Alta. when constructed].*[40]

Aircraft Repair Ltd. hanger. Ansons, Harvards, and Lend-Lease Bell P-39 Airacobras en route to Russia via Alaska.

Photo courtesy of Alberta Aviation Museum.

"Flying control western areas."

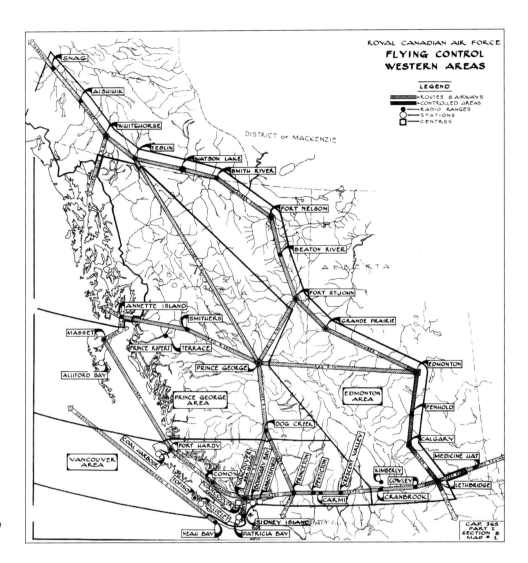

Courtesy Department of National Defence [Canadian Air Publication 365; see end note 42].

The United States would be responsible for "the maintenance, local airport control and defence of ... Edmonton Satellite ... [which] will be subject only to airways traffic control by Canada under mutually acceptable regulations." Eight flight strips along the Alaska Highway, fifteen others related to the Canol oil pipeline project from Norman Wells to Whitehorse, plus those on the Crimson Route in the northeast, all used exclusively by the Americans, were to be controlled in all respects by the USAAF. All this was adopted by the PJBD as its 32nd Recommendation.[41]

When the new system worked well in the West and in the North, it was extended across the country. By the end of 1943 the RCAF controlled all air movements in Canada, and did so for the duration of the war.[42] On the Northwest Staging Route, where atmospheric conditions rendered radio communications unreliable, some 2400 miles of land lines had to be installed, largely by American engineers.[43] What it meant in terms of flying control was summed up by Air Vice-Marshal T.A. Lawrence, Air Officer Commanding North West Air

Groundcrews service one of the Bell P-39 Airacobras being delivered to the USSR along the Northwest Staging Route.

Photo courtesy Department of National Defence [PMR 79-90].

Command, a new formation created in June 1944 to control the Northwest Staging Route and associated airfields in northwestern Canada:

> *The duty control officer in the airways centre in Edmonton can, by merely pushing one button, talk instantly to the Fairbanks control tower, or to any control tower between Edmonton and Fairbanks, or for that matter to Winnipeg, Calgary, Lethbridge, Great Falls, Montana or Vancouver. The system will work as smoothly ... as the ordinary inter-office telephone of any modern business building.*[44]

Although the British had not been involved in the negotiations with the Americans, or between the RCAF and the Department of Transport, they welcomed the introduction of a uniform set of procedures. Not only would this promote safety and efficiency; it would also strengthen the hold of Canada, and thus of the Commonwealth, on Goose Bay and Gander.

Confident that a good system of air traffic control had been developed in North America, and seeing the need for standardization, the government worked for an international agreement even before the end of the war. In March 1944 Howe explained the Canadian position:

> *It is obvious that air regulations dealing with such matters as traffic rules, safety and navigational aids should be as nearly as possible, uniform through the whole world and that an international authority must be set up and given the power to prepare regulations which would be accepted as standard by the members of that authority.*[45]

The development of a universal system of air traffic control thus became a major Canadian contribution growing out of the war. With a proposal by the United States more likely to be regarded with suspicion, Canada argued, with some British support, the merits of the Canadian-American system. Although most countries were reluctant to give up their own diverse practices the Canadian proposal, with some changes, was accepted for international air routes and Canadians went on to play a significant part in the co-ordination of international aviation.[46]

Procedures developed in western Canada thus formed the basis of the international system of air traffic control established in the postwar world. The little-known airway in the northwest played its small part in this story.

Throughout the war, and especially during the campaign in the Aleutian Islands, from May 1942 to June 1943, the Northwest Staging Route served as a crucial supply line. American expectations that the route would be the means of launching a northern air offensive against Japan proved illusory but led to an intensified drive to expand the capacities of the various staging posts. With the fading of the Japanese threat in the northern Pacific region, its chief military use was ferrying aircraft to the USSR, 2491 being delivered in 1943, 3148 in 1944, and 2143 in 1945.[47] The official USAAF history summed it up:

> *As seen by the planners in December 1941, the wintry air road*
> *northwest was essential for supplying and reinforcing the*
> *pitifully small garrison of American forces in Alaska. Such was*
> *its principal occasion for being until September 1942, and*
> *throughout the war it continued to deliver to the United States'*
> *armed forces in Alaska aircraft and aircraft supplies. For three*
> *years, however, from September 1942 until September 1945, this*
> *airway's primary function was to deliver lend-lease aircraft,*
> *nearly 8,000 in all, to the aircrews of the Soviet Union, waiting*
> *at LADD Field, Fairbanks.*[48]

A Siberia-bound Bell P-39 Airacobra being towed across the tarmac at an unidentified airfield on the Northwest Staging Route. The dozens of P-39s parked in the background give some idea of the heavy use made of the airway to deliver much-needed aircraft to both American and Soviet air forces.

Photo courtesy Department of National Defence [PMR 79-91].

If it had been used for nothing else, this would have made the route a key contributor to the Allied victory.

In many respects the wartime saga of the Northwest Staging Route was simply a good example of the Canadian war effort in microcosm. We generously offered to do what we could, all the while fretting about the cost to our treasury and to our sovereignty. In the end we need not have worried. We came out of this episode smelling and looking good. We helped our American friends get personnel and materiel to Alaska for their own use in our common defence and for onward transmission to our Soviet ally. In the process we obtained modern facilities in the North that we could and did put to good use after the war.

P-39 Airacobras being ferried to Alaska at rest on an unidentified aerodrome along the Northwest Staging Route. The presence of a twin-engine Avro Anson, much used in training, suggests that this airfield housed a British Commonwealth Air Training Plan School.

Photo courtesy Department of National Defence [PMR 76-460].

NOTES

[1]Recommendation No. 24, February 25-26, 1942, Stanley W. Dziuban, *Military Relations between the United States and Canada, 1939-1945* [Washington 1959], p. 357, and C.P. Stacey, *Arms Men and Governments: The War Policies of Canada, 1939-1945* [Ottawa, 1970], p. 346.

[2]Wesley Frank Craven and James Lea Cate, *The Army Air Forces in World War II, Vol. 7: Services around the World* [Chicago 1958; reprinted 1983], p. 152; Deane R. Brandon, "ALSIB: The Northwest Ferrying Route through Alaska, 1942-45, Part 1," *Journal American Aviation Historical Society*, Vol. 20, No. 1 [Spring 1975], p. 23.

[3]Stacey, op. cit., p. 379-82

[4]Tenth recommendation, Dziuban, *Military Relations*, p. 351; F/L E.P. Wood, "Northern Skytrails, Part X," *Roundel*, Vol. 1, No. 10 [August 1949], pp. 4-8. For details on the development of the Northwest Staging Route as a military airway, see Department of Transport [DOT] file 5150-32 pts 1 and 2, "Airports & Airharbours, Northwest Staging Route, General Correspondence," National Archives of Canada [NA], Record Group [RG] 12, Vol. 1405.

[5]Lieutenant-Colonel R.W. Hale, O.C. [Officer Commanding], 2nd Battalion, Edmonton Regiment, to District Officer Commanding [DOC], Military District [MD] No. 13, Calgary, 11 September 1941, enclosing "Interim Report on International Airports," 10 September 1941, and "F," Headquarters, MD 13, to Major-General R.O. Alexander, General Officer Commanding-in-Chief, Pacific Command, 12 September 1941, DHist 169.009[D106].

[6]Brandon, "ALSIB ... Part 1," p. 23; Craven and Cate, op. cit., *Vol. 1: Plans and Early Operations, January 1939 to August 1942* [Chicago 1948; reprinted 1983], pp. 303-4.

[7]Hale to Brigadier F.M.W. Harvey, DOC MD 13, 16 February 1942, DHist 169.009[D106].

[8]Hale, after seeing the route for the first time in several months, commented: "I found that there have been so many changes and improvements that I am out of date myself." Hale to Harvey, 16 February 1942, ibid. For more detail on improvements at each of the airfields by late 1942, see the facility reports in RCAF file S.50-50-8, DHist 181.003[D4823].

[9]A/V/M N.R. Anderson, for CAS, to AOC-in-C [Air Officer Commanding-in-Chief] RCAF Overseas, 26 January 1943, AFHQ file S.24-1-13 [Plans/JP], DHist 181.003[D4823]. See also other progress reports in RCAF file S.267-17-1 Vol. 4, "Aerodrome Facilities Reports," DHist 181.003[D5217].

[10]See, for example, minutes of meetings and related documents in RCAF file FS-N-25, DHist 181.009[D3293].

[11]PC 3758, 6 May 1943; Stacey, op. cit., p. 386. For a copy of Foster's instructions from the Prime Minister, as communicated to MD 13 in May 1943, see DHist 169.009[D106].

[12]"Progress Report, Canada-United States Joint Projects," 31 August 1943, DHist 181.003[D4823].

[13]Vincent Massey, *What's Past is Prologue: The Memoirs of the Right Honourable Vincent Massey* [Toronto 1963], p. 371.

[14]Lieutenant-Colonel E. Brown, Area Commandant, Prince of Wales Armoury, Edmonton, to AA & QMG [Quartermaster-General] MD 13, 19 June 1942, Major-General J.P. Mackenzie, QMG, Ottawa, to DOC MD 13, 14 July 1942, QMG to DOC MD 13, 20 July 1942, DOC MD 13 to Secretary, Department of National Defence [DND], Ottawa, 22 July 1942, QMG to DOC MD 13, 11 August 1942, DHist 169.009[D106].

[15]Brown to DAA & QMG MD 13, 25 August 1942, DHist 169.009[D106].

[16]W/C C.G. Durham, for AOC No. 4 Training Command, to AOC Western Air Command [WAC], 14 March 1944, and related correspondence, RCAF file S.202-1-173 Vol. 1, "Organization - North West Staging Route," DHist 181.009[D1315].

[17]Ronald A. Keith, *Bush Pilot with a Briefcase: The Happy-go-lucky Story of Grant McConachie* [Toronto 1972], 234-5. CPA ultimately became Canadian Airlines International.

[18]Brown to Harvey, 2 March 1942, DHist 169.009[D106].

[19]Ibid. Hale to Harvey, 3 March 1942.

[20]Canada, Parliament, House of Commons, Debates, 1942, Vol. 3, 2486.

[21]Dziuban, op. cit., p. 308.

[22]See, for example, DHist 169.009[D106].

[23]Dziuban, op. cit., p. 308.

[24]Ibid., pp. 309-10; *Minneapolis Morning Star*, Oct. 1943. For an account of Northwest Airlines responsibilities on the Northwest Staging Route, see Craven and Cate, *Plans and Early Operations,* pp. 357-8, and *Services around the World,* pp. 156-8. The close relationship of the airline with the USAAF is illustrated by the posting of a former Northwest vice-president, Colonel George E. Gardner, to Edmonton, as executive officer to the ATC commander there. Ibid., p. 157.

[25]Massey, op. cit., p. 371.

[26]Canada, Parliament, House of Commons, Debates, 1943, Vol. 1, p. 21.

[27]Ibid., 1944, Vol. 3, 2227; Dziuban, op. cit., pp. 358-9; RCAF file S.262-5, "Curtailment of US activities over the North West Staging Route," DHist 181.009[D3293].

[28]Canada, Parliament, House of Commons, Debates, 1944, Vol. 1, 980-1. In May 1944, the valuation placed on the Northwest Staging Route by the Canadian government was $31,311,196. The total value of US construction in joint defence projects in northern Canada at that time was $76,811,551. C.G. "Chubby" Power, Minister of National Defence for Air, to J.L. Ilsley, Minister of Finance, 17 May 1944, RCAF file FS-N-25, DHist 181.009[D3293]. This file contains detailed breakdowns of the cost of improvements made to support US air activities along the Northwest Staging Route, along with frequent concerned communications between Canadian officials about the ultimate cost to be born by this country.

[29]See RCAF file S.262-5, "Northwest Air Command Curtailment of US Activities over the NW Staging Route - Report of Meetings Joint Board of Defence," DHist 181.003[D3281].

[30]"Report of the Advisory Committee on Post-War Hostilities Problems, 'Post-War Canadian Defence Relationship with the United States: General Considerations,' 23 January 1945," paragraph 3, in James Eayrs, *In Defence of Canada, Vol. 3: Peacemaking and Deterrence* [Toronto 1972], p. 376. Some of the best sources on the handover of facilities from US to Canadian control can be found in DOT files, such as 6800-18 pt 1, "Stations, Radio, Government Owned, Northeast Staging Route, General," Sept. 1942 to Dec. 1947, NA, RG 12, Vol. 1222, and 5150 pts. 5 and 6, "Airports & Airharbours, Northwest Staging Route, General Correspondence," Aug. 1945 to July 1949, ibid., Vol. 1406.

[31]Massey, op. cit., pp. 396-7.

[32]Dziuban, op. cit., p. 356.

[33]"Western Air Command," unpublished narrative, nd, section 8, 1-4, DHist 74/3; WAC Headquarters [HQ], daily diary, DHist.

[34]"Sidelights on the JANCAN Agreement," especially paragraph 5, and "Joint Agreement between CNWSF, WAC, WDC and ATC, 17 Feb. 1943," WAC file 204-2-1 Vol. 1, "Ops, Operational Procedure & Control," DHist 181.002[D164].

[35]F/L K.A. Herchmer to S/L P.E. Willis, Secretary, JAN-CAN Committee, 25 May 1943, Herchmer to SASO [Senior Air Staff Officer], 29 May 1943, and G/C W.A. Jones, for AOC WAC, Vancouver to AOC, No. 4 Training Command, Calgary, 7 June 1943, DHist 181.002[D164].

[36]For exchanges between USAAF Ferrying Command officers and RCAF personnel on the Northwest Staging Route, see DHist 181.009[D1315].

[37]A/V/M L.F. Stevenson, AOC WAC to Secretary, DND for Air, Ottawa, 15 July 1943, DHist 181.002[D164]. See also Stevenson to air member for air services, 26 July 1943, and "Conference Held at North West Staging Route Headquarters, Edmonton, Alta., to Discuss 'JANCAN' Agreement as Formulated at San Francisco June 23, 1943," ibid. In fact, DOT officials were not impressed with the first RCAF graduates of DOT's Montreal-based air traffic control school who were posted to Northwest Staging Route stations. See DOT file 11-4-39 pt. 1, "Defence Measures and Regulations, Aviation, Traffic Control Officers - Northwest Staging Route," July 1942 to July 1943, NA, RG 12, Vol. 615. See also DHist 181.009[D5286].

[38]Stevenson to Sec. DND for Air, 26 July 1943, DHist 181.002[D164]. For more on NWSR air traffic control, see RCAF file S.202-1-173 Vol. 1, "Organization - North West Staging Route," DHist 181.009[D1315].

[39]Costello to AOC WAC, 4 August 1943, DHist 181.002[D164]. See also AFHQ to AOC WAC, X832 A2014, 4 August 1943, DHist 181.002[D106]. See also AFHQ to WAC, Signal A2780, 6 September 1943, ibid.

[40]"Minutes of Meeting Held at RCAF Headquarters, Lisgar Bldg., Ottawa, Ont. August 19, 1943," 3-4, DHist 181.002[D164]. See also A/V/M W.A. Curtis, for CAS, to AOC WAC, 11 April

1944, in which he wrote: "As the controlling authority on the Northwest Staging Route, it is still the responsibility of the R.C.A.F. to maintain close liaison with the United States Forces. Routine maintenance will continue to be carried out by the R.C.A.F., and every effort should be made by your Command to ensure that facilities, for which Canada is responsible, are properly maintained and operated. Any suggestions you may put forward with respect to the improvement of maintenance and control on the Northwest Staging Route will be welcomed by these Headquarters." On 6 May a WAC staff officer minuted this letter to the AOC: "Para 3. states that RCAF have no responsibility for construction on N.W.S.R. Para 4. states that RCAF is the controlling authority. Shall we accept then that we confine ourselves [in war [unclear]] to maintenance matters only[?]" The file contains no answer to this question. RCAF file 1-42-1, "WAC - Policy - Co-operation with US Forces - Defences of Pacific Coast - NW Staging Route," DHist 181.003[D5204]. For more on the RCAF assuming control of the Northwest Staging Route, see DHist 181.009[D3391].

[41]"Minutes of Meeting ... August 19, 1943," 4, DHist 181.002[D164]. See also Stacey, *Arms, Men and Governments*, pp. 346-7. The air traffic control question is covered in surprising detail in Dziuban, *Military Relations*, pp. 304-6.

[42]"Air Traffic Control: Sub-Committee Minutes," 20-30 Aug. 1943, DHist 181.002[D164]; R.C.A.F. Regulations for Control of Aircraft Movements [CAP 365, 2nd ed., May 1944], DHist 89/331.

[43]See the unpublished history of RCAF landlines by an unidentified author [circa 1945] in DHist 181.009[D1038]. For the teletype circuit on the route, see RCAF file S.9-3, DHist 181.009[D1050].

[44]Statement by Lawrence, 3 Feb. 1945, in Goddard, "North West Air Command," chapter 2, C, section 33, DHist 74/6. See also RCAF file S.1-18 Vol. 2, "Summary - Canada-United States Joint Projects," DHist 181.003[D5206], and RCAF file S.202-1-173 vol. 1, "Organization - North West Staging Route," DHist 181.009[D1315].

[45]Canada, Parliament, House of Commons, Debates, 1944, Vol. 2, 1578.

[46]J.R.K. Main, *Voyageurs of the Air: A History of Civil Aviation in Canada, 1858-1967* [Ottawa 1967], pp. 193-4. As a corollary, Montreal was made the headquarters of the Provisional International Civil Aviation Organization. Although Main says the choice was unanimous, "The final vote on the actual site was 27 for Montreal, 9 for Paris, 4 for Geneva, and 1 for China. After the vote had been taken the French graciously acknowledged the appropriateness of Montreal ...." Report of the Delegation to the First Meeting of the Interim Assembly of PICAO, 1946, Donald M. Page, ed., Documents on Canadian External Relations [DCER], Vol. 12: 1946 [Ottawa 1977], p. 523. See also the memo by the first secretary, "Mr. Symington's Visit to Washington," 10 April 1946, John Hilliker, ed., DCER, Vol. 11: 1944-1945 Part II [Ottawa 1990], p. 559. See also Canada, Parliament, House of Commons, Debates, 1945, 585-6. For more on the strides made in air traffic control during the war, see Carl A. Christie, *Ocean Bridge: The History of RAF Ferry Command* [Toronto 1994], especially chapter 12.

[47]Dziuban, *Military Relations*, p. 216. For more on the Northwest Staging Route, see John Stewart, "Canada and the Air Corridor to Alaska, 1935-42" [undergraduate thesis, Mount Allison University, Sackville, New Brunswick 1981], copy, DHist 81/332; K.C. Eyre, "Custos Borealis; the Military in the Canadian North" [PhD thesis, University of London 1981], pp. 82-95; Stan Cohen, *The Forgotten War: A Pictorial History of World War II in Alaska and Northwestern Canada* [Missoula, Montana 1981]; and Craven and Cate, op. cit., pp. 152-72. There are a large number of under-utilized files on the Northwest Staging Route at the National Archives, in DOT as well as DND holdings, RG 12 and RG 24, and also in some private collections like the A.G.L. McNaughton Papers, Manuscript Group [MG] 30 E 133, and those of S/L Joachim Jaworski, MG 30 E 214. In addition, DHist still holds several useful files on the subject.

[48]Craven and Cate, op. cit, p. 153. For more on the delivery of aircraft to the USSR, and also to the Royal Air Force, see Christie, op. cit., passim.

Blatchford Field: The War Years, 1939-1945

Mark Hopkins

In 1924 few Edmontonians could imagine the impact that two acres of the Hagmann farm would have on the city and the world. In response to a petition by W.R. [Wop] May and Harry Adair, Edmonton City Council designated a portion of the Hagmann estate to be set aside for the city's first airfield. On 16 June 1926, the federal government granted Edmonton the licence for Canada's first "Public Air Harbour." Later that same year council approved a motion to honour Ken Blatchford, Edmonton's aviation-minded mayor, christening the new airport Blatchford Field. On 8 January 1927, Blatchford Field officially opened with the arrival of two Siskin fighters from Royal Canadian Air Force No. 2 Squadron, stationed in High River. This was one of many firsts which would soon give Edmonton the unofficial title of "The Gateway to the North," a title which would take on new importance and significance during the Second World War.

In Europe, Hitler's armies rolled over Polish borders, taking the world to war in September 1939. The city of Edmonton was quick to recognize the potential use of Blatchford Field in the war effort, and offered Ottawa the use of its air harbour facilities. Ottawa was equally swift to respond; and Canada agreed to pay the city of Edmonton one dollar per annum for the duration of the war. Initially two criteria were established, the first being that Blatchford Field continue its operations as one of the nation's leading air-freight centres. Commercial business and services, especially to the north, were to continue as before. The second requested that Captain Jimmy Bell continue to manage the overall operation of the airport under the jurisdiction of the Royal Canadian Air Force. This met with full approval as Captain Bell already had been associated with, or been managing, the airfield for almost two decades with great success.

Matt Berry and Captain Jimmy Bell, ca. 1942.

Richard Finney
Photo Courtesy Alberta Aviation Museum.

Captain Bell could not foresee the events that were about to engulf Blatchford Field, which he had already watched grow from a cow pasture to one of the nation's leading commercial airports. In the next few years Edmonton would witness a virtual explosion of activity at Blatchford Field. It would begin with the development of commercial passenger services and related support industries, and rapidly lead to organization of the British Commonwealth Air Training Plan, the formation of the Northwest Staging Route, and construction of the Alaska Highway and Canol Pipeline. In a few short years Blatchford Field was to become the busiest airfield in North America.

Commercial Development 1939-1945

Without trivializing the contribution made by the smaller air services across the country, two airlines in particular stand out during this period; Trans-Canada Air Lines and Canadian Pacific Airlines. The government-owned TCA was formed in 1937, and in 1939 went to a wartime footing. The RCAF itself could not handle the transport of all wartime personnel, mail and cargo such as spare aircraft parts; soon TCA would be criss-crossing the country and eventually the Atlantic with mail and passengers. Between 1939 and 1946 it would grow from an average of 2,000 passengers and 367,000 pounds of mail to 300,000 passengers and 2,300,000 pounds of mail. TCA would make a vital contribution to the war effort and establish itself as one of Canada's leading post-war airlines.

Canadian Pacific Airlines was officially formed on 16 May 1942, after Canadian Pacific Railway purchased a number of smaller aviation companies. While TCA was concentrating on operating the long-distance transcontinental routes, Canadian Pacific Airlines concentrated on the short- and medium-range routes connecting western Canadian centres. Besides running five repair depots, CP Airlines was a vital asset which assisted in the construction of the Alaska Highway and Canol Pipeline. As the second significant post-war national airline, Canadian Pacific Airlines would be instrumental in opening routes to the Orient and beyond.

Perhaps one of the greatest civilian contributions to the war effort was that made by the men and women of Leigh Brintnell's Aircraft Repair Limited. Wilfred Leigh Brintnell was a familiar name to anyone associated with bush flying and Blatchford Field. A First World War veteran, he continued to pursue his love of flying and eventually rose to the position of chief pilot and General Manager of Western Canada Airways, and subsequently owner of Mackenzie Air Services.

In 1936 Brintnell suggested to General Airways and Wings Limited a mutual pooling of resources to create one maintenance and service facility. Since Mackenzie Air Service already maintained the best equipped facility on Blatchford Field the new organization was incorporated as a division of Mackenzie Air Services. The depot located at the north end of Blatchford Field would succeed in providing quality service to the cooperating airlines while equipping Edmonton with a repair facility, which Brintnell felt would be essential for the coming conflict in Europe. On 5 November 1937, Aircraft Repair Ltd. was incorporated in Alberta by Brintnell, with Harry Haytor as his manager.[1]

Canada entered the Second World War in September 1939 and quickly recognized the need for an organized operation utilizing technically skilled and mechanically proficient personnel, needed especially for aircraft repair and maintenance. While the RAF battled the Luftwaffe in the skies over England, damaged aircraft began to flood Canadian facilities such as Aircraft Repair. Brintnell, Hayter and the company's 100 employees received their first job, 100 battle-damaged Fairey Battles which had been badly mauled during the fall of France. Jimmy Bell provided space in an old hangar so the work could commence as soon as possible.

By 1941 the heart of a new federally funded Aircraft Repair was being constructed at the northern end of Blatchford Field. A rail spur would bring damaged aircraft and unassembled BCATP training planes into the heart of the facility. In addition Aircraft Repair ran a field service unit travelling to crash sites throughout the province, as well as repairing American aircraft which began to arrive in 1942.

During its peak Aircraft Repair would employ 3000 civilian workers, many of whom were women. For the first time Edmonton had large numbers of women working in traditional male jobs, in a plant that was regarded as the most active repair facility in the Commonwealth.

Shift change at
Aircraft Repair Ltd.

*Photo courtesy Alberta
Aviation Museum
[1993.96.51].*

At war's end Aircraft Repair had successfully completed 1,597 government contracts, worked on over thirty varieties of aircraft, including Ansons, Oxfords, Airacobras as well as various types of transport and passenger aircraft. On 27 February 1945, the company was reorganized into Northwest Industries Limited and today continues to service the aviation industry and the armed forces.

One account of this period notes that "[in] the final analysis, Brintnell and his staff may be counted as leaders amid one of the most important logistic and support service programmes of the war and were major contributors to the Allied victory."[2] Wilfred Leigh Brintnell was awarded the Order of the British Empire [OBE] for his work with Aircraft Repair.

The British Commonwealth Air Training Plan

In October 1939 discussions began between Canada, the United Kingdom, New Zealand and Australia concerning the implementation of a joint air-training plan in Canada. On 17 December 1939, the British Commonwealth Air Training Plan [BCATP] was officially established. By March 1945, when the Plan came to an end, it had graduated 131,553 of the 159,340 students who had begun training.[3] The RCAF would graduate 72,835; 25,547 would be pilots, 12,855 navigators, 6659 air bombers, 12,744 wireless operators [air gunners], 12,917 air gunners, and 1,913 flight engineers.[4] Included in the total were 42,110 RAF and Allied nationals, including 9606 Australians, 7000 New Zealanders, 2000 French, 900 Czechoslovakians, 677 Norwegians, 450 Poles, 450 Belgians and 400 Dutch.

At the outbreak of the war it quickly became apparent that Canada had taken on a tremendous responsibility considering the size and existing strength of the RCAF. Combining the permanent and Auxiliary Force would provide a total strength of 4061 personnel and aircraft totalling 270, of which many were obsolete. Early estimates indicated 40,000 personnel would be required to operate the Plan, and this did not include manning Canada's operational squadrons. Fortunately, the concept of a strategically located, comprehensive training plan had been discussed as early as 1936. Even before the official outbreak of hostilities the Department of National Defence had initiated steps to facilitate a quick response to the implementation of the plan. In early 1939 the Department of National Defence, in cooperation with the Department of Transport, already had begun a programme of facility planning; the Department of Transport would locate suitable airfields, while Defence would plan the construction of its facilities.

As the search for suitable training bases began, various cities began to lobby for BCATP facilities. The intense rivalry between Edmonton and Calgary had existed in sports since the Great War, and would now extend into the Plan. Since Ottawa's acceptance of Edmonton's offer of Blatchford Field, great things had been forecast for the city. Edmonton would house the largest and best of the BCATP programmes. By the spring of 1940 Mayor John Fry was becoming frustrated; despite the two promised schools, Blatchford Field seemed to be in the centre of a "sitzkrieg" while Calgary was a virtual hub of activity. Mayor Fry poured out his frustration in a letter to the Minister of Commerce. He wrote that "we are slighted for Calgary, Lethbridge, McLeod and Medicine Hat, who are all getting much larger programmes than we are, in spite of the fact that our airport more nearly meets the specifications than any other."[5] Ottawa's reply indicated that although progress appeared slow, improvements would continue in the near future.

While the implementation of the Plan seemed slow to some, several of its programmes had been operating since the summer of 1939. The Edmonton Flying Club had been offering combat flying courses to experienced pilots, before Canada's actual involvement in the war. By the summer of 1940 Edmonton had learned that Blatchford Field and the Edmonton area would host four of the Plan's schools. Located on the field would be No. 2 Air Observers School and No. 16 Elementary Flying School, with the No. 4 Initial Training School located at the University of Alberta and No. 3 Manning Depot located at the Exhibition Grounds. Plans also called for fifteen new buildings, including three hangars, as well as extension of the airport runways and airport boundaries. Under the plan 107 schools would eventually operate from 231 sites, with 23 schools operating between Edmonton and Lethbridge.

Canadian Airways pilots at No. 2 AOS, Blatchford Field, 7 April 1944.

Don Innes.
Photo courtesy Alberta Aviation Museum.

The BCATP was developed to maximize the resources available in the military and to utilize as much of the experienced civilian sector as possible. Schools such as No. 2 AOS were contracted to various civilian airlines. Each school operated under the Plan would receive certain government and RCAF assistance. The government would provide buildings, aircraft, certain equipment and operating expenses with each school allowed a five per cent profit — except AOS schools. The RCAF would contribute instructors in navigation, bombing, and other technical skills, as well as conduct the required courses. The operating company would supply pilots, mechanics, radio operators, guards, and aircraft service as well as all personnel, including storekeepers, clerks, parachute packers and stenographers.[6] On 19 July 1940 Canadian Airways [Training] Ltd. was registered in Alberta as a company with Wilfred R. May as manager.[7] Four months later, on 5 October 1940, the No. 2 Air Observers School officially opened in Edmonton.[8]

Training in a Link Trainer at No. 2 Air Observers School at Blatchford Field.

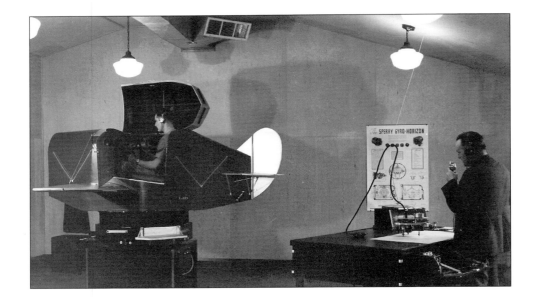

Photo courtesy Alberta Aviation Museum [1993.42.05].

While the prairies had the highest percentage of recruitment in the country, the experience of joining the forces is one memory that few seem to cherish. Having met the required academic standards or having completed wartime emergency training, the recruits would find themselves at a manning pool. In Edmonton it was designated No. 3 Manning Depot and officially opened 21 July 1941. By 31 August this depot already consisted of 19 officers, 156 staff, 1643 trainees and 45 civilians. No. 3 Manning Depot officially closed on 15 August 1944.[9]

The manning depot was a recruit's introduction to military life. The shock of drill, parades, medical examinations and interviews soon wore off. Those selected as gunners would move on to gunnery and bombing schools, the mechanically inclined were sent to St. Thomas, Ontario where they learned engine repair, aircraft-body design or instrument repair. Navigator students were sent to No. 2 AOS at Blatchford Field, while pilot trainees were sent to No. 4 Initial Training School [ITS] at the University of Alberta.

No. 4 ITS opened in the early part of June 1941 with the three student residences known as Athabasca, Assiniboia and Pembina Halls housing the station personnel, and the infirmary located in the basement of Athabasca Hall.[10] On 16 June 1941 the school's four Link Trainers arrived with the first fifteen students appearing on 20 June. By November of the same year four more Link Trainers arrived and courses averaging in excess of fifty students were starting almost every week. No. 4 Initial Training School closed operations in November 1944.

ITS training followed a strict regime of classes, physical training and drill. The school was strictly a ground school, with no flying but plenty of courses in aeronautics and mathematics. Included in the ITS schedule were the most rigorous medical exam to date, as well as time in the MSB, a low pressure chamber, and the first exposure to the famous Link Trainer. Candidates would eventually be interviewed and their future as pilots evaluated. Those that did not meet requirements were sent to a gunnery, air observer or technical school for further training. Those determined to demonstrate pilot potential were introduced to No. 16 Elementary Flying School and would at last find themselves at Blatchford Field. On 31 August 1944 No. 4 Initial Training School officially closed its doors.[11]

Blatchford Field hosted the two remaining schools located in Edmonton, No.16 Elementary Flying School and No. 2 Air Observers School. No. 16 EFS was managed and run by the Edmonton Training Flying School Ltd., incorporated in Alberta on 31 October 1940.[12] Moss Burbidge, winner of the McKee Trophy in 1932 for his outstanding contribution to aviation in Canada, would once again take charge of flight instruction at the flying club. Having served as instructor of the club from 1929 to 1938, he was once again asked to serve as chief instructor of No. 16 EFS in December 1939. Over the next two years an average of twenty single-engine aircraft would circle the city almost daily on training flights.

The standard EFS course consisted of eight weeks of navigation, gunnery and basic flight training. Included in this course were approximately fifty hours of flight time in single-engine Tiger Moths, Fleet Finches, Cornells or Harvards, and 126 hours of ground lectures.[13] Pilot trainees were expected to solo after eight hours of dual instruction, executing virtually perfect take-offs, landings, navigation and receivers before being allowed to move on to a Service Flying School. No. 16 Elementary Flying School closed in July 1942.

No. 16 Elementary Flying Training School, Blatchford Field, 1941.

Don Innes.
Photo courtesy Alberta Aviation Museum.

Anyone who had lived in Edmonton was not surprised to hear that No. 2 Air Observers School would be managed by Wilfred [Wop] R. May. Wop May was a First World War veteran of the Royal Flying Corps, and had been flying various aircraft out of Edmonton since 1919. Wop was known throughout Canada for his exploits, such as the hunt for the Mad Trapper or Rat River and the Little Red River Mercy Flight, both of which brought worldwide attention to Blatchford Field.

While No. 2 AOS did not officially open until 5 October 1940, a considerable amount of work had already taken place. The first day of August witnessed the arrival of seven Mk. 1 Avro Ansons, and by 29 October the Honourable J.C. Bowen, Lieutenant-Governor of the Province of Alberta, was on hand to present the James Richardson Trophy to Leading Aircraftsman J.B. Ruston, the most proficient student of the graduating class. By the end of the year four classes had graduated.

Mk. V Anson Trainer used by BCATP.

Photo courtesy National Archives of Canada [PA 64295].

No. 2 AOS served as a specialty training facility with three distinctive courses offered, each lasting twelve weeks. Navigation was the primary duty of an air observer, with bomb aiming and air gunnery as secondary duties. Also included was the wireless operator [gunner], a category in which recruits could enroll directly. All air observers who graduated would continue their training at a Bombing and Gunnery School or a Wireless Operators School.

The syllabus at No. 2 AOS consisted of air exercises in navigation, reconnaissance and photography. Ground instruction included maps and charts, dead reckoning navigation, compasses, meteorology, instruments, wireless, photography, reconnaissance, signals, drill and physical training, totalling some

385 hours of instruction. On the average students would receive about thirteen hours of flying time, although this would increase to 25 hours by 1944.[14]

Perhaps one incident best describes Wop May and his management of No. 2 AOS. Margaret Littlewood had obtained her pilot's and instructor's licences just before the start of the war. When she was unable to find work, a friend suggested that she contact the ten air observers schools operating under the Plan. She received letters of rejection from nine schools; however, Wop May not only offered her a position but sent train-fare to get her to Edmonton. She was immediately assigned to the Link Trainers, and although there was some initial resistance to a female instructor, she was soon part of the team. Between 1942 and 1944 Margaret Littlewood would instruct over 100 students, and would remain the only female instructor in the BCATP.

At first No. 2 AOS started training with seven Ansons. By 31 March 1941 the school had two Boeing 247Ds, two Lockheed 10As, and thirteen Ansons with 1770:30 hours logged in the air. That December found the school operating 28 aircraft, eight of which had bomb-gear installed. November 1943 represented the peak of No. 2 AOS operations, with 60 serviceable Anson Mk. 1s and one Mk. V, and eighteen additional Mk. 1s out of service.[15] No. 2 AOS officially closed its doors on 14 July 1944.

Captain Jimmy Bell must have found his position as airport manager challenging as 1941 rolled to a close. New buildings for No. 2 AOS were going up, Aircraft Repair was getting busy, TCA and other smaller airlines were expanding, and at any given time up to fifty BCATP airplanes were training over the field. With the Japanese attack on Pearl Harbor the pressure went up another notch; the Americans were coming!

Canadian Pacific Airlines crew and executive staff, No. 2 AOS, Blatchford Field, 1944.

Don Innes.
Photo courtesy Alberta Aviation Museum.

The Northwest Staging Route

During the 1930s Grant McConnachie, owner of United Air Transport, envisioned flying his aircraft from Edmonton to Shanghai. By 1939 McConnachie was operating commercial service to Fort St. John, Dawson Creek and Whitehorse, while completing a field at Fort Nelson and beginning one at Watson Lake. Logically the next step seemed to be through Alaska, over the Bering Sea, and down the coast of Siberia to China. Imperial Oil was already financing the project with a $100,000 line of credit. On 13 January 1941 McConnachie sold his airline, now called Yukon Southern Air Transport, to CPR, which he eventually would manage as president of Canadian Pacific Airlines.

On 22 June 1941 Germany launched an all-out assault on the Russian front. Within a month negotiations were under way regarding a proposed American lend-lease programme. Talks were still in progress when Japanese aircraft attacked Pearl Harbor on 7 December 1941. The following January, plans were made and permission granted by the Canadian government for the utilization of a route through Canada to Alaska. This route, pioneered by Grant McConnachie, would become known an the Northwest Staging Route.

Blatchford Field began to handle American aircraft within days of the attack on Pearl Harbor. C-47s loaded with troops and equipment began heading to Alaskan military bases through Alberta. To add to the confusion, on 14 February 1942 the United States and Canada directed work to begin on the Alaska Highway. A road would be built stretching 1523 miles from Dawson Creek to Fairbanks, Alaska, sending 10,000 American soldiers and over 16,000 civilian workers on the rails through Edmonton to the railhead at Dawson Creek.[16]

On 3 June 1942 the Japanese attacked Dutch Harbor in Alaska, and within days thirty United States Air Force DC-3s came screaming into Blatchford Field. Capt. Bell was almost at a loss as refuelling and parking virtually clogged all the airport's runways. Later in the month 500 aircraft passed through Edmonton, mostly en route to Alaska. The skies above Edmonton were buzzing, and of little comfort to Jimmy Bell was the fact that the Americans had not yet *officially* arrived.

On 14 August 1942 the USAF 7th Ferrying Group, 383rd Air Base Squadron was established with their headquarters in Edmonton. Detachments were located in Fort St. John, Fort Nelson, Grande Prairie, Watson Lake and Whitehorse. The 384th Air Base Squadron was located in Fairbanks with detachments in Northway, Tanacross, Big Delta, McGrath, Galena, Nome and Anchorage. The 385th Air Base Squadron was assigned to Great Falls, Montana with detachments in Lethbridge, Kamloops, Prince George and Calgary.[17]

Captain Bell must have been overjoyed when in late 1942 the government completed the new "state of the art" control tower and administration building. This complex featured a meteorological station, radio equipment that could maintain contact over a million square miles of territory, and offices for Bell, his staff, TCA, CPA, and Wing Commander Farrell of the Northwest Staging Route.[18] Meanwhile across the field, on the east side, the Americans were building four hangars, barracks and support buildings. While Captain Bell may have had new facilities, they soon would prove necessary as Blatchford Field was becoming the busiest airport in North America, with takeoffs and landings averaging one per minute at peak times.

Edmonton residents were shocked to learn that on 22 November 1942 the first highway convoy from Dawson Creek had arrived in Fairbanks, Alaska, only nine short months after construction began. By this time a new venture was under way, the Canol Pipeline. Alaska was in urgent need of oil and as Edmonton residents were learning, where there was American will there was a way. Completed almost as fast as the Alaska Highway, the 500 mile pipeline would extend from Norman Wells to a refinery in Whitehorse.

Captain Bell was finding his new facilities being worked to the maximum. On 29 September 1943 the field set a North American record with 860 planes passing through the field.[19] The American facilities on the east side of the field were nearing completion or ready for occupancy, and the congestion around the field forced BCATP aircraft to Penhold and Claresholm for their training flights. On one day 27 aircraft circled the city waiting for permission to land; on another occasion over 100 DC-3s were lined up waiting for the weather to clear; their cargo — live naval torpedoes.[20] To Edmonton residents it must have appeared to be a full-scale invasion. The airport was crowded, the streets were swarming with American personnel, hotels were always full and airport support buildings were overflowing into the west end and downtown. The Americans decided to build another airport to relieve the congestion.

Lend-Lease DC-3s and Bell P-39 Airacobras en route to the USSR over Northwest Staging Route, Blatchford Field.

Photo courtesy Alberta Aviation Museum [202927].

Eight miles north of the city the Americans started construction on a seven million dollar project. The new Namao airfield would feature two 7000-foot runways capable of handling the largest aircraft. At the same time the federal government continued to upgrade and invest in Blatchford Field. By 1944 six million dollars had been spent on the field with a further two million invested by the end of the war. The runways were upgraded with steel and concrete, increasing the field's ability to handle heavy transport aircraft. When No. 2 AOS closed its doors in July 1944, it provided more room for Northwest Staging Route personnel. Wop May was presented with the Medal Of Freedom, Bronze Palm for assisting with the Staging Route, as well as developing in 1943 an aerial rescue unit to save downed pilots along the route.

On 27 September 1944 the base at Namao was completed and American personnel were settling into their new facilities. One of the last functions of the American staff at Blatchford was to honour the person who had worked incredibly hard for them; Captain Jimmy Bell was awarded the American Medal of Freedom. The vacated facilities at Blatchford Field were taken over almost immediately by the Department of Transport and various commercial operations. Aircraft Repair Ltd. was reaching the end of their contract obligations and began laying off hundreds of workers.

In April 1945 Germany was defeated, and when a few short months later Japan surrendered, Jasper Avenue turned into a giant parade. Although the war was over, the American Lend-Lease programme did not officially end until September 1945. In the space of three years over 5066 fighters were delivered, 2618 P-39 Airacobras, 2397 P-63 Kingcobras, 48 P-40 Warhawks and three P-47 Thunderbolts. In addition, another 2860 bombers and transports travelled the

Aircraft Repair Ltd. hangar at Blatchford Field, with Lend-Lease Bell P-39 Airacobras ready for transport to the USSR. Russian pilots took over at Fairbanks, Alaska.

Photo courtesy Alberta Aviation Museum.

route, including 1363 A-20s, 732 B-25 Mitchells and 765 C-47s, C-46s and At-6s. The Northwest Staging Route must be considered one of the great achievements of the war. Pilots flew over 2000 miles of the worst terrain in North America, and some didn't make it. At the time the Commanding General of the Red Air Force was quoted as saying "[there] are graves of those who died among the snows of this route which mean as much to us as those at Smolensk, Stalingrad and Sevastopol. We feel they died fighting beside us."[21]

Blatchford Field would continue to do well. The American hangars would be taken over by various commercial operations. Two of these hangars still stand on the east side of the field bordering the Northern Alberta Institute of Technology. The hangar that housed No. 2 AOS would become the post-war home of the 418 [City of Edmonton] Squadron, and eventually the Alberta Aviation Museum. The site of Aircraft Repair Ltd., later Northwest Industries, is now a series of abandoned buildings on the far north end of the field.

The first five years after the war would prove even busier than thought possible. TCA and CPA would open new routes and services; construction of the DEW line would break traffic records set during the war; the RCAF established Canada's largest concentration of personnel and aircraft in Canada by establishing the Northwest Air Command in Edmonton.

Not even Wop May could have possibly imagined the glowing future of the cow pasture on which he had landed his Curtiss Jenny so many times only some twenty years before.

NOTES

[1]J.A. Villa-Arce, *Chronological History of Aviation in Alberta:1900-1961.* [Provincial Museum of Alberta, Human History Section, Edmonton: 5 February 1974. (Mimeographed)], p. 21.

[2]William Paul Ferguson, *The Snowbird Decades.* [Vancouver: Butterworth & Co., 1979], p. 73.

[3]W.A.B. Douglas, *The Creation of a National Air Force. The Official History of the Royal Canadian Air Force,* Volume II. [Toronto: University of Toronto Press, 1986], p. 293.

[4]Ibid, p. 293.

[5]Frank Dolphin, *History of the Municipal Airport.* [Unpublished manuscript: Alberta Aviation Museum, Archives Division, 1993] Ch. 4, p. 3.

[6]Department of Defence, Directorate of History, Record Group 24 [RG24]/D6771, 181.009, Vol. I, 1940, "Standard Form of Agreement for Operation of an Air Observer School at an Aerodrome Maintained by the Department of Transport." See also; "Schedule 11 to Foregoing Agreement," "Estimate of Costs upon which Remuneration under Schedule II is Based," and "Schedule of Wages."

[7]J.A. Villa-Arce, op. cit., p. 23.

[8]K.M. Molson, *Pioneering in Canadian Air Transport.* [Altona, Man.: D.W. Friesen & Sons Ltd., 2nd ed., 1975], p. 234.

[9]DND, DHist, RG24, Microfilm Reel 12380, "Manning Depot #3."

[10]DND, DHist, RG24, D5355, 181.003, "Historical Report to DMS [AIR], No.4 ITS," p. 1.

[11]Ibid, p. 5.

[12]J.A. Villa-Arce, op. cit., p. 24.

[13]Peter Conrad, *Training for Victory. The British Commonwealth Air Training Plan in the West.* [Saskatoon: Western Producer Prairie Books, 1989], p. 30.

[14]DND, DHist, RG24, D6771, 181.009, Vol. I, "Air Observers School Syllabus," 3rd ed., 15 May 1940.

[15]DND, DHist, RG24, FA104, Microfilm Reel C12,329, "# 2 AOS July 1940-1944."

[16]Stan Cohen, *The Trail of '42. A Pictorial History of the Alaska Highway.* [Missoula: Pictorial Histories Publishing Co., 1979; reprint ed., Altona, Man.: D.W. Friesen and Sons Ltd., 1993], p. 15.

[17]Stan Cohen, *The Forgotten War. Volume Two. A Pictorial History of World War II in Alaska and Northwestern Canada.* [Missoula: Pictorial Histories Publishing Company, 1988], p. 37.

[18]Eugenie Louise Myles, *Airborne from Edmonton.* [Toronto: The Ryerson Press, 1959], p. 259.

[19]James G. MacGregor, *Edmonton: A History.* [Edmonton: M.G. Hurtig Publishers, 1967], p. 265.

[20]Pierre Berton, *Runway to the World.* Muni News, Volume 7 Issue 1, 1994, p. 11.

[21]J.A. Foster, *The Bush Pilots.* [Toronto: McClelland and Stewart, 1990], p. 176.

Watching the War Fly By: The British Commonwealth Air Training Plan in Alberta

Patricia A. Myers

On 9 January 1941 the *Claresholm Local Press* reported "a real old time chinook" had blown in the day before making it feel more like June than January. That was bad news for the hockey players and curlers who depended on cold temperatures to keep their ice keen. But it was good news for the airfield under construction just outside of town. "Work is rapidly speeding up at the airport," the *Press* continued, "The gravel dump is already a small mountain.... High powered dump trucks rumble in and out of town on change of shifts at all hours of the day and night.... The lumber and cement is rapidly piling up on the grounds, being moved by truck from the local freight yards." The new airfield was to be the home of No. 15 Service Flying Training School of the British Commonwealth Air Training Plan.[1]

That Plan was an ambitious scheme to train air crew, drawn from air force enlistees from British Commonwealth countries, for the Allied war effort. It had its roots in the Imperial Conferences of the 1920s where the idea of cooperative air training had first been raised.[2] During the 1930s the Royal Air Force [RAF] and the Royal Canadian Air Force [RCAF] began to cooperate in a limited way. Canadians were accepted into the RAF in small numbers, while some British recruits were trained in Canada. As gathering war clouds threatened Europe during the late 1930s, the reemerging German air force caused Britain to think about expanding its own air-training capacity. Canada seemed safe, secure and a good distance away from its own vulnerable shores, making Canadian soil a good location for the necessary training facilities. Negotiations to get some kind of training scheme under way were begun, although progress at first was slow. Canada and Great Britain soon learned, however, that training would have to be well planned, and that the civilian flying clubs would have to be partners in the endeavour.

When Canada did not declare war on Germany until one week after Britain and France had done so, Prime Minister W. L. Mackenzie King was making a point: Canada would make her own decisions, and as much as possible participate in the war on Canada's terms. [3] Paramount in King's mind was preserving both Canadian independence and Canadian unity. He was adamant that Canada not be drawn into supplying unlimited land troops, fearing a repeat of the conscription battle like the one that had so divided the country during the First World War. King found the idea that Canada's major contribution to the war effort could be supplying and training air crew appealing for that reason.

Negotiations to formulate the British Commonwealth Air Training Plan [BCATP] were long and slow as the King government kept to its course of ensuring Canadian independence. In the end King wore the other parties down, and the deal that was signed on 17 December 1939 [King's birthday] included his demands that the Plan be run by the RCAF and that the formation of Canadian operational squadrons would be possible in the future. King also wrung financial concessions out of the British, including an agreement to help Australia and New Zealand raise the Canadian dollars they needed to pay their way in the Plan.

The BCATP was run by four training commands: No. 1 was headquartered in Toronto and administered western Ontario; No. 2, centred at Winnipeg, covered Manitoba, part of Saskatchewan and part of northwestern Ontario; No. 3 had headquarters at Montreal and administered Quebec and the Maritimes; No. 4, with headquarters in Regina until September 1941 when they were moved to Calgary, ran the programme in the rest of Saskatchewan, as well as in Alberta and British Columbia. Each command looked after every aspect of the Plan in its district, from pilot training right down to repair, maintenance and stores.[4]

The BCATP accepted its first recruits 29 April 1940 at No. 1 Manning Depot in Toronto, and stayed in effect until 31 March 1945 with few alterations. With the fall of France in June 1940 it was pushed ahead on a faster schedule, and some RAF schools were relocated onto Canadian soil. The agreement was amended in 1942, with the RAF units being integrated into the BCATP.

This scene was repeated at mess halls on BCATP stations across Alberta.

Photo courtesy Provincial Archives of Alberta: Alfred Blyth collection, [Bl.605/15].

Those first recruits followed a plan of study that changed little over the training scheme's lifetime. Some tinkering was done with the amount of time spent in each training phase and with the air observer/navigator duties, but essentially the original plan of 1940 endured until 1945. The Plan's mandate was to graduate all members of an air crew; pilots, navigators, bomb aimers, wireless operators, air gunners and flight engineers were all trained under its wing.

Although most of the young men who signed up started out wanting to be pilots, it was the job of their instructors and of the training regimen to ensure only those best suited to piloting graduated as pilots. At every stage in the process, including initial recruitment, trainees could be sent into one of the other streams.

The BCATP had a tremendous presence in Alberta. Factors that had made Canada attractive as a location for the Plan, primarily its distance from Europe and plenty of space, were certainly available in Alberta. The combination of seemingly limitless sky, clear weather, and low population density had ensured the prairies would be a prime location for air training. Each station, for example, not only had its airfield and a host of buildings, but an auxiliary airfield nearby as well. The Hon. John C. Bowen, Alberta's Lieutenant-Governor, while speaking in Edmonton in 1942, suggested that the success of Canada's bush pilots and of Canadian aces in the First World War were also factors that had led to the Plan being located in Canada. Alberta certainly could claim important roles for her aviators in both those instances. Peter Conrad has argued baser motives had a hand in determining exactly who got what training centres, maintaining that Liberal ridings received preference in the location of training facilities wherever possible.[5]

Alberta was quickly dotted with BCATP facilities. As well as the training command located in Calgary after September 1941, Alberta received No. 3 Manning Depot located in Edmonton; an Initial Training School [ITS] at Edmonton; Elementary Flying Training Schools [EFTS] at Lethbridge [later moved to High River], Edmonton, DeWinton, Bowden and Pearce; Service Flying Training Schools [SFTS] in Calgary, Fort Macleod, Claresholm, Vulcan, Medicine Hat, and Penhold; and a Flying Instructor School [FIS] at Vulcan that was later moved to Pearce. A Wireless School was located in Calgary and a Bombing and Gunnery School in Lethbridge, while Air Observers Schools [AOS] were run in Edmonton and Pearce. Finally, a repair depot and an equipment depot both were located in Calgary.

BCATP schools brought tremendous changes to their host communities, with the greatest changes occurring in the smaller communities. Airfields had to be carved right from the prairie soil, and barracks and huts rise from what had once been wheat fields. From the minute the location of a school was announced the effects started to be seen. The first sign of what was to come usually occurred when officials from the Department of Transport began to acquire land, and as survey crews marked out future runways and building locations. Construction equipment and workers followed. Small towns did not have the large construction companies required to do the earth moving, grading and excavation required by air training sites, so much of the construction was handled by outside companies who hired labour locally. In Claresholm, for example, earth moving and ground preparation for the Service Flying Training School was carried out by the General Construction Company of Vancouver. Almost twenty train-car loads of graders, steam shovels, rollers, trucks, and asphalt mixers rolled into the tiny town. Bennett and White of Calgary then took over when it was time for the buildings to go up. The Claresholm newspaper noted that many of the trucks used on the project were being operated by local owners.[6]

In Lethbridge, the story was the same for the construction of No. 8 Bombing and Gunnery School. Shoquist Construction of Saskatoon, Saskatchewan, acted as general contractor for the buildings and hired Alberta companies for various jobs. Freel of Lethbridge, for example, did the sheet metal work, while the painting was done by Palex Painters of Calgary.

The first impact on the towns was economic, and this influence lasted until the Plan ended. The BCATP construction boom would create hundreds of short-term jobs.[7] Tradesmen from tin smiths to electricians were needed, as were general workers to do jobs such as laying railway spur lines into the school sites or unloading pipe for the gas line. At one point, the *Red Deer Advocate* noted that 400 men were working on the Penhold Station. As the stations went up, other groups of workers came in waves. Electricians and plumbers replaced carpenters, for example, as the buildings took shape. This continued the pattern of migrant labour created by the Depression, where men had gone from town to town in the hope of finding work. The *Claresholm Local Press* reported at the beginning of construction, that "unskilled labour has poured in from hundreds of miles around, broke, and with no connections." Men working on the station, it was said, were continually being asked if any more jobs were available. Although the work of constructing a station required a great number of workers, the frantic pace went on for only a short time, and did not provide any lasting end to unemployment.

For the towns, though, the economic benefits did start immediately. "Vulcan Booming as Air Station Brings Big Payroll," a *Lethbridge Herald* headline cried during the construction phase. It claimed Vulcan was even busier than it had been during the biggest wheat boom years. Those building the stations were paid regular wages. On the first pay day, businesses stayed open in the evening so the workers would have no problem deciding what to do with their earnings. If they were from out of town, they needed to rent a place to stay. Boarding houses, basements and hotels were full for the first time in years. Not all landlords, though, were able to collect what they were owed; the Claresholm paper noted that some of the construction workers had "neglected" to pay their boarding-house bills before leaving town.

When the bases were up and operating, the economic benefits of having one located near your community were staggering. The first priority was housing; although the trainees and some of the instructors lived on the base, many of the other officers and employees wanted accommodation in town, especially if they were married and had brought their families with them. Appeals from local authorities to residents to open their homes to the newcomers were made on a patriotic basis as well as an economic one. It was argued that the income from rented rooms or suites would be welcome in many households. Residents were also urged to renovate as it was felt that this would make unused space more appealing to potential renters. Farmers as well as townspeople took in boarders and renters to ease the acute housing shortage.

Boards of trade assisted in trying to locate housing space within their communities, and in encouraging local citizens to make it available to BCATP personnel.[8] Furnished accommodation was particularly hard to find. The Vulcan board drew up a list of available rooms, and the Macleod Board of Trade also helped to place BCATP families. In the larger centres the story was the same. Many people in the area around the airport in Edmonton, for example, took in boarders connected with military activities.

Local people also found regular employment on the stations as many jobs did not require that they be done by military personnel.[9] Men and women worked as mechanics, truck and tractor drivers, janitors, stenographers and at a host of other occupations. A large part of their steady pay cheques remained in their communities.

Almost all businesses benefitted from increased revenue as the result of a station being located nearby.[10] BCATP trainees and members of the Royal Canadian Air Force Women's Division [RCAF (WDs)] were paid a daily stipend, and some of that found its way into local coffers. F. M. Anderson & Co. Ltd. of Vulcan advertised special stock for the RCAF, including khaki pants, "silver grey airforce broadcloth dress shirts, and regulation military dress Oxfords." Drug stores urged the new residents to come in and browse through their sundries and toiletries. Even garages and auto parts dealers sought to bring their products to the attention of the airmen and airwomen. Taxi companies, tailors, and barbers all aimed advertising at those connected with the BCATP. For example, the Claresholm Laundry offered free pick-up and delivery to the airmen. From postcards and souvenirs to send back home, to shoes and cologne, businesses strove to coax a part of airmens' and airwomens' pay from their pockets.

Aircraft repair at No. 2 Air Observers School in Edmonton, 1943.

Photo courtesy Provincial Archives of Alberta: Alfred Blyth Collection, [Bl.529/1].

The entertainment industry did particularly well. Movie houses, dance halls, and cafes near BCATP stations from Edmonton to Medicine Hat saw their business jump dramatically. Games rooms such as bowling alleys and pool halls also did a good business. Drug store soda fountains and main street restaurants plying home-style cooking sold everything from sodas to lemon meringue pie in great quantity. Beer halls did a good business, too, and many a young trainee had his first beer after joining up.

This is not to imply, however, that the stations with their staff and trainees were viewed only in a cold, economic light. There is much evidence to indicate the newcomers were heartily welcomed into their new communities. Civic authorities were among the groups in the forefront of the welcome extended to all those associated with BCATP stations. Mayors, boards of trade, and other officials took part in welcoming ceremonies in person, and urged residents to open their homes and hearts to the young men and women connected with the BCATP. The Mayor's welcoming address printed in the 4 August 1941 edition of the *Claresholm Local Press* is typical of the sentiment expressed toward the newcomers. "The Town of Claresholm gives Welcome," it proclaimed, and went on to extend "the unreserved hospitality of the town and rural communities" to the school's commanding officer and those serving under him. "It is with mingled pride and sublimation [sic]," he continued, "that we offer 'all out' co-operation towards the progress of this training and towards the happiness and comfort of the staff and student pilots." Civic support continued throughout the operation of the Plan, as boards of trade and civic leaders hosted dinners and put on other activities for the station officers and other personnel.[11]

The general populace joined in too, and did not let up until the Plan was closed down. From those who simply showed up at the train station to drive new trainees to the BCATP facility, to the thousands of Sunday pot roasts shared with homesick enlistees, communities pitched in to make the airmen and airwomen feel at home. While the BCATP built recreation halls on the stations, it left the furnishing and running of them to volunteers from the communities. The Legion and the YWCA stepped forward in this capacity, but so did much smaller, local groups from churches, women's groups, service clubs, and other organizations. From the United Farm Women to the Eastern Star Lodge, women in particular sewed curtains, staffed canteens, and put on turkey suppers. Others in the communities collected sports equipment and board games, ran dances, put on concerts, and led magazine drives for the stations.

Providing recreational facilities right in the towns was a point of real pride in the smaller communities. In Red Deer, the town bought a building and renovated it to make a recreational facility, while women's groups took turns staffing it every evening. This facility was very much appreciated by the BCATP personnel, and an article in the *Red Deer Advocate* in March 1942 put the weekly attendance at around 3700. Activities ranged from dances to "picture shows" and concerts. The games room was said always to be busy, and lots of writing paper and envelopes were handed out as well.

This community generosity did not go unnoticed. D.K. Yorvath, Managing Director of No. 5 EFTS in High River, for example, thanked that town through its newspaper in September 1942, expressing his appreciation for its friendship, cooperation, and support. He felt that High River had adopted each new class, and had helped to make their stays happy ones. For their part, BCATP staff and students gave a great deal back to their host communities. They took part in parades, put on concerts, gave Christmas parties for underprivileged children, and helped in war bond drives. They took part in sports days, and played against local sports teams.

Airmen and WD's take part in a parade in Calgary during the war. BCATP personnel were eager participants in community activities.

Photo courtesy Provincial Archives of Alberta: Harry Pollard Collection, [P6495].

Certainly one aspect of all this community activity was to provide wholesome, supervised activities for the legions of young men and women the BCATP had thrown into their midst. An advertisement for dances at a hall in Claresholm declared they were held in "clean, attractive surroundings," and were "capably controlled." Community authorities were concerned about the influx, every six weeks or so, of a new group of young men with money in their pockets and the spectre of an imminent departure to war on their minds. Romances blossomed quickly in this atmosphere. One women from a farm near Penhold recalled that she spotted an attractive RAF corporal playing in the dance band at the Penhold station. The next day she met him at a church social and dance in Red Deer, where he asked her to dance. A year later they were married. This experience, with some variation in the time it took to get to the altar, was repeated in all communities with BCATP stations.[12]

One of the side effects the BCATP had, especially on the smaller communities, was to turn the war into something of a spectator sport. Right from the beginning of construction, local residents watched developments closely. In Edmonton hundreds of curious people watched as planes for the Air Observers School arrived, and followed the later construction at the airfield. During the construction phase at Penhold, the best show from the spectator's point of view, according to the *Red Deer Advocate*, was watching the trusses for the hangar roofs go up. Each roof had 22 trusses and they were raised with drag lines. As construction proceeded at the bases, guards were posted and the public could no longer have unrestricted access to the site. In some smaller communities it took a while for this message to be accepted. In Claresholm residents had to be warned that the guards took their duties seriously and were armed.

Opening day was the first chance the communities got to see the stations in operation.[13] Each station went all out to make a good impression; most opening-day celebrations were held after the stations had been up and running for a few weeks, and often were held in conjunction with graduation ceremonies for the first class. The excitement building up to the big day was intensified by good press coverage. In Lethbridge 5000 people attended the opening of No. 8 Bombing and Gunnery School in November 1941; the official opening ceremony and speeches were followed by the "wings parade" where members of the graduating class received their wings. The grounds and some of the buildings then were opened to the public. The whole affair was very festive and featured formation flying, a parachute jump, and rousing band music provided by the band from the Service Flying Training School at Macleod.

Similar opening days were held at every station in Alberta, and they were attended by thousands of people. Curiosity about the stations and their activities naturally was high, created by months of construction followed by the frantic activity of the arriving staff and students. By opening day training planes would have been cruising constantly overhead, providing a thrilling spectacle for many residents. The excitement of opening days was usually repeated every year with equally festive anniversary open houses or carnivals. No.19 SFTS near Vulcan hosted a "Mammoth Free Carnival" in September 1944, featuring a wings parade, sports competitions including a baseball game against army personnel from Calgary, and a dance. There were also games of skill, raffles and fireworks. Conducted tours of the station were offered where the public could examine various pieces of RCAF equipment. People were "cordially invited to come at 1 p.m. and stay until 2 a.m." These events continued to be well attended throughout the existence of the training scheme.[14]

BCATP stations also encouraged local residents to become spectators in the sporting arena.[15] Airmen and airwomen held sports days where they competed in a variety of track and field events, while at open houses they frequently put on sports exhibitions. Throughout the year they played baseball, basketball, hockey, rugby and many other sports. They played inter-squad games against others at their station, as well as scheduled competitions against teams from other BCATP schools. Some teams played in local leagues and against teams from nearby

Hundreds of spectators filled this arena, probably in Edmonton, to watch a "wings parade" in May 1943. BCATP activities drew large, supportive crowds for the duration of the Plan.

Photo courtesy Provincial Archives of Alberta: Alfred Blyth Collection [Bl.543/1].

towns. Games were well attended by local residents, and received good coverage in the papers. The airmen's hockey team from No. 15 SFTS near Claresholm was credited with rekindling interest in hockey in that district. In February 1942, this team was challenging for the RCAF Service League title in southern Alberta, locked in a battle with a team from Macleod. When the final game was held in Lethbridge, a special train chartered to make the trip carried several hundred boisterous supporters from the base and town to Lethbridge to support their team.

Boxing was another sport featuring air force personnel that enjoyed good fan support among civilians. One "Mammoth Boxing Card" put on at the station near Vulcan in February 1943 featured a western Canadian welterweight champion. Tickets could be purchased at several places in town, including King's Drugstore and Bon and Monty's pool hall and barber shop. Wrestling or a fencing demonstration often rounded out the evening. Boxing cards almost always drew large enthusiastic crowds, and continued to be popular throughout the war years.

From watching aircraft dipping and droning overhead to joining in the cheers for a victorious hockey team, Albertans who lived near a British Commonwealth Air Training Plan facility had ring-side seats for one part of the war. On the whole it was a sanitized and glossy show. Apart from the relatively few times when novice or stunting pilots sent their planes spinning into the ground, the reality of war was far removed from BCATP stations. Instead, the daily round featured a continuous stream of healthy young men passing through their training requirements, parading through the streets, playing in a band, or engaged in robust athletic competition. At carnivals and open houses local residents peered into cockpits, marvelled at the orderliness of the parachute packing room, and enjoyed music and refreshments, all in the company of spotlessly turned-out airmen and airwomen. Local attention usually remained focused on the economic benefits, and some of the social ones, of having a BCATP station nearby.

While casualty lists filled the newspapers, and fear for loved ones fighting overseas was no less real, nearness to a BCATP station ironically reinforced the distance separating the towns' experiences from the conflict. When the cafes and bowling alleys were full, and you went off whistling to your job as a truck driver on the station, the war seemed quite far off indeed. Beginning in 1944, when it came time for the plan to be wound down, all communities with stations were reluctant to see them closed. Most lobbied the federal government in an attempt to keep the stations open in some capacity, whether as training facilities or as airports. Communities could see the end of the boom time, and were apprehensive about the future. One account of just how buoyant those boom years were can be found in *Wheat Country*, the Vulcan local history: the theatres ran every night except Sunday, restaurants were full, and for the first time in its history the bank stayed open past 5 o'clock to cash pay cheques. With the memory of the bleak Depression years still quite fresh, communities feared that the loss of BCATP facilities would mean a return to economic despair.[16]

While economic uncertainty seemed to cloud the immediate post-war picture in many communities, many also were not blind to some of the other more lasting effects of having the Plan in their back yard. The British Commonwealth Air Training Plan gave local people a real opportunity to contribute to the war effort on a very personal level. Buying war bonds was one thing, but singing songs around the parlour piano with young airmen and airwomen was quite another. Many friendships were made, and when the time came, many farewells were hard. Thirty years after the closure of No. 2 Flying Instructor School near Vulcan, residents continued to exchange Christmas cards and letters with now-distant friends made at the school. Some people connected with the plan took up residence in the host communities, often because of marriage, but for other reasons as well. Jock Palmer was typical of this process, moving to High River from Lethbridge with No. 5 Elementary Flying Training School when it changed locations. He stayed in High River, opening up an electrical repair shop there.[17]

The British Commonwealth Air Training Plan brought good times to the small Alberta communities near the stations. Town economies boomed, and the steady stream of sports, carnivals and other entertainments made for a very busy time. Local people could contribute directly to the running of the war effort, and were proud of what they had done. The BCATP brought the war closer, and at the same time made it seem very far away. When it was all over, townspeople wished the departing personnel "Farewell and Happy Landings," and hoped their towns could face the future with the optimism and economic benefits their wartime experience had brought.

NOTES

The author would like to thank Michael Payne, Stan Reynolds, Jack Reilly, Jack Manson and Byron Reynolds for comments on the chapter of her forthcoming book on the history of aviation in Alberta, from which this article is drawn. Called Sky Riders: An Illustrated History of Aviation in Alberta 1906-1945, *it is being published by Fifth House Publishers in the spring of 1995.*

[1] *Claresholm Local Press*, 9 January 1941.

[2] Several works discuss the genesis of the BCATP. See for example, Larry Milberry and Hugh A. Halliday, *The Royal Canadian Air Force at War, 1939-1945* [Toronto: CANAV Books, 1990]; F. J. Hatch, *Aerodrome of Democracy: Canada and the British Commonwealth Air Training Plan, 1939 - 1945* [Ottawa: Queen's Printer, 1983], pp. 1-12; and J. L. Granatstein, *Canada's War: The Politics of the Mackenzie King Government, 1939 - 1945* [Toronto: Oxford University Press, 1975], pp. 43-44. For general background on the Second World War in Alberta and Canada, see Howard Palmer with Tamara Palmer, *Alberta: A New History* [Edmonton: Hurtig Publishers, 1990]; Robert Bothwell, Ian Drummond and John English, *Canada 1900 - 1945* [Toronto: Oxford University Press, 1987]; and J. L. Granatstein and Desmond Morton, *A Nation Forged in Fire: Canadians and the Second World War 1939 - 1945* [Toronto: Lester and Orpen Denys Limited, 1989].

[3] King's position and fears, his expert manoeuvring, and the negotiations to formulate the Plan can be followed in detail in Granatstein, pp. 43 - 66. King's diaries are also useful. See J. W. Pickersgill, *The Mackenzie King Record.* Volume I, 1939 - 1944 [Toronto: University of Toronto Press, 1960], pp. 40-59. See also Hatch, pp.1-26.

[4] Several works discuss the details of establishing and implementing the Plan. See for example, Hatch, Chapter 2; W.A.B. Douglas, *The Creation of a National Air Force: The Official History of the Royal Canadian Air Force.* Volume II [Toronto: 1986)], pp. 220-224; Ted Barris, *Behind the Glory: The Plan that Won the Allied Air War* [Toronto: Macmillan, 1992)], pp. 33-34, 58-60. For the experience of those in the Plan, see Larry Milberry, *Aviation in Canada* [Toronto: McGraw-Hill Ryerson Limited, 1979]; Larry Milberry, gen. ed., *Sixty Years: The RCAF and CF Air Command 1924 - 1984* [Toronto: CANAV Books, 1985], pp. 97-114; and Spencer Dunmore, *Wings for Victory: The Remarkable Story of the British Commonwealth Air Training Plan in Canada* [Toronto: McClelland and Stewart, 1994]. Two good accounts of experiences in Alberta are John W. Chalmers, "Learning the Gen Trade," *Alberta History* [Summer 1994] pp. 2-20, and Murray Peden, *A Thousand Shall Fall* [Stittsville, Ontario: Canada's Wings Inc., 1979]. See also Mary Ziegler, *We Serve That Men May Fly* [Hamilton, Ontario: RCAF (WD) Association, 1973]. Daily diaries were kept at each BCATP station, and are now housed at the National Archives of Canada.

[5] Reported in the *Edmonton Bulletin*, 15 December 1942; Peter Conrad, *Training for Victory* [Saskatoon: Western Producer Prairie Books, 1989], p. 16.

[6] *Claresholm Local Press*, 10 October 1940 and 14 August 1941 [special opening section]. For Lethbridge, see *The Lethbridge Herald*, 7 November 1941 [special opening section].

[7] Construction of the various stations can be followed in the local newspapers through regular reports. See for example, the *High River Times, Vulcan Advocate, Lethbridge Herald, Red Deer Advocate* and *Claresholm Local Press* during the construction phase for each facility. For a discussion of the impact of the stations in Saskatchewan, see Brereton Greenhous and Norman Hillmer, "The Impact of the British Commonwealth Air Training Plan on Western Canada: Some Saskatchewan Case Studies," *Journal of Canadian Studies*, Vol. 16, Nos. 3&4 [Fall/winter, 1981], pp. 133-144.

[8] *Vulcan Advocate*, 14 May 1942; *Lethbridge Herald*, 15 November 1941; For Edmonton, see Lori Yanish and Shirley Lowe, *Edmonton's West Side Story: The History of the Original West End from 1870* [Edmonton: 124th Street and Area Business Association, 1991].

9 See for example, "Wanted" advertisement, *High River Times*, 12 June 1941.

10 Local newspapers were full of advertisements from businesses hoping to get a part of the BCATP bonanza. The editions celebrating the official opening of each station are particularly rich. See for example, *Vulcan Advocate*, 5 November 1942.

11 *Claresholm Local Press*, 14 August 1941. Community participation, including the development of recreation facilities, can be followed in the newspapers. See for example, *Lethbridge Herald*, 7 October 1941 and 20 November 1941; and *Red Deer Herald*, 27 August 1941, 3 September 1941, and 4 March 1942. The role of the Legion in setting up recreational facilities can be found in Clifford H. Bowering, *Service: The Story of the Canadian Legion* [Ottawa: Dominion Command, Canadian Legion, 1960].

12 *Edmonton Journal*, 11 October 1994, "War-time romance with 'cute' RAF man blossomed into a lifetime of happiness"; Gordon Wagner's memoir, *How Papa Won the War* [Courtenay, B.C: Flying - W- Publishing Co., 1989], is full of examples of what townspeople feared. He details the earthier pursuits during his time at BCATP facilities in Alberta.

13 For examples of opening day activities, see *High River Times*, 25 September 1941, *Claresholm Local Press*, 21 August 1941, and *Lethbridge Herald*, 10 November 1941.

14 *Vulcan Advocate*, advertisements, 7 September 1944 and 14 September 1944.

15 Sporting events can also be followed in the newspapers. See for example, *High River Times*, 6 August 1942, and *Vulcan Advocate* sports columns on 14 January and 4 February 1943. Various publications put out by the stations also covered the wide range of sporting activities available. See for example, *The Penhold Log*, Vol. IV, No. 2, August 1943 in the Red Deer and District Archives, Red Deer; and *A History of No. 5 E.F.T.S.* [February 1945], in the library collection of the Glenbow Archives, Calgary.

16 See the *High River Times*, 26 October 1942, for an example of civic action to keep the stations functioning; *Wheat Country: A History of Vulcan and District* [Vulcan and District Historical Society, 1973], pp.105-106.

17 *Wheat Country*, p.106; *High River Times*, February 1945. See as well, *Vulcan Advocate*, 12 April 1945, "Farewell and Happy Landings."

"Every Kitchen is an Arsenal": Women's War on the Home Front in Northern Alberta

Catherine C. Cole

Women made many significant contributions to Canada's war effort. In Alberta, at least five hundred women entered the armed forces. Mary Dover of Calgary was a Lieutenant Colonel in the Canadian Women's Army Corps [CWAC], and headed the country's largest training centre. The Alberta Women's Service Corps [AWSC] was established at the beginning of the war to train women in military discipline, first aid, transport, clerical, commissariat, and other duties. Women formed auxiliary units to the Veterans Volunteer Reserve and participated in activities such as rifle practice, first aid training, social events and fundraising. In addition to their military and paramilitary efforts, women on the home front contributed voluntary service through agencies such as the Women's Institutes [WI], the United Farm Women of Alberta [UFWA], the Red Cross, the Imperial Order of the Daughters of the Empire [IODE], the Young Women's Christian Association [YWCA], and various church groups. Some women also started non-affiliated groups with the single purpose of contributing to the war effort.

A national census undertaken late in 1939 registered women for Emergency Services, and they trained for opportunities which might arise during the war. These women worked in wartime industries such as the Great Western Garment Company and Aircraft Repair Ltd. in Edmonton, and filled men's traditional roles teaching, in local businesses, and on the farms. Between 1940 and 1942 the number of male family members working on farms across the nation dropped by 13.2 per cent and the number of male hired hands dropped by over 40 per cent.[1] No matter what type of war-work women were engaged in, all the while they thought about their husbands, fiancés, sons or daughters serving overseas, and worked to make their time more bearable, and towards a shortened war.

During the war many women replaced men working in the farm fields.

Photo courtesy Provincial Archives of Alberta [PAA Bl. 639/5].

Women's Wartime Concerns

The outbreak of war brought an abrupt end to the Great Depression. It provided an abrupt change of focus for women, from money and security anxieties, to fear for loved ones and uncertainty for the future. Women's pages of newspapers continued to relate fashion tips and information about health, nutrition, child care, weddings, the comings and goings of society's elite and other social events, but many articles had a new focus. Serialized novels had wartime titles such as "Girl at the Front" and "So Your Husband's Gone to War." Most of the organized social events reported were now fundraisers in one form or another, or efforts to entertain servicemen stationed in the region, or their wives and mothers. The daily lives of women changed as well. One of the first changes noted on the home front was that marriage became more popular; 200 more couples married in 1939 than in 1938, an increase of about 50 per month since the outbreak of war. The records office noted that the "[majority] of the would-be grooms told office clerks that they wanted to get married before joining the army so that their wives would be able to get allowances."[2] As the war progressed, many aspects of their lives were regulated by government, and women felt more and more demands upon their time and their emotions.

Newspapers were critical of the federal government's response to the war, writing that Canada seemed slow to respond to the emergency. Women's voluntary service organizations, on the other hand, already were experienced in war-work from the First World War, and immediately mobilized their members, who began knitting, fundraising, and providing a broad range of comforts for soldiers. Women initiated numerous means to assist the war effort, and were always anxious to support broader societal efforts, but an editorial in the *Edmonton Journal* titled "Why Ignore the Women?" questioned the lack of recognition of women's contributions by Ottawa.

> *The women of Canada are just as anxious to help their men smash Hitler and all his works as are the women of the British Isles to help their men. In Britain, the government has organized its eager women to assist in almost every phase of their country's war effort. In Canada, the government does not seem to know or care that the women can and want to help.*[3]

Capt. B. Farnham sells stamps to women during a war savings stamps campaign in Edmonton.

Photo courtesy Provincial Archives of Alberta [FAA Bl. 591/2].

As the years passed, and more and more men were called into active service, the abilities and contributions of women become more important. Each year saw women coping with additional responsibilities. Many women were left on their own to raise their children and handle family finances, in many cases for the first time. Women, as the primary purchasers in families, were encouraged to buy British and Empire-made goods to assist the economies of the allies. They were urged to save their spare change to buy war savings stamps, and were responsible for both the buying and the selling of war savings stamps. Aluminum salvaging began in the summer of 1941, and salvage of fats began in 1942. "Every Kitchen is an Arsenal" was a slogan in the campaign to collect fats and bones, and posters and leaflets proclaimed that "If everyone in Canada saves as little as two ounces of waste cooking fat in a week, it will produce the glycerine required for the

"Every kitchen is an arsenal." Women and children collecting fats in Edmonton during July 1943.

Photo courtesy Provincial Archives of Alberta [PAA Bl. 590].

gunpowder to smash Adolph, Benito and Tojo!"[4] Edmonton children were given a free theatre ticket for every two pounds of fat collected, and women in the Citizens Volunteer Bureau coordinated the campaign. Rural areas also participated in the salvage programmes and forwarded their salvage to central depots; grain elevators doubled as collection depots throughout the rural west. Rationing began in February 1942, with sugar limited to 3/4 pound per person per week. Within months, tea, coffee and butter also were rationed, effectively ending the popular "Afternoon Tea" fundraisers. The following year, the rationing was extended to include meats other than fish and poultry, preserves and alternative sweeteners.

While many of the changes in women's lives were viewed as temporary, or "for the duration," early in the war women recognized that many changes would be permanent. Encouraging increased settlement in the west had long been seen as desirable, and one aspect of women's club work had traditionally been to welcome new settlers to an area and assist them in adapting to the Canadian way of life. These women faced difficult questions during the war. For many, the war was being fought to support democracy, a British democracy. And many women's groups felt that all people who chose to live in Canada had an obligation to support the cause. For example, the UFWA voted to revoke an agreement giving Hutterites and their descendants the privilege of not fighting when Canada was at war because they "felt that at a time of crisis there should be no group with special privileges."[5] Friction between groups was acknowledged as a problem. Mrs. Harvey Agnew of Toronto stressed to a meeting of the YWCA the importance of home front activity, and "referring to the quarrels between Canadians and Immigrants said women should take a share in unifying the various peoples of Canada."[6] The IODE was one of many organizations which from the first days of the war addressed the concern of a pending refugee problem. Provincial President Mrs. R.C. Marshall stated that "Canada's wide-open spaces will inevitably give us a refugee or immigration problem. In the past we have shouldered some duties in connection with Canadianization. We must decide what we will do for immigrants in the future."[7] Some refugees were welcomed with open arms; an *Edmonton Journal* survey found that there were hundreds of women in Alberta who were willing to take British or French refugee children.[8] The idea of bringing in "guest children" from Britain came from a woman who had formerly lived in Fort Saskatchewan, but who was then living in British Columbia. Mennonites, although opposed to war on religious principle, offered to help with the refugee problem through the Red Cross. As the war progressed through Europe, Albertans with European connections initiated fundraising to assist survivors overseas and, in some cases, beginning with dispossessed Finns in the winter of 1940, efforts to bring refugees to Canada. The IODE had assisted in the acculturation of immigrants prior to the war and voiced concerns, shared by the AWI and other women's groups, about the ability of immigrants to adopt Canadian values. They passed a resolution that "anti-British aliens" should be expelled from Canada at the end of the war as the public's concern about a "Fifth Column" of enemy spies grew.[9]

Voluntary Service Organizations and "Home Comforts"

In addition to the established agencies, each with their own missions in peacetime, some women formed informal groups for the duration. The *Edmonton Journal* periodically reported the organization of new groups with names like the "Broadview Club" and the "Homefront Guild." Gertrude Poole, wife of Ernest Poole of Poole Construction Limited, opened her home to a group of about 40 Edmonton women who knit and sewed articles for the Red Cross. [The Poole family moved to Edmonton in 1932, and has made many contributions to the community, including the donation of significant collections of paintings, some of which are shown in the photograph of the workshop, to the Edmonton Art Gallery, and decorative arts to the Provincial Museum.]

Existing women's organizations included war-related projects among their initiatives. The YWCA offered support and amusement to young girls who were facing additional responsibilities due to the war, and was instrumental in finding

Mrs. E.E. Poole's sewing room showing garments provided for European refugees.

*Photo courtesy
Provincial Archives of
Alberta [PAA A4651].*

housing for women moving to the cities to take positions in the work force. Other organizations provided entertainment for the mothers and wives of servicemen. However, most voluntary service organizations directed their energies towards "home comforts" and fundraising.

By 1939 there were hundreds of Women's Institute branches in rural communities and urban centres throughout the province. They followed a prescribed annual programme, which included speakers on a variety of topics, instruction in various handicrafts, and fundraising for community efforts. The war once again provided an opportunity for members to serve their country as they had during the First World War, and to fulfill their motto "For Home and Country." In her 1941-1943 Report on Legislation and International Relations for the AWI, Mrs. D.W. Patterson made the following observation.

> *Much grief and toil will be our lot before the fighting is over. In
> our own small way, Alberta Women can work and pray, can
> bravely endure, in the dark days ahead, and can keep informed
> and alert in preparation for the brighter future that must emerge
> from the crucible of war.*[10]

Branches focussed their attention on war work, not just in terms of fundraising, producing articles for the Red Cross, and sending parcels overseas, but also within the programme itself. Often branches omitted the lectures and educational aspects of their meetings during the war, but when lectures were included they were on war-related topics such as "Causes Leading to the European War," "Post War Settlements," "Canadianization," "Women's Place in War-Time," "The Naturalization of Women," "Patriotic Work done by Women's Organizations," and "Know our Allies." These talks were either prepared by local women or were borrowed from the provincial loan collection. The handicraft aspect of the programme centred around knitting and sewing for inclusion in parcels for local soldiers or for the Red Cross.

Women in the AWI worked to make soldiers and civilian victims of the war more comfortable. They made quilts as fundraisers and for use overseas through the Canadian Women's Institute's "Blankets for Britain" campaign; made garments for refugee children; knitted socks and other garments for servicemen and servicewomen; purchased chocolates, gum and cigarettes to send overseas; wrote letters to local boys serving overseas; made "ditty bags" and purchased toiletries such as soap, toothbrushes, razor blades, hairbrushes and combs to fill them with; and made "housewives," or sewing kits, which they filled with buttons, thread, needles and yarn; and baked cookies and fruit cakes.[11] The Fort Saskatchewan WI sent parcels regularly to local boys on Christmas, birthdays, and in-between, and to prisoners of war. Even though sugar and fruit were rationed, members donated their own portions for use in baking cakes. Two members made 74 Christmas cakes during the war [they were the only two with mixmasters, according to Helen Thorne, then secretary of the Home Comforts Fund]. The cakes were shared with others in their units by the local boys, and the women's efforts were very much appreciated by the soldiers. The Fort Record printed many letters of thanks, including those from Malcolm R. MacCrimmon, who wrote that:

> ...[the] cake was just grand, the fellows in the band didn't give me a minutes rest until they all had a bit of it. They thoroughly enjoyed every part of it as did I. The socks are swell, in fact I think I'll save them for Sunday wear.
>
> You have no idea how much the fellows look forward to a parcel from Canada over here. It means a lot to them and its ever so good of you women to think of them.[12]

Fred Taylor also wrote, expressing his thanks.

> Socks around here are a bone of contention and to have extra ones is to be the envy of the hut. After I showed them to the boys I had to lock them up or some one would have borrowed them before I had a chance to wear them myself.[13]

Membership in various organizations frequently overlapped. In Fort Saskatchewan the women's organization of the Red Cross became the nucleus for the local branch. At first it met in the Council Chambers, and later in the O'Brien Watt store, where materials were distributed and finished goods collected every week. The output was prodigious; from Fort Saskatchewan, then a town of only 900, the WI and other local townswomen combined to send thirteen shipments to the Red Cross in 1942 alone. The total output included: 974

garments and knitted articles, five quilts and comforters, 76 pairs of seamen's socks, 440 pairs of service socks, 29 pairs of mitts and gloves, 76 sleeveless sweaters, hospital supplies, pyjamas, gowns, baby clothes and layettes.[14]

The womens' institute reported that:

> *Anyone who could wield knitting needles was conscripted to fill the quota. Even if they were unable to use knitting needles, they were quickly taught. The women prisoners in the Provincial Gaol were given instruction by Mrs. McLean, the warden's wife and a good institute member, and a great quantity of knitting was obtained in this way [500 articles in the first two years of the war].*[15]

Other incarcerated volunteers were inmates in the Ponoka provincial mental hospital who contributed by making ski suits for children.

While the Canadian Red Cross Society was not strictly a women's organization, knitting and fundraising efforts for the Red Cross were primarily women's contributions. At the outbreak of the war, the National Headquarters urged dormant local branches across the country to be placed on a wartime basis immediately. In September 1939 there were only 47 active branches of the Red Cross in Alberta; within six months there were 325 branches with thousands of women active.[16] Other women's organizations experienced similar increases in membership. While most people supported their work, the Red Cross inevitably became the target of some criticism during the war. The Red Cross was concerned about the quality of goods produced, and approved the use of particular patterns and yarns, and issued knitting instructions through the newspapers as well as knitting booklets to reach readers in rural areas. For example, the "Lux

The "Lux knitting book," and its war supplement of instructions for knitting woolens approved by the Red Cross and IODE for men in service, was promoted through window displays such as this one at Eaton's in Edmonton, October, 1942.

Photo courtesy Provincial Archives of Alberta [PAA Bl 430].

Knitting Book" was available by sending one box top and 35 cents to the Lux company, and was promoted through window displays. Red Cross members questioned the value of producing socks of inferior materials and at a meeting in Fort Saskatchewan "a sample sock was displayed, showing that after a few washings by the boys, it had shrunk so badly that it was impossible for a grown up to wear it."[17] Members of Parliament argued in the House of Commons about the merits of hand-made versus machine-made socks. The superiority of hand-made socks was eventually conceded but Walter Kuhl, MP for Jasper-Edson, complained that women were wasting their time knitting for the war effort.

> *The basic fact was that one knitting machine could make 3,000,000 loops in the time the human hand took to make 300.*[18]

Other criticisms were made of the way the materials were collected and distributed. The organization responded, saying:

> *If your neighbour tells you the Canadian Red Cross Society is selling the socks and sweaters that patriotic women knit for the soldiers and sailors, it's a Nazi lie. The Red Cross has never been able to obtain proof that socks so made are being sold for 49 cents a pair, or any other price. The canard has been officially denied a score of times, but is still circulating.*[19]

The Red Cross requested that groups fill specific quotas of articles, and many groups set targets for numbers of knitted goods. One chapter of the IODE established a "Socks for the Soldiers" drive, with a goal to produce at least 500 pairs of socks for Edmonton soldiers per month.

Women from Imperial Oil packing parcels for overseas.

Photo courtesy Provincial Archives of Alberta [PAA Bl. 807].

Knitting was pervasive; the Junior Hospital League even left yarn in the beauty salon of the Hudson's Bay Company store for women to knit afghan squares while their hair dried.[20] The importance of the knitting cannot be exaggerated. For the women, knitting was a concrete expression of their ability to assist men at the front and refugees who had lost their homes; unable to care for them personally, women worked constantly to keep them warm. For the soldiers and refugees, the hand-knitted goods prevented illness and no doubt in many cases death, and signalled that women in Canada cared. From the various women's organizations throughout the region, Red Cross goods were sent to the depots at the Hudson's Bay Company annex in Edmonton or the Tegler Building, where they were sorted and forwarded to eastern Canada. By February 1943, twenty million articles had been sent overseas from Canada through the Red Cross since the beginning of the war.

> *Sometimes they were handed to the men directly, whenever they walked into the Red Cross headquarters in London, but the majority went in great bales from the warehouses, where they were stored on arrival from the ships, to the troop clothing stores where they were distributed by the units themselves.*[21]

The IODE, AWI and other organizations also sent goods overseas, independent of what they sent through the Red Cross. In this way women were assured that they had "played their part in the victory of the battle of London."[22]

Fundraising

For a nation just pulling out of the Great Depression, financing the war was a critical task. Popular support was essential, and vast sums of money were raised throughout the province. For example, the first Red Cross drive raised $80,000 in Edmonton and $130,000 throughout northern Alberta; the provincial goal of $150,000 was more than doubled. Smaller-scale initiatives such as bake sales, card parties, concerts, raffles, teas, and dances were conducted by women's agencies for related causes. They established funds with names such as the "Emergency War Fund," "Russian Fund," "Jam for Britain," "Overseas Cigarettes Fund," "Home Comforts Fund," "Navy League Fund," and "Seeds for Britain."

The War Charities Act of 1939 regulated the agencies authorized to conduct fundraising for the war effort. Six months into the war over 400 war-service organizations had registered in Ottawa under the act. Attempts to coordinate the efforts of the disparate groups were critical. In Edmonton, when twelve organizations met to co-ordinate services, "several speakers warned that the public was becoming irritated by the increasing number of war service appeals and emphasized that it was advisable to make one co-ordinated appeal."[23] Co-ordinated fundraising for social services in Edmonton led to the establishment in 1941 of the "Community Chest," the forerunner of the United Way.

Fundraising efforts were sometimes coordinated beyond the local level. For example, Alberta branches of the IODE participated in a national effort to raise $100,000 through a "buy-a-warplane campaign" to purchase a Bolingbroke bomber. Similarly the City of Edmonton, Alberta collaborated with the City of Edmonton, England, to raise $25,000 to donate a Spitfire to the Royal Air Force. In 1941, six national agencies, including the YWCA and the IODE, cooperated to form the Canadian War Services Fund Campaign, the only campaign then authorized to collect funds for Canadian men in uniform.

Photographs printed in the *Edmonton Bulletin* and reprinted in the *Fort Record* highlighted family commitment to the war effort as each member filled a different role. Mrs. MacCrimmon feeds her hens and turkeys, while her son Malcolm served in the pipe band of the Scots Guards at Buckingham Palace.

Photo courtesy Provincial Archives of Alberta [PAA Bl.627/4] [Reprinted from Fort Record *29 September, 1943*].

"Victory Bond" campaigns held at intervals throughout the war reached both workers and those at home as people were encouraged to buy bonds to help raise the funds required to maintain the armed forces. Individual women took on projects to raise funds to purchaseVictory Bonds. For example, Mrs. MacCrimmon kept hens at Fort Saskatchewan and bought bonds with her egg-money.In Edmonton, over 600 women canvassed door-to-door, reaching other women in their homes. "[Whatever] their responsibilities, they are out to win this war and feel that the War Savings campaign is one of the most concrete ways of showing what they are made of."[24]

Women in Paid Labour

Women entered the paid labour force in greater numbers than ever before, and in numbers not reached in the postwar years until the 1960s. The Second World War marked the beginning of the urbanization of the population of Alberta; a part of that shift consisted of young women moving to the cities to take temporary positions that had opened up because of the war. For example, 200 Edmonton

Women working at Kenn's Garage in January 1940. Many women assumed jobs traditionally held by men during the war.

Photo courtesy Provincial Archives of Alberta [PAA Bl.685/2].

women enrolled in the first mechanics class offered by Dominion Motors Ltd. as part of the wartime Women's Auxiliary Motor Service Plan.[25] When the first 25 women graduated, Mr. Frederic Webster of General Motors said: "As your fathers, brothers or sons lay down their peace-time jobs to take up the fight you will have equipped yourselves to step into their positions and release them for the grimmer tasks of war."[26]

Whether it was a case of taking the civilian jobs of men who had enlisted, or working in plants on government contracts, women were anxious for the opportunity to serve their country, to fulfil a personal desire to work outside the home and to provide much needed income for their families. While the West received relatively few war contracts compared to Central Canada, such contracts were significant to the Albertan economy as their value exceeded $20,000,000 annually. Edmonton lobbied Ottawa to establish war industries locally, and firms that received

Women work beside men servicing aircraft at No. 2 Air Observers School in Edmonton, February 1943.

Photo courtesy Provincial Archives of Alberta [PAA Bl. 529/3].

war contracts included Aircraft Repair Ltd. and the Great Western Garment Company [GWG].

Aircraft Repair Ltd., with its motto "To keep 'em flying," assembled and repaired Avro Anson and Harvard airplanes, and handled maintenance and overhauls on 25 to 30 different types of planes, for the British Commonwealth Air Training Plan. The firm expanded from 25 to 2500 employees between its beginnings in April 1941 and October 1943. Women worked alongside men making up forty per cent of the work force. Some women, like Frances Woodruff, had a brother in the RCAF, and although unable to serve in the forces, were determined to do their part.

A company float in the sixth "Victory Loan" parade challenges other firms to match GWG's subscription of 17% of its payroll to the 5th Victory Loan.

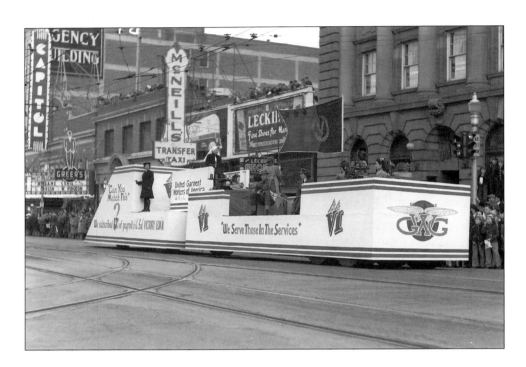

Photo courtesy
Provincial Archives of
Alberta [PAA Bl. 732/1].

At GWG women also were performing an essential war service, and during the war they were unable to resign unless they enlisted in the armed forces. The firm received nearly $4,000,000 worth of government war contracts between 1940 and 1945, and up to 25,000 articles of military clothing were produced weekly. After the difficult years of the Great Depression, the war years were a time of expansion, as GWG became the largest garment manufacturing company in the British Empire. The company built an addition to its Edmonton plant at 10305-97 Street [now the Army & Navy building] to accommodate the staff needed to meet increased production quotas. During these years the firm produced a broad range of garments, including army combination overalls, army khaki shorts, army cotton battle-dress uniforms, army khaki shirts, army trousers, RCAF combination overalls, RCAF shirts, and prisoner-of-war uniforms. Of 488 workers, 425 were women. They worked piece-work, three shifts, 24 hours a day, 7 days a week. The *Edmonton Journal* praised their contribution in 1942.

*In the fullest sense of the term, they were key war workers,
ranking with the employees of munitions plants and women in
the armed forces. Their job was a vital, important one, and they
performed it with energy, devotion and skill.*[27]

Before the war, positions within the company were assigned on the basis of gender: women were seamstresses and "foreladies" while men were machinists and cutters, or "knife pushers" as they were called. Changes in technology paralleled changes in organizational structure; as machinery became lighter-weight and easier to operate, it enabled women to assume positions previously held by men. When men enlisted, women were able to take over these functions for the duration. For example, cutter Louis Kabesh left to join the Navy in 1943 and re-joined the firm after the war.[28] During his absence overseas, his job had been performed by women employees.

Conclusion

After the jubilant celebrations of V-E and V-J Days, the transition from wartime to peacetime was gradual rather than immediate. While the government continued to issue contracts to GWG to produce clothing for the Netherlands, many women lost their jobs in other industries as men returned to resume their pre-war lives. In voluntary service, women continued to provide "Home Comforts" for the men remaining overseas, assistance to European refugees, and welcoming teas for war brides. An account of the Fort Saskatchewan Women's Institute describes this postwar readjustment.

*While it was true the war was over, and things were slowly
returning to normal, some changes had been made within the
[Alberta Women's] Institute which would remain permanent.
One of these was the emphasis placed on overseas relief. The
aftermath of war had left such chaos and despair, and such a
legacy of human suffering, on a scale which had never before
been experienced, that the branches determined to do what they
could to alleviate it, in whatever way they could.*[29]

Many of the changes that had been made to Albertan society were permanent, while others such as the lessons of self-sacrifice and frugality were lost as Albertans were encouraged to become greater consumers in order to fuel the post-war economy. For women unable to participate on the battlefront, participation on the home front was a means of supporting their husbands, sons and daughters, and helping to speed victory. The ideal of service — for home, king and country — was a natural expression of the womans' wartime role.

Notes

[1]*Fort Record*, 23 September 1942.

[2]*Edmonton Journal*, 2 January 1940.

[3]*Edmonton Journal*, 16 January 1941.

[4]Advertisement in the *Fort Record*, 10 March 1942.

[5]*Edmonton Journal*, 22 January 1940.

[6]*Edmonton Journal*, 1 June 1940.

[7]*Edmonton Journal*, 13 March 1940.

[8]*Edmonton Journal*, 1 June 1940.

[9]*Edmonton Journal*, 17 May 1940.

[10]Mrs. D.W. Patterson, "A.W.I. Report on Legislation and International Relations, 1941-1943. Twenty-Third Provincial Convention." *Twenty-Third Report, A.W.I. Convention*, p. 67. [PAA 74.1 RG 229 Box 9].

[11]Dorothy Hosegood, née Sissons, to Catherine Cole, 18 November 1989, quoted in Catherine C. Cole and Ann Milovic, "Education, Community Service and Social Life: The Alberta Women's Institutes and Rural Families, 1909-1945," in *Standing on New Ground: Women in Alberta*, Catherine A. Cavanaugh and Randi R. Warne, eds. [Edmonton, University of Alberta, 1993], p. 29.

[12]*Fort Record*, 29 January 1941.

[13]*Fort Record*, 24 December 1941.

[14]*Fort Record*, 3 February 1943.

[15]Helen Thorne, personal interview; Mrs. C.C. Bodill, "History of the Women's Institute, Fort Saskatchewan, Alberta, founded 1915," [unpublished manuscript].

[16]*Edmonton Journal*, 26 February 1940.

[17]*Fort Record*, 25 March 1942.

[18]*Edmonton Journal*, 8 June 1940.

[19]*Fort Record*, 5 June 1940.

[20]*Edmonton Journal*, 12 March 1941.

[21]*Fort Record*, 24 February 1943.

[22]*Edmonton Journal*, 1 March 1941.

[23]*Edmonton Journal*, 14 May 1940.

[24]*Edmonton Journal*, 2 March 1941.

[25]*Edmonton Journal*, 10 April 1940.

[26]*Edmonton Journal*, 15 November 1940.

[27]*Edmonton Journal*, 18 April 1942.

[28]Personal interviews; Louis Kabesh, Lillian Morris.

[29]Mrs. C.C. Bodill, op. cit.

Volunteer War Service in Alberta, 1939-1945

Donna Alexander Zwicker

During the war years, Canadian women played a major part in maintaining the home front. When Prime Minister W.L. Mackenzie King appealed for volunteers, women's organizations were quick to offer their assistance. Auxiliary service groups and special committees of national women's clubs provided comforts and extras, first for men's and later for women's services. Fund-raising campaigns launched by clubs and other concerned groups in aid of the war effort involved activities such as "tag days," and the sale of war savings stamps and Victory Bonds. Civic groups also ran consumer programmes which were tailored to wartime needs.

Plans for the organization of volunteer work were shaped by the Canadian experience during the First World War. Dr. E.H. Coleman, with the office of Under Secretary of State for External Affairs, explained the development of volunteer work during that war in a letter:

> *The outbreak of the war in 1914 found the charitable and philanthropic organizations in Canada quite unprepared for a war effort. Inevitably, at the outset, there was an overlapping of activities and I am afraid there were instances of waste and misdirected effort. As time passed, the sphere of activity of the various organizations became more clearly defined. I think early in 1917 the Government called a meeting of the heads of women's organizations in Ottawa in connection with national service. In the autumn of 1917 there was passed a special Act dealing with War Charities, with the view of eliminating those which were not conducted in a manner conducive to effective work.[1]*

The government's desire to recognize the volunteer work of women was matched by women's willingness to make a positive contribution to the war effort. As early as June 1939, the National Council of Women placed itself at the disposal of the government.[2] On 13 September 1939, the National Council of the Young Women's Christian Association [YWCA] wrote to Mackenzie King, offering the same services they had performed in the Great War.[3] In the same month, Lady Tweedsmuir, wife of the Governor-General, also was contacted by a number of organizations such as the Catholic Women's League [CWL], the Canadian Red Cross Association [CRCA], the Imperial Order of the Daughters of the Empire [IODE], the YWCA, the Canadian Women's Press Club and various Jewish groups.[4] In her reply to these groups, Lady Tweedsmuir thanked them for their interest and informed them that their services would be called upon.

The Department of National War Services [DNWS] was set up on 12 July 1940, to organize and control volunteer war work. Its immediate responsibility was that of national registration, but its function was also "to organize and promote different forms of voluntary assistance to the war effort; and to coordinate existing public information services of the government and use them with any necessary additions to secure 'the utmost aid from the people of Canada in the national emergency'."[5] Later the department was placed in charge of supervising war charities and the National Salvage Campaign.

One of the first areas for which volunteers were needed was "auxiliary service work." Special auxiliaries to local regiments sprang up, and clubs formed auxiliaries within their own organizations to aid servicemen and women. These clubs provided a range of services for the enlisted personnel, including hostess houses, leave centres, field comforts, camp libraries and a magazine service. When Alberta regiments were formed, such auxiliaries filled their specific needs as well.

Red Cross Reception Centre, Calgary.

Photo courtesy Glenbow Archives, Calgary [NA-4987-4].

The concept of service through hostess houses, recreational huts and leave centres was rooted in the Canadian experience during the First World War. In each case, work was done by volunteers and costs were covered by fund-raising projects organized by the YWCA.[6] On 22 May 1944, a War Service Committee was formed within the Y's organization to oversee this wartime work. By November, Mrs. Agnew, president of the national YWCA, was able to write to the Minister of National War Services that seven hostess houses were in operation, and that sixteen more had been requested by Army and RCAF camps. While the YWCA had operated eight hostess houses during the First World War, by the end of the Second World War there were 38 in existence.[7]

Alberta had three hostess houses during the Second World War. One was in Camrose, one in Claresholm and a third was located in Fort Macleod.[8] As in the previous war, their function "was to provide an official meeting place — with a hostess in charge — for women relatives and friends visiting men on Active Service."[9] The YWCA organized these houses and operated them with the help of community churches and service organizations. Service wives who lived in the community were provided with facilities for social contact with other service families in their camp district. Activities included sewing for the Red Cross, handi-crafts, cooking and nutrition classes, educational courses in such things as baby and child care, and recreational activities like bridge, concerts and dances.[10]

Calgary and Edmonton did not have any hostess houses, but Calgary and Banff were designated as leave centres, and were among the twelve across the country that provided a place for female military personnel to rest while on leave. Over 250,000 servicewomen stayed overnight in such places from January 1943 to June 1946. Most of the centres "were large residences or former hotels; at Banff, a beautiful summer home was leased for this purpose."[11]

Since Edmonton had such a serious housing and hotel accommodation shortage during the war, the local YWCA was particularly active in assisting female military personnel through its room registry service.[12] In 1942, Edmonton's volunteers listed 462 rooms and placed 2321 people in overnight accommodation.[13] The following year they referred over 6000 people, including 1313 servicemen and 82 servicewomen, to approved rooms.[14]

One of the most demanding tasks that Edmonton YWCA members performed was meeting incoming trains and buses, and providing service people with assistance. Between April 1939 and April 1940 they met 1439 trains at all hours of the day and night, and helped 887 travellers in making their connections.[15] In 1942 the number of trains they met increased to 1786, and in 1943 to 2667.[16]

Refreshment centre on Calgary railway station platform, 1945.

Photo courtesy Glenbow Archives, Calgary [NA-4987-10].

In Calgary, women undertook the work in cooperation with the Royal Canadian Legion and the Red Cross. Among their concerns were the veterans on the hospital trains, which were sometimes unscheduled, adding further to their burdens. Still, under the direction of Mrs. F.C. Naylor, they met the veterans and did small errands such as sending urgent telegrams, mailing letters, helping soldiers off the trains, locating friends in the city, and generally trying to "make them feel that Calgary [was] not a strange city without a soul."[17]

The Imperial Order of the Daughters of the Empire, with a membership of 30,000 women across Canada, represented an impressive work force. By November 1939, the national IODE had organized a project for the purchase of field comforts and cigarettes. From the beginning, the Alberta Chapter was very much involved, with over 100 local chapters organized under its direction, and located in various communities. Each chapter was kept busy distributing field comforts, cigarettes and books to servicemen. For example, in the fall of 1940 it provided the men at Currie Barracks with 2200 laundry bags, and purchased a large supply of cigarettes for them; it also sent 8000 cigarettes to the Field Battery in Lethbridge.[18] In the same year the Alberta Chapter spent $33,000 on supplies for use in Canada and abroad. One account described their effort in the following way:

> *Of this amount approximately $3,392 has been used for field comforts and $9,525 for the bomber fund. More than 260,000 cigarettes have been purchased and sent to men on active service, and cases of clothing have been sent to Lady Tweedsmuir, who is in charge of the field comforts of the order in London.*[19]

Throughout the remainder of the war the flow of field comforts and cigarettes to Albertan and other Canadian servicemen continued.[20] Another IODE project was the collection of books for camp libraries. In 1940, the Barriefield Camp at Kingston, Ontario, received 1000 books, while other Canadian camps and troop ships also became the recipients of reading material. The IODE collected and distributed 76,500 books in 1941, twice that number in 1942, and 294,505 between April 1945 and 1946. A total of 1,404,831 books were made available to the services during the war years.[21]

Mrs. R.M. Beatty of Red Deer was in charge of the book programme in Alberta. Under her direction, 3000 books [at 22¢ each] were purchased from a Vancouver firm in 1941, to supplement those that were donated.[22] Radio stations CJCA and CFRN encouraged Albertans to contribute, as did Imperial Oil Ltd., which, besides giving the IODE commercial time during the nation-wide hockey broadcasts which it sponsored, organized drop-off depots at many of its service stations.[23] The Postmaster-General also made a national appeal for books and set up drop-off depots at many local post offices, including those in Calgary and Edmonton.[24]

Additional reading material came from the Council of Jewish Women, which began collecting magazines in Alberta during August 1941. During the summer of 1942 this group distributed 25,000 magazines to manning depots, observer schools, camps in Red Deer, Grand Prairie and Camrose, American soldiers in Alaska and in Edmonton, to the HMCS Nonsuch barracks, the Wings Club, the naval station at St. Joseph's College, the soldiers' ward at the University of Alberta Hospital, and the Legion Hut.[25] In December 1942, the Edmonton Council of Jewish Women alone distributed over 13,000 magazines.[26]

Women's groups also entertained Canadian and Allied soldiers who were temporarily stationed in their locality. In Calgary, the Loyal Orange Benevolent Association ladies organized dances and card games for the new trainees of the Royal Air Force.[27] In 1941, the Annie MacDougall Chapter of the IODE invited over 60 airmen of the British Commonwealth Air Training Plan to a tea soon after their arrival.[28] At Christmas, Calgary and Edmonton homes were opened to all the forces, especially to those men who were far from home. In Edmonton, between 500 and 600 invitations were extended in 1942.[29] The next year over 377 servicemen accepted invitations to spend their Christmas leaves in local homes. In addition, 3252 meals were provided for "the boys" in transit, or for those who were unable to get leave during the festive season.[30]

Women's groups associated with churches were very active in giving assistance to the services. The Catholic Women's League supported a large number of worthy projects, particularly the Red Cross.[31] More than 60,000 ladies from the United Church Women were enrolled in 1018 war service units across the country. Many women of both the Protestant and Catholic faiths collected articles for hospitals, bomb victims and the armed forces overseas.[32]

Women also formed a variety of auxiliaries. One of the largest was the Women's Auxiliary to the Navy League of Canada. A branch was started in Alberta in October 1941. Invitations were sent to women's clubs and to relatives of those in the Royal Navy, Royal Canadian Navy, Mercantile Marines, Royal Canadian Naval Volunteer Reserve, and the Sea Cadets. The purpose of the auxiliary was to provide "comforts and needed supplies for those training in Canada and for men of the Navies and Mercantile Marine entering ports both on the Atlantic and Pacific Coasts."[33] The major project carried out by the local auxiliaries involved filling ditty bags for men in the naval services. At a meeting in Calgary, 35 women's group leaders agreed that their organizations could fill 400 bags in a short time, while a Navy League group formed in northern Alberta, with headquarters in Edmonton, decided that they could get 1000 bags filled.[34]

The Alberta Navy Mothers' club, working closely with the Navy League, knitted goods for the ditty bags or made the bags from stiff cotton for other clubs. In Edmonton, in September 1942, the Navy Mothers donated twenty bags to the 100th Avenue War Service Group, which in turn made the food and articles to put in the bags before turning them over to the Navy League.[35] The Navy Mothers also gave financial support to the Navy League projects such as Robert

House in Victoria, which was opened to entertain men of the Navy who were stationed there or docked in the port temporarily.

There were service clubs which were not specifically attached to any one branch of the armed forces. The 100th Avenue War Service Group, organized in November 1940 by concerned Edmonton women, met in a member's home to sew and raise funds for the war effort. They not only made goods but also sent parcels, Christmas gifts, and letters to the boys overseas. The Ceiling and Visibility Unlimited Club, comprised of civilian and servicemen's wives in Edmonton, began in the same year to raise funds for a variety of wartime causes.[36] Most auxiliaries catered specifically to one local regiment or unit, and as new units were formed in the three services, more new auxiliaries sprang up. An article in the *Edmonton Journal* described these new clubs:

> *Their activities vary to some extent, but a common feature is the raising of money to send comforts to men on service. Some have garden parties and bridges. Others arrange dances. Still others resort to sales of home cooking and rummage. But whatever the source of income may be, it all goes to make the men more comfortable in their fight for freedom.*[37]

There were sixteen auxiliaries in Edmonton by the summer of 1942.[38] Wherever a unit was formed, an auxiliary seemed to follow even in the rural communities. Stettler, in central Alberta, proudly sent men to war from a locally raised Tank Battalion unit, and many of these would be killed or wounded during the Dieppe Raid. In the spring of 1941, a ladies auxiliary to the battalion was formed by relatives and friends of the district men who were serving in it. The auxiliary organized raffles, bake sales and other fund raising activities.[39] Stettler and Edmonton were typical of a national trend, in which local auxiliaries formed around units in their own community. The clubs added a personal touch which helped to boost morale and show the servicemen that their friends, family and community members stood behind them.

Alberta women raised funds for a great number of worthy charities and government-sponsored savings and loan campaigns, especially through what were known as tag days. Donations were collected in exchange for tags depicting support for the war effort. In Edmonton 29 tag days were held in 1940, with proceeds totalling $20,950, while in the following year a few more tag days were added, and $30,733 was collected by the sponsoring organizations.[40] For example, Protestant women's church groups held a tag day in October 1941, with the proceeds going to provide parcels for soldiers.[41] The Ladies Auxiliary to an Edmonton regiment raised $660 at a tag day, to fill parcels and buy cigarettes for Christmas parcels for their boys.[42] The Twentieth Century Club, in conjunction with the Stagette Club and the Women's Liberal Club, had over 100 women canvassing on their tag day. This group raised $300, and the proceeds were sent to the Merchant Marines, the Queen's Canadian Fund and a few other national funds for soldiers and refugees.

Tag days became so numerous across the country that measures were taken to restrict them. Businesses and individuals simply found it too difficult and bothersome to be exposed to so many tag days, although they were all held for worthy causes. Consequently, in 1941 a Community Chest was organized in Edmonton to take care of civilian charities and to reduce the number of such events. In one instance seven auxiliaries agreed to combine their work in one tag day. The result was only 30 tag days in Edmonton during 1942. Finally Ottawa intervened with national controls aimed at better organization, and the reduction of tag days. In a letter to local representatives of the National War Service Organization, Judge T.C. Davis, Associate Deputy Minister, Department of National War Service, explained that

> *As a matter of national policy the Government of Canada decided that it would be desirable first of all to have appeals for peace-time objectives, made, so far as possible and practical, in the fall months of the year, and appeals for aid for the War Service Auxiliaries made in the spring of the year, thus, leaving the balance of the year free for the Governmental appeals for War Savings [and] Victory Loans....*[43]

In the spring of 1942 the new programme was put into operation, and the Canadian War Service Fund was created at the suggestion of the Canadian Legion, IODE, Knights of Columbus, Salvation Army, and the YWCA. These organizations cooperated with the Canadian Red Cross Society and the Navy League of Canada in a public appeal with a goal of twenty million dollars. The plan was to turn this money over to the provinces, for distribution to local branches of these groups.

The Community Chest organization also began a major fund-raising drive that year at the request of the federal government.[44] First organized in 1917, it was not until 1941 that it once again became the only major fund-raiser for community organizations in seventeen cities.[45] Major centres such as Calgary and Edmonton got behind the local campaigns to raise money. In Edmonton, supporters canvassed nearly 22,000 homes for donations; at the same time, the people were informed that they would not be called upon for another year to donate to the 28 local organizations funded by the chest.[46]

The government-sponsored Salvage Campaign, begun in 1942, was one of the local projects which collected funds throughout the year for the Canadian Red Cross, the Canadian Legion, the Young Women's Christian Association, the Young Men's Christian Association and the war work of the Knights of Columbus and the Salvation Army. Many commodities such as iron and steel, fat and bones, newspaper, broken glass and rubber were urgently needed by factories producing war materials. An Ottawa press release explained how the proceeds from the sale of these materials would be used:

> *The kind of local work which is to be financed from the salvage*
> *plan includes the welcoming of the boys and girls on active*
> *service when they come to town, the provision of entertainment and*
> *recreation and in the many ways in which it is possible, the*
> *helping out of the families and dependents of those on active*
> *service.*[47]

Women and children were asked to participate in the programme as their patriotic duty. In Alberta, depots were set up in Edmonton and Calgary for the collection of these goods. The depots operated year-round, calling for newspapers, fat, bones, rags and rubber. Block captains were appointed for different sections in the cities, facilitating better administration. Women also ran a phone committee to help coordinate the pick-ups. In one Calgary collection drive, three train-car loads containing salvaged newspapers, rubber and glass were shipped to factories in the East. Unlike some central Canadian drives, tin was not collected in Alberta because the province was too far away from factories which could process it at a reasonable cost. The campaigns were always geared to existing markets and the availability of salvage material in the region.

The model for Canadian salvage campaigns seems to have been those launched in Great Britain by the Salvage Department, in cooperation with local housewives and children. Information was given to British women through the media and poster campaigns. Thousands of depots for the temporary storage of salvage were set up across the country in empty warehouses. Agatha Dore wrote a description of the British situation:

> *People put their pride aside and carry from time to time all the*
> *salvage they can gather, old newspapers, bottle caps, rubber*
> *goods, matches, rags, cartons, [and] paper boxes.... At these*
> *depots, volunteers sort, bundle and prepare for shipping all the*
> *salvage which is sent to the dumps where it is sold.*[48]

The British campaign operated on a larger scale than that in Canada, since the situation there was more desperate, and there were more people available to be called upon. In Britain there were "about 200,000 persons enrolled as 'Salvage Stewards',"[49] many of whom were engaged in many other volunteer activities as well. The Canadian government also tried to control charitable organizations' projects which raised funds for war work outside the larger campaigns. The main way of monitoring the activities of the groups was through the revival of the War Charities Act in 1939. On 20 June 1941, the War Charities Act was amended to make it more applicable to the needs of the Second World War. The new amendments included a call for detailed financial accounts for every registered fund which collected money from special projects such as carnivals, bazaars, shows, exhibitions or other entertainment. Any fund with receipts over $2000 was required to have an outside audit performed by a professional accountant, while those with receipts less than $2000 needed only the certification of a bank manager or accountant. The new regulations ensured that the government was made aware of any fund-raising scheme that was successful, and it helped to avoid repetition of fund-raising for similar or overlapping causes.[50]

Many of the funds registered under the War Charities Act provided relief for war-torn countries. There was a Polish Relief Fund which sent clothing to Polish refugees who had fled their country to live in remote areas of Russia.[51] The Russian Relief Fund and the Chinese Relief Fund also found strong support in Canada.[52] The Mrs. Winston Churchill Fund and the Queen Charlotte Maternity Hospital Fund, both in Great Britain, appealed for help from Canadian organizations.[53] Alberta organizations contributed to a great number of similar charitable causes besides their own projects.

Bundles for Britain and the Bomber Fund were run almost entirely by women's organizations. The Canadian Business and Professional Women's Club was particularly supportive of the Bundles for Britain campaign. New and used clothing was collected nationally by branches of the organization and shipped to Britain to aid bombed-out victims of the air war. Groups from Saskatchewan to Victoria sent their collected articles to the Vancouver club for shipment overseas. Manitoba sent its contributions abroad with another group known as V Bundles of Manitoba, while the rest of the country sent their contributions through Saint John, New Brunswick. In all, "more than 400,000 new and used articles of clothing were sent to the British Isles."[54] The club in Edmonton sent at least one bundle of clothing every month as their contribution, and in Calgary, under the supervision of Miss Cassie Kippen and Miss Evelyn Banborough, they cleaned, packed and shipped over 1000 articles.[55]

The IODE, formed in 1899, had a long history of contact with Britain and was among the most active of the Canadian clubs during the Second World War. In 1940 the Order purchased a Bolingbroke bomber to be given to the Canadian government as a symbol of their dedication to Canada's war effort. Within the first six weeks, more than $100,000 was raised for the bomber.[56] Each province shared in the fund raising for the plane, with Alberta chapters contributing their share of the cost.[57] Extra funds were collected so that $300,000 could be sent to the British Ministry for Air, and a further $50,000 was sent to Australia to be used in the purchase of a Hurricane fighter plane.[58]

Women's clubs also supported the two most significant government schemes to raise money for the war effort, when they were asked to sell war savings stamps and certificates, as well as Victory Bonds.[59] These campaigns were inspired by the highly successful "Tap Loan Plan," a savings and loan campaign designed to raise funds for the war effort in Great Britain. Through these schemes the Canadian government sought to encourage a national savings plan for the average wage earner, and at the same time gather additional revenue for war needs. As Frederick I. Kerr and Wilfred H. Goodman have described it, the government:

> *hoped to kill several birds with one stone, viz., to stem inflation by curtailing current spending; to encourage the people to save now so that their post-war spending power might be increased; to stimulate war consciousness through self-denial and, while accomplishing the foregoing, to augment the federal war chest.*[60]

The sale of stamps and certificates began in May 1940 with the sale of 25-cent War Savings Stamps and War Savings Certificates in denominations of $5, $10, and $25, with a limit of $500 per individual in any one year. These stamps could only be cashed by conversion into War Savings Certificates, which bore no interest, but yielded a premium of 25 per cent at the 7 $1/2$ year maturity, which was tax free.[61]

A further adaptation of the British savings and loans campaign was put into operation in Canada in October 1941. It was known as the War Weapons Plan, and linked the sale of savings certificates directly to the purchase of ships, planes, guns and munitions. Each region of the country was assigned certain goals calculated in terms of their fund-raising for a specific objective.[62] The *Edmonton Journal* clearly reflected the Edmonton region's goal:

> *The plan is to increase regular war savings to the point where Edmonton can buy a bomber plane every month. A bomber costs $100,000. This type of campaign is being conducted throughout the dominion with various cities and areas working toward different objectives, all expressed in terms of war weapons rather than in sums of money.*[63]

During the campaign, Alberta businesses and clubs threw their support behind the cause. Eighty per cent of Edmonton businesses participated in the buying and selling of stamps and certificates. Clubs such as the Stagette Club, Citizen's Volunteer Bureau, Women's Canadian Club and wives' auxiliary clubs took turns canvassing neighbourhoods and selling from booths.[64] Again the IODE was a major sponsor of the drive, with national sales reaching $183,576 in five years.[65]

In the autumn of 1941, the federal government introduced the programme for the sale of Victory Bonds, with campaigns to be held at six-month intervals. The First Victory Loan Campaign was held from 2 June to 22 June 1941. Its national objective was $600,000,000, but total sales amounted to $838,820,250.[66] The second campaign, held from 10 February to 7 March 1942, was equally successful. In Edmonton, over 800 women were involved, including 500 from the IODE.[67] During the Fifth Victory Loan Campaign, over 50 underwriters were hired on commission to sell the bonds in the city.[68] While women's groups were gradually replaced by the underwriters, they were of course still asked to purchase bonds.

Women were involved in urban volunteer bureaus which were organized in Winnipeg, Toronto, Montreal, Saskatoon, Edmonton, London, Woodstock, Quebec, Cornwall, Fort William, Sault Ste. Marie, and St. Catharines. In Edmonton, the Citizen's Volunteer Bureau encouraged workers from all walks of life to participate in the salvage campaigns, the selling of stamps and bonds, blood donor clinics and "make-over" clothing projects. It was also involved in other wartime issues such as rationing, price ceilings, nutritional information and housing.[69] A co-ordinating body was set up to assist existing comunity organizations when extra volunteers were needed, and to avoid the duplication of local help projects. Women's names, together with their available free hours and their affiliations with other active wartime groups, were registered with the bureau.[70] Edmonton's first project placed 200 people in the salvage campaign as truck drivers and sorters.[71] By the spring of 1943, there were 405 Edmonton women registered for service with the Citizen's Volunteer Bureau. In addition, it was able to call upon 800 workers to help with the rations board's distribution of ration books, and another 300 helpers were found when a fats drive was held in schools for the salvage committee.[72] Throughout the war, the bureau proved to be a successful addition to the community's war organizations and their many projects.

The rationing of sugar, tea, coffee and meat came to Canada between June 1942 and May 1943, and women's organizations were soon involved in assisting the federal government in the distribution of ration books, saving the enormous handling costs. In Calgary, 50 school teachers at Victoria School arranged southern Alberta rationing coupons according to districts.[73] In Edmonton, 3611 volunteers collected application cards for rationing coupons, 1500 women recorded the information on cards, and a combined force of 3000 volunteers, and the Local Council of Women, picked up the ration cards for distribution. The overall project was overseen by the IODE's provincial chapter. Again and again, during the remainder of the war, the women rendered valuable service in the rationing programme.[74]

Sometimes it was necessary to educate the women themselves to accept the government's rationing policy, as there were sometimes complaints about the need to share rationed foods. However, Byrne Hope Sanders, director of the consumer branch of the Wartime Prices and Trade Board, met with a positive response when she sent letters to the presidents of national women's organizations requesting that, in the interests of rationing, they dispense with afternoon tea at their gatherings.[75]

In the case of meat, the limit was two pounds weekly for each person. The *Edmonton Journal* told women that meat rationing "would assure every civilian in this country an equal share of the supplies that are available after obligations have been met to the United Nations, Canada's armed forces and others who may be in the front lines."[76] Of all the beef, veal, pork, mutton and lamb produced in Canada in 1942, 40 per cent was sent to Great Britain, ten per cent to other Allied countries, and the remaining 50 per cent was made available to Canadian citizens on a rationed basis. Fish and poultry were never rationed.

Tin was one rationed commodity. By October 1942, the tin cans available had been cut by 180,000, and by December products such as tobacco, coffee, honey, paint, syrup, edible oils, liquid wax, wax paste, jam, shoe and metal polish, grease and lubricant oils were no longer being packaged in tins.[77] Slogans such as "250 tubes of toothpaste supply the same amount of tin needed for a Bolingbroke Bomber" helped to encourage people to accept the new restriction.[78] Fewer luxury items such as evening gowns, hats, furs and cosmetics were manufactured, and in some cases production ceased altogether. However, Albertans knew that

Canada's rationing was much less severe than that in Great Britain, where bombed areas relied on mobile kitchens and canteens for meals and where everyone was on strict meat and clothing rations.[79]

However, shortages did exist in Canada, and as a result the government supported community nutrition programmes. The *Calgary Albertan* carried a series titled "Weekly Wartime Nutrition Hints," financed by Swift Canadian Co. Ltd.[80] When Dr. Max Cantor, assistant professor of biochemistry at the University of Alberta, addressed a public meeting sponsored by the Calgary Adult Education Council, he pointed out that Canada was facing definite nutritional problems. Cantor quoted a survey of four Canadian cities, one of which was Edmonton. "In Edmonton," he said, "it was found in many cases there was not sufficient food available to furnish the needed calories for energy or even satisfactory amounts of most food constituents."[81] Following the British and American examples, Canada therefore took steps to improve the diet of its citizens.

Alberta groups responded by forming information classes on nutrition for women. The volunteer bureau in Edmonton signed up women who wished to attend nutrition courses.[82] The public was free to attend classes sponsored by the Edmonton Home Economics Association in conjunction with the Local Council of Women and several social agencies.[83] Beginning in 1940, special nutrition classes were held for expectant mothers, and wives of privates in the armed forces, since they comprised a group considered to be much in need of information on healthy and inexpensive food.[84] In Calgary, weekly meetings were held at the Calgary Gas Company Auditorium, under the auspices of the Red Cross and the local Home Economics Association, "the purpose of which was to instruct Calgary housewives in the buying and cooking of the proper kinds and amounts of foods to provide adequate and healthful diets for their families."[85]

The Consumer Branch of the Wartime Prices and Trade Board [WPTB] was formed in January 1942 to keep the cost of living down, and to ensure that consumer goods reached all people equally. A meeting was called by Donald Gordon, chairman of the Trade Board, with the heads of 18 national women's organizations, "to enlist the support of Canadian women in guarding the price ceiling."[86] One hundred and ninety-five cities and towns developed a consumer branch with a women's subcommittee to bring their concerns and problems forward. Alberta towns with less than 5000 people appointed 1000 liaison officers to work with the subcommittee throughout the province on important issues. These liaison officers and members of the committee were organized in the Women's Regional Advisory Committee [WRAC]. Members were elected by any approved organization, or in response to a demonstrated need in any locality.[87]

There were other action groups within the cities that either approached the WRAC or the Consumer Branch of the WPTB. In Calgary, the Women's Home Security League pressed the board for price controls, while rising prices on food, clothing and rental accommodations in both Calgary and Edmonton remained major issues.[88] It was the women of the community who formed such groups and sat on committees like the WRAC which ensured that inflation was kept in check by reporting unnecessary price increases.

Edmonton matched bustling eastern centres in population growth during the war years. Its population increased by 30 per cent between 1941 and 1943. Housing shortages occurred due to the influx of Americans connected with the Alaska Highway project, the increasing number of military men and their families who were stationed in and around Edmonton, and the Social Credit government's legislation prohibiting the National Housing Act from constructing houses in Alberta. In July 1943, there were virtually "no suites, housekeeping rooms, offices, [or]warehouse space of any kind for rent."[89] Wartime Housing Limited, a crown corporation set up to build houses in areas of need that were connected with war industry or troop stations, was permitted to build 250 homes in the fall of the year. Local builders were allowed to construct 500 more homes to keep the shortage within acceptable measures. Although Calgary was not hit as hard as Edmonton, there were shortages of accommodations in that city as well, which also were met in part by the building of wartime houses through Wartime Housing Limited.

The burden of community and civic efforts was largely carried by women while the country was at war. Women's organizations remained active between 1939 and 1945 in volunteer work supporting men's and women's units stationed in Canada and abroad. Women volunteers helped to make leaves more enjoyable for service personnel, and raised funds for comforts and extras for the armed forces. Fund-raising campaigns were hosted by a wide range of organizations. Local causes, national funds and overseas relief work were among the many areas into which women channelled their energies. When the government introduced large-scale fund-raisers such as War Savings Stamps and Certificates, and Victory Bonds, women's organizations heartily supported the cause. Rationing coupons and consumer self-help programmes were carried out by volunteers. In short, women from all across the country helped to make victory a reality. While the methods differed slightly from region to region, and from city to city, it must be said that women maintained the home front while the nation was at war.

NOTES

[1]National Archives of Canada [NAC], Records of the Governor General's Office, 1774-1966, Record Group 7 [RG7], [hereafter cited as NAC, RG 7, G 26], Vol. 107.

[2]Rosa L. Shaw, *Proud Heritage* [Toronto: The Ryerson Press, 1957], p. 160.

[3]NAC, RG 7, G 26, Vol. 107. Letter of 13 September 1939 to Prime Minister King from Helen Agnew, President of the YWCA.

[4]NAC, RG 7, G 26, Vol. 107, passim.

[5]Gwendolen M. Carter, "Organization and Work of the Canadian War Administration," *British Commonwealth at War*, ed. W.Y. Elliot and H.D. Hall, [New York: 1943], p. 334.

[6]Josephine P. Harshaw, *When Women Work Together: A History of the YWCA in Canada 1870-1976* [Toronto: Ryerson Press, 1966], pp. 155-156.

[7]Mary Quayle Innis, *Untold the Years* [Toronto: McClelland and Stewart Ltd., 1949], pp. 174-175.

[8]Ibid., Appendices - Table VII.

[9]Harshaw, op. cit., p. 161.

[10]Ibid., p. 162.

[11]Innis, op. cit., p. 179.

[12]Ibid., p. 178.

[13]Provincial Archives of Alberta [PAA], Young Women's Christian Association file, *President's Report*, 30 April 1940.

[14]PAA, YWCA file, *Yearly Report, 1943.*

[15]PAA, YWCA file, *Secretary's Report, 1940.*

[16]PAA, YWCA file, Yearly Reports, 1943 and 1944.

[17]*Calgary Herald*, 11 December 1943.

[18]PAA, Imperial Order of the Daughters of the Empire file [IODE file], Box 1, file 6.

[19]Glenbow Archives [GA], Mrs. J.A. Mathers, collector, Scrapbook 1936-1942.

[20]PAA , IODE file, Box 1, files 6 - 7.

[21]*The Imperial Order Daughters of the Empire Golden Jubilee 1900-1950* [Toronto: T.H. Best Printing Co. Ltd., 1950], pp. 78, 86.

[22]Ibid., p. 86; PAA, IODE file, Box 1, files 6 - 7.

[23]*Golden Jubilee*, p. 79; PAA, IODE file, Box 1, file 7.

[24]NAC, Records of the National War Services, 1939-1954, Record Group 44 [RG 44], Vol. 8, file 25.

[25]*Edmonton Journal*, 18 September 1942 .

[26]Ibid., 12 January 1943.

[27]*Calgary Albertan*, 22 November 1941.

[28]Ibid., 5 November 1941.

[29]*Edmonton Journal*, 18 December 1941.

[30]Ibid., 9 January 1943.

[31]Ibid., 14 October 1941.

[32]Ibid., 19 April 1943; 17 January 1943.

[33]*Calgary Albertan*, 3 October 1941.

[34]Ibid., 7 October 1941; 22 October 1941. The ditty bags held two or three of the following knitted articles: socks, helmet, scarf, mitts, sweater, seaman's long stockings; as well as the following additional suggestions: hard candy, nuts, dates, figs, cocoa, sugar, tins of fruit juice, soup, chewing gum, small towel, wash cloth, soap, handkerchief, comb, razor blades, cigarettes, tobacco, paper and envelopes, flashlight, games, puzzles, and first-aid kit.

[35]The Navy Mothers' Club grew from a handful of women to 444 members in Edmonton by January 1943. This was a typical phenomenon among women's auxiliaries. See also PAA, 100th Ave. Service Group file.

[36]PAA, Ceiling and Visibility Unlimited Club file.

[37]*Edmonton Journal*, 25 September 1941.

[38]Ibid., 22 August 1942.

[39]Ibid., 23 April 1943.

[40]Ibid., 9 February 1942; 21 March 1942.

[41]Ibid., 17 October 1941.

[42]Ibid., 3 October 1941.

[43]NAC, RG 44, Vol. 27.

[44]Ibid.

[45]Innis, op. cit., p. 190.

[46]*Edmonton Journal*, 9 October 1941.

[47]Ibid., 9 March 1942.

[48]Agatha Dore, *Women's Volunteer Services for Civil Defence* [Ottawa: Edmond Cloutier, 1944], p. 10.

[49]Mrs. Jules Laine, *Selected Voluntary Organizations in the United Kingdom* [Ottawa: Edmond Cloutier, 1944], p. 10.

[50]For a copy of the regulations see PAA, Ceiling and Visibility Unlimited Club file.

[51]*Golden Jubilee*, p. 72.

[52]PAA , Edmonton Home Economics Association, file 49, passim.

[53]Both the Edmonton and Calgary chapters collected for the Churchill fund. The 100th Avenue Service Group sent donations to the hospital funds.

[54]Elizabeth [Bess] Forbes, *With Enthusiasm and Faith-History of the Canadian Federation of Business and Professional Women's Clubs 1930-1972*. [Ottawa: Canadian Federation of Business and Professional Women's Clubs, December 1974], p. 43.

[55]*Edmonton Journal*, 26 March 1943; Forbes, op. cit., p. 26.

[56]Charlotte Whitton, *Canadian Women in the War Effort*. [Toronto: The MacMillan Company of Canada Ltd., 1942], p. 31.

[57]PAA, IODE file, Box 1, file 6.

[58]*Golden Jubilee*, pp. 70-71.

[59]For a good explanation of war savings see C.H. Herbert, "Why War Savings," No. 7 in a *Contemporary Affairs Series* [Toronto: The Ryerson Press, 1940].

[60]Frederick I. Kerr and Wilfred H. Goodman, *Press Promotion of War Finance* [Toronto: Southam Press, 1946], p. 29.

[61]Ibid., p. 28.

[62]Sale of War savings stamps and certificates up to December 1945 reached approximately $370,000,000 .

[63]*Edmonton Journal*, 9 October 1941.

[64]Ibid., 4 October 1943.

[65]*Golden Jubilee*, pp. 72-73.

[66]Kerr and Goodman, op. cit., p. 39.

[67]*Edmonton Journal*, 14 February 1942.

[68]Ibid., 18 October 1943; 4 October 1943.

[69]R.M. Farquharson, "Manning Pool for Women," *Saturday Night*, 58, No. 32 [8 May 1943].

[70]*Edmonton Journal*, 1 April 1943.

[71]Ibid., 13 January 1943.

[72]Ibid., 13 March 1943.

[73]*Calgary Albertan*, 30 July 1942.

[74]*Edmonton Journal*, 26 June 1942; 22 June 1942.

[75]*Calgary Albertan*, 9 September 1942.

[76]*Edmonton Journal*, 10 May 1943.

[77]Ibid., 28 October 1942.

[78]*Calgary Albertan*, 12 August 1942.

[79]Dore, op. cit., p. 9; Margaret Biddle, *The Women of England* [Boston: Houghton-Mifflin Company, 1941], pp. 37-38.

[80]*Calgary Albertan*, 26 January 1943.

[81]Ibid., 14 March 1942, p. 10.

[82]*Edmonton Journal*, 15 March 1942.

[83]GA, Alberta Home Economics Association file, Box 5, file 64.

[84]PAA, Edmonton Home Economics Association, file 49.

[85]GA, Alberta Home Economics Association, Box 5, file 64.

[86]*Calgary Albertan*, 22 January 1942.

[87]GA, Consumer Association of Canada file, Box 1, file 33.

[88]*Calgary Albertan*, 13 August 1942.

[89]Reg. T. Rose, "Edmonton: Boom Town . . . Plus," *Canadian Business*, 16, No. 86 [July 1943], p. 86.

Der Deutsche Kriegsgefangener auf Alberta*: Alberta and the Keeping of German Prisoners of War, 1939-1947

John Joseph Kelly

During the Second World War, some 38,050 German military personnel, merchant seamen and refugees experienced the hospitality of the Mackenzie King government, while they were being held in prisoner of war camps across Canada.[1] In a little-known aspect of Canadian history, the largest POW camps in this country were situated in Alberta, just outside the cities of Lethbridge and Medicine Hat. This is the story of how Alberta played a major role in the Canadian war effort by housing those German POWs whom Britain could not take because of her geographical proximity to the battlefields of Western Europe.

Throughout the spring of 1939, as the international political climate deteriorated with the German takeover of the remnants of Czechoslovakia, the Royal Canadian Mounted Police were working on a list of individuals in Canada who were to be arrested upon the outbreak of war, as well as those organizations, and their newspapers, which were to be outlawed. These included the following groups:

> ....members of the German National Socialist Party (N.S.D.A.P.), each of whom undertook to obey implicitly and without question the order of the Fuehrer and his representatives

> ....male members of the Deutsche Arbeitsfront, which consisted of German nationals who described themselves as 'true followers of the Fuehrer.' Like members of the N.S.D.A.P., they were recent immigrants to Canada, and were nearly all of military age, and thus under German law were liable for compulsory service in the German Army

> ....male German nationals resident in Canada, who were not known formally to be members of either the N.S.D.A.P. or the Arbeitsfront, but who, from their political and social associations, business and industrial connections and other opportunities for espionage, were believed to be persons who could not safely be allowed at large in time of war

> ....and naturalized Canadian citizens of German birth or members of a racial organization, who identified themselves with Nazi propagandist activities so that they could not be regarded as loyal citizens of Canada. They were all persons of influence in their communities and were leaders of the Deutscher Bund, the Canadian Society for German Culture [2]

*The German title is "German Prisoners of War in Alberta."

With the British declaration of war on 3 September 1939, the RCMP swung into action, and over the next six weeks they incarcerated some 358 individuals felt to be of questionable loyalty, predominantly from the metropolitan centres of Toronto, Montreal, Vancouver and Regina.[3]

There had been a historical precedent set during the First World War, when Canada had interned or placed on parole some 10,000 aliens, and had housed German combatant prisoners in Fort Henry, at Kingston, Ontario.[4] However, upon the outbreak of war in September 1939, the Canadian government did not expect to be called upon to exercise a similar function. It believed that only about 400 civilians would need to be interned, and to handle this relatively small influx, only two camps were to be opened: one located on the site of the former relief camp at the forestry reserve near Petawawa, Ontario; and the other at the Kananaskis Forest Experiment Station, approximately fifty miles west of Calgary, and thirty miles east of Banff, near Seebe, Alberta.[5] These sites were chosen because the government did not wish to spend too much money on what it felt was going to be a short-term, limited venture. This viewpoint was set forth in a letter from the Under Secretary of State, Mr. E.H. Coleman, to Mr. H.R.L. Henry, private secretary to Prime Minister Mackenzie King, in which he wrote:

> *....the number of enemy aliens interned will not be large and it is earnestly desired that every possible economy should be exercised in setting up stations or camps.... [It] would be manifestly wasteful to set up this expensive organization in every section of the country....*[6]

It was felt at this time that accommodation for two hundred men at each site was sufficient, and that the internees could provide valuable work for the wartime economy at both these locations.[7] The Kananaskis camp was the first to open, as a receiving station, with Major J.W. Stagg as the Commandant, and a guard of 29 men. By October 1939, there were 150 prisoners in the camp, with room for more if it was needed at a later time.

These first prisoners were not prisoners of war in the strictest sense of that phrase. Those who would be designated "Prisoners of War Class I" were to have been captured in warlike operations, and were to be covered under Articles 1 and 81 of the Geneva Convention of 1929. The enemy aliens now resident in the camps would be referred to as "Prisoners of War Class II," and would not be entitled to the special rights and privileges accorded to combatant prisoners. They were to be subject to the same laws as the members of the Armed Forces of Canada. Prisoners were not to be employed on work having a direct connection with the war effort. For that work not directly related to the war effort which they could do, the pay rate for prisoners was fixed at twenty cents per day, a rate based on the cash allowance made to members of labour camps run by the Department of National Defence during the Depression in the 1930s. No access to newspapers was allowed, as it was felt that news of Allied defeats would hearten the internees. Representatives of the Protecting Power [the Swiss] were permitted to visit the prisoners. The most severe form of disciplinary action allowed for civilian internees would be confinement in the detention barracks for a period not exceeding 28 days. In November 1939, it was decided that the Canadian authorities would go as far as to allow the Geneva Convention to be applied to the civilian internees.[8]

For example, on 7 December 1939, two internees escaped from the Kananaskis camp, cutting their way through the wire, and remaining on the loose for five days. They were tried before a military court in Calgary and sentenced to two years imprisonment without hard labour.[9] A similar escape in September 1940 netted another two-year sentence for each of the two prisoners.

Of course, the German aliens at Kananaskis did not enjoy their incarceration. They nicknamed the camp "Kan-A-Nazi," and constantly complained about their treatment. On the other hand, the Canadian authorities went out of their way to point out that the prisoners often were receiving better care than Canadian citizens on the home front. Newspapers were quick to pick up on the story, and to take note of the treatment that was afforded the prisoners:

> *....More than 150 persons of German descent held in this resort country camp have the best of food, excellent clothing and quarters, enough light work to keep them in fine physical trim, and a wide choice of recreational facilities....The reporters ate a lunch from the prisoners kitchen, and it was obvious why the men had gained an average of ten pounds in weight since being received at the camp. Some gained twenty-five to thirty-five pounds....*[10]

In June 1940, the British government asked the Canadian government to accept some 4000 interned enemy aliens from England, along with another 3000 prisoners of war who had been captured at that time. An internment panic had hit the British authorities because of the reports of Fifth Column activity in the Low Countries. With Britain seen as the last bastion of defence against the German onslaught, the Churchill government felt that the custody of so many potentially dangerous individuals in areas that might soon be the scene of active military operations would put a serious burden on the fighting ability of British military forces. Canada, on the other hand, was unprepared to accept this number of prisoners, as they had expected to handle only Canadian civilian internees imprisoned under the Defence of Canada Regulations. But in the end the King government agreed to the British request. Fourteen permanent camps were established across Ontario, Quebec and New Brunswick to meet this demand, with another three temporary sites set up so that the prisoners could be processed and moved along. None of these sites were actual prisoner of war camps, but were organized around existing buildings, such as empty factories or mills, which already possessed facilities for heating, sewage and lighting, and were located near a rail line. All could be occupied with a minimal outlay of cost, which was essential to the government.[11]

Once the Canadian government had set the precedent of taking prisoners from the British government, requests became more frequent. Another one thousand German Luftwaffe POWs arrived in January 1941. In September 1941, a further request to house 2,010 POWs was sent, to be followed in December 1941 by a petition to dispose of four thousand German prisoners captured in the North African campaign. The government agreed to both these requests, but immediately realized that this acceptance now exhausted the capacity of the existing system of camps in Canada. The Prime Minister wrote:

> ....*consideration will have to be given to the establishment of new, larger camps designed to hold thousands, instead of hundreds. Canadian authorities are considering plans for such units to take 10,000 P.O.W. each.*[12]

The tented camp at Ozada.

Photo courtesy John Joseph Kelly.

On 6 May 1942, Camp 133 was opened at Ozada, Alberta under the command of Colonel Carson A.V. MacCormack O.B.E. It was located on the Morley Flats, some two-thirds of the way from Calgary to Banff, just off the main Canadian Pacific Railway line, and near the point where the Kananaskis River enters the Bow River. The camp itself was 1 1/8 miles square, with eight guard towers on each side, totalling some 28 towers. The enclosure was surrounded by a single wire fence. Inside the enclosure, there were about 3400 tents, in which prisoners were "housed." Ozada was indeed a "temporary" camp, to be used only until the larger, more permanent camps were ready. In writing about this period, the Camp Interpreter noted:

> *....Unfortunately that summer and fall [1942], the weather was terrible, almost continuous rain and some snow [due to altitude] every month of our stay. Everything was under canvas and there were no permanent buildings....*[13]

The German prisoners complained bitterly to the Swiss Consul General that the accommodations in the camp were in direct contravention of the articles of the Geneva Convention. After studying the issue, the Swiss Consul General sided with the Canadian authorities, and pointed out that the Veterans Guard of Canada, most of whom were veterans of the First World War who were charged with guarding the prisoners, also were living in tents, and that therefore no blame could be placed on the Canadian government for living conditions in the camp. This was not good enough for the German prisoners, and the atmosphere in the camp steadily deteriorated into what would become known locally as "The Battle of Ozada."

The matter came to a head during the latter part of July 1942, when six German Luftwaffe prisoners who claimed to have been promoted to the rank of officer began to wear the badges of officers, and claimed that Canadian "other ranks" [non-officers] were required to salute them, in the same way that German "other ranks" and NCOs [non-commissioned officers] were required to salute Canadian officers. The Camp Commandant, Colonel MacCormack, ordered all of them to have these rank badges removed by 21 July. When they refused to do so by that day, MacCormack sentenced them to the maximum 28 days detention for "refusing to obey an official order," in a building built within the wire enclosure just outside the main gate of the camp. In retaliation for this sentence, German prisoners in the compound seized Lt.-Col. G. Armstrong, MC, the second in command, with two other officers and a staff sergeant, all of whom were conducting their early morning inspection at the time they were captured. The Canadian personnel were held as hostages for six hours, until they were released by an armed platoon of Veterans Guards which had marched into the compound to rescue them. Tension continued to be high in the camp after this incident, and during the next week the German prisoners refused to parade for the daily count or to appoint a new camp leader, claiming that Feldwebel Steutzel, their main leader in this conflict, remained the German camp leader. MacCormack responded by declaring Ozada to be a detention camp, and the POWs then were placed on rations of bread and water. The six German prisoners went on a hunger strike, and refused to consume even the bread and water rations. It was not until 29 July that the German prisoners chose a new camp leader who was acceptable to Colonel MacCormack, and that full rations finally were sent in to the prisoners. The six identified as trouble makers were sent to other POW camps, where two later were court martialled for inciting the POWs to mutiny, resulting in three-year prison sentences for each of them.

As cooler heads prevailed, life slowly returned to normal at Ozada. Over the next six weeks, five more loads of prisoners arrived out of the Libyan desert, and by the end of September 1942, there were somewhere between 12,000-13,000 men in the tented camp. The night of 21 October 1942 saw a severe windstorm lash the camp, blowing down many of the prisoners' tents; this was followed by a six-inch snowfall which caused great discomfort throughout the camp. In November 1942, another gale succeeded in bringing down most of the tents in the camp. Temperatures stayed below the freezing point, and over several nights the water main had to be thawed after freezing over. There were no tears shed on 10 December 1942, when the prisoners started their move from Ozada to the newly erected camps at Medicine Hat and Lethbridge.[14]

However, several of the German prisoners planned to stay behind and make a break for freedom once everyone had departed. Four sergeants of the Wehrmacht [German Army] had dug a tunnel four feet long, and two feet square, which led to a dugout over which a ground sheet had been placed, covered with gravel to conceal the excavation. These soldiers hoped to survive on supplies which they had previously taken into the dugout, but their efforts were to prove unsuccessful. The Camp authorities had anticipated some such attempt at hiding out, as it was a familiar trick that had been used successfully by British POWs during the First World War. A fully equipped guard detail had been left at the camp to prevent anyone from getting out, and on 28 December 1942, after eighteen days, the German prisoners surrendered, none the worse for wear despite a very cold Christmas.[15]

Colonel Eric Kippen [Commandant at Lethbridge] and unidentified officer [on right] at Lethbridge POW camp, February 1945.

Photo given to John Joseph Kelly by Colonel Kippen, ca. 1977.

The Medicine Hat and Lethbridge camps were built at a cost of $2.3 million each, and were the first in this country to be designed exclusively for use as internment sites for POWs. Both were located close to the necessary sources of fuel, energy, water, sewage, and electricity. Each of the four sides of the enclosure had a length of 2,500 feet, and occupied an area of some 143.5 acres (58.1 hectares). There were 36 dormitories in each camp, with dimensions of

160' x 36' x 10', each being able to accommodate 350 men in double bunks. There were two large recreation halls, measuring 145' x 140', each with a seating capacity of three thousand men. Each camp boasted six "educational huts" [24' x 120'], six workshops of the same size, six packing storage barracks [120' x 48'], and six mess halls and kitchens, measuring 150' x 63', of which a space of 63' x 36' was used for kitchen space. The capacity in each dining hall was 800 men. Cooking and heating in the dormitories was done by natural gas.

What was life like "behind the wire" for the German prisoners in these Alberta camps? The German combatants prisoners were subject to treatment under the International Convention Relative to the Treatment of Prisoners of War [Geneva Convention]. Charges could be sworn out against a prisoner, and the Camp Commandant then could deal with the matter by a detention of not more than 28 days, or confinement to quarters not exceeding fourteen days. Articles 54 to 59 of the Geneva Convention stated that such detention meant confinement in a cell, lighted by daylight, with facilities for remaining out of doors or taking exercise for at least two hours per day. Prisoners in detention would be allowed to read and write, and to send and receive letters, but they were not to receive parcels. The use of "dark cells" to confine prisoners was prohibited. For what transgressions could a prisoner be put in detention? At Ozada, one German received 28 days for giving a false name when asked, while another received 28 days for spitting a mouthful of water on a Canadian soldier "as a joke." Two other prisoners received 28 days for attempting to escape from Ozada.

The Geneva Convention ensured that combatant prisoners were housed in buildings or huts having dormitories, a prescribed amount of air space for each individual, and fittings and bedding material of the same minimum requirements as for depot troops of the Detaining Power, in this case the Canadian Army. Other regulations ensured that the food be equivalent in quality and quantity of that for depot troops, and that an infirmary be provided in every camp.

German Prisoners-of-War at the Wainwright Camp library, 1 October 1945.

Photo courtesy Provincial Archives of Alberta [PAA BI 983/4].

Each prisoner of war was clothed by the Canadian government, at no cost to himself. They received a pair of leather boots, a pair of gum boots, three pairs of socks, two pairs of winter underwear, one winter cap, one summer cap, one mackinaw overcoat, woollen mitts, a winter coat and trousers, as well as various necessities such as razors and shaving brushes.[16] Prisoners were permitted to wear their badges of rank and decorations. However, once their uniforms were worn out, they were issued with the standard type of internment clothing, consisting of lined or unlined blue denim, characterized by special markings in order that they could be identified if an escape were effected. These special markings included a red stripe down the right pantleg, while the back of the coat had a fourteen-inch red circle set into the cloth. The German prisoners were angered, and viewed these identification markings as a stigma. Ironically, the concept of marked clothing originated in Germany during the First World War, when British officer-prisoners had to wear a yellow stripe inserted in the trouser leg and a yellow band on each arm. At any rate, the government was not going to change its views, as unmarked civilian clothing would have facilitated the escape of the German POWs.[17]

Article 12 of the Geneva Convention permitted the establishment in each permanent internment camp of a canteen for the use of the prisoners. Goods supplied to the canteen were to be sold to the prisoners at local market prices. The officers' mess was permitted to provide beer at the discretion of the Camp Commandant. Profits from the canteen were accumulated to defray the cost of recreational, educational and other facilities, which were to be provided for the benefit of all the prisoners. However, any damages to the camp caused by the German prisoners would be deducted from the canteen profits.

German prisoners' canteen at the Wainwright Camp, 1 October 1945.

Photo courtesy Provincial Archives of Alberta [PAA Bl 983/b].

Upon their arrival in the camp, the prisoners lost all their monies and effects to the authorities. These were duly inventoried and put into safekeeping, to be returned upon release or parole. Article 86 of the Geneva Convention allowed for the representatives of the Protecting Power, that is, the Swiss, to visit the prisoners. They would intervene on the part of the prisoners, and act on any complaints set forth by them. Similarly, a representative of the International Red Cross Committee was also allowed access to the camps, and it was the IRCC which brought comforts and supplies to the prisoners, working to help the prisoners' mental and physical well-being.

Each combatant officer POW was permitted to write four postcards and three letters per month, whereas "other ranks" were permitted four postcards and two letters per month. Protected personnel [medical personnel, padres, and members of the forces who did not bear arms] were permitted double that quota. No postal charges were made in the country of origin or destination for parcels and correspondence addressed to POWs, although regular airmail rates had to be paid by the prisoners if they made use of airmail. Prisoners were also permitted to send telegrams and overseas cables at their own expense. All letter mail to and from POWs was censored in the Ottawa Post Office, where censors were instructed to watch for any details of potential intelligence value, and to pass these on to their military intelligence officers. Prisoners were allowed to receive postal parcels containing foodstuffs and other articles intended for consumption or clothing, as well as consignments of books.

Mixed medical commissions consisting of three members [two Swiss and one Canadian] went around to the different internment camps to examine sick and wounded prisoners, and to make appropriate decisions regarding their welfare. Approximately 1165 sick and wounded German prisoners were repatriated to the Fatherland through the activities and recommendations of such medical commissions.

In the summer of 1943, the Minister of Labour was authorized to use German prisoners of war in agricultural and other labour projects which were not related to the war effort. Article 3 of the Geneva Convention authorized a belligerent country to employ prisoners of war as workmen under certain specified circumstances. Article 29 said that no prisoner was to be employed on work for which he was physically unsuited. Articles 31 and 32 noted that no prisoner was to be employed on work having any direct connection with the war effort, nor on dangerous and unhealthy work. Article 30 ensured that one day of rest per week was to be required. Pay was twenty cents per day, and NCOs could be compelled to undertake only supervisory work, for which they did not have to be paid. Article 34 noted that the duration of the daily work was not to exceed that for civilian workers employed on the same jobs, which was usually eight hours.[18]

The main gate at
Lethbridge POW
Camp, with a work
party of prisoners
leaving through it in
October 1944.

*Photo given to John
Joseph Kelly by Colonel
Kippen ca. 1977.*

The government felt that it was important to keep the prisoners occupied:

> *....Everyone...realizes the importance of finding work for the
> prisoners. It is essential to employ all of them, if possible, all the
> time. They will be happier if they are occupied. It will improve
> their morale and as a result it will be easier to handle the
> camp....*[19]

Prisoners who were kept busy did not have time to plot escapes. As well, the
public undoubtedly would be angry at the knowledge that these men were being
cared for at the expense of the taxpayer without doing any work.

On the other hand, it was realized that the German prisoners could supply a
large labour force that could work relatively inexpensively. Some five hundred
prisoners at the Lethbridge camp were designated to be used in the local sugar
beet fields. Only "other ranks" would be employed, and they had to volunteer to
be able to work on the projects. The agreed-upon pay was $2.50 per working day
for each prisoner. Any company which used this prison labour would deduct one
dollar for each prisoner and accompanying guard who were fed and boarded, and
a further fifty cents per day was credited to the account of the prisoner of war so
that he could make purchases from the camp canteen. Other labour projects
included a hundred men hoeing crops near Lethbridge, a wood-cutting project
employing some two hundred men in South River, Alberta, and an irrigation
project needing an additional one hundred men at Brooks, Alberta. Some of the

prisoners were allowed to reside on the farms of their employers at night, and then return to the work projects in the morning. One of the biggest problems faced by the authorities on these projects was the tendency of the German POWs to try to slow down production. This problem was finally alleviated in the spring of 1945, when detention camps were set up to punish these trouble-makers. In fact, these labour projects became so successful that during 1945 about 2,200 POWs were employed in sugar beet work and the hoeing of other crops; further arrangements were made to supply Ontario with POW labour for the beet fields located around the city of Chatham.

Work party of German POWs harvesting sugar beets near Lethbridge, Alberta, October 1944. Note POW clothing on the nearest German prisoner, highlighted by the red circle in the middle of his back.

Photo given to John Joseph Kelly by Colonel Kippen ca. 1977.

Once the prisoners had started working the authorities appear to have realized, with chagrin, that a valuable commodity had been allowed to loiter in the POW camps for several years at public expense, without any use being made of their labour-saving potential. For the minor sum of fifty cents per day, great work could be accomplished in the areas of beet harvesting, farming and lumbering. The Receiver General of Canada received the following monies from the POW employers[20]:

1943 [7 months] $155,948.15

1944 [12 months] $675,108.47

1945 [12 months] $2,427,123.81

Sugar beet harvest tonnage was also quite impressive: [21]

> *1944: 18,344 tons of sugar beets giving a sugar content of 6,545,000 pounds.*

> *1945: 66,814 tons of sugar beets giving a sugar content of 22,704,000 pounds*

The labour projects would be deemed an unqualified success. One author noted:

> *....to some basic industries, the infusion of this labour was a veritable life giving plasma enabling them to revive and continue their vigorous contribution to the nation's war effort.*[22]

Even though prisoners were labouring on these projects, and the government was able to save money by utilizing them, neither side forgot that these were combatant prisoners whose duty was to escape from Canada and return to Germany to fight again. During the war, about a hundred German prisoners made their escapes from Canadian internment authorities, with most such incidents occurring when the German prisoners walked away from labour projects upon which they were employed. In November 1946 there were still some 23 German prisoners "at large," eighteen months after the cessation of hostilities. At the Medicine Hat camp the authorities found a home-made short wave radio, with the radio antenna threaded through the clothes line. There was a short wave radio at the Lethbridge camp as well; until May 1945 this set was completely portable, and was moved from hut to hut. However, it was not very efficient, and only occasionally would it pick up German stations. To compensate for this shortcoming, a larger set was built by three prisoners, and was assembled inside a building partition in the music instrument repair shop. The parts came from men who had been on the outside on labour projects, and all the parts were "home-made." For example, the tuning knobs were made from the tops of Listerine bottles, while the headphones were taken from German air force helmets.[23] Messages would be smuggled into camps, written in indelible pencil on wax paper, in nutshells, in sausages, in cigars, and in tin cans. In one case at Lethbridge, in October 1944, a letter was sent to the camp inside a loaf of bread, which was detected only when the loaf was sawed through by the camp authorities. The information had been allowed through by the German censors in the hope that it would get through to the prisoners. However, the war news was so bad from Germany that the camp authorities let it through to demoralize the prisoners even more. Camp authorities also found a home-made air rifle at Medicine Hat, instruments rigged up for low-power high-voltage electric charges, short wave radio antennae made from bedsprings, and even explosive belts! A search at the Medicine Hat camp during September 1944 also turned up "secret writing" materials, as well as complete directions from Germany as to their use and purpose. This kit included a solid type of ink that had previously only been used by the German Secret Service. It seemed obvious to the camp authorities that an extensive organization had been set up in Germany to make use of intelligence information gathered by the prisoners.

Colonel W.J.H. Ellwood [Commandant at Medicine Hat POW camp] seated at his desk. Colonel Ellwood was Medicine Hat's Commandant from August 1944-1946.

Photo given to John Joseph Kelly by Colonel Ellwood ca. 1977.

The Canadian authorities had a great fear of a "Gestapo element" in the camps, and this fear was confirmed with the murders of German prisoners at the Medicine Hat camp on two occasions: 22 July 1943, and 10 September 1944. In the first case, the murder of August Plaszek, a Military Court of Inquiry noted:

> ....*The guilty party or parties were not discovered, but a good many P.W., strongly Nazi, who either assisted in, connived at, or approved of the hanging, were uncovered. Some of these, all strongly Nazi and some Gestapo, had been troublemakers at Lethbridge and Ozada, and it is evident that they were anxious to get control of the camp from the slightly more moderate Nazi group previously in control.*[24]

An Intelligence Report, gathered from the scrapbook of a German POW, backs up the assessment of the Court of Inquiry:

> ....*And now, a little "Gestapo" has also come into existence, which sternly saw to it that all the soldiers of the camp behaved as exemplary Nazis.... Some P.W. were tired of being duped any more by these uniformed tramps and got together to bring about an overthrow of these elements. But through treachery, the camp police got wind of this, and a few of those revolutionists had to leave the camp. The mob got hold of one of them, dragged him into the recreation hut, and strung him up on one of the rafters here without any trial whatever, after he had first been stoned half to death. Thus did Gefreiter Plaszek, having done his duty towards the Fatherland at the front, die the hero's death.*[25]

In the second case, Karl Lehmann was dragged into the classroom where he had taught French language classes to some of his fellow prisoners. Here, the best boxer in the camp struck Lehmann once on the jaw, injuring him and causing him to bleed. Then they hanged him from a gas pipe in a corner of the room, where his body was not found until the next morning.[26] The authorities spoke of a "Geistige Betreung" [Spiritual guardianship], which had both a "spiritual" control over the hearts of the prisoners, and a Gestapo control over the prisoners' minds, exercised through education in the camps, political censorship, morale and ideology.[27] Throughout the last few years of the war prisoners were constantly seeking the protection of the Canadian authorities, and there appears to have been some truth to the military assessment that:

> ....a group of P.W. ... were trying to maintain Nazi doctrines among the P.W., and there was a lot of talk about organizing a "Werewolf" organization. They were transferred to Neys on April 18, 1945, and things calmed down....[28]

With the war winding down the Canadian government did not see fit to accept any more prisoners from Britain, though the British requested that Canada accommodate another fifty thousand prisoners.[29] The Canadian government felt that with the prisoners it was already holding, it was more important to classify them by their degrees of pro- and anti-Nazi fervour, in order to facilitate their ultimate repatriation back to Germany. It was felt that no prisoners would be returned until after the end of the military occupation of Germany, which would be at least 1 ½ years after the cessation of hostilities. The PHERUDA programme was established in each camp, and classified prisoners as being "Black" [strong Nazi], "White" [anti-Nazi], or "Grey" [neutral or moderate]. This was done on the basis of interrogating prisoners about their political leanings, their attitude towards Hitler, their education, their religion, their usefulness for the purposes of labour, their dependability, and their attitude [rated from pro-Allied to anti-Allied]. The basic test of "whiteness" was the willingness of the prisoner to cooperate with the Canadian authorities in different ways. The Whites were to be repatriated first, the Greys second, and the Blacks were to be sent back to the defeated Fatherland last of all.

However, in deciding the basis upon which the remaining prisoners were to be repatriated, the requirements of the labour projects prevailed over all other interests. German prisoners were still in demand, and a large number of companies were still utilizing prisoner labour even after the end of the conflict. At the war's end, some 11,115 POWs were still employed on various labour projects organized by the Department of Labour. The German prisoners continued to work on these projects in order to purchase items from the camp canteen for which they had no other means of obtaining money, and for the chance to get out from behind the barbed wire. The Intelligence Officer at Wainwright, Alberta, noted:

> ...A great number of P/W have approached the Interpreter Officer in order to obtain work on a works project. Almost every

> *P/W O.R. wants to get out....they had noticed the cordial relation between Canadian officers and men, and consider this as a living example of democracy, therefore they would like to get out and work for Canadians or Canadian firms.[30]*

The prisoners also knew that by working they might gain the experience and training in trades that would be of help to them when they were forced again to earn a living back in Germany. Also, the products that they were gathering, like cabbage, radishes and potatoes, were consumed largely by the prisoners themselves. It was not until February 1946 that the first 2755 POWs were repatriated to Germany, but the exodus continued throughout that spring, so that by the end of July 1946 only 4400 prisoners were left in Canada to provide labour for the sugar beet harvest. Some six thousand Germans had by this time made written application to stay in Canada, but Article 75 of the Geneva Convention stated that all prisoners of war were to be repatriated as soon as possible after the war, so these hopes were never realized.

The final 4400 prisoners were evacuated in November 1946, a move that sparked protests from Alberta farmers. By the first week of January 1947, all the prisoners were gone from Canada, save for some sixty of them who were either in hospital or in jail. Another 162 had died in captivity, and their bodies are interred in a special area of Woodland Cemetery in Kitchener, Ontario.

Could it be said that Alberta played a key role in the Canadian war effort by housing German POWs during the war? The answer must be an unequivocal "yes." Over sixty per cent of all German prisoners of war who were sent to Canada were interned in Alberta camps. Kananaskis was used from the opening day of the war, while the three largest camps, located at Ozada, Lethbridge and

An exhibition of handiwork by German POWs at either Medicine Hat or Lethbridge.

Photo courtesy John Joseph Kelly.

Medicine Hat, were not only the biggest POW camps in Canada, but the latter two were also the only camps built expressly for the purpose of holding German POWs. The problem with these camps was that they were so large that most of the prisoners were anonymous to camp staff, a situation which led to a constant battle between them and the camp Gestapo as to who would truly control the camps. The ability to offer outside employment and a cash salary to the prisoners was a boon to the Canadian authorities who sought to ensure that the POWs remained cooperative. That there was still a demand for prisoner labour some eighteen months after the end of hostilities speaks volumes about the success of this programme.

And what of the German prisoners who spent those years incarcerated in the Canadian West? Major Henry Smith of the Veterans Guard of Canada, a participant at "the Battle of Ozada," wrote:

> *....Generally speaking, we treated the P.O.W. really too well compared to how British and Canadian P.O.W. in Germany were treated. No doubt plenty of complaints were made, but most of them were minor, and more of a "nuisance" than genuine....I personally do not know of any case where P.O.W. were genuinely mistreated, and any complaints of such, which might have been made to the Swiss Consul...did not go any further after being investigated: they were just gripes to try and cause trouble.....Any "crimes" committed by a P.O.W. were tried by Commandants, and in worse cases by courts martial, and I often heard P.O.W. say that we treated them fairly....*[31]

This view was shared by Colonel E.D.B. Kippen who was a Camp Commandant during the war:

> *....A great many of them* [former German POWs in Canada], *I understand, immigrated to Canada during the next few years* [after the war]. *I think this is all first class evidence in favour of their treatment here....*[32]

The delegate from the International Red Cross, Mr. Ernest Maag, also shared a generally positive view of prisoners' treatment:

> *....With regard to hygiene and salubrity, the camps in Canada met...the most modern requirements....[It] must be stated that the general health was so good and the death rate among prisoners was so small that the record regarding Article 15 of the Geneva Convention must be described as excellent....*[33]

The final word should go to a former POW who wrote to Colonel Kippen almost two years after the war to express his feelings:

> *....I shall always appreciate the ever so correct and considerate attitude of the Government of Canada, and the Military Authorities towards P.O.W.s. This is meant to be a simple act of gratitude to fairness met in enemy hands. I honestly believe that many a former P.O.W. will agree with me, if I say, that your country has done a lot to show Germans in Canadian custody the value of democratic life. The results of this attitude, I hope, will prove to be of stimulating value, in rebuilding our own country....* [34]

Notes

[1] Directorate of History, Department of National Defence, File 113.3P4 (D2), Directorate Narrative, 5 September, 1945.

[2] National Archives of Canada, [NAC], W.L.M. King Papers, MG26, J1, Vol. 273, p. 231084, "International Security Measures Taken on the Outbreak of War," 2 December, 1939.

[3] NAC, Director of Internment Operations, RG6, L, Vol. 10, File 4-1-5 (1), Inspector D.C. Saul, RCMP to Director of Internment Operations, 20 October 1939.

[4] NAC, Secretary of State Department, RG6, D1, Vol. 21, p. 1, W.D. Otter to the Minister of Justice ["Internment Operations 1914-1920"], 30 September 1920.

[5] NAC, Director of Internment Operations, RG6, L, Vol. 11, File 4-3-1, General Panet to Lt. Col. Desrosiers, 11 September 1939.

[6] NAC, W.L.M. King Papers, MG26, J1, Vol. 265, p. 225543, E.H. Coleman to H.R.L. Henry, 25 September 1939.

[7] NAC, Director of Internment Operations, RG6, L, Vol. 11, File 4-3-1, General Panet to Lt. Col. Desrosiers, 23 November 1939.

[8] NAC, Director of Internment Operations, RG6, L, Vol. 12, File 5-1-2, W. Stuart Edwards to General Panet, 17 November 1939.

[9] NAC, Director of Internment Operations, RG6, L, Vol. 12, File 5-1-2, Lt.-Col. Hubert Stethem to the Department of External Affairs, 30 July 1940.

[10] Lorne Bruce, "1940 German Prisoners Highly Satisfied With Alberta Internment Camp Life," *Nelson Daily News,* 13 March 1940, p. 4.

[11] NAC, W.L.M. King Papers, Vol. 292, p. 247153, Mackenzie King to Vincent Massey, 10 June 1940.

[12] NAC, Director of Internment Operations, RG6, L, Vol. 10, File 4-2-1, Mackenzie King to Vincent Massey [#37], 7 January 1942.

[13] Major Henry Smith [Ret.], Veterans Guard of Canada, personal communication to the author, 21 August 1976.

[14] Ibid.

[15] NAC, RG 24, Microfilm Reel C-5395, Brigadier Harvey DOC, MD 13, to the Secretary, Department of National Defence, 29 December 1942.

[16] NAC, Director of Internment Operations, RG6, L, Vol. 1, File 1-1-6, Colonel Hubert Stethem to the Department of External Affairs, 19 March 1941.

[17] NAC, Director of Internment Operations, RG6, L, Vol. 2, File 1-2-7, Colonel Hubert Stethem to the Department of External Affairs, 29 January 1941.

[18]NAC, Director of Internment Operations, RG6, L, Vol. 1, File 1-2-3, Assistant Director of Internment Operations to Angus MacDonald, 7 August 1940.

[19]NAC, Director of Internment Operations, RG6, L, Vol. 1, File 1-2-3, General Panet to the District Officers Commanding, 6 August 1940.

[20]NAC, Department of Labour, RG27, Vol. 965, File 24, History Projects PW.

[21]Ibid.

[22]Ibid.

[23]NAC, RG 24, Microfilm Reel C-5416, Colonel E.D.B. Kippen to Headquarters of MD #3, 27 September 1945.

[24]NAC, Directorate of Prisoners of War, File H.Q.S. 7236, "Case of hanging by his fellow prisoners of P.W. Sdt. PLASZEK, August."

[25]NAC, Directorate of Prisoners of War, Intelligence Report, File 26-H-44, 14 November 1944.

[26]Douglas Sagi, "My Fuehrer I Follow Thee," *The Canadian Magazine*, 4 January 1975, pp.1-4.

[27]NAC, RG24, Microfilm Reel C-5365, Camp Intelligence at Lethbridge, Colonel E.D.B. Kippen to Headquarters MD 13, 2 April 1945.

[28]NAC, RG24, Microfilm Reel C-5365, Camp Intelligence at Lethbridge, Intelligence Report for April 1945, 11 May 1945.

[29]NAC, Minutes of the Cabinet War Committee, RG2, 7c, Vol. 16, Meeting of Monday 11 December 1944.

[30]NAC, RG24, Microfilm Reel C-5365, Summary of Camp Intelligence for Wainwright, Alberta for month of June 1945.

[31]Major Henry Smith [Ret.], Veterans Guard of Canada, personal communication to the author, 21 August 1976.

[32]Colonel E.D.B. Kippen, personal communication to the author, 16 August 1976.

[33]Directorate of History, Department of National Defence, File 382.013 [D13], Report of the Red Cross Delegate on Internment Operations in Canada, pp. 222-223.

[34]Anonymous letter to Colonel E.D.B. Kippen, 26 March 1947.

In the 18 years since the initial research for this material was undertaken, the government documents of the period have been re-numbered at the National Archives of Canada.Researchers interested in doing further reading in this area should consult Barbara Wilson's *Guide to Second World War-Prisoners of War-Internment Operations*, which provides specific references to the Alberta camps in Record Group (RG) 24 holdings.The Archivist presently responsible for these records is Mr. Paul Marsden.

Ideological Battles in Medicine Hat: The Deaths of August Plaszek and Karl Lehmann

Danial Duda

The second largest mass hanging in Canadian history occurred in Lethbridge, Alberta on 18 December 1946.[1] Five men were hanged for committing murder; one was a sex murderer, while the other four were members of the German Wehrmacht. These four Germans were prisoners of war, and had murdered a fellow prisoner, Karl Lehmann, on 10 September 1944 in Internment Camp No.132 Medicine Hat. Lehmann's murder was the second to happen in the Medicine Hat camp. On 22 July 1943, August Plaszek had been killed by fellow POWs, and three men were charged for it. One was hanged, another's sentence of hanging was commuted to life imprisonment, and the third man was acquitted. Both murders were a result of arguments over political ideology, and threats or perceived threats of an overthrow of the internal camp leadership.

Each POW camp had a spokesman or leader whose duty was to communicate concerns of the prisoners to the camp authorities. A large camp like Medicine Hat was very efficient financially, but its size prevented the Commandant and his staff from getting to know many prisoners; the camp leader and his staff had greater control over fellow POWs. In the case of the two murders, the camp authorities were ignorant of what was happening until it was too late.[2] It was also a long and arduous process for the RCMP to bring the guilty parties to trial. Plaszek's murderers were charged 26 months after the incident and Lehmann's

August Plaszek,
27 June 1942.

Photo courtesy Glenbow Archives, Calgary [NA-5012-1].

were charged 19 months later.[3] Major E.H.J. Barber later reported that "[to] prevent further such breaches of the law an order was issued that any P.W. having any knowledge of an attack or intended attack on any other P.W. would be held guilty of an offence unless he reported the matter to the Military Authorities."[4] The prisoners did not like this order, but there were no more murders. It would have helped the Canadian authorities if they had told the POWs that they were subject to Canadian law while detained in Canada as stipulated in Article 45 of the Geneva Convention.[5] Perhaps it might have saved the lives of Plaszek and Lehmann.

August Plaszek was born 30 January 1903. Before he joined the French Foreign Legion, he was a farmer near Nordlunen, Germany. He was Roman Catholic. He was 5' 5 $^1/_4$" tall and weighed 150 lbs. In the 1930s, Legionnaires who returned to Germany were re-educated in Nazi ideology and then inducted into the army. Plaszek was in the 361st African Regiment that was brought into the North African campaign by Erwin Rommel, the infamous leader of the Afrika Korps. The troops in this regiment were ex-Legionnaires and Rommel believed that their previous experience in Africa would be an asset. In 1943 the 361st was almost wiped out at Tobruk, where Plaszek was captured by the British. He, along with the remnants of his regiment, would eventually be interned at Medicine Hat. The irony of the situation was that had Plaszek stayed with the French Foreign Legion, he would have been fighting his home nation.[6]

These ex-Legionnaires would meet in an open area by the soccer field in the Medicine Hat compound. They would reminisce about their past and discuss what their future might hold. The leading Nazi elements despised this group, thinking that they could have fought better for the Fatherland. They were also believed to be the leaders of the communist sympathizers. Those men who were outspoken against the Nazis were at first terrorized; notes, excrement in their food, and a death's head drawn on their pillow were just the beginning of the terror process. The next step would be isolation from the main body of prisoners, and the last step was torture.[7]

On 21 July 1943 Camp Leader Eilsterman called a meeting of his hut leaders. They believed that this group of men met regularly to plan an overthrow of the camp leadership. It was intended to have the leaders of the group transferred to another camp. Four men were to be interrogated the next day: Christian Schultz, Max Weidhauer, Afonse Burkhardt, and August Plaszek.[8] The first to be questioned was Weidhauer and the next man was Schultz. After his interrogation, Schultz was being escorted back to a detention hut to await further questions. Before they reached the hut, Schultz made a dash for the warning wire and reached it before the mob of prisoners caught him. He begged to be let across the wire and a guard in the closest tower fired a warning shot that stopped the mob. Four guards then entered the compound, two helping Schultz climb the wire as the mob of six to eight hundred men blocked the way to the main gate. They then took two of the guards hostage until the Camp Leader ordered the men to let the guards go.[9]

The wire around Camp Wainwright, similar to those around the Kananaskis, Lethbridge and Medicine Hat camps. It was the wire on the right, the warning wire, that saved Christian Schultz, but which led to August Plaszek's death.

Photo courtesy Provincial Archives of Alberta [PAA Bl.983/2].

Losing Schultz raised the ire of the mob to a fever pitch. The prisoners returned to the interrogation hut and a small group entered it and dragged out August Plaszek. The surprised victim was then beaten and taken to the recreation hall where he was hanged.[10] It took 26 months for the RCMP to obtain enough evidence to lay charges. With a mob action, who was responsible? No one would speak out until well after the war was over and the threat of reprisals was gone. The investigation was carried out in four camps: Kananaskis, Lethbridge, Medicine Hat and Neys, Ontario. Three men were charged with the murder: Werner Schwalb, Adolf Kratz, and Johannes Wittinger.[11]

Werner Schwalb was born on 11 June 1915 at Sausenheim Pfalz, a county in the French occupied zone 20 miles west of the Rhine. He was single and a baker and cook in civilian life, living in Rheinphaiz. He joined the German army on 2 November 1937 and received the Iron Cross, First Class in the French campaign. In North Africa, Schwalb was captured at Solomn in Egypt by a South African unit attached to the British Eighth Army. Before arriving at Medicine Hat, he was interned at Ozada and Lethbridge.[12]

Adolf Kratz was born on 19 July 1921 in Koblenz, Germany. Before he entered the army in 1940, he was a carpenter in Cologne. In 1941 he was transferred to the Russian Front for six months, after which he fought in North Africa. Kratz was captured by the Free French Forces at Tobruk on 29 May 1942 and eventually arrived in Canada in August of that year as a POW. His first camp was Ozada, then Lethbridge and finally Medicine Hat. He participated in the Department of Labour work projects working in the sugar beet fields of southern Alberta.[13]

The recreation hall where August Plaszek was hanged.

Photo courtesy Provincial Archives of Alberta [PAA A10974].

Johannes Wittinger was captured by the same unit that captured Kratz at Tobruk. Wittinger was born on 6 June 1915 in Kratz, Austria and worked as a truck driver in Grafendorf, Austria before being drafted in 1940. He had been wounded in the arm in what action he saw, and he was awarded the Iron Cross, Second Class for this. He was married and had a five-year-old daughter.[14]

Each man was tried separately. Schwalb's trial began on 25 February 1946, with Kratz's trial next and Wittinger's finishing on 21 June 1946. The details of the event unfolded between the three trials. The key witness that saved Kratz and Wittinger was Schwalb, who testified at Wittinger's trial that they were nowhere near the murder scene when it happened. Because of this evidence, Wittinger was found not guilty and two days before he was to hang, Kratz's sentence was reduced to life imprisonment.

Schwalb's sentence of hanging was carried out on 26 June 1946, although he was willing to testify in the Lehmann murder trials that had begun in May 1946. Schwalb died as a German soldier, his last words being "My Führer, I follow thee."[15]

The motive behind the Lehmann murder was similar to that of Plaszek's; however, the goal was to eliminate one man and not to cause the breakup of a group. Karl Lehmann was a professor of languages at the University of Erlangen, a stout middle-aged man, 5' 9" and 195 lbs. The Tunisian campaign was his last before he was captured and shipped to an English POW camp before being sent to Canada. In Camp Oldham, Lehmann began to speak out against the Nazi regime and to forecast that Germany would lose the war. During his stay in Oldham, the Roman Catholics in the camp asked the local priest, who was German-speaking, if he would come and say mass and hear confessions. An altar and confessional were set up in a recreational hall; but, the Gestapo element in the camp made sure that one of the walls of the confessional was a fake wall.

Canadian Veterans'
Guard leads the
funeral procession for
murdered POW
August Plaszek.

*Photo courtesy Glenbow
Archives, Calgary
[NA-5078-7].*

The Gestapo clique then listened in on the confessions and used this information
for blackmail. During Lehmann's confession, a man by the name of
Perzonowsky was behind the fake wall. He would be one of the men
charged and found guilty of murdering Lehmann.[16]

Lehmann was sent to Canada by the British authorities to protect him from the
Nazis because of his political views. In 1942, he came to Canada with another
shipment of POWs that was also carrying Perzonowsky. Both men ended up in
Medicine Hat.[17] It would be two years before the murder took place, and during
that time Lehmann carried on with his speeches forecasting German defeat to
whomever wanted to listen. For his anti-Nazi views, Lehmann was labeled as the
leader of the communists in the camp. He encouraged anyone who would want to
discuss this to come and listen to him, including the ex-Legionnaires. This did
not bode well for him with the Nazi leadership in the camp.[18]

The event that gave the Nazis permission to act was a speech that Hitler made
after the failed assassination attempt on his life which occurred on 20 July 1944.
In his broadcast speech he told all the Nazi faithful throughout the world to do
their duty and get rid of any traitor in their midst. The POWs in Medicine Hat
heard the speech by short wave radio. It also became known that one of the
perpetrators of the assassination plot was none other than Field Marshall Erwin
Rommel, the Afrika Korps commander greatly admired by the ex-Legionnaires.[19]
With this order from the Führer, and the evidence of his outspoken views back in
Oldham which continued at Medicine Hat, Lehmann became an automatic target
for the Nazis; the one who gave the order to get rid of him was Perzonowsky.[20]

Ironically, the spark that led to the actual murder was struck by the Canadian
authorities. German POWs were being segregated by their political ideology and
given colour classifications to tell them apart: "Whites" were pro-democratic,
"Greys" probably could be convinced to become democratic, and "Blacks" were

definitely Nazi.[21] Whites also helped the Canadian authorities spread democratic ideals because the detaining power was not allowed under the Geneva Convention to do so directly. The ardent Nazis found out that they were being shipped out of Medicine Hat to Neys, Ontario on 11 September 1944.[22]

On the night of 10 September, Lehmann was asked to go to the hut where he gave lectures and meet someone who wanted to talk to him. When he arrived there were four men waiting for him: Bruno Perzonowsky, Willi Mueller, Heinrich Busch and Walter Wolf. They beat Lehmann and then hanged him. The next day all four were off to their new home in Neys.[23]

The hut where August Plaszek was questioned before his murder. It was in a similar hut that Karl Lehmann was beaten and hanged.

Photo courtesy Provincial Archives of Alberta [PAA A 10973].

Sergeant-Major Bruno Perzonowsky, the ring leader, was born in Johannesburg, East Prussia. He was captured on 14 April 1941 when his bomber went down in Wales; his sixty completed flights earned him the Iron Cross, First Class. Before joining the Luftwaffe in 1935, he was a policeman in Elbing, East Prussia. His wife and daughter lived in Kragemfurt, Austria during the war. He arrived in Canada on 1 January 1942 and was interned in Montieth, Medicine Hat and Neys.[24]

Sergeant Willi Mueller was born in Kleina, a province of Gorerotz. He was captured near Glasgow on 6 May 1941 when a Spitfire shot down his bomber. He had won the Iron Cross, both First and Second Class and had completed 87 operational flights. Before he joined the German Kriegsmarine in 1935 he had been a mechanic in Rosetz. Within the year, he transferred to the Luftwaffe. He was single.[25]

Sergeant-Major Heinrich Busch was born in Burgon, Frankfurt-am-Main. The collision of his bomber with barrage balloon wires led to his capture in Norfolk, England. He had completed twenty six operational flights and was awarded the Iron Cross, Second Class. He was a clothing store clerk before signing up with the Luftwaffe in 1934. He arrived in Canada in January 1942 and was interned in Montieth, Medicine Hat and Neys. He was also single.[26]

Sergeant Walter Wolf was captured at Halfaya Pass in North Africa on 17 January 1942. He was married but had no children. He had received the Iron Cross, Second Class. Before enlisting at the age of 19 in 1937, he was a financial tax inspector. After the French campaign, he was transferred to a unit in the Afrika Korps. Arriving in Canada on 26 May 1942, he was interned at Ozada, Lethbridge, Medicine Hat and Neys.[27]

As with the Plaszek murder trials, all four men were tried separately. They were arrested on 6 April 1946; the preliminary hearings began on 1 May and finished on 15 May. On 24 June Perzonowsky was the first to be tried, two days before Schwalb was to hang for Plaszek's murder. Next to be tried was Wolf, then Busch, and finally Mueller. All four were found guilty and sentenced to hang. The main line of defence was that all four were following orders and had executed a man who was believed to be a traitor. This was not a strong enough argument and a court of appeal upheld the decision of guilty on 16 October 1944; however, there were two stays of execution. On 18 December, all four men were hanged, at the same time as a sex murderer was executed. When the four POWs found out that they were to die with a sex murderer, they asked if they could die by firing squad, the sentence of a court martial. Their request was refused. The night before the executions, three of the prisoners tried committing suicide by slashing their wrists with razor blades that were probably smuggled in with books. The guards stopped them in time and after they were bandaged up at the hospital, they were taken to the gallows. It was the second largest mass hanging in Canadian history, the largest happening during the Riel Rebellion when eight natives were hanged at Battleford for their actions in Riel's cause.[28]

These murders are tragic examples of what a powerful and ruthless clique can do in an enclosed environment like a POW camp. Even with the humane treatment carried out by the Canadian authorities following the provisions of the Geneva Conventions, the life of a prisoner was by no means always safeguarded from the horrors of war. A clear example of this was shown in a scrapbook that scouts [unarmed members of the Veterans Guard of Canada who patrolled within the barbed wire and watched for any illicit activity] captured in the Medicine Hat camp. Seventy per cent of the POWs never had better conditions than at Medicine Hat. Those who became the leaders often despised the war and the German leadership until they were sent to Canada; with the "good life" here, they "gathered behind a red swastika banner."[29] The Nazi hierarchy flourished and everyone was watched by everyone else. No one could have his own opinion. There were leaders appointed for everything: huts, sections, sports, and special groups. In July 1943 several officers from the Bowmanville camp in Ontario arrived. They allegedly had "brought with them a communication from the most senior German officer in Canada, Lt.-Gen. Schmidt."[30] Thereafter all affairs were carried out by the Gestapo element as if ordered by General Schmidt. During his preliminary hearing, Walter Wolf gave evidence that General Schmidt gave orders to destroy any traitors after the 20 July 1944 attempt on Hitler.[31] Some POWs who were tired of the Nazi ways began to get together and plan an overthrow of the camp leadership. Treachery led to this group's demise and one was killed in the recreation hall. "Thus did Gefr. [Private] Plaszek," it was observed, "having done his duty towards the Fatherland at the front, die the hero's death." [32] Beatings were daily occurrences, and those who felt threatened sought protection from the Camp Commandant.[33] According to this soldier, life in Medicine Hat was not a pleasant way to wait out the war, though most of the prisoners had it better than Canadian POWs in Germany.

By January 1947 all German POWs had been repatriated to Germany except some 60 prisoners. Most of these were too ill to travel at this time while some who had successfully escaped were still at large. Others, like Adolf Kratz, were serving their jail sentences for whatever crime they had committed. Kratz was released in 1955 following representations made by family and friends. One plea was that his 74-year-old mother needed someone to support her. Before he left for Germany, Kratz would play a key role in the British Columbia provincial election of 1960. During that general election Donald Riggan, a Social Credit candidate in the riding of Delta, would be accused of having a criminal record. He confirmed these allegations and said that there was a good reason he had this record. In 1949 a member of the RCMP approached him and asked him to commit a crime in Alberta and be caught at it. He could then plead guilty and be sent to the penitentiary in Prince Albert, Saskatchewan, where he would "obtain vital information from a 'brilliant Nazi scientist named Adolf Kratz' who was serving a sentence for murder...."[34] It was only one week before the election when this patriotic episode in Mr. Riggan's life was disclosed to the public. Jack Weeks, the deputy warden of the Prince Albert Penitentiary, said he remembered both Kratz and Riggan; but Kratz was almost illiterate, and the prison records described him as a 22-year-old German who was a private in the Afrika Korps and a carpenter in civilian life.[35] This description did not fit that of a "brilliant Nazi scientist." The RCMP would not confirm the story for Mr. Riggan.[36] The voters did not believe him either and he lost by 4000 votes.[37]

With the deportation of Adolf Kratz to Germany, the history of the murders at Medicine Hat came to a close. Though the general experience was a good one for German POWs in Canada, the strong Nazi element in some camps, especially at Medicine Hat, made life a living hell for some. Thus the war that was being fought in Europe had its effects even on the bald Alberta prairie; until the Nazis were totally defeated, those prisoners who held contrary political views were not safe. Even the Geneva Conventions, designed to protect those victims of war who were at the mercy of the enemy, could not protect the POW that thought differently from his comrades. At times the idea that "a regimental number is not a piece of information, but a man, and a man in trouble" could not go far enough to protect everyone; at least it did not for August Plaszek and Karl Lehmann.

NOTES

[1] Douglas Sagi, *My Fuhrer, I Follow Thee* in *The Canadian Magazine/The Calgary Herald*, 4 January 1975, pp. 2,6.

[2] Major E.H.J. Barber, *Memorandum on Internment Operations 27 June 1947*, File 382.013(01); Department of National Defence, Directorate of History [Ottawa], pp.14-15.

[3] David J. Carter, *Behind Canadian Barbed Wire: Alien, Refugee, and Prisoner of War Camps in Canada 1914-1946*, [Calgary: Tumbleweed Press Ltd., 1980], pp.220, 260.

[4] Major E.H.J. Barber, op. cit., p.15.

[5] Ibid. See also Dietrich Schindler and Jiri Toman, eds., Chapter 36 "Convention Relative to the Treatment of Prisoners of War. Signed at Geneva 27 July 1929." *The Laws of Armed Conflicts: A Collection of Conventions, Resolutions and Other Documents* [Geneva: Henry Dunant Institute, 1973], pp.261-288.

[6] Department of National Defence, *Directorate of History*, File 113.304(D6), "POWs and Internees, Canada: Press Releases"; Sagi, op. cit., p. 4 ; Carter, op. cit., pp.217-220.

[7] John Melady, *Escape From Canada! The Untold Story of German POWs in Canada 1939-1945* [Toronto: Macmillan, 1981], p.168.

[8] Carter, op. cit., pp. 240-246.

[9] Ibid.

[10] Ibid. ; Melady, op. cit., pp.168-171.

[11] Carter, op. cit., p. 220.

[12] Ibid., pp. 239-240.

[13] Ibid., p. 240.

[14] Ibid.

[15] Ibid., p. 252.

[16] Melady, op. cit., pp. 179-179; Carter, op. cit., pp. 257-270.

[17] Melady, op. cit., pp. 178-179.

[18] Ibid., pp. 180-181.

[19] Carter, op. cit., p. 257; Sagi, op. cit., p. 6.

[20] Carter, op. cit., pp. 257-270.

[21] See John Joseph Kelly, "Intelligence and Counter-Intelligence in German Prisoner of War Camps in Canada During World War II," *The Dalhousie Review*, 58(2) [Summer 1978], pp. 285-294 and Don Page, "Tommy Stone and Psychological Warfare in World War Two: Transforming a POW Liability into an Asset," *Journal of Canadian Studies* 16(3&4) [Fall-Winter 1981], pp. 110-120.

[22] Melady, op. cit., p. 181.

[23] Carter, op. cit., pp. 257-270.

[24] Ibid., p. 261.

[25] Ibid.

[26] Ibid.

[27] Ibid.

[28] Ibid., pp. 257-270; Sagi, op. cit., p. 6.

[29] John Joseph Kelly, *Prisoner of War Camps in Canada 1939-1947* [MA Thesis, University of Windsor, 1976], p. 175.

[30] Ibid., p. 176.

[31] Provincial Archives of Alberta, Accession No. 83.323, File No. 1 [Walter Wolf file].

[32] Kelly, op. cit., p. 176.

[33] Ibid., pp. 175-177.

[34] Provincial Archives of Alberta, Accession No. 78.139, File No. 19 [Newspaper Clippings].

[35] Ibid.

[36] Ibid.

[37] Elections British Columbia, *Electoral History of British Columbia 1871-1986*, p. 269.

Redeeming the War on the Home Front: Alberta's Japanese Community During the Second World War and After

David J. Goa

Most of the essays in this volume touch on service in the midst of "the terrors of history." For many of the people who are the subject of these reflections, the service is, as the title suggests, "for king and country" whether or not this was conscious in their minds at the outset of the war. The terrors of history[1] tend to bring out the best and the worst in human nature; so it is not surprising to find remarkable expressions of service and selflessness by so many men and women who responded to the call of their sovereign and country, who entered the fields of battle or served the war effort on the home front.

There are several other forms of service which we glimpse when we reflect on Canadians who found themselves the subject of the terrors of war, not because they had to face the enemy abroad, although there were Japanese, Italians and Germans alike who did serve in the Canadian forces, but because they were defined by the state as "the enemy within." They were enemy aliens whether or not they were citizens by adoption or birth. They were enemy aliens because, as far too often happens in human affairs, the war set to flight common sense and made it mandatory that judgement be exercised solely on the grounds of race and national origin. War has a levelling effect and its terror tends to spread throughout society.

At the heart of this essay is an argument that the many Japanese women[2] removed from the West Coast, beginning in February 1942 through the exercise of the War Measures Act, and resettled in Picture Butte and other towns of southern Alberta, were in service as well. Their service has also proven itself of singular value to Alberta and the civil life of Canada. What these women served, initially without the support or assistance of their husbands or older sons, was their children and the remnant of a shattered community. They were required by the particular way the terrors of history were being played out in their life in Canada to bring some modicum of stability to young lives, to work in the sugar beet fields for income and nurture the Japanese community's relationship with the farming community of southern Alberta, and slowly to build a new world in a country which had rejected them in the most thorough way. What I want to touch on are the cultural sources which contributed to the remarkable way the Japanese in Alberta put their world back together after it was so shattered. I will explore how two of these sources, the neo-Confucian value of family and the Buddhist insight into the fleeting character of life, made it possible for a group of Canadian citizens defined as "enemy aliens" to build a new community and nurture the civil life in the heartland of southern Alberta. The depth of Japanese cultural memory and the value formation of their religious faith and practice have been an unspoken source for the making of community.

The Japanese Communities of Southern Alberta

When the war broke out in 1939, there were 540 people of Japanese ancestry living in Alberta. Most of them were farmers and were well established citizens of Calgary, Raymond, Lethbridge, Taber, Hardieville and Redwater. A number of the young men of the Nisei, or second generation, saw the war as an opportunity to serve "King and Country" and to demonstrate their loyalty to Canada. In British Columbia the Nisei were refused when they attempted to join the army. If they were allowed to enlist, the argument went, they would be entitled to vote and given all the rights and responsibilities of citizenship. In Alberta, however, the attitude was considerably different and seven Nisei enlisted in the army in 1940.[3]

Ann and David Sunahara[4] argue that there was some fear in the Alberta Japanese community early in the war that their fledgling community, which had made Alberta their home for many years, would now start to receive the kind of hostile treatment they saw the German and Italian citizens of Alberta receiving. This fear proved groundless and the *Calgary Herald* and the *Lethbridge Herald* cautioned the public not to discriminate against Japanese-Albertans. The editor of the *Calgary Herald* wrote, in the rhetoric of the time, that "the yellow peril does not necessarily crouch under every yellow skin," while the *Lethbridge Herald* reminded its readers of the contribution of the Japanese community to southern Alberta. Both newspapers argued that this community had supported the Red Cross over the years, and its leaders had made public declarations of loyalty to Canada.[5]

The attitude was very different in much of British Columbia, with its larger and quite prosperous Japanese community. The hostility that developed during the early years of the war culminated with the federal Cabinet order in February 1942, to remove every man, women and child of Japanese ancestry residing within 100 miles of the Pacific coast.[6] Of course, this accounted for the vast majority of the Japanese citizens of Canada. Soon the British Columbia Security Commission was set up to administer the relocation of these communities, and it was under their auspices that many came to Alberta.

The Alberta sugar beet growers approached the Security Commission and requested the resettlement of Japanese families in Alberta, to work as labourers in the sugar beet fields. The shortage of manual labour due to the war, and a threatened strike by sugar beet workers, prompted W. F. Russell, secretary of the Alberta Sugar Beet Growers' Association, to make this request upon hearing in February 1942 of the Cabinet order to be administered under the War Measures Act. Here was an opportunity to get low-cost labour for the sugar beet fields, and perhaps a relatively attractive option for displaced Japanese as well.[7]

Local and regional opposition did arise when the growers' request became known and the first Japanese arrived.[8] The argument that British Columbia was exporting its problems to Alberta was put forward from a number of quarters. Ann and David Sunahara describe the situation in early 1942:

Japanese-Canadians
arrive at Picture Butte
from Mission, British
Columbia, April 1942.

*Photo courtesy City of
Lethbridge Archives and
Records Management.*

*In March 1942, the Beet Workers Union, city and labour
councils, local Canadian Legion branches, boards of trade, and
citizens' committees throughout southern Alberta demanded that
Japanese from British Columbia not be admitted to the province,
and if they were admitted, that they be guarded by the army and
removed from the province after the war. Southern Albertans,
who for years had Japanese neighbours, were not immune to the
wartime hysteria. Careful to distinguish between "their"
Japanese and Japanese British Columbians, residents of
Raymond, Lethbridge and Taber held public meetings to protest
the proposed movement of Japanese British Columbians into
southern Alberta. This, they felt, was just a way of exporting
British Columbia's problem to Alberta.*[9]

The Sunaharas have suggested that the beet growers played both ends against
the middle in their argument for bringing this potential labour force to Alberta.
In Alberta they argued that the Japanese were not a threat to public security,
while in British Columbia they argued that the Japanese were a security threat
and should therefore be moved to the interior of Canada. It was a convenient
argument calculated to acquire cheap labour.[10] The government of Alberta also
entered the debate and made a formal request to the federal government that
they insure that relocated Japanese be returned to British Columbia following
the war.[11]

For many within the Japanese community, coming to Alberta and working in
the beet fields was preferable to the internment camps and working on road
gangs.[12] It offered the possibility of reuniting family members, working in
agriculture for a wage, and with the promise of reasonable housing and schooling
for children, it seemed preferable as an interim solution to the shacks in ghost
towns in the isolated mountain valleys of British Columbia.

Many of the Japanese who came to Alberta had family farms in the Fraser Valley, while others had been involved in the fishing industry along the coast. They saw the journey to Alberta as a short exile which offered a reasonable standard of living and more freedom than the alternatives in British Columbia. This image was short-lived, however. When they disembarked at places like Picture Butte in southern Alberta, they were received by local farmers and driven, usually by horse and buggy, to the farm. Characteristically they were housed in granaries or chicken coops, and almost immediately began the demanding and back-breaking labour in the sugar beet field. They were required to work on the farm to which they were assigned.[13] Travel was restricted, and internees were not allowed to augment their income when the sugar beet season was over with work in the local urban centres. There were also local ordinances prohibiting Japanese families from moving into town. The Sunaharas poignantly describe the immediate response of the Japanese labourers.

> *The response of the displaced Japanese to the conditions on the sugar beet farms was typically Japanese. After lodging their protest with the British Columbia Security Commission, they worked to better their lot. With building materials given them by the Commission, they tried to repair the granaries and shacks they were living in. Even after making repairs, however, their housing remained woefully inadequate for a prairie winter. Often three generations would be crowded into an uninsulated granary. A coal stove would occupy one end of the shack and a sleeping platform the other. In this one room, grandparents, parents, and children ate, slept, and worked. One mother of ten remembers that the conditions: "made you very angry. But anger killed the sorrow and the hurt, and the anger itself was destroyed by making a living. I became too busy to be angry."[14]*

Ann and David Sunahara have analyzed the conditions closely and argue that ninety per cent of the 2664 Japanese from British Columbia "were virtually impoverished by the spring of 1943." Only fifteen per cent had found work during the previous winter; forty-two per cent were on relief, and many more "were borrowing against their next year's beet contracts to avoid the humiliation of having to ask for relief."[15]

The Japanese community responded to these challenges early in their tenure in Alberta.[16] Led by Seiku Sakamoto, the English-language secretary of the Japanese Camp and Mill Workers Union in British Columbia prior to the war, they tried to join local vegetable growers' cooperatives. When this attempt was frustrated they organized the Beet Workers' Association for the workers living north of the Oldman River, as well as a second organization, the Shinwa Kai or Benefit Association of Raymond, Alberta. These organizations took up a variety of issues and worked for better conditions. In the 1943 contract negotiation between beet growers and their Japanese workers, they requested that workers have the right, which had been prohibited under the initial agreement, to move to other farms.[17] Their other major concern had to do with the education of Japanese children. Since the Alberta and federal governments could not agree upon which level of government was responsible for their education, they sought a solution in the delegation of that responsibility to the local school boards. These boards, ignoring the contribution made by the Japanese workers to the local tax base, charged $70 a year for each Japanese high school student.[18]

The Takeyasu family harvesting sugar beets near Picture Butte in 1943.

Photo courtesy City of Lethbridge Archives and Records Management.

Two themes are apparent in this brief sketch of the conditions among the 2664 Japanese who were moved to southern Alberta in 1942. They were faced with the strenuous labour in the sugar beet fields, and the need to build an interim environment which provided the stability necessary for a decent life. For the Japanese the challenge was enormous. They had to make their way in an entirely new circumstance. They had lost their homes, possessions, livelihood and community. For many, it must surely have seemed that they had also lost the nation of their birth or the nation they had adopted. Despite the clear fact that they were faithful citizens, war had pitted their nation against their ancestral homeland.[19] Links with Japan were cut off, and they were called upon to rethink their place in Canada and their relationship to Japan. Another striking theme emerges from this period. The coming to southern Alberta of 2664 Japanese people to work in the sugar beet industry in the midst of the war was for the local population an extraordinary event. Virtually overnight the social and cultural environment of this part of the province was transformed. Such a large influx of unwelcomed people would be a challenge. However, the coming of the Japanese under such adverse circumstances, under suspicion of being national enemies during wartime, was a challenge to the region like none other. When we consider the challenge to the Japanese people who came and to the local community which "hosted" them during wartime, we are forced to ponder the values that made it possible for both communities[20] to remake a social world in a healthy and nurturing way.

The evacuees who came to Alberta were fortunate to be entering a context where the local reputation of the Japanese was excellent and where there already were several Japanese community institutions established. The Alberta Japanese community played an important mediating role in the resettlement process. Within a short time of their arrival in Alberta the Reverend Shinjo Ikuta and the Reverend Yutetsu Kawamura helped the evacuee communities establish Buddhist Churches under the auspices of the Jodo Shinshu Buddhist Church of Canada. Churches were established in Picture Butte, Taber and Coaldale. Along with the church, a Kobai Kumiai or cooperative store was established to import Japanese food for local consumption. The church became a centre of religious life as well the centre for the social and cultural life of the Japanese community, providing clubs for teaching kendo and judo as well as other forms of education and entertainment for children and adults alike.

Contributions to Civil Life

In the five decades following the war the Japanese communities which have remained in southern Alberta have both built their own strong institutions and worked diligently within the civil life of the region. A number of local residents have served on the town councils,[21] in the local service clubs[22] and on the marketing boards for the sugar beet and potato growers[23] in the region. Many families have developed fine farms, established businesses, and made professional contributions in virtually all fields.[24]

At the civic level southern Alberta has benefitted enormously from the contribution of its Japanese citizens. Two examples stand as vivid reminders of a community which sought to transform the terrors of history into the building of a wholesome public life in cooperation with its neighbours. In the 1960s the town of Raymond established a Cemetery Day complete with a non-denominational service in memory of the deceased in the community. The Town Councillors

Kendo-Japanese fencing class at Raymond Buddhist Church, ca. 1948.

Photo courtesy Folklife collections, Provincial Museum of Alberta [PH75.7.399].

decided to establish this day because of what they had for years observed within the Japanese Buddhist community. A major Japanese and Buddhist festival day is called Obon, a day set aside for remembering and honouring one's deceased relatives and friends.[25] The Japanese at Raymond occasionally went in procession through the streets to the cemetery on the edge of the town, held their service of thanksgiving in the cemetery, and danced the Obon odori back through the streets to the Buddhist Church on main street for the festive gathering. Members of theTown Council observed this ritual of regard for the fleeting character of life and respect for all those who have clothed us in life and bequeathed the world to us. Their questions about the meaning of Obon led to a inquiry to see if it would be appropriate for the town to adopt this festival as a civic cemetery day. As a consequence, the town of Raymond regularly goes to the cemetery on Obon, Japanese and others alike, and spends the day remembering and honouring relatives, friends and ancestors.

A second remarkable response to the war, internment, and evacuation, is the Nikka Yuko Japanese Garden, a Canada-Japan friendship garden built for the Canadian Centennial in 1967. This jewel adorns the City of Lethbridge and invites all who enter to experience the deep sense of interdependence of all nature and the beauty and wonder of nature and of the work of human beings cultivating nature. The garden was developed through the initiative of Alberta's Japanese community, led by Reverend Yutetsu Kawamura and the civic leaders of Lethbridge. It is dedicated to the friendship between two nations, Canada and Japan; however, many who visit the garden would never know about the communal experience that lies just below the surface and provided the ground for the creation of Nikka Yuko. The garden exists, not because of the friendship between our two nations, although thankfully that friendship has also come, but because the Japanese Buddhist sensibility looks to bring forth something of gentle beauty even from hostility and hardship. The lotus blossoms, the dearest of Buddhist symbols, capture this sensibility in the garden at Lethbridge. The roots of much human experience are to be found in the mire of history; in some circumstances, tragedy and terror are the ground for beauty, the blossoming of new life. In the experience of the Japanese community of southern Alberta, this is anything but a sentimental image.

The Spiritual Sources of Culture and Community Life

A special sensibility made it possible for the Japanese community of southern Alberta to accept harsh circumstances and to work for a recognition of the interdependence of all nature, including all peoples, enemies and friends alike. This sensibility has its source in the teachings of a prince of the Sakya clan of northwestern India, Siddhartha Gautama, a man who has come down through history as the historical Buddha. Legend and historical sources suggest that he was born some 2500 years ago [624 and 448 B.C.E. are the usual suggested dates], and taught a gospel grounded in the experience of the three inescapable evils that afflict humankind: age, disease, and death. He taught that everything was suffering [*sarvam duhkham*]: "birth is suffering, decay is suffering, sickness is suffering," everything impermanent is suffering. When we experience life as suffering, the source of this experience [and this became his second truth] is desire, or tanha. If you wish to overcome experience in bondage to suffering, you must recognize that suffering is rooted in desire. This desire, such a fundamental motivation for human feeling and action, is ultimately the desire to make things permanent which are in their nature impermanent. You will need to suppress this desire, the Buddha taught, if you wish to be free of suffering. Establishing one's life and sensibilities on the recognition of this connection between desire and suffering, and moving to a recognition of the interdependence of all things in an ever-changing nature, including our historical experience, is the Eight-fold Path which Buddhist tradition developed.

The Buddhist Church of Canada[26] established four congregations in southern Alberta during the war period; there are now seven congregations in the province. These four churches were the centre of community life. The various services which focus the meditation of devotees are structured around contemplation of the fleeting character of life. There is a set of memorial services for those relatives and friends who have died, and a set of festivals which recall the life and teaching of the Buddha and Shinran Shonin [1173-1262 A.D.], the reformer who rejuvenated a portion of Japanese Buddhism in the thirteenth century. The Buddhist Church of Canada is a part of the Jodo Shinshu wing of Japanese Buddhism. The Jodo Shinshu tradition, recalled in the text, chants, sermons, plays and symbolic gestures of the festivals, cultivates the key Buddhist insights and the teachings which flow from them. The insight into the connection between suffering and desire and the teaching about the interconnectedness of all nature are at the centre of all these services.

In Japanese homes as well, this insight and teaching are central. Most of the homes in southern Alberta have a butsu dan, a home shrine, where offerings of thanksgiving are placed on a daily basis and where prayers are offered to the

Celebration of the opening of the Raymond Buddhist Church, ca. 1929.

Photo courtesy Folklife collections, Provincial Museum of Alberta [PH75.7.383].

A service for the arrival of a shrine. This shrine was brought to Raymond Buddhist Church from Royston Buddhist Church due to relocation of Japanese from the coast, ca. 1943.

Photo courtesy Folklife collections, Provincial Museum of Alberta [PH75.7.402].

Amida Buddha in gratitude for life with all its impermanence, for the insights and teaching of Buddha and Shinran Shonin, and in thanksgiving for relatives and friends who have died. Butsu dan also were built in the internment camps and used there on a daily basis.[27]

At the heart of the cultural life of Alberta's Japanese community is meditation, cultivating within the faithful a regard for the impermanence of life, thanksgiving for life, and an awareness of how our desires can so easily deepen our suffering and estrangement from the possibilities of the present. For the 2664 evacuees moved to Alberta during 1942, the Buddhist Church provided a language of meaning for the historical events which appeared to tear their life apart. It brought the central teaching which flows from the insight into suffering, the teaching that all life is interdependent, to the centre of consciousness and provided a ground upon which to accept without passivity, to act, not out of a sense of victimization as so often happens, but out of a sense of interdependency, and to build a stable and fruitful community in service to its own children and to the larger public good.[28]

The sensibility which led the Japanese community in southern Alberta to cultivate a commitment to a civic vision has its roots in another dimension of Japanese culture which traces its roots back to China and another spiritual and civic leader, Confucius [probably born in the second half of the sixth century B.C.E.]. Scholars of Japanese culture have noted the deep influence of Neo-Confucian thought in shaping Japanese family and civil life.

The Confucian world view understands each person's goal as "the pursuit of the excellency of their humanness [jen yi] by the correct and proper accomplishment of their social duties [li]."[29] This pursuit is shaped by the educational process within the heart of the culture. It nurtures a direct parental

The community kitchen in the camp in Slocum, British Columbia.

Photo courtesy National Archives of Canada [C-24452].

love for all those who are younger, and a reverence, called filial piety, for those who are older and in positions of authority. Within the Confucian tradition a breach of the rules of filial piety is the only definition of sacrilege. This view is articulated in a famous passage in the Hsiao Ching, in which the following words are put in the mouth of Confucius.

> *The master said, "Filiality is the root of virtue, and that from which civilization derives....The body, the hair and skin are received from our parents, and we dare not injure them: this is the beginning of filiality. [We should] establish ourselves in the practice of the true Way, making a name for ourselves for future generations, and thereby bringing glory to our parents: this is the end of filiality. Filiality begins with the serving of our parents, continues with the serving of our prince, and is completed with the establishing of our own character."*[30]

Family and community are woven together through filial piety. During the war years with the hardships of living in granaries and chicken coops, often without the presence of father and older sons, this fundamental value of respect and honour for parents gave a stability to Japanese families that is remarkable. The importance of respect for the state, even when the state had treated one's community so badly, remained intact. The goal of filial piety, after all, was to establish the character of each citizen, including the character of the young children within the community. In reviewing this period and the Japanese response to the way they were treated, it is striking to notice that there was virtually no rioting, criminal activities or incidents of rebellion against the circumstances in which the community found itself, much less rebellion against the state. The behaviour of adults, teenagers and children alike was usually impeccable, and the explanation lies deeper than merely the fear of state suppression. At the same time, the beet workers did organize and make their concerns and needs clear, attempting to change the intolerable conditions which adversely affected some of their members. Following the war many Japanese decided to stay in southern Alberta and set about building community institutions and entering into the civil life of the region. The cultural sources of filial piety run deep and were more than a match for the trauma of a decade.[31]

I was first welcomed into the Japanese community while doing field research for the Provincial Museum of Alberta about fifteen years ago. In conversations with a number of elderly men and women about the shape and meaning of their cultural life, the occasional comment was made about the evacuation and their place in Canada. My attempts to pursue this avenue of conversation rarely developed beyond the obvious historical facts. Within the last two years I have returned to Picture Butte, Lethbridge, and Raymond to discuss the historical experience of the community. To my considerable surprise we have talked at length about the evacuation, resettlement in Alberta during the war years, and the implications for their life and the lives of their children. The apology of the Canadian Government on 22 September 1988 for the treatment of Japanese Canadians caught by the dreadful circumstances of war and identified as a potential national security risk has opened the door to the memory of the war years. Canada's recognition of and apology for its wrongful treatment of the Japanese was welcomed by the community. A number of people talked about how they can now speak to their children about the pain and difficulty of those years and to each other and their neighbours about its joys. The shame of Canada has been lifted by the apology and the Japanese community, with its high cultural regard for the "prince", as Confucius put it in the Hsiao Ching — its high regard for nation and government — can open to the memory of those years and speak about its terrors and joys.

Rev. S. Ikuta and family. His son, Kyojo, was ordained to the ministry of the Buddhist Church of Canada. He is the second person from the left.

Photo courtesy Folklife collection, Provincial Museum of Alberta [PH75.7.382].

For some years I have wondered why none of the studies of the Japanese experience in Canada has reflected on the sources within Japanese culture which were used by the community to address the difficulties of the war period. In a discussion with Rev. Kyojo Ikuta,[32] a long-time Jodo Shinshu Priest in Calgary, I raised the theme of the spiritual sources in Buddhism and Neo-Confucianism which were drawn upon to help the Japanese rebuild a shattered world. Rev. Ikuta suggested that the emphasis on social justice issues in the interpretations of the war years had its roots in the human rights legislation of Canada and the ethical concerns of Christians. Ikuta stated that most of the Japanese interpreters of the period and many who were involved in working for an apology by the Canadian government were Christian. For them, understandably, the social justice issues were in the foreground. Glimpsing the spiritual sources within Japanese culture was an important part of completing our understanding of the war period and its effect on the community, as well as the response of the community. This response has intrigued me for many years. At the heart of Buddhism, and in the very structure and purpose of family and community life, as rooted in the ancient ideas of Confucius, lie the keys to understanding how the Japanese were able to act in such a redemptive way. In so doing the elders of this community in southern Alberta have educated the character of us all.

NOTES

[1] For a discussion of his ideas regarding "the terrors of history," see Mircea Eliade, *Myth and Reality*, [New York: Harper and Row, 1963], passim.

[2] Many women were evacuated to Alberta with their younger children on the understanding that they could be joined by their interned husbands and older sons at a somewhat later date. It fell to the women to work through the initial stage of resettling in Alberta and to lay the foundations for a new life. Canadian immigration policy, from its beginning in 1907, established a set of restrictions which made it very difficult for women to join their husbands.

[3] Ann and David Sunahara, "The Japanese in Alberta," in Howard and Tamara Palmer, editors, *Peoples of Alberta: Portraits of Cultural Diversity* [Saskatoon, Saskatchewan: Western Producer Prairie Books, 1985], p. 402. This is the finest essay on the history of the Japanese community in Alberta. I am indebted to it for many of the details and the historical argument of this section of the paper.

[4] Ibid., pp. 394-412.

[5] Ibid., 402.

[6] See Ann Sunahara's extensive discussion of this act and its implications in *The Politics of Racism: The Uprooting of Japanese Canadians in World War II*, [Toronto: Lorimer, 1981].

[7] For a thorough account of the Alberta experience see David Iwassa, *Canadian Japanese in Southern Alberta, 1905-1945*, [Research Paper, University of Lethbridge, 1972].

[8] For a remarkable account of the evacuation experience see the unpublished memoir by George Takeyasu, *1942 Evacuation: A Recollection*, available in the Folklife Archives of the Provincial Museum of Alberta.

[9] Ann and David Sunahara, op. cit., p. 403.

[10] Ibid.

[11] Premier Ernest Manning was lobbied by civic groups, the Union of Alberta Municipalities, and the Alberta Federation of Labor to insure that displaced Japanese be returned to British

Columbia at the end of the war. The sugar beet industry, faced with another labour shortage at the end of the war, pressured the Premier to keep the Japanese in Alberta. Manning agreed in March 1946 to permit them to stay, but kept his decision quiet. On the 26 March 1948 Premier Manning announced that all Japanese residents of Alberta were entitled to full citizenship rights.

[12]Many of the women who came to Alberta in the spring of 1942 commented that a primary motivation for coming was the possibility that their husbands would be freed from internment and be able to join them. See recorded interviews in the Folklife Collections, Provincial Museum of Alberta, conducted during 1994.

[13]Most of the Japanese I have interviewed on this issue speak well of the farmers for whom they worked. Their contracts, however, could make it extremely difficult for anyone who was working for a difficult and abusive farmer to seek an alternate place of employment.

[14]Ann and David Sunahara, op. cit., p. 405.

[15]Ibid., p. 406.

[16]Ibid., pp. 406-408.

[17]The Growers' Association refused this request, arguing that its agreement with the British Columbia Security Commission compelled each Japanese family to stay on the farm to which they were assigned. In 1943 after the beet contracts were negotiated, and completed, all the workers refused to work until permission was given for those workers who wished to transfer to other farms.

[18]Ann and David Sunahara, op. cit., p. 407.

[19]In a number of interviews with members of the Japanese community in southern Alberta I have explored their memory of Canadian propaganda about the Japanese, endeavouring to understand how this effected them. Since they were not allowed to have radios or subscribe to newspapers, they were curiously insulated from the media campaigns to mould wartime Canadian perceptions of their community.

[20]The author is currently exploring both the values which formed the bases of the Japanese response to the evacuation, and those that informed the southern Alberta farming community which "hosted" the evacuees. The hypothesis of the study is that the need for labourers in the sugar beet fields is only one reason this potentially volatile circumstance remained peaceful. A set of religious and civil values were also at work within the southern Alberta farming communities as a stabilizing force.

[21]Muneo Takeda and Mac Nishiyama have both served on the Raymond Town Council.

[22]The Lions Club has been quite popular within the Japanese community. From the early 1950s various members of the community have held offices of significance, including Mac Nishiyama, who rose to Deputy District Governor, and Hiede Karaki, who held provincial office. Reyko Nishiyama served as Division Commissioner and on the Provincial Council of the Girl Guides of Alberta, as well as on the Board of the Raymond and District Museum.

[23]Norris Taguchi, long-time President of the Picture Butte Buddhist Church, served on the Potato Growers' Marketing Board for a number of years.

[24]There are far too many contributions to mention. The work of Robert Hironaka, research scientist with the federal Agricultural Station, Lethbridge, stands as an example of local commitment of national significance.

[25]For a complete study of the ritual life of the Japanese Buddhist community of southern Alberta see David J. Goa and Harold G. Coward, "Sacred Ritual, Sacred Language: Jodo Shinshu Religious Forms in Transition", in *Studies in Religion/Sciences Religieuses* [Vol.12, No.4 1983], pp. 363-379.

[26]Mark Mullins, *Religious Minorities in Canada: A Sociological Study of the Japanese Experience* [Queenston, Ontario: The Edwin Mellen Press, 1989].

[27]There is a Butsu dan made in one of the internment camps in the Folklife Collections of the Provincial Museum of Alberta.

[28]See Mac Nishiyama's essay "A Devotee's Reflection on Jodo Shinshu Buddhism," in David J. Goa, ed., *Traditions in Transition: World Religions in the Context of Western Canada* [Edmonton, Alberta: Provincial Museum of Alberta, 1982], pp. 59-61.

[29]*The Eliade Guide to World Religions*, Mircea Eliade and Ioan P. Couliano [New York: Harperand Row, 1991], p. 92.

[30]Scripture of Filiality I; Hsiao Ching, quoted in Laurence G. Thompson, *Chinese Religion* [Belmont, California: Wadsworth Publishing Company, 1989], p. 42.

[31]About 1300 young Japanese-Canadian men were moved to work camps along the Yellowhead-Blue River Highway. Three temporary camps were located near Gauche and Decoigne, west of Jasper townsite, in mid-1942. A brief sit-down strike occurred at Decoigne in March 1942 to protest living conditions in the camp. This in turn prompted the movement of the 8th Canadian Divisional Headquarters to Jasper. See Bill Waiser, "Labour Camps in Western Canada's National Parks, 1914-1945", Canadian Heritage, Parks Canada, *Research Bulletin No. 309* [September 1994]; also Provincial Archives of Alberta, 66.166/1446.

[32]Interview with Rev. Kyojo Ikuta, March 1993.

Tears in the Garden: Alberta's Ukrainians During the Second World War

Peter Melnycky

Canada's entry into the Second World War was to have profound effects on all its citizens, including the country's numerous ethnic minorities. The Ukrainians, one of Canada's largest ethno-cultural communities, figured prominently in the national mobilization for the war effort. The 1941 census recorded 305,929 Ukrainians in Canada, and during the course of the war their loyalty was subjected to the same sort of scrutiny that had been directed towards them during the Great War of 1914-1918. In spite of this, Ukrainian-Canadians, both individually and as a community, were to make a significant contribution to the war effort. The intent of this paper is to examine the Ukrainian-Canadian community in Alberta during the Second World War, and to summarize its record of war service.

By 1941 the Ukrainian community in Alberta had been established for almost five decades since the first settlement of the 1890s. The third-largest demographic group, after the British [English, Scottish, Irish] and Germans, Ukrainians numbered 71,868 in 1941, with an overwhelming 58,470 [81.36 %] living in rural areas, and only 13,398 [18.64 %] living in urban centres. Almost 60 per cent of urban Ukrainians lived in Edmonton [6668 or 49.76 %] and Calgary [1164 or 8.68 %]. This rural predominance was reflected in a work force that was primarily agricultural. Two-thirds of Alberta's Ukrainians were Canadian born.[1]

The war effort was supported by most political factions within the community, especially after the Soviet Union's entry into the conflict against Germany in 1941. Edmonton's Ukrainian Catholic *Ukrainski visti* [Ukrainian News], the major Ukrainian periodical published in Alberta, declared:

> *We, Canadian Ukrainians, as loyal subjects of Canada, await the command of our government and stand on guard for our fosterland Canada, and the whole British Empire, by the side of other Canadian patriots. All our service — for the King, for Canada, and for the bright future of the invincible British Empire!*[2]

Early on in the war, Ukrainian-Canadians enlisted voluntarily in such large numbers that, in 1941, Joseph Thorson, Minister of National War Services, noted that Ukrainians, especially in certain districts in Saskatchewan, were enlisting out of all proportion to their population. The English-language press estimated there were 35,000 Ukrainians in the armed forces, a figure which was accepted as the minimum number who served during the war. The press also noted that Ukrainians made up 10 % of the Canadian contingent sent to defend the garrison at Hong Kong.[3]

Ukrainian Orthodox
Chaplain Rev.
Captain Michael Fyk
and family, 1943.

*Photo courtesy
Provincial Archives of
Alberta [PAA GP 907].*

In recognition of these high levels of enlistment, the military established a separate chaplaincy, with seven priests of the Ukrainian Catholic and Orthodox churches to minister to the needs of their faithful. In February 1942, Rev. S.B. Sawchuk of Winnipeg was the first Ukrainian Orthodox priest to be appointed chaplain for Ukrainian Orthodox personnel of all services in the prairie provinces,[4] while Rev. Michael Pelech was the first to act in this capacity for the Ukrainian Catholic servicemen.[5] Rev. Michael Fyk was the second Orthodox priest appointed to the chaplaincy.[6] Ukrainian servicemen also received leave for Christmas holidays according to the traditional Eastern rite Julian calendar rather than the Gregorian calendar recognized by the Latin rite Catholic and Protestant churches, as well as the Canadian government.[7]

Alberta's Ukrainians were among the first Canadian soldiers sent overseas to Europe; Michael Hunka shipped out from Halifax in December 1939.[8] In Edmonton, the local branch of the Ukrainian National Federation made particular efforts to ensure a Ukrainian presence in the Canadian military. Members enlisted to form a separate platoon within the Second Battalion of the Edmonton Regiment, Canadian Reserve Army. In January 1942 the Ukrainian National Home in Edmonton hosted a traditional Ukrainian Christmas Eve dinner for the Ukrainian platoon, and for twenty Ukrainian-Canadians training there with the Royal Canadian Air Force. Former Member of Parliament Michael Luchkowich and Vegreville MP Anthony Hlynka addressed the guests, and together toasted the Ukrainian-Canadians who had fallen in the defence of Hong Kong.[9] The *Ukrainski visti* echoed these sentiments, running block messages on its editorial page calling for Canadians to *"Vidomstit Hong Kong"* [Avenge Hong Kong].[10]

A month later the Ukrainian platoon hosted a second banquet intended to encourage continued enlistment in the Canadian military. Attending were Edmonton Police Chief A.G. Shute, Lieutenant Parlee, Officer Commanding, the Ukrainian platoon, Lieutenant-Colonel R.W. Hale, Officer Commanding, 2nd Battalion, Edmonton Regiment, with Major Fry of the Edmonton Regiment. During the banquet, Radway teacher Volodymyr H. Kupchenko, the son of a prominent Ukrainian National Federation activist, announced his intention to enlist, suggesting that "[any] able-bodied young man should be ashamed of wearing civilian clothing at this stage of the war....The freedom we are enjoying in Canada is too precious to be lost through complacency on our part."[11]

In spite of the record of Ukrainian enlistments, and the outward displays of patriotism by the Ukrainian community in the form of various war bond and loan drives, there were still voices within the dominant social strata prepared to target that community as "foreign" and "alien." Even as the community celebrated those volunteering for service overseas, and mourned those who had already made the supreme sacrifice for their country, there were some who continued to see Ukrainian-Canadians as an alien threat to the country. Slogans appeared which were reminiscent of nativist sentiments expressed two decades earlier during the Great War. Having immigrated to Canada from the Austro-Hungarian Empire, Ukrainians were suspect, were required to register with the authorities, were disenfranchised and in some cases were interned.[12] The community defended itself against such unfair criticisms. In the Alberta Legislature, William Tomyn, Willingdon's Member of the Legislative Assembly for the Social Credit party, rejected negative sentiments against Ukrainians and people of "other nationalities" as hateful attacks, wounding peoples' hearts in ways that would be difficult to heal.[13]

The politics of Ukrainian organizations in Canada which sought the establishment of a unified and independent Ukraine were not always in harmony with the policies of Canada and its allies. The Ukrainian left supported German and Russian dismemberment of interwar Poland, while the Ukrainian right recognized neither Polish nor Soviet rule over Ukrainian lands. As a consequence, organizations on both ends of this spectrum came under the scrutiny of the Defence of Canada Regulations. Misgivings about the loyalty of Ukrainians became particularly focused during the 1942 plebiscite called to release Prime Minister Mackenzie King's government

Private John Nykolaychuk, Barich, Alberta.

Photo courtesy Provincial Archives of Alberta [PAA GP 2184].

from previous pledges to avoid conscription for overseas service. In Alberta the sole riding to register a clear No vote was Vegreville, a constituency in which Ukrainians formed a majority of voters, and where the sitting Member of Parliament was Anthony Hlynka of the Social Credit Party.[14] In anticipation of the plebiscite, an editorial in the *Vegreville Observer* set the tone for the special scrutiny which was to follow:

> *The electoral district of Vegreville is somewhat unique in that at least 80 per cent of the qualified voters are of Ukrainian descent. Vegreville electoral district comes about the closest in all Canada to having a solid mass of voters of non-Anglo-Saxon descent (except of course, the electoral districts in Quebec, which are in a different category). The vote in Vegreville will, therefore, give a close indication as to the feeling of those "foreign-born," or of "foreign-born" descent in this crisis which has descended on the country of their adoption — Canada. Thus the eyes of Canada will be anxiously directed towards the result in Vegreville.*[15]

Every segment of the organized Ukrainian community favoured releasing the government from its conscription promises. The Ukrainian Canadian Committee urged a unified Yes vote to allow the government to freely explore all military avenues required for the welfare of the nation.[16] The *Ukrainskyi holos* [Ukrainian Voice] newspaper, published by the Ukrainian Self Reliance League, and the voice of the large Orthodox community, was adamant that not a single vote should be neglected and urged all "in light of their own interest as Canadian citizens concerned about the welfare of Canada" to vote "Yes."[17] In Edmonton the local Ukrainian Canadian Committee formed a group under Peter Lazarowich to promote a Yes vote, and former MP Michael Luchkowich addressed the community on the subject over radio stations CJCA and CFRN. *Ukrainski visti* made its own position clear in its editorial, "Let Us Vote 'Yes'."[18]

In spite of the official unanimity of Ukrainians towards the plebiscite, the community was in fact quite fractured along political lines. In the riding of Vegreville in particular, there were several reasons why the vote went heavily against the Liberal government's plebescite. During the war years, one of the most powerful organizations within Alberta was the pro-communist Ukrainian Labour Farmer Temple Association [ULFTA]. This group condemned fascism, but applauded the German-Soviet Non-Aggression Pact of 23 August 1939 and, while not openly opposing Canada's participation in the war, was nevertheless suppressed by the Canadian government. On 4 June 1940, the Defence of Canada Regulations outlawed the ULFTA and its newspapers. Many of the association's properties were seized and disposed of and 33 of its leaders interned. After Germany's attack on the USSR on 22 June 1941, the ULFTA reappeared as the Ukrainian Association to Aid the Fatherland, and later as the Association of United Ukrainian Canadians. While the association was officially in favour of a Yes vote during the 1942 plebiscite, there was nevertheless a substantial community of interest among the Ukrainians of Alberta that had reason to vote No as a protest over specific losses suffered at the hands of the Liberal government.[19]

Auto mechanics in training at Smoky Lake, Alberta during the war.

Photo courtesy Provincial Archives of Alberta [PAA G978].

Vegreville had a history of support for non-traditional protest parties. Between 1925 and 1949 the riding was represented by United Farmers of Alberta and Social Credit Members of Parliament. Both on the provincial and federal levels, the Social Credit party took a non-committal attitude towards the plebiscite, which many interpreted as a whisper campaign against a Yes vote. John Horn Blackmore, Social Credit Leader in the House of Commons, was critical of the government and its plebescite but offered no advice on how Canadians should vote. The *Calgary Herald* criticized Blackmore for being "Out Of Step," and concluded that if some Canadians decided to cast negative votes as a result of his speech "it would not be surprising." In Alberta, Premier William Aberhart refused to cooperate with Yes committees, or to declare his position on what he saw as a federal matter.[20] Vegreville MP Anthony Hlynka called for a conscription of wealth and industry, and not only manpower. Ultimately he declared himself to be in the Yes camp, and urged all Ukrainians to vote Yes for very pragmatic reasons: "If it is shown after the vote that Ukrainians in the Vegreville riding voted negatively, then some circles and individuals will ascribe to Ukrainians opposition to military service beyond the borders of Canada [and] sentiments in some circles would be against Ukrainian Canadians. For this reason I personally will be voting 'Yes'."[21]

Across Canada the Yes side garnered 64 per cent of the votes tallied, while in Alberta this rose to 70 per cent. In Vegreville a total of 14,512 votes were cast; 5471 [37.69 %] in favour of releasing the government, and 9041 [62.30 %] against, the latter figure being the largest percentage voting No outside Quebec. Athabasca also registered a majority No vote, although by a margin of less than 50 votes, and with five polls failing to receive ballots due to the Spring breakup.[22]

Ukrainskyi holos reacted critically to the results of the vote. An editorial entitled "Shame and Sorrow" chastised Ukrainians for voting contrary to the advice of their leadership and foresaw potentially catastrophic consequences for the community.[23] Edmonton's *Ukrainski visti* rejected any collective responsibility for the Vegreville vote, blaming instead "disloyal" Ukrainian communists for the results.[24] Conversely the Communist *Ukrainske zhyttia* [Ukrainian Life] attributed the results to the influence of Ukrainian National Federation "fascists" under the direction of MP Anthony Hlynka.[25] What emerged from this debate in the community was an overall position that the plebiscite was not in fact a vote on patriotism, but rather a vote of confidence or lack thereof in the Liberal government. It was felt that Ukrainian enlistment figures spoke louder than the plebiscite results, and that Ukrainians, out of the 1,500,000 Canadians who had voted No, should not become scapegoats for exercising their franchise as their consciences dictated.[26]

The *Vegreville Observer* interpreted the plebescite as a vote for or against Hitler, as well as a test of loyalty to Canada for Ukrainians and other non-"Anglo-Saxons," and condemned the results in Vegreville as a disgrace and an indication of a Hitlerian fifth column in Alberta. Historian Howard Palmer points out, however, that outside of such inappropriate outbursts in the heat of the moment, there was no "concerted public attack on Ukrainians," and the absence of "sustained commentary" was attributable to the Ukrainian community's clear commitment to the war effort in spite of the plebescite results. Their sizable numbers within the Canadian military argued that "any charges of disloyalty to Canada could easily be dismissed."[27]

The Ukrainian Canadian Committee [UCC] protested attempts to ignore the community's record of service on the home front and in the armed forces, and to ascribe disloyalty to Ukrainian-Canadians based on the results of a free and open plebiscite: "Imputing Nazi sympathies to them is an injustice and an insult. It has caused a great deal of resentment and is not conducive to national unity which is paramount at this critical time of war."[28] Albertans participated in the first Congress of Ukrainians in Canada, held in Winnipeg during June 1943, which called not only for a redress of the discrimination suffered by the community in the past, but for a new social contract in which the nation-building of Ukrainians would finally be recognized. UCC president Rev. W. Kushnier expressed the community's frustration that even in the nation's time of emergency, when Ukrainians were offering the lives of their sons "and the sacrifice of what little wealth" they possessed, they were still not spared from attacks against their patriotism.[29]

Congress participants reiterated that the sacrifices of their sons and daughters in the war effort were to be the final word on the loyalties and rights of Ukrainians in Canada. Congress records note that hundreds of Ukrainians were part of the First Canadian Division. An estimated 11.4 % of Ukrainians in Canada were in uniform, a figure above the national average, and many had already made the supreme sacrifice at Hong Kong and Dieppe. Several hundred commissioned officers among the Ukrainian-Canadians in all branches of the military included Squadron Leaders and a Lieutenant-Colonel.[30]

There were complaints at the commencement of the war that Ukrainians had difficulty gaining admittance into the RCAF, especially as aircrew, and that they faced discrimination and impediments to promotion within the officer corps.[31] The dislocation and alienation experienced by farm boys from fairly homogeneous settlement blocks, suddenly thrown into the regimented atmosphere of training camps, was exacerbated by incidents of prejudice. One veteran recalls such an incident:

> *[In Winnipeg] I was looking for a friend and mistakenly I walked into another barracks, and a guy asked my name and I said, "Pawliuk." And he said, "Oh, a bohunk." That's what he said, right off the bat. And I said, well, what could I say? I was just one among the whole barracks full of them. But I recall little things like that very clearly, because it did hurt me. I felt, gee, I am as much Canadian as anybody else. I spoke no other kind of language except English, I did all the things that everybody else did, and why should I be called something different?[32]*

Just as the response of Alberta's Ukrainians to the 1942 plebiscite lacked unanimity, the response to military service also showed a spectrum of reactions. In addition to the thousands of men and women who enlisted to serve their country, there were those who did not serve until called and still others who refused to serve at all in a war in which they did not believe.[33] Canada's Ukrainian-language press preferred to give prominence to those who served. However, it expressed bitter irony when a countryman from Edmonton, Peter Joseph Olienik, was awarded the Distinguished Flying Cross but had his name transformed into a more acceptable "Irish" derivative [O'Lienik] by some members of the Canadian press.[34] Home front contributions to the war effort also were publicized. Alberta's Ukrainians contributed generously to the various Victory Loan Bond, War Savings Certificate, and War Service Fund drives in fifteen districts, in which they made up at least 50 per cent of the population. The Fourth Victory Loan Campaign raised $923,000 in these districts, with Radway exceeding its quota by 198.6 %, Smoky Lake reaching 136.8 % and Vegreville 121.3 %. Ukrainians also participated in the varied forms of Red Cross and Service Club work through projects such as sewing, knitting, packing overseas parcels, tag days, teas, and exhibitions.[35]

Although the estimated number of Ukrainian-Canadian men and women serving in the forces numbers between 30,000 and 50,000, there are in fact no precise data on either the overall figures or the number of recruits from Alberta. In 1946, a commemorative almanac honouring Ukrainian-Canadians in the military listed 252 Ukrainian Albertans wounded in action, 168 killed in action, 68 missing in action and 16 prisoners of war.[36] One of the few verifiable figures on enlistment indicates that of 551,273 enlistees completing occupational history forms, 12,389 listed Ukrainian as a spoken language. Of 43,580 Alberta enlistees, the largest language group registered, other than English, was Ukrainian with 2265 respondents. Of 730,000 personnel of the Canadian Army [Active] from 1939 to 1945, 75,887 [10.80 %] knew English and another language other than French.[37]

"Pilot Mandrek," 1942.

*Photo courtesy
Provincial Archives of
Alberta [GP. 1921].*

For the thousands of Alberta's Ukrainians from all walks of life who enlisted in the forces, the RCAF was an especially popular branch of service, due to the presence of British Commonwealth Air Training Plan facilities in Alberta. Women performed many important functions, ranging from nursing sisters, filing clerks, aircraft repair personnel, band leaders and truck drivers, to aircraft recognition instructors. Perhaps one of the most interesting careers was that of Nadia Svarich of Vegreville, who headed up the Canadian Women's Army Corp's 38-piece military band, the only such brass band in the British Empire.[38]

In many cases the war saw a second generation of Alberta's Ukrainians serving with Canada's armed forces, as had their fathers. Todosi [Tony] Gregoraschuk of Lac Bellevue served with the Canadian Army at Calgary during the First World War, while his son George was on active duty with the RCAF in Europe during the Second World War.[39] In the same district, Harry Chmilar served with the Canadian Expeditionary Force for three years during the First World War; his son William served in the RCAF during the second war, and was assigned to the Pathfinder Force with RAF Bomber Command, and awarded the Distinguished Flying Cross.[40] Eli [Alex] Cherniwchan of the Vilna district fought with the Canadian army in France during 1916. Two decades later, four of his sons served in the army and one in the navy.[41] John Holowaychuk, who arrived in Canada as a twelve-year-old in 1898, settled near Lamont and served with the Canadian Army during the First World War. In 1940 John and his wife Tekla's son, Louis, left his job with Zeidler's in Edmonton to enlist with the RCAF, and after his training in Canada he went overseas. On the night of 10 June 1944 he was killed over France. He was buried at Theuville, France under the name "Pilot Officer L. Holoway, Age 29."[42]

William James "Rip" Klufas, one of the highest ranking Ukrainian-Canadians to serve with the RCAF, was born in 1915 at Radway. His parents were John and Mary [née Lazowski], immigrants who arrived in Canada in 1910. Of six children born into the family, three sons became teachers and served in the Canadian armed forces during the Second World War. Rip obtained his permanent teaching certificate in 1936, and was teaching at Wayne school when he signed up with the RCAF in 1941. He joined RAF Bomber Command overseas as a navigator, and rose to the rank of Squadron Leader, and later Base Leader. His decorations included the Canadian Volunteer Service Medal and clasp, the Air Observer Badge, the Defence Medal, Operational Wings, the Aircrew Europe Star, the 1939-45 Star, the War Medal 1939-45 and the Distinguished Flying Cross, which was presented to him by King George VI at Buckingham Palace. William's brothers Harry and Peter served in the Canadian Army, the former with the Canadian Military Headquarters staff in London.[43]

Squadron Leader William J. Klufas, DFC.

Photo courtesy Ukrainian Canadian Archives and Museum of Alberta [Ph 72-213].

Another interesting RCAF career was that of an Ispas native, Flight Lieutenant Alec Pawliuk, who enlisted in 1942. Pawliuk flew Halifax bomber missions as a navigator until he was shot down over Berlin in January 1944. What followed was fifteen months' captivity as a POW, with some 2000 Allied officers, in Stalag Luft III, the camp now infamous for "The Great Escape" which took place on 25 March 1944. Pawliuk himself joined the next escape group, named "X Organization," which worked on a tunnel for about six months before the camp was evacuated in the face of advancing Allied forces. Pawliuk was liberated by British troops on 2 May 1945.[44] Also confined at Stalag Luft III was Edmontonian F/O [Flying Officer] Carl Rudyk, who enlisted in May 1943. In England he was posted with an RAF Lancaster Bomber Squadron, and was shot down returning from a raid on Berlin. He spent a year in Stalag Luft III, where his wounded right leg was amputated.[45]

One Ukrainian-Canadian airman shot down over occupied Europe who avoided entry into a POW camp was F/O William Poohkay of Morecambe. Born 17 September 1915, Poohkay enlisted with the RCAF on 1 July 1941, graduating as an Observer. He was posted overseas in December 1942 with the 427 "Lion" Squadron. During his 37th bombing raid, on 28 June 1944, his plane was shot down over France en route to bomb targets in Luxembourg. Parachuting safely into a barley field not far from an enemy aerodrome near Rheims, Poohkay used his skills as a farm boy to live off the land for several days. Using the French he

Flight Officer William Poohkay.

had learned at school and from neighbours in Alberta, Poohkay contacted a French family and the officials in the village of Juzancourt, and eventually linked up with the "Maquis," or French underground. He was given the code name "General Foch" and fought with the French underground deep in the Ardennes forests until the area was liberated by General George S. Patton's army. He was awarded the 1939-45 Star, Aircrew Europe Star, France and Germany Star, Defence Medal and Canadian Volunteer Service Medal.[46]

In the European theatre of war Alberta's Ukrainians were among those who initiated the Ukrainian Canadian Servicemen's Association, Active Service Overseas [UCSA], conceived during Ukrainian Christmas celebrations in January 1942, and formally established a year later in Manchester. The association aimed to promote social contacts, to attend to the needs and interests of Ukrainian-Canadian men and women of all three services, and to arrange annual meetings each January, whenever possible, in addition to periodic festivals and get-togethers. The UCSA also planned a complete registry of Ukrainian personnel on active service, as well as casualty lists. The care for graves of fallen comrades and the posting of next-of-kin on burial locations was offered, as well as welfare to prisoners of war through aid and correspondence. Alex Olynyk, Joseph Gula and Nestor Holychuk, all of Edmonton, were among the association's 23 original members. Other Albertans played important roles within UCSA and its London club; Corporal Anne Cherniawski of Vegreville was Director of the club, while LAW [Leading Airwoman] Emily Winiarski of Edmonton and Lance-Corporal Helen Kozicky of Calgary were active as directors of association and club activities.[47]

The second annual meeting of the UCSA was held in Manchester on 2 May 1943, to celebrate both Mother's Day and Ukrainian Easter. Ukrainian servicemen attended the celebrations and meetings hosted by the local Ukrainian club, the only such institution in Britain at the time. Candlelit tables featured traditional fare such as Ukrainian sausage [kubassa], honey cake, cottage cheese and painted Easter eggs [pysanky], some of which had arrived from Canada. Among the celebrants was local British war bride and widow Camille Marchuk, whose Canadian husband Harry Slusar was killed in the assault on Dieppe. Private Slusar arrived in Canada in 1906 as a five-month-old child, and as an adult taught Ukrainian and music in Calgary before enlisting with the Royal Hamilton Light Infantry. Slusar wrote his wife shortly before he went into action :

This may or may not be my last means of communicating with you as I expect to be in action against the Jerries any time now.

Whatever happens to me is left in trust with God. This is one time I appreciate your prayers which you have always devoted to me. The thing we are about to carry out looks crasy [sic], however, there are possibilities of all kinds....Whatever happens, I was with the boys. If it is a success we will have something to talk about; if otherwise, it's within God's hands....[48]

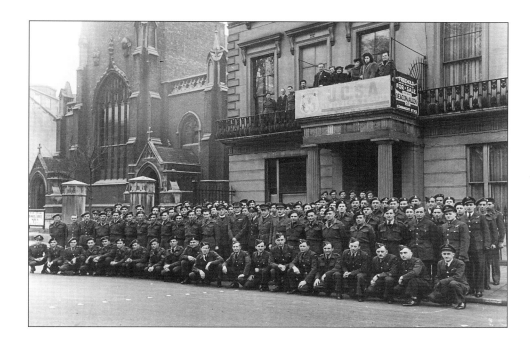

Ukrainian Canadian Servicemen's Association members in front of their London headquarters, November 1945.

Photo courtesy Ukrainian Canadian Archives and Museum of Alberta [Ph 309-23].

The servicemen's home communities in Alberta did not forget them during their festive gathering. Anna Pidruchney wrote from Smoky Lake and forwarded a list of prospective recruits for the association, which she thought would "go down in Canadian history and the history of the Ukrainian-Canadians as a most necessary and welcome institution." A parcel arrived from Vegreville MP Anthony Hlynka, while the Ladies Society of the Ukrainian Orthodox Church in Edmonton advised that a shipment of 1000 cigarettes was on its way.[49] An evocative plea from Innisfree widower Olexa Kuzyk asked that members attend to the grave of his only son, RCAF F/Sgt. Eugene Kuzyk, killed in action on 22 September 1942 and buried at Dishforth, Yorkshire:

On the occasion of your Easter festival I ask you, his brothers-in-arms, to remember and to pay tribute to him and to all Ukrainian-Canadians who have laid down their lives in this war for the cause of freedom and democracy. I humbly ask you to be so good and kind as to care for my son's grave; and on the first possible occasion, please lay a wreath on it.[50]

During 1943 the UCSA sought to acquire permanent quarters in London and appealed to Ukrainian-Canadians for support through one of its prominent

Alberta members. Volodymyr H. Kupchenko taught at various schools near Radway between 1936 and 1942, before enlisting with the Canadian Army. Upon completion of his training in Victoria, with the rank of 2nd Lieutenant, he joined the Sherbrooke Fusiliers Regiment [Armoured Division], attaining the rank of Captain. He was wounded in Antwerp and again at Caen on D-Day. In addition to stressing the need for a hostel in London, Kupchenko complained of the absence of Ukrainian chaplains among active service troops at the front, a problem which "cried to heaven for attention."[51]

> *For two and three years we have not heard the Divine Liturgy in our language, despite the fact that death is buzzing above our heads. We plead, we demand from You at least two chaplains of the Greek Catholic and Greek Orthodox faiths, or do you expect us to fight a war and die without even a word of comfort?*[52]

The UCSA was to organize a total of eleven "get-togethers" during the course of its existence. The association newsletter published casualty lists, honour rolls and decoration dispatches. In August 1944, a service club and hostel were opened in London at 218 Sussex Gardens, Paddington. The association attained a membership of 1500, and a nominal roll of 3000 Ukrainians in the Allied Forces who were accepted as associates.[53]

After the Allied landing at Normandy in 1944, Ukrainian-Canadian servicemen gathering at the UCSA club related stories of encountering the more than one million Ukrainian refugees swept up in the conflict; among *Ostarbeiters* [forced labourers from eastern Europe] working in German factories and as farm labourers, among the inmates of German concentration camps, among the mass

V-E Day celebrations in Smoky Lake, 8 May 1945.

Photo courtesy Provincial Archives of Alberta [PAA G 1241].

of refugees on the continent and among captured enemy personnel. Touched by these encounters, they committed themselves to helping these people by establishing the Central Ukrainian Relief Bureau [CURB], and later the Ukrainian Canadian Relief Fund and the Canadian Relief Mission for Ukrainian Refugees [and War Victims]. Ukrainian-Canadian servicemen acted as couriers, delivering mail from the refugees to the Americas, and aiding the flow of food, clothing and medicine into the refugee camps. A census was initiated to collect accurate data on all Ukrainian refugees, while Ukrainian-Canadian military dentists and doctors provided services and supplies to refugees in the camps. Furthermore, when it became apparent that some refugees were in danger of forced repatriation to the Soviet Union, theUCSA and CURB defended them before British liaison officers attached to Soviet Repatriation Commissions.[54]

Remembrance Day lunch for veterans at the Ukrainian National Home, Smoky Lake, 11 November 1946.

Photo courtesy Provincial Archives of Alberta [PAA G 475].

Upon the conclusion of hostilities in Europe, servicemen stationed in Europe disbanded UCSA and reconstituted themselves within Canada, in close co-operation with the Canadian Legion, as the Ukrainian Canadian Servicemen Veterans Association. Separate branches of the Royal Canadian Legion which united veterans of Ukrainian descent were established in Montreal, Toronto, Winnipeg and Edmonton. In Edmonton No. 178 Norwood Branch was formed in 1946. Membership quickly grew to over one thousand, and the branch commenced its proud and varied record of community service, including support for the Ukrainian Canadian Committee, the Ukrainian Cultural Heritage Village, and the promotion of Ukrainian studies within the schools of the province and at the University of Alberta. Another continuing commitment is support of the Ukrainian Canadian Museum and Archives in Edmonton, where a special collection has been established to commemorate the military service of Canadians of Ukrainian descent.[55]

V-J Day Parade in
Smoky Lake,
15 August 1945.

*Photo courtesy
Provincial Archives of
Alberta [PAA G 1293].*

The Ukrainian community in Canada felt that its record of service and sacrifice during the war would finally earn them acceptance within the country. In the words of Vegreville MP Anthony Hlynka, "These young men have with their blood purchased and guaranteed for us a permanent place of equality in this nation."[56] Proud of their record of service, Ukrainian-Canadians in Alberta took a more assertive attitude towards their position as citizens[57] and sought to influence government policy in areas of immigration, culture and education. This was reflected in their significant influence upon governments, which adopted multiculturalism as a defining concept for the country, the introduction of Ukrainian-language classes and bilingual schools throughout the prairie provinces, and the establishment of centres of Ukrainian studies such as the Canadian Institute of Ukrainian Studies at the University of Alberta.

The Second World War acted as a crucible in which Ukrainians continued to forge the character of their identity within Canada. It was an experience shared in common with fellow Canadians, yet to which they brought their own particular perspective. Alberta's Ukrainians registered a proud record of service and sacrifice dedicated not only to stopping aggression in Europe but to the promotion of a more tolerant and equitable society in Canada. When considering the participation of Alberta's Ukrainian community in the war effort, one might ponder the politics of war, the strategies and heroics of military efforts and the exhilaration of triumph; yet as in all wars, one is struck most of all by the deep sense of personal loss suffered by those who made the ultimate sacrifice during the conflict. It is perhaps fitting that the final words on the topic of the contribution of Ukrainian Albertans to the war effort be left to the simple reflections of Mary Feschuk, one of the many women who made the most profound and bitter of contributions to the war effort in a son who would never return home.[58]

> *...the war was on and our oldest, George, was nineteen. He had been working in Three Hills and had earned enough money to buy a little car. Soon we heard of local boys being called to the army or joining up. It was very sad for us, because we knew that he would go also. He spent some time in Canada receiving training and was able to come home from time to time....When the boys in his regiment signed up to go overseas he did too; he didn't want to be left behind. On December 23, 1944 he left home and with the Edmonton regiment went overseas. He wrote many letters home saying, "Cold, poor grub, frozen toes," and "if ever I get home, I'll have much to talk about," but this was not to be....I happened to be in the hospital in Smoky Lake when the telegram came. It was...delivered to the farm where my husband was. I was not told until I got home from the hospital that our son was killed in action on April 25, 1945....I didn't expect this, but it had happened to a few local boys before him. We thought it might be a mistake, that he would come home or write, but he never did....My whole world fell apart. Relatives, neighbours and friends came to comfort us, but there was no comfort. The only comfort I had was from little Darlene who was only four. She would say, "Mama — don't cry" and try to wipe my tears, but there was no stopping them....they were never wiped away....They fell in my garden, in the milk pail, in the bread dough.... During this time of grief and sorrow, our last child, Evaunrie, was born. I still had tears enough to bathe her with. She was a tiny baby but healthy and she kept me busy...knowing nothing of the sorrow around her.*

NOTES

[1]N.J. Hunchak, *Canadians of Ukrainian Origin: Population, Series No. 1*, [Winnipeg: Ukrainian Canadian Committee, 1945], pp. 47, 49, 54, 57, 67-68; William Darcovich and Paul Yuzyk [eds.], *A Statistical Compendium on the Ukrainians in Canada, 1891-1976*, [Ottawa: University of Ottawa Press, 1980], p. 66.

[2]*Ukrainski visti*, 5 September 1939, cited in Watson Kirkconnell, *The Ukrainian Canadians and the War*, [Toronto: Oxford University Press, 1940], p. 15.

[3]*Ukrainski visti*, 16 December 1941, cites *The Toronto Evening Telegram* and the *Toronto Star*. See also Paul Yuzyk, *The Ukrainians in Manitoba: A Social History*, [Toronto: University of Toronto Press, 1953], pp. 192-193.

[4]*Ukrainskyi holos*, 18 February 1942.

[5]Ibid., 18 March 1942.

[6]Ibid., 9 June 1943.

[7]Ibid., 9 December 1942.

[8]Ukrainian Canadian Museum and Archives, Edmonton Photograph File:72-319.

[9]*Ukrainski visti*, 25 November 1941; 13 January 1942.

[10]Ibid., 10 March 1942.

[11]*Edmonton Bulletin*, 9 February 1942, cited by Myrna Kostash, *All of Baba's Children*, [Edmonton: Hurtig Publishers, 1977], p. 303; *Novyi shliakh*, 18 February 1942.

[12]See Peter Melnycky, "The Internment of Ukrainians in Canada," in Frances Swyripa and John Herd Thompson [eds.], *Loyalties in Conflict: Ukrainians in Canada during the Great War*, [Edmonton: Canadian Institute of Ukrainian Studies / University of Alberta, 1983].

[13]*Ukrainski visti*, 24 February 1942, "Posol Tomyn pro dovhy, shkilnu systemu i pro napady na chuzhyntsiv."

[14]See J.L. Granatstein, *Conscription in the Second World War, 1939-1945: A Study in Political Management*, [Toronto: The Ryerson Press, 1969]; J.L. Granatstein and J.M. Hitsman, *Broken Promises: A History of Conscription in Canada*, [Toronto: Oxford University Press, 1977]. For a discussion of the Ukrainian community and the plebiscite see Thomas M. Prymak, *Maple Leaf and Trident: The Ukrainian Canadians during the Second World War*, [Toronto: Multicultural History Society of Ontario, 1988], and Howard Palmer, "Ethnic Relations in Wartime: Nationalism and European Minorities in Alberta During the Second World War," *Canadian Ethnic Studies*, Vol. XIV, No. 3 [1982], pp. 1-23.

[15]Cited in *Calgary Herald*, 20 April 1942.

[16]*Ukrainskyi holos*, 25 March 1942.

[17]Ibid., 22 April 1942.

[18]*Ukrainski visti*, 14 April 1942.

[19]John Kolasky, *The Shattered Illusion: The History of Ukrainian Pro-Communist Organizations in Canada*, [Toronto: PMA Books, 1979], pp. 27-33, 37, 181, 185, 244.

[20]*Calgary Herald*, 7 April 1942, "Affirmative Vote on Plebiscite Not Assured"; 18 April 1942, "Aberhart Not Interested in Plebiscite Vote"; 23 April 1942, "One Political Group Leader Is Out of Step"; 24 April 1942 "Plebiscite Was Provincial Matter on February 10."

[21]*Novyi shliakh*, 22 April 1942, "Zaklyk posla Antona Hlynky do ukraintsiv okruhy Vegreville."

[22]Howard Palmer, op. cit., pp. 17-19; Thomas Prymak, op. cit., p. 163; and *Edmonton Journal*, 15 May 1942, for final figures in Athabasca and Vegreville.

[23]*Ukrainskyi holos*, 6 May 1942, "Sorom i Shkoda."

[24]*Ukrainski visti*, 12 May 1942, "Komunisty vidvichalni za vyslid pliebistsytu."

[25]*Ukrainske zhyttia*, 7 May 1942, "Sprava zalezhyt teper vid uriadu."

[26]*Ukrainski visti*, 12 May 1942; *Kanadyiskyi farmer*, 6 May 1942, "Pliebistsyt i Ukraintsi"; 13 May 1942, "Dalshi zavvahy pro resultat plebistsytu"; *Ukrainskyi holos*, 13 May 1942, "Ispyt Dozrilosty."

[27]Howard Palmer, op. cit., pp. 17-19.

[28]*Ukrainskyi holos*, 6 May 1942.

[29]*First All-Canadian Congress of Ukrainians in Canada*, [Winnipeg: Ukrainian Canadian Committee, 1943], p. 26.

[30]Ibid., pp. 40-51.

[31]Ibid., p. 50; Thomas Prymak, op. cit., pp. 133-135.

[32]Cited in Kostash, op. cit., p. 351; see also p. 294.

[33]Ibid., pp. 48, 51, 294-295, 308-309.

[34]*Ukrainskyi holos*, 18 March 1942, "Vidznachennia dlia ukrainskoho irlandtsia" [Award for a Ukrainian Irishman]. See also 16 December 1942, and *Edmonton Journal*, 14 March 1942; *Ukrainski visti*, 8 December 1942.

[35]*First All-Canadian Congress....*, pp. 43-44, 46-47, 51.

[36]Rev. Ihor Shpytkowski [ed.], *Almanakh kanadiiskykh ukrainskykh voiakiv*, [Winnipeg: "Buduchnist natsiia," 1946].

[37]Thomas Prymak, op. cit., pp. 131-32.

[38]William Kostash "For King and Country," in Anton Chomlak et al., *Ukrainians in Alberta*, [Edmonton: Ukrainian Pioneers' Association of Alberta, 1975], pp. 215, 219-20.

[39]*Dreams Become Realities: A History of Lafond and Surrounding Area*, [Lafond: Lafond Historical Committee, 1981], pp. 409-412.

[40]Ibid., pp. 247-248.

[41]Emily Odynak et al., *Voices of Yesteryears: Vilna and District History*, [Vilna: Vilna and District Historical Society, 1991], p. 351.

[42]Steve Hrynew [ed.], *Pride in Progress: Chipman, St. Michael, Star and Districts*, [Chipman: Alberta Rose Historical Society, 1982], pp. 223, 381-84.

[43]*In Search of Greener Pastures: A History of Radway and Area, Volume Two*, [Radway: Radway and Area Historical Archives Association, 1993], pp. 622-625.

[44]"A Prisoner of War: One Man's Memoirs of the Great Escape" in Mike Kostek [ed.)], *Down Memory Trails: A History of Two Hills and Surrounding Area*, [Two Hills: Two Hills Historical Society, 1986], pp. 237-238.

[45]George Lupul et al., *History is Everything That We Have Done: 45 Years with Norwood Legion Branch # 178*, [Edmonton: Norwood Legion Branch #178, 1991], p. 402.

[46]William Kostash, op. cit., pp. 216-219; George Lupul, op. cit., p. 389; Emerson Lavender and Norman Sheffe, *The Evaders: True Stories of Downed Canadian Airmen and Their Helpers in World War II*, [Toronto: McGraw-Hill Ryerson, 1992], pp. 132-33, 242.

[47]For a history of the association see Gordon B. Panchuk [ed.], *Memorial Souvenir Book I: Souvenir Memorial Books (UCSA-UCVA) and Ukrainian Branches of the Royal Canadian Legion*, [Montreal: Ukrainian Canadian Veterans Association, 1986]; Lubomyr Y. Luciuk [ed.]. *Heroes of Their Day: The Reminiscences of Bohdan Panchuk*, [Toronto: The Multicultural History Society, 1983]; George Lupul et al., op. cit., pp. 27-34; William Kostash "For King and Country," p. 221.

[48]*UCSA News Letter*, Vol. 1, No. 4, [January-February-March 1944], p. 8.

[49]Panchuk, *Memorial Souvenir Book...*, pp. 40-46.

[50]Ibid., p. 43; *Ukrainskyi holos*, 14 October 1942, Petro Zvarych "Na vichnyi spomyn Ukrainskykh Voiakiv"; *Ukrainski visti*, 17 October 1942, "Svizha mohyla ukrainskoho letuna na Angliiskii zemli."

[51]*Ukrainskyi holos*, 21 October 1942, Isidore Gorsesky et al., *Ukrainians in Alberta: Volume Two*, [Edmonton: Ukrainian Pioneers' Association of Alberta, 1981], pp. 176-177; *In Search of Greener Pastures....*, pp. 1094-1097.

[52]*Ukrainskyi holos*, 1 September 1943, "Lyst vid voiakiv zza moria do batkiv u Kanadi."

[53]George Lupul et al., op. cit., p. 34.

[54]Stanley Frolick, *Between Two Worlds: The Memoirs of Stanley Frolick*, [Lubomyr Y. Luciuk and Marco Carynnyk, eds.][Toronto: The Multicultural History Society of Ontario, 1990], pp. 122-130.

[55]George Lupul et al., op. cit.; John Sorochan, "Royal Canadian Legion, Norwood Branch 178, Edmonton, Branch," in Chomlak, *Ukrainians in Alberta....*, pp. 225-227.

[56]*First All-Canadian Congress....*, p. 86. See also pp. 88, 110-111, 163.

[57]Kostash, op. cit., p. 308.

[58]Compiled from "Memoirs of Mary [Waselenchuk] Feschuk," in *Our Legacy: History of Smoky Lake and Area*, [Smoky Lake: Smoky Lake and District Cultural and Heritage Society, 1983], p. 432; and *By River and Trail: The History of Waskatenau and Districts*, [Waskatenau: Waskatenau and Districts Historical Society, 1986], p. 695.

The Veterans Volunteer Reserve: Alberta Nativism in Two World Wars

Ken Tingley

The Veterans Volunteer Reserve [VVR] was created by the Alberta government during the spring of 1940.[1] This was a period of great excitement, and even panic, for many Albertans, who each morning opened their newspapers to read of the increasingly shocking successes of the German forces in Europe. By June much of western Europe, including Paris, had been occupied, and Britain was holding out alone on its island bastion. In this atmosphere, Alberta Premier William Aberhart was persistently and publicly criticized by ex-servicemen's organizations for a perceived laxity and lack of "preparedness." On 17 June 1940, Walter R. McLaren, provincial president of the Canadian Legion, called upon the Aberhart government to follow the lead of other provincial governments, such as that in neighbouring Saskatchewan, and "organize a provincial civil security force."[2]

In this heated political atmosphere, and in response to such direct pressure, Aberhart called a meeting with Lieutenant-Colonel Frederick F.C. Jamieson, the chairman of the ex-servicemen's general committee which was demanding more direct involvement for veterans in home defence. Meetings were held on 18 and 19 June, in which Aberhart met not only McLaren, but Lieutenant-Colonel William F.W. Hancock, commander of the RCMP Edmonton Division, and Deputy Attorney-General George B. Henwood.[3] The civil security force which resulted from these meetings appears to have been largely the creation of Jamieson, who pressed it on Aberhart over the misgivings of the military and the RCMP. It was an immediate political response to the growing demands of the increasingly powerful "returned-men's" organizations of Alberta.[4]

VVR members from Byemoor and Endiang, wearing their medals from the Great War, with VVR caps and armbands.

Photo courtesy Hugh L. Wallace.

During the Second World War the VVR would become the last publicly acceptable organization to give expression to the nativist sentiment in the province. Most of its members were veterans of the Great War of 1914-1918, and their political views after 1940 reflected this fact. As such, VVR members often voiced most directly public concerns regarding "enemy aliens" and "subversives" who might form a fifth column in their midst. While their fears proved to be largely unfounded, their views were an important part of the political landscape on the Alberta home front, and were heard in almost every community throughout the province, where its numerous battalions, companies and platoons were located. Between 1940 and 1945 the VVR enrolled over 7000 members, with a total strength of 5500 at its peak in 1941.[5]

Nativism was well established in Alberta before the outbreak of the First World War, and its prevalence in certain districts and among certain groups during the period from 1914 to 1918 established the pattern which would be repeated during the Second World War. First identified as a force in the political history of the United States, nativism referred to "the amalgam of ethnic prejudice and nationalism, and unlike racism involved prejudicial attitudes toward 'white' ethnic and religious minorities." Alberta historian Howard Palmer describes the situation in 1914:

> *The Germans, who formerly had been counted among western Canada's most desirable citizens, now became the most undesirable. Immigrants from the Austro-Hungarian Empire, including Austrians, Croats, Poles, Hungarians, Czechs, Slovaks, and Ukrainians, also found themselves under intense suspicion even though few had any loyalty to the [Austro-Hungarian] Empire. Indeed, many had come to Canada to escape military service demanded by Austrian imperial authorities.*[6]

Citizens of enemy countries, and "enemy aliens" who were not yet naturalized Canadian citizens, had their languages suppressed in community churches and schools, their newspapers and mail censored or suppressed, lost their jobs, and had to turn in their firearms and report regularly to the police. Naturalization was suspended for the duration of the war. E.A. Mitchner, leader of the provincial Conservative opposition, suggested to Prime Minister Robert Borden that the "enemy alien born," who had voted against the Alberta Conservatives in the 1917 provincial election, should be disenfranchised, fearing they had "the balance of power to defeat most of our candidates in the Province." The Wartime Elections Act met such concerns when most "enemy aliens" naturalized after 31 March 1902 were disenfranchised.[7]

Nativism in Alberta frequently was concentrated in its most vocal and public form among the province's returned men and reservists. "Home defence" units were formed among Edmonton's reservists in 1915, and in 1916 mobs of veterans attacked German businesses in Calgary. In the provincial capital, the Hudson's Bay Company formed a "Home Defence" unit among its managers and employees; most were with the 101st Fusiliers, while others represented the 19th

Alberta Dragoons or Legion of Frontiersmen. As the *Edmonton Bulletin* reported, "There is no class distinction when the cause of Empire is the consideration and all stand united." The Leduc Home Guard was organized just south of Edmonton in 1916, with infantry and mounted infantry companies, while such units were formed in other "foreign districts" as well.[8]

Prejudice directed at "enemy aliens" in Alberta had abated somewhat by 1916, at least in the rural districts where they were needed to solve the problem of wartime labour shortages. However, when larger numbers of returned men began to appear in the province in 1918, demands for further restrictions on "enemy aliens" increased once more. This may have been caused by renewed fears following German victories, after the Russian Revolution released troops from the Eastern Front, and before the full impact of American involvement in the war had been felt. On 15 January 1918, the newly formed, and already politically powerful, Great War Veterans Association [GWVA] aroused nativist passions and spread fear among Alberta's ethnic community when it passed several unnecessarily inflammatory resolutions at its Edmonton convention. These declared that all "enemy aliens" should be forced to work at employment of national importance, and if necessary that they be interned in order to compel them to that end. All those disenfranchised under the Wartime Elections Act should be required to report to the authorities every 30 days as well, while "such Enemy Aliens [should] not be permitted to proceed outside a certain radius [of their homes] without permit from the proper authorities." An additional income tax on aliens also was demanded. Naturally these comments caused consternation in many districts. On 24 January 1918, a public meeting was held at the Ruthenian Hall in Vegreville, where some 200 disenfranchised Ukrainian farmers and local businessmen met to discuss the GWVA resolutions. This meeting was led by Andrew Shandro, the MLA for Whitford, as well as Peter Svarich, Thomas Perepeletza and other community leaders. At the conclusion of the meeting it was decided to send a delegation to Ottawa in an effort to forestall further punitive measures against "enemy aliens." That February J.G. McCallum, MLA for Vegreville, and Andrew Shandro met Prime Minister Robert Borden, Premier Charles Stewart and former Alberta Premier A.L. Sifton; their fears were somewhat alleviated at this meeting by assurances that no such measures were anticipated.[9]

Despite the fact that the "enemy alien" population of Alberta had already experienced harsh treatment during the war, the authorities expressed surprise that they would take the GWVA resolutions seriously. A.P. Sherwood, Chief Commissioner of the Dominion Police, directed the Royal North West Mounted Police [RNWMP] to take all possible steps to contradict rumours of homestead confiscation and cancellation of land contracts, which apparently had begun to flourish at the same time as the GWVA convention. Sherwood concluded that "undoubtedly such rumors will create a spirit of unrest amongst the Alien Enemy population to the detriment of the country." Superintendent T.A. Wroughton, commanding RNWMP G Division in Edmonton, dispatched his special agent George Effenberger to investigate the Vegreville situation. His conclusion was that the majority of settlers "are ignorant and cannot read or write and therefore have to depend [for] their news on the gossip, hence the splendid opportunity for hair-raising rumors and reports." Wroughton, never one to seek out the subtleties of a situation, merely questioned Shandro's patriotism and offered the opinion that he was "nothing more or less than a grafter." Constable Armitage, in charge of the RNWMP Coutts Detachment in southern Alberta, suggested that the government's provision of seed grain to "alien" farmers in southern Alberta when they lost their crops in 1917 should have allayed any fears regarding confiscation. Corporal Schultz of the Andrew Detachment sent circulars to the Greek Catholic and Orthodox churches in his district in an effort to forestall parishioners' anxieties, but the seeds of distrust and fear had been sown by the returned men of the GWVA. Two decades later they would flower in a less extreme form of nativism, as the Albertans on the home front endeavoured once more to accommodate the domestic stresses and tensions released by another global conflict.[10]

One of the first VVR parades held at McLennan, 1940.

Photo courtesy Provincial Archives of Alberta [PAA 66.166/1532].

It was the veterans of Alberta who once again expressed concerns regarding loyalty of the "enemy alien" population most persistently and in the most extreme terms during the early years of the Second World War. Rallies were organized by "returned men" at many locations throughout Alberta, at which they became increasingly outspoken in their demands that the Social Credit government and the federal government institute restrictive and punitive measures to control a "fifth column." Clearly they feared that such a movement would grow to dangerous proportions within the ethnic settlement blocs [or "enemy alien" districts], and would repeat the recent successes of the European Quislings. This fear was expressed publicly in locations such as Consort, in east-central Alberta, where shortly after the formation of the VVR, a mass meeting of veterans was organized to form a home defence unit. After the meeting its chairman reported to the provincial Attorney-General that there were many German "aliens" in the district, and warned Aberhart that the concerns of local citizens would soon have to be addressed. The Consort group was immediately referred to the VVR, which it soon joined. Numerous resolutions regarding the fifth column threat were passed at a similar meeting in Clyde, located north of Edmonton, three days before the VVR was established. These veterans from Westlock, Barrhead, Athabasca, Boyle, Dapp and other district locations soon joined the new provincial Reserve organization, where they felt that their concerns could be addressed best. A typical meeting of 400 people in Olds, chaired by Percy Leask, the local Legion president, called upon the government to intern all aliens merely suspected of subversive activities. In 1940 such suspicions would have cast a very wide net. A VVR unit was organized by Absalom Clark Bury, a local barrister and veteran of the RNWMP and militia, who had served as adjutant at an internment camp in Jasper National Park during the First World War. Thus many VVR organizers ensured that their units would be characterized by a strong anti-alien bias. In fact, constraints placed upon this bias by VVR Headquarters were required in several instances to control the nativism endemic to certain districts.[11]

Robert Underwood, who commanded the Coronation unit, best expressed the role of the VVR at this time when he reported that his men cooperated with the RCMP, "especially with respect to the utterances or actions of foreigners." Once again, the terms "foreigner" and "enemy alien" were applied broadly to those who were not "Anglo Saxon" or "British," and who might in fact be naturalized citizens, but who did not speak English; these terms frequently were applied within the broadest nativist tradition by VVR members. Between 1941 and 1943 several units, such as those located in Acadia Valley and Dapp, became almost totally inactive with the exception of intelligence gathering duties among the "foreigners" in their districts. Major Alexander Gibson described the means by which the Lamont unit under his command, situated "in the heart of a foreign settlement, German on the west and Ukrainian on the other three sides," planned to observe the district by "cooperating with the R.C.M.P. in a quiet way." Major Ronald C. Arthurs, VVR Executive Director, preferred that his organization maintain a public presence in the "foreign" districts in this way, although the RCMP were not always keen to receive his assistance. In June 1940, William Tipper, Section Leader in Byemoor, complained that while there were "not half enough [RCMP]...they seem to resent any assistance that our local constable and Legion members are quite willing to offer them in this district."[12] The RCMP appear to have remained distrustful of VVR assistance for the duration, perhaps concerned that their more excitable elements would be difficult to control in the absence of strict military or police constraints.

Ensuring loyalty in "enemy alien" districts was accomplished by the VVR in several ways. The Millet Company [E Company, Wetaskiwin and District Battalion] compiled township maps for the districts where their members lived; each section was designated by the name of the resident farmer, with either the letter L [for loyal] or D [for doubtful or disloyal]. In the Peace River country, and throughout northern Alberta generally, Reserve members remained vigilant as well. Harold Duncan, the Smith merchant who commanded the VVR unit in that town, reported that "all our section men are foreign and as the bridge that goes over the Athabasca river is the only outlet to the Peace River country, I think something should be done to see that this particular bridge is safeguarded." Duncan concluded with the warning that several of these railway section hands had access to dynamite for clearing log jams on the river. Even magistrates and justices of the peace were scrutinized. L.A. Shearer, the notary public and insurance agent who established a Reserve unit in Fairview, complained that Magistrate Stewart had shown leniency to the "known nazi" Julius Weber on the charge of possessing unregistered firearms at his farm, in the "German district" near Hines Creek. Fred Udell, Commander of the Waterton unit in southwestern Alberta, reported to Major Arthurs that Justice of the Peace Harold Oland "was not at all sympathetic with the British," and that he expressed his views openly. When Oland left Waterton to subcontract with his brother at the Prisoner of War Camp located in Lethbridge, Udell expressed alarm:

> *I consider him to be a very dangerous man to be working any Gov't construction job especially an Internment Camp or Empire Training Centre and not at all worthy of holding a J.P. position. [He] is a man with a very sneaky and cunning way of working to get information and using it when opportunity arises. I think steps should be taken to watch him close [sic] and think he should be prevented from obtaining work around any Gov't project.*

Such recommendations, frequently based upon personal animosity, were acted upon in many cases. When Charles Nash, the Killam postmaster who led that town's VVR unit, learned that an "alien" named Kurt Bittner from Edmonton had been hired by the local Beaver Lumber yard, his confidential report was followed up by an RCMP visit to the lumber yard, and Bittner was fired.[13]

The VVR also kept its eyes open for the distribution of literature which was prohibited by the Defence of Canada Regulations, or films which might incite subversive activities. The Brooks Company [Lethbridge and District Battalion] spent much of its effort during late 1940 collecting "subversive literature" distributed during the nights in that town and the surrounding area. In Wainwright "prohibited literature" was the object of periodic searches during the following year. E.J. "Buffalo Bud" Cotton, the unit commander, reported an additional benefit of such searches:

> *Although no offence of this nature was found, it had its desired effect, in so far as [sic] suspected subversive elements being aware that literature of all kinds are [sic] being closely watched.*

When the film *I Was A Spy* was shown in Looma, just southeast of Edmonton, on a Saturday night in early October 1940, the Looma VVR reported to the RCMP that it included depictions of Allied aircraft bombing a church. John DeVries, the Western Divisional Manager for Sovereign Film Distributors, almost immediately reported to Robert Pearson, Chief Censor for Alberta, that all bookings of that film had been cancelled "in strong foreign districts" of the province. On 22 June 1944 the Ukrainian Canadian Association screened a Ukrainian-language film in Wildwood. E.W. Phillips, the VVR commander, although not certain what the film's narrative contained, was concerned that it might be subversive, and therefore felt that it posed a danger. Such concerns sometimes led to extreme reactions. Alfred Giddings, the Waskatenau commander, reported that his unit had passed a resolution in January 1941, requesting that the provincial VVR "use their influence to have all foreign languages forbidden to be spoken in all public buildings and public meeting places." He observed that "at times, in some of the stores and places of business, there is not a word of English spoken."[14]

While monitoring "enemy aliens" to ensure that they reported to the RCMP as required by the Defence of Canada Regulations, some confusion developed due to inconsistencies in some districts. John Payne, who commanded the small Cherhill section attached to the South Edmonton Battalion, noted that there was "quite a lot of dissatisfaction about the way the Aliens have to report," and indicated that those who lived in the Rochfort RCMP Detachment area were required to report once a month, while those in the Westlock Detachment area were only required to report annually:

> *[There] are men who are neighbors and one has to go to*
> *Barrhead once a year and the other goes to Cherhill or Rochfort*
> *once a month. Now the V.V.R. here [Cherhill] passed a*
> *Resolution that all enemy aliens be compelled to report to the*
> *police at least once a month, and to have the Law [Defence of*
> *Canada Regulations] enforced because some of there [sic]*
> *people are getting quite snotty.*

Delinquency in signing up for national service registration was of concern to the VVR as well. Men convicted of such delinquency frequently were sent to Alternative Service Work Camps. Sometimes they would be released to work, but after 1943 were required to donate a percentage of their monthly salary to the Red Cross under Order-in-Council 246 [1943], as well as Order-in-Council 1977 [1944] and Order-in-Council 2821 [1944]. The location of these men was reported to Robert English, the Registrar for Division M, Mobilization Branch, National War Services, at his Edmonton office, and efforts subsequently would be made to ensure that these penalties were paid. Hoarding by aliens was another concern. In October 1942 the Jarvie unit reported a suspected case in which sugar, tea and coffee were being hoarded on a homestead some six miles west of their community. When the RCMP investigated, they seized these items and laid a charge of illegal possession.[15]

Although North American nativism was at its height during the early twentieth century, and had declined by the 1930s, its spirit was revived by the excitement and uncertainty of the Second World War. Elements of the nativist bias characterize the attitudes and expressed opinions of many VVR members, most of whom had formed their views of "enemy aliens" during the First World War, when Alberta nativism was at its peak. Consequently, the nativist sensibility determined the focus of VVR concerns in most areas. Franklin Sissons, reporting for the Bon Accord unit, felt that there was little possibility of subversion there, as "the district is mostly Anglo-Saxon." In such districts it was easy to make up VVR units out of what one leader termed "a few of the right spirited townsmen." On the other hand, David Glass reported that about 90 per cent of the population near Rocky Rapids was "alien," and therefore "quite favorable to Hitler." A VVR presence in such districts was considered important, since the disloyalty of its inhabitants was usually assumed on the basis of its ethnic background. When Thomas Allison, who farmed near Beaverhill Lake, asked to join up, he was attached to the Vegreville company. Major Arthurs reported to the Vegreville commander that Allison appeared to be the only enrollment from the Mundare area, "and of course Vegreville is the nearest unit established to that hotbed of enemy aliens."[16]

Waskatenau VVR platoon, 1941.

Photo courtesy
Provincial Archives of
Alberta [PAA G.1097].

Animosity toward political radicalism and union organization went hand in hand with nativist ethnic prejudice, and so special attention was focused upon the mining towns during the war. Major Arthurs, writing to the Mercoal branch of the Canadian Legion, cautioned that "[with] the very large foreign element in your district it is essential that some one should keep an eye open for any improper conduct." John Davies, the Canadian National Railway section foreman in Mercoal, immediately forwarded a list of seventeen men working at the coal mine, who he suspected of evading military service. Almost all had East European names. Ted Conger, the Mercoal postmaster, and an employee of the Mercoal Mercantile Company, acted informally for the VVR after 1941 by keeping an eye on mine employees and monitoring their mail. Joseph Holroyd, a VVR "correspondent" in the Coal Branch, carried out surveillance of the "foreign population" as well. The threat of subversion also was stressed by the Sterco unit, "especially as a large percentage of the employees at the Foothills Collieries are of Foreign or Enemy Alien origin, and to a much lesser degree at Coal Valley and Sterco." Similar concerns about the coal fields had been typical of the First World War as well. In 1917 the Brazeau Collieries near Nordegg had requested police guards be provided by Sir Percy Sherwood, Chief Commissioner of Dominion Police: "We do not like to contemplate what the position would be if there were no policemen at the mines, as we have found that the presence of one or two policemen there during the last few years has had most satisfactory results." In June 1940 the *Edmonton Journal* reported that over 60 per cent of the Nordegg population was of German or Italian descent, and that the police were busy registering "aliens." Nevertheless, the RCMP stressed that none was giving any trouble, and that many of the Italian miners professed anti-fascist sentiments. However, memories persisted of the 1917 coal strike, when the United Mine Workers of America had shut down all the mines in District 18. Fearing any organization which might lead to similar labour unrest, the authorities paid special attention to the mining districts.[17]

Finally, another element of nativism which coloured the VVR approach to its duties was the moralistic tone which sometimes grew from what Howard Palmer describes as its goal of "achieving a pure, Christian society." In a regular unit commander's report, the commander of the Wildwood unit scrutinized the morals of his neighbours, and fumed: "A woman leaves her husband, and has a family of her own, moves in with another man and bares [sic] him a child and goes by his name. Is this not a very bad example to our growing generation and what can be done?"[18]

Women with the Veterans Volunteer Reserve Auxiliary march in Wainwright on Dominion Day, 1942.

Photo courtesy Provincial Archives of Alberta [PAA 66.166/1660].

The widespread presence of the nativist bias among VVR members produced a tendency toward vigilantism in several instances. One such case involved Lewis Rinas, who sat on the Pioneer Municipal District Council and operated an auto wrecking business in Thorsby. Rinas was charged with making subversive statements in a Thorsby beer parlour on 4 July 1940, and was tried in Leduc before Magistrate Robert C. Young; prosecution was handled by Constable Mitchell of the Breton RCMP Detachment. The accused pleaded guilty to the charge, was sentenced to three months imprisonment under the Defence of Canada Regulations, and taken to Edmonton to serve his sentence. However, in ten days Rinas was granted bail and appealed his conviction, and the appeal was upheld by an Edmonton court. At this point the VVR became very concerned and took a hand in the case. Geoffrey Mealing, a Thorsby teacher who commanded the local platoon, complained to Major Arthurs:

*Unless we can get more support from our courts, we have our
choice of moving out of the country altogether or going "Klu
Klux Klan [sic]." I cannot urge upon the executive too strongly
the necessity of making strong representations to the Dominion
and Provincial Governments about enforcing the Defence of
Canada Regulations, and of treating these men as enemies,
rather than as citizens who have broken a traffic regulation.*

Several days later Arthurs replied that he had called a meeting with
Lieutenant-Colonel Hancock, his fellow VVR Board member, and the officer
commanding RCMP K Division:

*A thorough discussion took place with regard to the conditions
existing in the Thorsby district. As a result of the interview, I
may state confidentially that Lt. Col. Hancock is arranging for a
check-up on certain individuals in the area and it remains now
for us to wait and see what action is taken.*

A retrial of Lewis Rinas was ordered shortly thereafter, and on 23 November
1940 he was convicted of two charges under the Defence of Canada Regulations,
and sentenced to serve out the remainder of his sentence, two months and twenty
days. The trial was held in Thorsby Police Court, with Magistrate Young presiding.
In the Rinas case the threat of violence appears to have forced the more stringent
application of wartime regulations through the agency of the VVR.[19]

Examples of intimidation may be seen in the operation of the Wainwright unit
as well. "Buffalo Bud" Cotton, its Commanding Officer, reported unit support for
the Red Cross and War Service League:

*Any parties being lukewarm or opposed to assisting these
organizations, were questioned by the members, who set them
right.... This has had a tendency for those that are in doubt
regarding rumors or misleading reports to turn to the V.V.R.
members for confirmation.*[20]

One man could sometimes establish a VVR presence in a district, and through
his quasi-official status impose his own personal prejudices there. The Wildwood
unit, located west of Edmonton near Chip Lake, was set up by such a man.
James MacFarlane Gilroy offered his services to the VVR on 23 June 1940, and
represented the Reserve there until he joined the Veterans Guard of Canada in
1942. After training as a medical student in Edinburgh, Scotland, he joined the
Gordon Highlanders in 1912, and was sent to France with the First Battalion on
14 August 1914. Taken prisoner by the German army at Bertry, France, on 27
August 1914, with his battalion, company and platoon commanders, he escaped
to Holland on 19 May 1917. After reporting to the War Office, he was transferred
to the 2nd Battalion, Black Watch [RH] in June 1918, and served in Palestine
until January 1920. Gilroy later immigrated to Alberta, where he worked as a

reporter for the *Edmonton Bulletin* and *Edmonton Journal* between 1926 and 1935, when he left to live and write at Northville, near Wildwood. His experiences during the First World War clearly had left him deeply suspicious and angry, and this soon became apparent when he joined the VVR. [21]

Gilroy felt that only one Scandinavian in his entire district was loyal, and the Swedish settlers and lumber mill workers especially were a concern for him. "The others are all Communists and hate Britain and the Empire," he reported, "though they have got land, work, relief or a living and education for their families under the Union Jack." Only three other men joined his unit, but one French veteran held a position at the Northville lumber mill, and in the fall of 1940 indicated his intention to "as far as possible...only take on returned men." Gilroy also reported weekly meetings held at the "Ukrainian" pool hall in Wildwood, where it was rumoured that moonshine alcohol was drunk, and all sorts of anti-British comments apparently could be heard. He sent a memorandum listing the names of seven Swedes, Danes and Ukrainians to VVR Headquarters, in which he indicated they were being watched closely and occasionally "tongue lashed" for "anti-British utterances." One Ukrainian man apparently expressed the opinion that Hitler would "free the Ukraine," but this appears to have been the most overtly subversive comment reported. For example, the principal evidence against one Carl Oberg seems to have been that he once turned off a radio broadcast regarding "the visit of Their Majesties" in 1939. On another occasion Harold Feldhaus, a German settler from north of Wildwood, met Private Walter Phillips, a local serviceman who was the son of the Wildwood VVR commander. Feldhaus reportedly commented to Phillips and his father that "the other side is no worse than this." This was a fairly thoughtless remark, under the circumstances, and enraged Gilroy, who wrote a lengthy report to Major Arthurs, in which he recommended "that should Feldhaus be found guilty [of the remark], he be interned for [the] duration subsequent to completion of his prison term." John Malzen, a Swedish logging contractor near Niton, verbally abused Gilroy for reporting Feldhaus during an angry confrontation some time later. During all of this Gilroy complained that he was receiving little cooperation from the Evansburg RCMP Detachment in rooting out subversives. It may be assumed that they sensed Gilroy's potentially inflammatory and disruptive role among the various ethnic groups in their district.[22]

Any "alien" who received a job outraged Gilroy; any internal ethnic bickering led to lengthy reports in which he outlined his fears of darker underlying subversive explanations. In July 1941, William Belkovski was accused of leading a Free Ukraine movement, taunting Poles following the German invasion of Poland, and responsibility for acts of arson in the area. By the end of the summer feelings had become so strained that Major Arthurs advised Gilroy to exercise some restraint:

> *Capt. Stewart-Irvine [Arthurs' Adjutant] has informed me of your feelings in that district, and although occasionally one's feelings are strained to a point where one is apt to take matters in his own hands, we must remember that we are living in a free country and must show an example to the foreign element.*

However, Gilroy was not unduly swayed by appeals to British justice, expressing the view that an unsatisfactory situation would persist "until the day the gentlemen from Ottawa wake up and dispense with providing the anti-British elements with all the safeguards of British justice." He continued in the same vein:

> *It is tragic to read in the papers of 878 persons being interned in*
> *all of Canada. There could be ten times that number interned*
> *right in the northern half of this province. Subversive elements,*
> *whether aliens or not — though the great majority are aliens —*
> *should be arrested on suspicion, held incommunicado, and tried*
> *secretly by an officer of the Royal Canadian Mounted Police,*
> *interned for the duration of the war and deported.*

Apparently this tirade had been caused when, during the previous week, Gilroy's squad, while "having a beer to kill a few minutes before the opening of the meeting," were "accosted by a drunken Swede" who swore at them. During 1942 numerous unsubstantiated reports were filed, with Gilroy expressing the opinion that informants were in personal danger and could not testify. In August he entered the home of Dominick Mostovich, in search of unregistered arms, without the benefit of a warrant. Soon after this he began a campaign for "British-only" postmasters. At this point the VVR was saved further embarrassment when Gilroy enlisted in the Veterans Guard of Canada.[23]

While James Gilroy represents the virtually unconstrained spirit of nativism, many other VVR men exercised a more balanced approach. Reginald Leaske, the Beaverlodge photographer and Secretary of the local Canadian Legion branch, warned Major Arthurs that several VVR men were "irresponsible, giving imaginative statements regarding activities of certain local aliens, which ultimately proves really a matter of personal dislike." P.L. Beeson, while commanding the Rumsey unit, took the view that "all known Aliens are or seem to be behaving themselves, tho' there are a lot of Central Europeans, honest workers in here this year, who while talkative seem harmless." In other units attitudes changed as the war progressed. Sidney Hancock, at Seba Beach, complained early in the war that "we have several aliens that are not to be trusted," and was instrumental in having Max Poluschuk of Sundance sentenced to four months hard labour for statements calculated to restrain enlistments. However, by 1944 the unit commander, E.L. Fage, felt that "a little enlightenment of the sort of evidence necessary to obtain a conviction" would clean up "some of the peculiar ideas several of the men had." By 1943 the excitement and suspicion surrounding the alien threat had declined. E.B. Atkins, for example, filed the following report for the Rumsey district during the spring of that year:

> *Regarding the intelligence work there is little to report, the*
> *aliens that report at this office do not show any rancor and are*
> *very pleasant to deal with, the women especially. [At] the first*
> *they were, or rather some were, kind of surly at having to report,*
> *but for over a year they have been pleasant to deal with, and I*
> *think that is a good sign, although I have my eyes open to*

possible deception. [Careful] inquiries from the neighborhood
fail to disclose any alien meetings, such as were formerly reported.
[Another] thing, German children that come into the office are very
nice and have a smile. [I] find children reflect the parents' attitude.

There may have been some truth to the observation made by William Osler, while commanding the Gleichen unit, that the VVR was "of considerable benefit to the community, as it provides an outlet for those who are suspicious of neighbours, and prevents the spreading of false rumours against those who are endeavouring to be loyal British subjects, although of foreign origin." As demonstrated by a comparison of the various VVR units, this appears to have depended upon the personalities and prejudices of the veterans involved, and the success with which they could be observed and controlled by VVR Headquarters and the RCMP.[24]

During its five-year history the VVR performed many duties to prepare for home defence, as well as other wartime activities on the home front. These included salvage campaigns, Air Raid Precautions duties, guarding downed aircraft from British Commonwealth Air Training Plan facilities, promoting Victory Loan drives, and similar tasks. However, the main reason that the VVR was created in 1940 was to act as a deterent to feared fifth column activities, especially in the "enemy alien" districts of rural Alberta. Its members were largely drawn from among the veterans of the First World War, and the manner in which they carried out their principal duty reflected the strong nativist prejudice of the group. The VVR remained the strongest voice of nativism in Alberta throughout the war.

NOTES

[1]This paper is excerpted from *The Veterans Volunteer Reserve 1940-1945: An Auxiliary Constabulary on the Alberta Home Front*, an Occasional Paper to be published by the Provincial Museum of Alberta in 1995. See Maurice F.V. Doll and Ken Tingley, "The Veterans Volunteer Reserve in Alberta, 1940-1945," *Alberta Museums Review*, Vol. 15, Issue 2 [Fall/Winter 1988], pp. 20-22.

[2]*Edmonton Journal*, 17 June 1940.

[3]The Veterans Volunteer Reserve was created on 19 June 1940, by provincial Order-in-Council 844/40, pursuant to the Constables Act [1922]. Hon. George Henwood was the first VVR Board Chairman; the Board included Hancock, Jamieson and McLaren. When Henwood resigned as Deputy Attorney-General, he was replaced by Henry Jackson Wilson, who on 20 July 1943 became Chairman of the Board. Otherwise Board members remained the same from 1940 until 1945. Its Executive Officer was Major Ronald C. Arthurs MC, a veteran of the 49th Battalion, Canadian Expeditionary Force, and Secretary of the Provincial Secretary's department.

[4]For an account of the beginning of the VVR, see "'An Example to the Civilian Population': The Establishment of the Veterans Volunteer Reserve in Alberta," a paper which I presented at the Edmonton and District Historical Society's Alaska Highway Commemorative Symposium in June 1992. This paper will be published by the EDHS in 1995 as part of its Alaska Highway publication tentatively titled *Three Northern Wartime Projects: The Northwest Staging Route, the Alaska Highway, and Canol.*

[5]*Provincial Archives of Alberta [PAA], 79.107/31-D*, Major R.C. Arthurs, Memorandum: "To C.F.R.N., Edmonton, The Veterans Volunteer Reserve," 13 September 1945.

[6]Howard Palmer, *Patterns of Prejudice: A History of Nativism in Alberta.* [Toronto: McClelland and Stewart, 1982], pp. 6-7.

[7]Ibid., pp. 47-50.

[8]*Edmonton Bulletin*, 30 October 1915; *Edmonton Journal*, 7 October 1916.

[9]National Archives of Canada [NAC], RCMP Records, Record Group 18 [RG 18], 550/148-1918, Supt. T.A. Wroughton, Commanding G Division RNWMP, "Confidential Report: Re: Unrest Among Enemy Alien Population, Soda Lake District, Alberta," 11 March 1918; *Vegreville Observer*, 30 January 1918, "Ruthenions [sic] Protest Against G.W.V.A. Resolutions"; *Edmonton Bulletin*, 19 February 1918, "Premier Promises Written Assurance to Dissipate Rumours Circulating in North Alta."

[10]NAC, RG18, 550/148-1918, A.P. Sherwood, Chief Commissioner, Dominion Police, to Comptroller, RNWMP, 11 February 1918; George E. Effenberger, Special Agent, RNWMP, Report, "Re: Unrest Among Aliens in Soda Lake District, Alta.," 18 February 1918; Supt. T.A. Wroughton, Confidential Report to the Commissioner, RNWMP, 15 February 1918; Corporal R. Armitage, Report to Supt. P.W. Pennefather, 1 April 1918; Corporal A.R. Schultz, Report to Supt. T.A. Wroughton, 25 February 1918.

[11]PAA, Attorney-General's Papers, 66.166/1647, Consort Unit Commander's Reports, July 1940; *Edmonton Journal*, 11 June 1940, 30 May 1940; PAA, 66.166/1603, Olds Company, Registration Form, A.B. Bury.

[12]PAA, 66.166/1647, Robert Underwood to R.C. Arthurs, 27 September 1940; 66.166/1550, A.R. Gibson to C.A. Edie, 6 September 1940; 66.166/1646, W.J. Tipper to R.C. Arthurs, 23 June 1940.

[13]PAA, 66.166/1572, Millet Unit Commander's Report, January 1941; 66.166/1543, H.E. Duncan to R.C. Arthurs, 2 July 1940; 66.166/1545, L.A. Shearer to R.C. Arthurs, 12 July 1940; 66.166/1665, F. Udell to R.C. Arthurs, [January] 1943; 66.166/1608, Killam Unit Commander's Report, April 1942.

[14]PAA, 66.166/1624, Hilliard Ridley, Brooks Unit Commander's Reports, 1940; 66.166/1660, E.J. Cotton, Wainwright Unit Commander's Report, 2 November 1941; 66.166/1452, J. DeVries to Robert Pearson, 28 October 1940; 66.166/1501, E.W. Phillips, Wildwood Unit Commander's Report, [1944]; 66.166/1551, A. Giddings, Waskatenau Unit Commander's Report, January 1941.

[15]PAA, 66.166/1613, J.A. Payne to R.C. Arthurs, 22 January 1941; 66.166/1460, R.C. Arthurs, Correspondence with R. English, Registrar, Division M, Mobilization Branch, National War Services, Edmonton, 1944; 66.166/1619, F.L. Poritt, Jarvie Unit Commander's Reports, 1942.

[16]PAA, 66.166/1632, F.M. Sissons, Bon Accord Unit Commander's Report, 31 December 1943; 66.166/1509, E.B. Atkins to R.C. Arthurs, 5 May 1941; 66/166/1553, D.H. Glass to R.C. Arthurs, 27 June 1940; 66/166/1574, R.C. Arthurs to H.S. Hurlburt, 5 September 1940.

[17]PAA, 66.166/1540, J.G. Davies, Mercoal Unit Commander's Reports, 1940-1941; R.C. Arthurs to J.G. Davies, 22 October 1940; 66.166/1505, L.D. Dunaway to R.C. Arthurs, 23 October 1942.

[18]Howard Palmer, op. cit., p. 43; PAA, 66.166/1617, E.W. Phillips to R.C. Arthurs, 3 March 1942.

[19]PAA, 66.166/409, G.R. Mealing to R.C. Arthurs, 25 October 1940; R.C. Arthurs to G.R. Mealing, 29 October 1940; *Edmonton Journal*, 23 November 1940.

[20]PAA, 66.166/1660, E.J. Cotton, Wainwright Unit Commander's Report, 28 November 1941.

[21]PAA, 66.166/1535, Chip Lake Unit Commander's Reports, 1940.

[22]Ibid., J.M. Gilroy to R.C. Arthurs, 14 August 1940; 10 October 1940; 4 December 1940; 8 March 1941; 13 April 1941; June 1941; 21 May 1941.

[23]Ibid., J.M. Gilroy to R.C. Arthurs, 14 July 1941; R.C. Arthurs to J.M. Gilroy, 15 August 1941; J.M. Gilroy to R.C. Arthurs, 12 July 1941.

[24]PAA, 66.166/1593, R.E. Leaske to R.C. Arthurs, 24 August 1940; 66.166/1501, P.L. Beeson, Rumsey Unit Commander's Report, 28 September 1940; 66.166/1544, S. Hancock to R.C. Arthurs, 26 June 1940; E.L. Fage, Seba Beach Unit Commander's Report, 31 March 1944; 66.166/1509, E.B. Atkins, Chauvin Unit Commander's Report, 31 May 1943; 66.166/1618, W. Osler, Gleichen Unit Commander's Report, 30 September 1940.

List of Contributors

David J. Bercuson, Ph.D.

Dr. David Bercuson has written, co-authored or edited over twenty books. He recently published *True Patriot: The Life of Brooke Claxton*, a biography of Canada's Minister of National Defence from 1946 to 1954. His book, *Canada and the Birth of Israel*, received the J.L. Segal Cultural Foundation Award in 1986. In 1994 he published *Battalion of Heroes: The Calgary Highlanders in World War II*. In 1989 he was appointed Dean of the Faculty of Graduate Studies at the University of Calgary.

Steven Boddington

Steven Boddington is presently completing his Ph.D. in Educational Foundations at the University of Alberta. He works as a historical consultant, and has a special interest in military history. He presented parts of the paper on "The Friendly Invasion" at the Edmonton and District Historical Society's Alaska Highway Commemorative Symposium in June 1992.

N. Frank Chiovelli

Frank Chiovelli has a longstanding interest in aerostation, the study of lighter-than-air aircraft. He has owned his own hot air balloon operation, as well as being a hot air balloon pilot with Richard Demers' Cloud Chaser Ballooning. His interest in the Japanese balloon bomb offensive against North America dates from 1979, and he has since been researching the subject through government documents and oral history sources.

Carl A. Christie, Ph.D.

Dr. Christie is Senior Research Officer with the National Defence Headquarters Directorate of History. He was part of the team which researched and wrote the official history of the RCAF between 1977 and 1986. His *Ocean Bridge: The History of the R.A.F. Ferry Command* will be published by the University of Toronto Press in 1995.

Catherine Cooper Cole

Catherine Cooper Cole is former Curator of Western Canadian History at the Provincial Museum of Alberta. She is currently in the Ph.D. programme at Leicester University, and is completing a research project for the Fort Saskatchewan Museum on women's home front activities during the Second World War.

Michael Dawe

Michael Dawe is Senior Archivist at the Red Deer and District Museum and Archives. He recently wrote a very popular history of his community.

James Dempsey

James Dempsey is Director of the School of Native Studies at the University of Alberta. His Master's thesis assessed the role of natives from the prairie provinces in the First World War. At present he is completing his Ph.D. at the University of East Anglia, and is writing his thesis on Blackfoot warrior representational art.

Maurice F.V. Doll

Maurice Doll is Curator of Government History, Provincial Museum of Alberta. Alberta's military history forms a significant component of the Government History Program, and is reflected in such projects as *The Poster War: Allied Propaganda War Art of the First World War,* a travelling exhibit developed by the Cultural Facilities and Historical Resources Division, Alberta Department of Community Development. This exhibit opened at the Provincial Museum in 1993 and has been touring since. Maurice Doll also edited and co-authored a book of the same title.

Danial Duda

Dan Duda works for the University of Alberta Library System, and has previously worked at the Provincial Archives of Alberta. He holds a B.A. Honours in History from the University of Alberta, and retains his fascination with military history.

Harris Field

Harris Field enlisted in Calgary in July 1941, returning to Alberta as a Captain in the Loyal Edmonton Regiment in October 1945. He worked with the legal firm now known as Field and Field Parraton until his retirement.

David Goa

David Goa is Curator of Folklife at the Provincial Museum of Alberta, and has authored and edited numerous studies and books on the religion and cultural life of the peoples of western Canada. He is currently completing a book and series of videos on the ritual life of Eastern Christian culture for the Canadian Museum of Civilization.

Mark Hopkins

Mark Hopkins is Curator at the Alberta Aviation Museum. He has previously held positions at the Provincial Museum of Alberta [Government History Program], Alberta Historic Sites Service, and the Canadian War Museum in Ottawa. His great interest is military history and collecting militaria.

Bruce Ibsen

Bruce Ibsen is City Archivist at the City of Edmonton Archives. He is Past President of the Archives Society of Alberta and the Friends of Geographical Place Names of Alberta. His interests include most aspects of local history with an especially keen interest in sports history.

John Joseph Kelly

John Kelly teaches in the history department at Our Lady of Mount Carmel School, Mississauga, Ontario. He wrote his Master's thesis on German prisoners of war held in Canada, and has since retained a strong interest in the subject.

Jeff Keshen

Jeff Keshen is currently an SSHRC Postdoctoral Fellow in the Department of History at the University of Alberta, and is researching the impact of the Second World War on morale and morality on the Canadian home front.

Carrielynn Lamouche

Carrielynn Lamouche lives on the Gift Lake Métis Settlement and is coordinator of the Social Security Reform Committee. She is a self-appointed historian researching and recording the lives of Métis who served in Canada's armed forces during the Second World War. While recording oral histories she has gained tremendous respect for Métis elders and she is working towards the establishment of a museum devoted to the preservation of Alberta Métis settlements history.

David Leonard, Ph.D.

Dr. David Leonard is Provincial Archivist at the Provincial Archives of Alberta. He is the author of several works on the development of northern Alberta, such as *A Builder of the North West: The Life and Times of Richard Secord*. His latest book, with Victoria L. Lemieux, is *A Fostered Dream: The Lure of the Peace River Country, 1872 - 1914.*

Catherine J. Lewis, R.N., S.S.C.D.

Catherine Lewis is an active community environmentalist, writer and research assistant. Educated at McGill University and Royal Victoria Hospital, she has been a Registered Nurse since 1945, and in 1951 joined the Victorian Order of Nurses.

David J. Lewis, B.A., M.D., F.R.C.P.(C)

Dr. Lewis is a retired psychiatrist and educator, and served with RCNVR and RCNR between 1941 and 1968. Now a Lt. Cdr. RCNR [Rtd], Dr. Lewis served with Combined Operations landings at Dieppe, North Africa [Algiers], Sicily, Normandy, Arramanches, HMC LCI(L) 311 in command; also on the Triangle Run, with HMCS Border Cities Kapuskasing. Following a distinguished academic career at McGill University [Emeritus Professor, 1985] and the University of Calgary, his special interests now are medical history and the history of Canadian Naval Combined Operations during the Second World War. Dr. Lewis is presently engaged in the research for a book on the history of Combined Operations.

W. Bruce McGillivray, Ph.D.

Dr. W. Bruce McGillivray is Assistant Director, Curatorial and Collections Administration at the Provincial Museum of Alberta. Dr. McGillivray's background as a systematist makes him a strong advocate for museum-based research. His current interest is in using multimedia to bring museum collections and their information out to the public.

Peter Melnycky

A graduate of the University of Manitoba, Peter Melnycky has been a historian with the Historic Sites and Archives Service of Alberta since 1982. He has researched and published on the history of Ukrainian settlement in Alberta and Canadian internment operations during the First World War. With Bohdan S. Kordan, he co-authored *In the Shadow of the Rockies: Diary of the Castle Mountain Internment Camp, 1915-1917.*

Sean Moir

Sean Moir is a historical research consultant. He is Past President of the Edmonton and District Historical Society, and as such has been very active in organizing historical programmes in Edmonton. At present hechairs the organizing committee for the EDHS conference, "Edmonton's Bicentennial: Historical Reflections," to be held in May 1995. His interests include the social, legal and police history of Alberta.

Jessie Morrison

Miss Jessie Morrison joined the Royal Canadian Army Medical Corps in May 1941, and in July 1944 served in Normandy with No. 10 Canadian General Hospital. She retired in 1967 after a long and successful career as a caregiver.

Patricia A. Myers

Pat Myers is a historian with the Historic Sites and Archives Service of Alberta. She recently completed *Sky Riders: An Illustrated History of Aviation in Alberta*, which will be published in 1995.

Bob Oliphant

Trained in portraiture as an academician, Bob Oliphant later turned to commercial art, which became his life's career. As Canadian Director and Chairman of the Education Committee, National Electric Sign Association, he was able to travel widely in the United States and Canada, lecturing on art and graphic design.

Phyllis M. Patterson

Phyllis Patterson joined the RCAF (WD) on 19 March 1942, and went overseas on 9 July 1943. She recently completed a biography of her famous grandmother, Mrs. W.H. [Eda] Owen, Edmonton's "Weather Lady." She is also working on *One Woman's War*, an account of her wartime experiences.

Rodney Pike, C.D.R., R.C.M.B.R., C.D.

Cmdr. Rodney Pike was born in Vancouver in 1912 and has lived in Edmonton since 1915. He graduated from the University of Alberta with a B.A. in Economics in 1936. He began work with Canada Life that year and joined the Edmonton Half Company of RCNVR as Active Probationary Sub Lieutenant the following year. In August 1939 he was called up for Active Duty. After the war Cmdr. Pike became the first Commanding Officer of HMCS Nonsuch in Edmonton and worked for Canada Life as Manager of the North Alberta Branch. Following his retirement in 1972 he became a Director of the Canadian Executive Service Overseas.

Stanley G. Reynolds

Stan Reynolds has operated one of the most successful car dealerships in Alberta since 1945. He is well known as a collector of vintage agricultural, automotive and aviation items. His numerous donations of such artifacts to the Provincial Government formed the nucleus of the Reynolds-Alberta Museum in Wetaskiwin.

Reginald H. Roy, C.D., Ph.D., F.R.H.S.

Dr. Reg Roy is one of Canada's best-known military historians. For some time he has been Professor of Military History and Strategic Studies at the University of Victoria. Dr. Roy began his career as a historian as part of the team which helped prepare C.P. Stacey's *Official History of the Canadian Army in the Second World War*. Among his publications is *1944, The Canadians in Normandy,* published on the fortieth anniversary of the D-Day invasion.

Kenneth W. Tingley

Ken Tingley was appointed a Research Associate at the Provincial Museum of Alberta in 1988. He has been a historical resource consultant in Edmonton since 1973. His *Veterans Volunteer Reserve: An Auxiliary Constabulary on the Alberta Home Front* will be published as an Occasional Paper by the Provincial Museum of Alberta in 1995.

Donna Alexander Zwicker

Donna Zwicker wrote her Master's thesis on the subject of Alberta women during the Second World War. She lives in Calgary, and has retained her interest in history. She recently served as Vice-President of the Historical Society of Alberta.